FRIENDS

FRIENDS

Understanding the Power of our
Most Important Relationships

Robin Dunbar

Little, Brown

LITTLE, BROWN

First published in Great Britain in 2021 by Little, Brown

3 5 7 9 10 8 6 4 2

A CIP catalogue record for this book
is available from the British Library.

Hardback ISBN 978-1-4087-1173-6
Trade paperback ISBN 978-1-4087-1174-3

Typeset in Garamond by M Rules
Printed and bound in Great Britain by Clays Ltd, Elcograf S.p.A.

Papers used by Little, Brown are from well-managed forests
and other responsible sources.

Little, Brown
An imprint of
Little, Brown Book Group
Carmelite House
50 Victoria Embankment
London EC4Y 0DZ

An Hachette UK Company
www.hachette.co.uk

www.littlebrown.co.uk

For
Freddie, Arthur, Edie, Eva, Rufus and Theo

Contents

	Preface	1
1	Why friends matter	3
2	Dunbar's Number	25
3	Making friends with your brain	48
4	Friendship in circles	68
5	Your social fingerprint	95
6	Friends in mind	111
7	Time and the magic of touch	132
8	Binding the bonds of friendship	157
9	The languages of friendship	175
10	Homophily and the seven pillars of friendship	200
11	Trust and friendship	228
12	The romance of friendship	252
13	The gendering of friendship	274
14	Why friendships end	300
15	Friendship as we age	320
16	Friends online	342
	Further reading	361
	Index	405

Preface

M ost of the research described in this book was carried out by the many graduate students, postdoctoral researchers and research fellows, as well as many external collaborators, who have worked with me over the past three decades. They are too many to name individually here, but the story owes everything to their individual and collective efforts, their friendship, and their enthusiasm. This was very much a communal endeavour, forged in bonds of friendship and a great deal of fun. Without their contributions, this story would have been very short. To all of them, a heartfelt thanks. Much of this was made possible by research grants from the UK's EPSRC and ESRC research councils (the *DTESS* project), the University of Liverpool, the University of Oxford, Magdalen College's Calleva Research Centre, the British Academy (a Research Professorship and the *Lucy to Language* project), Aalto University (Finland), the EU'S FP7 and Horizon 2020 programmes (the *SOCIALNET, ICTe-Collective* and *IBSEN* projects) and the European Research Council (the *RELNET* project), as well as individual research fellowships funded by the Royal Society and the EU's Marie Curie programme. Other contributions for specific studies came from the Holocaust Memorial Day Trust, CAMRA (the Campaign for Real Ale), the Big Lunch Project and Thomas Fudge the Dorset Bakers. Last but not least, John Archer kindly read chapter 13.

1

Why friends matter

The journalist Maria Lally described her experiences as a thirty-something mum moving out of the bustling London lifestyle that she had enjoyed since first starting work for a quieter life with her young family in the Surrey countryside. She very quickly realised not only that she did not know anybody in the village but that it was going to be difficult to make friends because everyone else was already embedded in longstanding friendships. 'I vividly remember,' she wrote, 'listening to two women arranging to go for a coffee, and I could have cried ...' That's something most of us could empathise with. We seem to spend so much of our time peering, like lonely Victorian waifs, through misty windows into cosy, warm rooms full of laughter and people happily absorbed in relationships of one kind or another.

Friendship and loneliness are two sides of the same social coin, and we lurch through life from one to the other. What has surprised medical researchers over the last decade or so is just how dramatic the effects of having friendships actually are – not just for our happiness, but also for our health, wellbeing, and even how long we live. We do not cope well with isolation. Friendship, however, is a two-way process that requires both parties to be reasonably accommodating and tolerant of each other, to be willing to spare time for each other. Nowhere has this been so obvious as in the modern world. Just when we might think social life couldn't get better, suddenly we find ourselves in the midst of a plague of loneliness.

A study of nearly 4,000 men in Australia carried out for the Movember Foundation in 2014 reported that men with few friends and low social support experienced most psychological distress. The ones that were especially vulnerable were those whose friendships were based on nothing more than a common interest, such as a sports club: as participation in the activity fell away, as members married, had children or moved away, so those who remained lost friends, and these weren't easily replaced. Loneliness is turning out to be the modern killer disease, rapidly replacing all the more usual candidates as the commonest cause of death. Why is this? Or, to put the question the other way around: if you don't already believe that friendship is good for you, let me see if I can persuade you.

Thanks be to friends

Perhaps the most surprising finding to emerge from the medical literature over the past two decades has been the evidence that the more friends we have, the less likely we are to fall prey to diseases, and the longer we will live. Julianne Holt-Lunstad, who leads the Social Connections and Health Laboratory at Utah's Brigham Young University and specialises in the impact of social connections and loneliness on our life chances, provides us with some particularly compelling evidence. She examined 148 epidemiological studies that provided data on factors that influenced people's risk of dying.

There are two things I like about this study. First, between them these 148 studies sampled over 300,000 patients. That's an enormous number of subjects by any standards, and means that the findings are likely to be very robust. Second, it is very hardnosed: its outcome measure is whether or not you survived. So many studies use rating scales of the kind that ask, rather vaguely, 'On a scale of 1–5, how much do you like X?' (I hold my hand up to that as much as anyone else), and these are always at the mercy of the subjectivities of how different individuals interpret the wording of a question or feel on that particular day. Does my rating of 'I'm very happy today' mean the same as yours? Does it even mean the same this week as I felt last week? Using whether you died or not as its criterion avoids this trap completely because there can be no argument: either you survive or you die. No ifs, buts, whens or howevers.

Among the factors included in the analysis were all the usual suspects beloved by your doctor: How overweight are you? How much do you smoke? How much alcohol do you drink? How much exercise do you take? How polluted is the air where you live? Have you had the flu vaccine? What rehabilitation regime are you on? Have they given you any drugs? In addition, however, they looked at a series of measures about the person's social world. These included things like: Are you married or single? How much do you participate in social activities? How many friends do you have? How involved are you with your friends or with the wider community you live in? Do you *feel* lonely or socially isolated? How much emotional support do you feel you get from other people?

The big surprise was that it was the social measures that most influenced your chances of surviving, and especially so after heart attacks and strokes. The best predictors were those that contrasted high versus low frequencies of social support and those that measured how well integrated you were into your social network and your local community. Scoring high on these increased your chances of surviving by as much as 50 per cent. Only giving up smoking had anything like the same effect. It will no doubt get me into trouble with the medical profession, but it is not too much of an exaggeration to say that you can eat as much as you like, drink as much alcohol as you want, slob about as much as you fancy, fail to do your exercises and live in as polluted an atmosphere as you can find, and you will barely notice the difference. But having no friends or not being involved in community activities will dramatically affect how long you live. That's not to say that all these other things make *no* difference, of course. Rather, the point is that, by comparison with the number and quality of the friendships you have or whether or not you give up smoking, the individual effects of all these other variables that your friendly neighbourhood doctor worries so much about are really quite modest. You will certainly do yourself a favour by eating better, taking more exercise and popping the pills they give you, but you'll do considerably better just by having some friends.

In an analysis of data from some 38,000 people aged fifty and over, Ziggi Santini and his colleagues at the Danish National Institute of Public Health in Copenhagen found that people who had more close friends and/or were more actively involved in outside clubs and organisations (church, voluntary organisations, educational activities, political and civic groups) experienced much less depression than those who were less socially involved. Up to a point, you could trade these two social factors off against each other – having more friends and fewer activities was as good as having fewer friends and more activities – but trying to do too much had detrimental effects, most likely because you stretched yourself too thin and didn't invest enough in building *quality* relationships. Being a social butterfly flitting from one friendship or activity group to another isn't the same thing psychologically as having a few close friends with whom you spend most of your time. You are likely not to feel part of a group, and so to feel lonely even though you think you are socially very busy. And maybe that's the message here: it is the sense of relaxedness that comes with spending time with friends that is important, as opposed to rushing madly around spending just a few minutes here and a few minutes there.

In another of her studies, Julianne Holt-Lunstadt looked at the effects of loneliness on how long people could expect to live once they had reached their sixties. She collated data from seventy studies, with just short of three and a half million people sampled over an average of seven years. Controlling for the age and gender of the people involved, as well as how healthy they were at the start of the study, factors like social isolation, living alone and *feeling* lonely increased your chances of dying by about 30 per cent. In other words, people who had many friends or were living with someone else (it doesn't *have* to be a spouse!) or felt more engaged with their local community lived longer than those who didn't score so highly on these. And we cannot blame this effect on the fact that people with debilitating illnesses or disabilities had fewer friends or felt lonelier because they could not get out of the house, since the researchers were able to hold these particular effects constant.

Even more persuasive evidence comes from a series of very elegant studies undertaken by the sociologists Nick Christakis and James Fowler (then both at Harvard University, but since moved on) using data from the Framingham Heart Study – a longitudinal study over many decades of a single community of nearly 12,000 people in Massachusetts. The study had originally been set up in order to investigate the factors that predisposed people to having heart disease, and included all the adults in the community. Everyone was followed up over a period of thirty years from the early 1970s to 2003. The friendship data in this community are not completely ideal (they were simply asked to name their best friends), but, because they had the entire community mapped, Christakis and Fowler were able to reconstruct not just who was friends with who, but also who were the friends of whose friends, as well as the friends of friends of friends. They were able to look at changes in people's behaviour or health status as a consequence of the changes that occurred in the behaviour or status of their friends, and of the friends of their friends, and so on.

They found that your chances of becoming happy, depressed or obese in the future, as well as the likelihood that you would give up smoking, were all strongly correlated with similar changes in your closest friend. There was a smaller but still significant effect due to the behaviour of your friends' friends, and a modest but just detectable effect due to the friends of your friends' friends, but nothing beyond that. When you look at their graphs for the community as a whole, it is blindingly obvious that happy people cluster together and that unhappy people cluster together. If your friends are happy, you are more than likely to become happy too. You could even see happiness spreading slowly through the population: if someone's friends were happy in one sample, there was an increased likelihood that they too would switch from being unhappy to happy in the following samples.

This was especially true if the friendship was reciprocal – in other words, the two people had both listed each other as a friend. If the friendship was not mutual – in other words, only one person had listed the other as a friend – the effect was negligible. Although the presence of a non-depressed friend also significantly reduced your chances of feeling depressed, a depressed friend was *six* times more likely to make you depressed than a happy friend was to make you happy. Female friends had an especially strong effect on the spread of depression.

Among the other effects they were able to document was a strong spatial effect. If you had a happy friend who lived within a mile of you, you were 25 per cent more likely to become happy. And you were 34 per cent more likely to be happy if your next-door neighbour was happy. I don't know what it says about this particular community, but, ominously perhaps for the future of the American family, the impact of a happy spouse or sibling was much lower than the effect of your neighbour – only about 8 per cent and 14 per cent respectively! Perhaps this just reflects the high divorce rate in the USA. Much the same was true for diagnoses of clinical depression. The presence of a depressed friend or neighbour significantly increased the number of days on which you felt depressed in a subsequent time period.

One of the best-established effects, at least in folk wisdom, is that married couples often die within a relatively short time of each other. This was certainly true of my parents: my mother died six months to the day after my father, despite the fact that both had been pretty active and, given that both were in their eighties, were in generally good health and sound mind. Felix Elwert and Nick Christakis examined data for nearly 400,000 married couples from the American Medicare database. For men, the death of their spouse was associated with an 18 per cent increase in the chances of dying in the immediate future, and the death of the husband increased the wife's risk of dying by 16 per cent. The causes of death were surprisingly specific. For men, the prior death of their wife from whatever cause increased their chances of dying from chronic obstructive pulmonary disease (COPD), diabetes, accidents, infection/sepsis and lung cancer by 20 per cent, with much lesser effects for other causes. For women, the prior death of the spouse increased their risk of dying from COPD, colon cancer, lung cancer and accidents. For neither sex was the risk of Alzheimer's disease or Parkinson's disease significantly higher, and nor was this the case for cancers that normally had very rapid progress and poor prognosis (such as pancreatic, prostate and liver cancers).

In many ways, family are just a special kind of friend and so play the same role. In 1947, the epidemiologist Charles Spence began a longitudinal study of infant health in Newcastle-upon-Tyne. Just over 1,000 babies born in May and June of that year in the city were followed up in detail over the first month of life, and then intermittently until age fifteen years. One of the strongest effects to emerge from this study was that the rates at which the children fell ill, or even died, were significantly affected by the size of their extended families: those who had more relatives were ill much less often and survived better. During the early 2000s, we sampled seventy-four young mothers with a two-year-old toddler living in Liverpool, recording both the mother's illnesses and those of their infants, as well as how often they contacted individual family members and friends, over the course of a year. Those who reported higher frequencies of contact with close family had lower illness rates (not what you would expect if social contacts caused the spread of disease), especially if these contacts were with very close relatives. This was also true for their toddlers. In other words, once again, people with large extended families suffered fewer problems.

A number of famous historical cases provide more insights into the benefits of family. In these historical cases, we don't usually know how many friends people had, but we often do know who their family members were, not least because they shared the same surname. In 1607 (a decade and a half before the more famous Pilgrim Fathers landed further north at Plymouth Rock), 104 English colonists put ashore at a site they named Jamestown (after the reigning king, James I) in present-day Virginia. Unfamiliar with the local plants and animals, and unable to clear enough of the forest to plant the European crops they had brought with them, they suffered starvation and high death rates, and would have died out completely but for the help given to them by the local Indians (of whom the young Pocahontas became the most famous). It was the ones that came as a family (and their servants) that did best, and the strapping young men travelling alone that did worst. In another of the iconic events in American folklore, the ninety-strong Donner Party set out from Missouri by wagon train in 1846 to cross the Sierra Nevada mountains to begin a new life in California. Delays along the route resulted in their being trapped in the mountains when winter closed in. Many of them died before they were rescued the following spring, but once again it was the young men travelling alone that died and the children and families travelling together that did best. There was something about being embedded in the warmth of a family circle that buffered them against the worst of the terrible privations that these migrant groups experienced.

We don't know exactly how friendship creates these health benefits, but there are several possibilities, all of which might work. One is that friends turn up with bowls of chicken soup when you are sick and do lots of other nursey things for you. (Incidentally, a study by Stephen Rennard and his colleagues at the University of Nebraska Medical Center found that chicken broth has very good anti-bacterial properties, so it really does do you good, just as grandma always said.) Another is that friends cheer you up when they visit and just make you feel better psychologically, and that takes the stress out of being ill and helps you get over it faster. In effect, friends act like a virtual aspirin, taking away the momentary symptoms that are wearing you down and making you depressed. However, there is a more interesting possibility that is related to the brain's endorphin system. Endorphins are neurochemicals that are chemically similar to morphine (the name is in fact a contraction of 'endogenous morphine', endogenous meaning 'the body's own') and, as we shall see in chapter 8, they are activated by many of the things that we do with our friends, such as laughing, singing, dancing, and even stroking each other. Dipak Sarkar of Rutgers University found that endorphins stimulate the release of the body's natural killer (or NK) cells, one of the white blood cells that act as the immune system's shock troops in searching out and destroying the bacteria and viruses that make us sick. It seems that the endorphins triggered by the presence of friends tune the immune system and give us enhanced resistance to the bugs that are responsible for many of the diseases that so discomfort us.

Although we are, subconsciously, probably well aware of its importance, we tend to underestimate the significance of psychological wellbeing as the bedrock on which our success in life is founded. If our sense of wellbeing is significantly diminished for any length of time, we are likely to slide into depression, and that leads to a downward spiral into ill health. If our mood is positive and everything is upbeat, we are not only more willing to engage with others socially but we approach everything we do with optimism and enthusiasm. We'll work harder to get even the most boring tasks done. It isn't hard to see how happiness, a sense of positivity and a 'can do' attitude can spread rapidly through a population in the way that Nick Christakis and James Fowler found in the Framingham Heart Study.

With a little help from your friends?

So far, I have emphasised the health benefits of having friends. That's because this finding has really caught everyone completely by surprise. No one had expected it – even if somewhere deep down in our subconscious we must have had some inkling that this was the case. However, good health and engagement with the community are not the only benefits we gain from friendships. Perhaps the most obvious is the fact that friends are willing to help us out when we are in need not just of emotional support but also of more mundane things like help with moving house or the loan of money or tools. In small-scale traditional societies, help with harvesting or house-building has always been important. These tasks are invariably on a scale that is beyond the individual, and help from family and friends is essential for their successful completion. Close friends will be more willing to do this without expecting you to reciprocate, but mere acquaintances will be more concerned to strike an 'I'll help you out now, providing you come and help me tomorrow' deal.

Oliver Curry carried out a number of studies on the altruistic behaviour of friends. In one of these, he asked people to think of a specific person in their social network, and rate how close they felt to them emotionally and whether they would be willing to lend them a sum of money or donate a kidney to them if they were in need of it. They had to nominate two family members and two unrelated friends, one of them a male and one a female in each case, in different groups of friends – best friends, good friends and just friends (but nothing special). As it happened, the sex of the person didn't make much difference, but both the measure of emotional closeness and the two altruism measures showed a steady, consistent decline as you moved from the closest to more casual friends. Family members were always rated higher than friends at every step, however, leading us to refer to this as the 'kinship premium': most people (though not necessarily all) will give precedence to a family member over a friend. We feel a sense of obligation to our friends and that sense of obligation seems to come from the fact that we spend a lot of time with them. This was born out in another study by Max Burton who asked people to rank their friends in order of how likely each of these would be to help them out if asked and then say how emotionally close they felt to each of them, and how often they saw them socially. He found that the people we feel most emotionally attached to and see most often are precisely the people who are most likely to help us out.

In other words, friends do a lot for us and we invest in them to ensure that they do.

The strength of weak ties

In an influential and much cited paper entitled 'The strength of weak ties' published in 1973, the American sociologist Mark Granovetter proposed that our social world can be divided into two kinds of relationships – strong ties and weak ties. We have only a few of the first type, with the bulk of our relationships being of the second type. It was the weak ties that he was particularly interested in. His suggestion was that these provide an information network through which we garner knowledge about opportunities that we might never otherwise come across if we had to find them for ourselves. The kind of things he had in mind were information about job opportunities, cheap deals in supermarkets, new films we might find interesting, a new up-and-coming stand-up comic or a music event we might like to attend. In effect, having friends allows us to search a much wider area than we would be able to do on our own. In their book *Connected*, Nick Christakis and James Fowler estimated that, until around 2010, 70 per cent of Americans met their life partner through friends or family, with most of the rest having known each other from school or college. In the last decade, this old village introduction service has, inevitably, been overtaken by internet dating sites which now account for around 40 per cent of couples. Even so, 30 per cent still met through the age-old route of family and friends, with casual meetings in bars and clubs (almost certainly in the company of friends) adding another 25 per cent.

In small-scale hunter–gatherer societies, these weak ties might allow us to find out about sudden concentrations of prey at distant waterholes, or learn that a certain grove of trees is just about to come into fruit. These kinds of resources are often quite ephemeral. Deer or antelope can congregate for few days on a patch of lush grassland, but then move on elsewhere once this has been grazed out. Most trees have a very concentrated fruiting period that lasts only a couple of weeks. The more people you have wandering randomly about your territory, the more likely someone is to chance upon a tree whose fruits are just about to ripen. If you had to search the whole area on your own, you might well not have chanced upon this particular grove until after the crop had been eaten out by other birds and mammals – or the fruits had ripened, fallen to the ground and begun the business of sprouting.

No one, least of all Mark Granovetter I suspect, is exactly sure just who he was referring to when he talked about weak ties. Did he mean our more casual friends, or did he mean the acquaintances with whom we might have the occasional beer after work but whom we would never invite home? He never specified, probably because he saw all these as one gigantic, interlinked social network – friends of friends of friends of friends, a bit like

Facebook. The gossip network ensures that information percolates down to us as one friend tells another about their new discovery, until eventually we all hear about it. Although the transmission of information may sometimes be slow, it will eventually reach us. Sometimes these weak ties can even provide us with benefits that are much more interesting than simply where the cheapest petrol is this week. I'll come back to this in a later chapter, because it turns out that, in fact, the circle of friendships involved in this kind of information exchange is a great deal smaller than Granovetter imagined.

Loneliness is a warning signal

So important is it to be part of a social group, that when we find ourselves alone or an outsider we typically feel lonely, even agitated, and will actively work to try and remedy the situation. Few of us could cope with living completely isolated on a desert island with no prospect of rescue. Even the rather disagreeable Scottish seaman Alexander Selkirk (the original on whom the Robinson Crusoe story was based) was overjoyed to be rescued after spending four years alone on what is now officially known as Robinson Crusoe Island. Loneliness takes its toll on us, and we do our best to look for opportunities to meet people. Being part of a group makes us feel properly human. We feel more relaxed when we know we belong. We feel more satisfied with life when we know we are wanted.

John Cacioppo was a pioneering neuroscientist at the University of Chicago who, along with his colleagues Gary Berntson and Jean Decety, founded what has since become known as social neuroscience. John came to be particularly interested in loneliness, and much of his later work was devoted to trying to understand the neurobiological correlates of loneliness and their functional consequences. During the course of this work, he came up with the idea that loneliness is actually an evolutionary alarm signal that something is wrong – a prompt that you need to do something about your life, and fast. Even just the perception of being socially isolated can be enough to disrupt your physiology, with adverse consequences for your immune system as well as your psychological wellbeing that, if unchecked, lead to a downward spiral and early death. Much of John's argument for this can be found in his engaging book *Loneliness: Human Nature and the Need for Social Connection*, co-written with William Patrick.

That loneliness really does have adverse consequences for your immune system was shown by Sarah Pressman and her colleagues at Pittsburgh's Carnegie Mellon University. They found that loneliness among freshmen students resulted in a reduced immune response when the students were given a flu vaccine. Their immune system was depressed and didn't rise to the challenge of the vaccine in the way it should have done in order to bestow proper immunity. In other words, despite having had the vaccine, they would not have been so resistant to future invasions by the flu virus. There was also an independent effect of the number of friends they had: those with only four to twelve friends had significantly poorer responses than those with thirteen to twenty friends. These two effects seemed to interact with each other: having many friends (a large social group of nineteen or twenty friends) always seems to buffer you against a weakened immune response, but feeling lonely *and* having few friends results in a very poor immune response. Friends are genuinely good for you, even at the physiological level of your immune system.

I remember being told by someone who came up to me after a lecture I had given at a book festival that he had spent many years in the army but had never been so ill as when he was back in civilian life after leaving the forces. The military make great efforts to turn their units into family affairs because that creates a level of bonding that ensures that the men stick together through thick and thin on the battlefield. By arranging life so that men eat, sleep, train and socialise together in the same small unit (usually the company, typically 120–180 men), they create a deep sense of bonding among them. The result, it seems, is much lower levels of general illness than we would see in the everyday civilian world.

David Kim, James Fowler and Nick Christakis used a subsample from the Framingham Heart Study where blood samples had been taken from volunteers to look at the correlation between sociability and risk of illness. They found that people with fewer contacts in their social network had elevated fibrinogen concentrations in their blood, while those who had many social contacts had low fibrinogen levels. Fibrinogen is a chemical that facilitates blood clotting so as to prevent excessive bleeding when a blood vessel is ruptured. It also facilitates wound healing and tissue repair more generally, and because of this its levels usually rise when the body faces challenges like inflammation, tissue injury and some cancers. Moreover, because high concentrations of fibrinogen can result in excessive blood clotting, they increase the risk of thromboses if levels remain high for any length of time. High concentrations of fibrinogens in the blood thus imply poor health, so this is very direct evidence that having friends buffers you against ill health as well as against the future risk of heart attacks and strokes. In another study, Andrew Steptoe, Jane Wardell and their colleagues analysed longitudinal data for 6,500 British men and women in their fifties and found that social isolation (but not self-reported feelings of loneliness) was a significant predictor of the risk of death over the following twelve years, even when controlling for age, sex and physical and mental health: being socially isolated increases by about 25 per cent the risk that you will die in the next decade.

So pervasive are the effects of loneliness that it even reduces neural connectivity and neural plasticity in rats if they are isolated when young. In particular, it can irretrievably alter the function of the prefrontal cortex (the front part of the brain where all the clever stuff, and especially the clever *social* stuff, is done), as well

as its myelinisation (the laying down of the fatty sheaths around
neurons that enable them to transmit signals faster and more
efficiently). Once the damage is done, it's done. In humans, short
periods of loneliness rarely have any long-term adverse effects, but
persistent loneliness is correlated with increased risk of Alzheimer's
disease, depression and dementia, as well as poor sleeping habits
(which in turn often have adverse psychological consequences).

In a recent study, Tegan Cruwys and her colleagues at the
University of Queensland, Australia, analysed data from the UK
Longitudinal Study of Ageing (ELSA) that repeatedly sampled
around 5,000 people from the age of around fifty. Included among
the health and wellbeing questionnaires was one about involvement in clubs and societies – everything from political parties,
trade unions and tenant associations to church, hobby groups,
music groups and charities. They found that people who belonged
to more groups were less likely to experience bouts of depression.
And this wasn't simply because depressed people don't join social
groups: they could follow individuals from one sample to the
next, and this showed that depressed people who belonged to no
groups at the start of the sample reduced their risk of depression
in a later sample by almost a quarter if, in the meantime, they
joined even one group. If they joined three groups, it reduced
the risk of depression by almost two-thirds. As they commented,
'membership of social groups is both protective against developing
depression and curative of existing depression'.

Similarly, Claire Yang and her colleagues analysed data
from four large longitudinal American health databases. They
found that, in each of four age groups (adolescents, young
adults, middle age and old age), people who were more socially
integrated had better adjusted biomarkers for physiological
function: lower systolic blood pressure, lower body mass index
(a measure of fatness), lower C-reactive protein indices – the
latter another measure of inflammation. In adolescence, lack of
social engagement had as big an effect on risk of inflammation

as lack of physical activity. In old age, lack of friends had a bigger effect on risk of hypertension than the usually cited clinical causes like diabetes. Even more worrying, the effects of social relationships on these physiological measures of good health during adolescence and young adulthood persisted into old age. In a longitudinal study of 267 males, Jenny Cundiff and Karen Matthews found that the more socially integrated a child was at age six years, the lower their blood pressure and body mass index two decades later in their early thirties. This result held up when they controlled for race, body mass index in childhood, parental socio-economic status, childhood health and extraversion. In other words, social engagement during childhood has consequences, direct or indirect, that last well into adulthood. That's a pretty sobering thought.

In another study, Anne-Laura van Harmelen and her colleagues looked at the impact of negative family experiences before age eleven on the risk of depression at age seventeen in nearly 800 British teenagers. They found that negative childhood experiences significantly increased the risk of depression at age seventeen. Negative family experiences included poor parenting styles, emotional, physical or sexual abuse, lack of affection or parental engagement, family discord, family financial problems, family deaths, family criminality or unemployment, and parental psychopathology. A second effect was due to bullying during childhood: higher frequencies of bullying by family members negatively affected the number of friends the children had at age fourteen, and having fewer friends at fourteen in turn increased the risk of depression at seventeen.

John Cacioppo's claim was that the magnitude of these effects is so great, and the fitness consequences so devastating, that it should not surprise us that natural selection has produced a mechanism that alerts us to the existence of the problem – a kind of evolutionary alarm bell. That there might be an evolutionary dimension to this is suggested by the fact the loneliness has been linked to both the oxytocin receptor genes (at least in adolescent girls) and the serotonin transporter gene – two neurochemicals in the brain that play an important role in regulating social behaviour. People who carry one particular variant of these genes are more likely to experience loneliness even in the middle of a crowd.

My own very modest contribution to this particular story was due to Ana Heatley Tejada. In a series of experiments carried out in Mexico and in Oxford, she found that perceived empathy in the way a stranger responds to you in a stressful situation results in a reduced sense of loneliness, as well as positively affecting physiological responses such as heart rate; in contrast, being on your own or with an unsympathetic stranger increased the sense of loneliness and the physiological responses. We respond instantly to how we perceive the situation. In addition, how lonely someone felt in this situation was affected by their attachment style (whether they were naturally warm and effusive or cool and stand-offish in their interactions with friends), the number of close friends they had and how much they valued close relationships. Interestingly, in a comparison between the Mexican and British subjects, she found that the quality of relationships with the nuclear family was very important in counteracting feelings of loneliness in the British subjects in particular. However, it seemed that the much larger extended families characteristic of Catholic Mexico generally buffered people against poor relationships with nuclear family members, whereas the British with their typically much smaller families did not have enough relatives to provide that protection.

All in all, social isolation is not good for us, and we should make every effort to avoid it. Being social and having friends carries many psychological and health benefits. Friendship protects us against disease as well as cognitive decline, allows us to be more engaged with the tasks that we have to do, and helps us become more embedded within, and trusting of, the wider community within which we live. That may be especially important in the contemporary world where the community may be heavily populated with strangers whom we don't know particularly well, if at all. Friends represent a source of help and support when we need it, as well as providing a group of people who are willing to give up their time (and perhaps even money) to socialise with us. So, if friends are good for you, how many friends is enough? Can you ever have too many friends? The next chapter will provide the answer. Before I do so, however, I should say something about how and why I became interested in friendship as a topic – in a word, how it was that this book came to be written at all.

By way of explanation . . .

Like many ideas in science, this book and the story it has to tell is a personal odyssey. It came about by accident. I had spent the better part of twenty-five years studying the behaviour of wild animals – mainly monkeys and an intensely monogamous miniature antelope (the klipspringer) in Africa, as well as feral goats on the Isle of Rum off the northwest coast of Scotland and the Great Orme in the northwest corner of Wales. My interests throughout these early decades focused on social evolution – why species have the particular social systems they do. Humans were, at best, only a very superficial interest, and then only because I had spent the first twenty years or so of my life immersed in the richly multicultural environment of East Africa. Nonetheless, it seems obvious to me now that this early casual exposure to as many as four very different human cultures all at the same time on a daily basis was an important catalyst both for my developing the sensitivities needed for careful observation of any species' social world and for the decision, many years later, to add humans into the mix.

What I learned from watching monkeys close up was that they are intensely social in a way that most other mammals and birds simply are not. There is a great deal of subtlety going on beneath the surface, and one needs to be tuned in to appreciate its significance. Just how subtle this can sometimes be is illustrated by a photograph I have of an adult female gelada baboon being groomed by her two daughters, one aged about three years (a teenager on the brink of puberty), the other an eighteenth-month-old juvenile. All around them, animals sit in huddles grooming. The mother has her head down on the ground and her bottom in the air while the younger daughter grooms the backs of her thighs. Her head is turned away to the right, and she very likely has her eyes closed as she enjoys being groomed in the warmth of the early morning sunshine. She is as relaxed as perhaps only a mother can be under the ministrations of her daughters. Peace . . . serenity . . . can life ever get better?

It is the behaviour of the older daughter that attracts attention. She sits on her younger sister's left side beside her mother's haunches. She has her right hand inserted in front of her sister's forehead and is gently pushing her away so that she can take over grooming Mum. It is her head that is the giveaway. It is tilted to the left and down: she is watching the back of her mother's head intently as she eases her younger sister out, carefully checking that Mum hasn't noticed. She wants Mum to come to after the relaxation and intimacy of being groomed to find that it is her older daughter that has been providing her with the morning's ministrations, not the younger one. When Mum turns to groom her groomer in return, as she surely will, it will be the older daughter that receives it, so that she can in her turn relax and doze off under the attentions of the hairdresser. She knows full well that her sister is likely to protest if she is too forceful, so she must ease her out with gentle firmness so that the youngster becomes distracted and drifts away to entertain herself or find another yearling to play with. If her sister protests or her mother happens to turn her head and notices, there will surely be maternal hell to pay.

It is this kind of subtle, fleeting interaction that is so typical of the monkeys and apes. Without knowing the dynamics of the relationships involved, without being there at *that* particular moment and realising what is going on, the casual observer can never hope to have any appreciation of the subtlety of primate social life. Blink, and you will have missed it. Without the benefit of several years spent sitting with the animals getting to know them as individuals just as you would a group of humans, I would never have understood the significance of what was going on before my eyes.

The 1990s, however, pretty much put a stop to fieldwork of this kind. The economy was in one of its downturns, and research of this kind came very low on any government's funding priorities. For want of anything better, I turned my attention to humans, doing more or less the same kinds of things that I had always done on monkeys using the same kinds of observational methods. In the midst of all this, I lit upon what, at the time, seemed to be four unrelated ideas – all in the same year. These were the Social Brain Hypothesis (the claim that a species' brain size determines, or more correctly constrains, the size of its social group), what later came to be known as Dunbar's Number (the limit on the number of friends you can have), the importance of social grooming for bonding in primates, and the gossip theory of language evolution (that language evolved to allow us to exchange social information as a partial solution to the time constraints of social bonding). With the benefit of hindsight, it later became obvious that these are, in fact, part and parcel of the same phenomenon – friendship. They form the framework around which this book hangs.

Looking back on this, I realise I was very lucky. Though a psychologist by background, I had spent half my research career as a zoologist and evolutionary biologist. As a result, I ended up with a foot in two camps that don't often talk to each other. That can make for awkward stresses (not least having to keep up with two completely unrelated literatures), but it placed me in the rare position of being able to see the world from two ends of the microscope at the same time. Fortunately, evolutionary biology is, of its nature, a multidisciplinary field and its core theory – Darwin's theory of evolution by natural selection – naturally weaves these different strands together into a coherently unified whole. I will not elaborate on this here because I say a great deal more about it in my book *Evolution: What Everyone Needs to Know*. But appreciating this may help to explain where I am coming from and how I got to be there.

*

The story so far, then. It seems that having friends is genuinely good for us, and not having friends doesn't do us any favours. There is an important caveat in this, of course, and it is highlighted by the phrase 'having friends'. The important thing about friends is that you need to have them *before* disaster befalls you. One reason is that, as we shall see later, people are only likely to make the effort to help you *if* they are already your friend. We are all *much* less likely to help strangers or people we know only slightly – despite what we sometimes claim. Making friends, however, requires a great deal of effort and time. It is not something you can just magic up over a cup of coffee – not least because everyone else is already embedded in friendship networks of their own, and to make time and room for you as a new friend means that they will have to sacrifice a friendship with someone else.

So how many friends is enough?

2

Dunbar's Number

Being a fan of BBC TV's brainbox *QI* programme, I happened to be watching it one evening when Stephen Fry, the programme's long-running host, asked the panel if they had ever heard of 'Dunbar's Number'. When they all looked blankly at him, he explained that it was the limit on the number of friends you can have, and this limit was 150. And borrowing an analogy I had used in an earlier book, it was, he suggested, all the people you would not hesitate to go over and sit with if you happened to see them at 3 a.m. in the Departure Lounge at Hong Kong airport. They would immediately know who you are and where you stand in relation to them, and you would know where they stand in relation to you. Your relationship has a history. No introductions needed. At this point, his regular panellist and comedy foil, the comedian Alan Davies, threw up his hands in mock despair and quipped: 'But I only have five!' He was not as far off the mark as he thought. We do indeed typically have around five intimate friends, but we also have 150 friends-in-general.

In fact, it seems that Dunbar's Number, or The Dunbar Number, has acquired its own popularity. If you try googling it, you will get 34.8 million hits. Perhaps the most amusing of these is a video on YouTube showing a young Dutch woman having the faces of all her friends being tattooed on her arm. You can check

it out at https://www.youtube.com/watch?v=ApOWWb7Mqdo.
Remarkably, the human arm is just long enough to fit the faces
of all her 152 friends – surely a triumph of evolution, and proof
of Darwin's theory if ever we needed any! Alas, it was in fact a
publicity stunt by an Amsterdam tattoo artist. Which, in many
ways, makes it all the more interesting: it seems that Dunbar's
Number had filtered its way even into the world of tattoo artists.
I like to think this is evidence of how scientifically well read the
Dutch are!

So what counts as a friend? Perhaps we need to decide what we
mean by the word so that we know what we are trying to count.
I am going to stick to everyday common-sense definitions – that's
to say, what the word 'friend' means in our face-to-face world.
Though we distinguish between friendships of different strength,
and we all have Alan Davies' handful of very close friends, it seems
to me that the broader sense of friendship we have shares many
similarities with family relationships – except, of course, that we
can choose our friends whereas, for better or worse, we have no
choice at all over whom we get as family. In many ways, these
relationships are all about a sense of obligation and the exchange
of favours – the people you wouldn't feel embarrassed about asking
for a favour and whom you wouldn't think twice about helping
out. Genuine friends are the sort of people you would *like* to spend
time with if you had the chance, and would be willing to make the
effort to do so. You know their names – not just their first names,
but their surnames as well. You know where they live (they are
in your address book), and you know all about their immediate
family, where they have lived in the past and the jobs they have
done. Casual acquaintances, and that includes at least some of
the people you work with, don't belong in this group because they
are not the sort of people you would go out of your way for; you
wouldn't make an effort to have them as part of your more intimate *social* world. To be sure, you might buy them a drink in the
pub on occasion, or you might even lend them a book that you

didn't mind losing. But you won't be willing to do any favours that involve major costs or risks for you.

Counting your friends by number

In trying to think of the best way of finding out how many friends people had, I originally had the idea of using Christmas-card lists. There were two reasons for this. One was that in the days before email and WhatsApp, sending Christmas cards to old friends was a genuine exercise in maintaining friendships, at least in Britain. (Americans always looked rather askance at this, by the way, since this wasn't something they did in such an all-consuming way.) As December got under way, most of us began to think about whom to put on the list of people we would send a card to. That often involved a great deal of agonising. Did they send us one last year? Have we really lost touch with them? They told us they were moving, but did they ever bother to send us their new address? The very fact that people asked these questions suggests that they were very carefully evaluating the quality of their friendships. After all, cards cost money, not just to buy the card but to pay the postage, and these costs rapidly stack up as you add more people to your list. Being included on a Christmas-card list was thus a marker of a genuinely meaningful relationship. The second reason for using Christmas-card lists was that it was something that happened once a year on a very regular cycle. A year without con- tacting someone seemed to be a natural Rubicon. If it's been more than a year since I made the effort to contact you, am I really ever likely to do so again after that? Most people we asked thought not.

So I persuaded Russell Hill to run a survey that asked people to tell us whom they were sending cards to that particular Christmas. We wanted to know not just how many cards people sent but who was in the household concerned, when they had last contacted each of them and how emotionally close they felt to each one.

Although we explicitly asked them to exclude their doctor, lawyer, butcher and baker, and any other purely business acquaintances, some people are always likely to be more generous than others in whom they send cards to. Still, it seemed like a reasonable criterion. Even so, completing our questionnaire for every single person in your Christmas-card list, adults and children alike, was a lengthy and tedious task to put it mildly, and that alone was likely to discourage them from including people frivolously.

The average number of friends yielded by this first sample was 154, including children. Our respondents had sent an average of sixty-eight cards, for an average of roughly two and a half recipients per household. There was, inevitably, a lot of variation across even this sample. Some people sent cards to fewer than twenty people, while the highest was 374. There was, however, a very strong peak at around 120–170, with rapidly declining tails on either side. In other words, the great majority of people sent cards to around 150 people, and, although some people did send cards to more than 200 people, they were relatively few in number.

Several decades earlier, Peter Killworth (a British oceanographer) and Russell Barnard (an American anthropologist) had put together an innovative attempt to estimate the size of people's social networks. They had had the idea of exploiting the 'six degrees of separation' that had been popularised by Stanley Milgram in the 1960s – a nice example of how science often proceeds by borrowing an idea used in one context to study or explain something in an entirely different context. In 1929, the Hungarian writer Frigyes Karinthy had written a short story called 'Chains' in which he argued that it was possible to reach any random person in the world in under six contacts. (I was once taken to have a beer in the café in Budapest where he is said to have written this.) Milgram had the idea of testing Karinthy's speculation and showed, in an iconic experiment, that it did indeed require only six contacts to connect any two randomly chosen people in the USA. He did this by asking a number of people in the Midwest to send a letter to a specific person that they did not know personally who lived in Boston on the east coast, and to do this by hand starting with someone they did know – who would in turn be asked to do the same. So, for example, you know that your uncle Jim is an airline pilot, so he is likely to know another pilot flying the Boston route for the same airline, and he in turn would likely know someone in Boston who knows someone in the same company that the target person works for, and so on. This was a real experiment and the people at each step in the chain had to add their names onto a list on the envelope. It turns out that you almost never need more than six people in the chain linking you and any other randomly chosen person. You are never more than six 'handholds' away from anyone else in the world.

Killworth and Barnard were interested only in that first step in the chain – whom do you give the letter to. The logic is precisely that these are people you would feel comfortable about asking a favour of – the key definition of a friend that I suggested earlier. They gave subjects up to 500 different target individuals elsewhere in the USA, and they wanted to know when subjects ran out of new people to ask and started recycling names, since that would identify the limit on the size of their social network. The average from two experiments turned out to be 134. Given that you probably wouldn't start many chains with young children, including these would bring the total up to around 150 or so. The range was roughly 30–300, which is remarkably similar to what we had found in our Christmas card study. Later, two of my collaborators at Manchester University, Alistair Sutcliffe and Jens Binder, asked 250 students and staff to tell them how many friends and family they had. They left the definition quite open so as not to bias people into giving a particular number. The average was 175, with the usual wide range.

Meanwhile, Russell Hill discovered that you can download data on the number of guests at weddings in the USA from The Knot's Real Wedding Surveys website. The average number of guests was 144, and this had been remarkably consistent across the whole of the last decade. Interestingly, in an earlier sample of American wedding data, Galena Rhoades and Scott Stanley at the University of Virginia had concluded that marriages that had 150 or more guests at the wedding were more stable and outlasted those with smaller guest lists, with very small weddings (those with fewer than fifty guests) doing worst. They thought this might have had something to do with the fact that declaring your love before more people made it more difficult (or embarrassing?) to have to say a few years later that the marriage had failed. If so, that seems to imply a remarkable degree of forethought: it implies that the number of people you invite to your wedding reflects your intuition as to how long the relationship is likely to last, and presumably you both have to agree on that. To be honest, I think that is unlikely. Perhaps a less cynical explanation might be that couples who invite a lot of people to their wedding are embedded within a larger network of family and friends who help to buffer them through the subsequent ups and downs of the relationship.

In the meantime, I became involved in a collaboration with Kimmo Kaski and his research group at Finland's Aalto University. A bluff and eternally enthusiastic statistical physicist with an interest in everything, Kimmo is the walking epitome of the sociable scientist – so much so that my co-author index increased dramatically after I began to collaborate with him, thanks to all the introductions he provided me with (a phenomenon I thought deserved a special name, so I gave it the name *Kaski's Katapult* to reflect the way your social network was launched onto a higher plane). Through Kimmo, we were lucky enough to gain access to a very large national mobile-phone dataset containing a year's phone-call records for some 6 million personal subscribers (20 per cent of all telephone subscribers in one very large European country – and it wasn't the UK or Finland, in case you are wondering). Of course, many of the calls people make will be business calls or calls to statutory or freephone (0800-) numbers. It is easy enough to filter most of these out (at least if you're a computer scientist), and, by adopting the criterion that a call to any number must have a reply from that number to be counted as a relationship, we ended up with what is still a very large sample of nearly 27,000 people with complete phone records. (I should add, by the way, that we have no idea what was said in these phone calls, as that is not recorded: we know only what number they called or were called by.) The average total number of people called was around 130, which, allowing for the fact that you are unlikely to be phoning any of the young children in the families you know, is close enough to 150 to be very encouraging. Once again, the range of variation in the number of people called was between 100 and 250.

In fact, this number turns up all over the place as a natural group size for human communities. The first place I had looked for it was in the size of communities in small-scale societies (hunter–gatherers and traditional horticultural societies). The average community size for a dozen or so of these was 148.4. A later study of a different dataset by Marcus Hamilton at the University of New Mexico came up with a value of 165. It also seems to have been the typical size for early medieval English villages. We know this from the Domesday Book, the complete census that William the Conqueror commissioned in 1086 AD in order to find out what he had managed to grab at the Battle of Hastings twenty years earlier – mainly so that he could determine how much tax he should be receiving. This unique document covered every county in England. Every house, field, plough, cow and horse was recorded, along with who owned it. The only thing it didn't record, because it didn't relate to taxes, was the number of people living in each house. However, historians have estimated the size of villages by multiplying the number of houses by the average size of a family at the time. The average village size was almost exactly 150 in each and every county in England and Wales.

Seven centuries later, the Church of England was making a

big effort to record births (or, rather, christenings), marriages and deaths (burials). Although time, human carelessness, the climate, insects, floods and fires have destroyed some of the church archives in which these were recorded, a great many have survived, giving us a rich collection of historical records about village life in the eighteenth and nineteenth centuries. From these, historical demographers have been able to reconstruct family sizes, fertility and mortality rates, and longevity, and how these changed over the centuries. More interesting for us is that they have also been able to use these records to determine the actual size of villages based on the number of people alive at any given time. Seven centuries after the Domesday Book, the average village size in England in the 1780s was still only 160.

Another historical example has recently been provided by the Italian economists Marco Casari and Claudio Tagliapietra. They used historical records to determine the size of communities in the Trentino region of the Italian Alps over the five centuries between 1312 and 1810 AD. These records are particularly good because they are based on the minute books of the grazing associations that regulated who could use the community's grazing land. Over 500 years, the average size remained astonishingly stable at around 175 people, despite the fact that the population of the region as a whole increased from 83,000 to nearly 230,000. In other words, as the population increased, the officials preferred to split the associations so as to keep them manageably small rather than allowing their size to escalate out of control. The reason for doing this was not because they would run out of land (there was, after all, enough land available for new associations to be set up) but because it got too difficult to control the members when the association's size became too large.

A modern example of this is offered by the Hutterites, the Anabaptist Christian sect whose members settled in the Dakotas and southern Canada after emigrating from central Europe in the mid-nineteenth century. Their communalistic lifestyle is based around communally owned farms managed democratically by the community as a whole (well . . . OK . . . the men of the community). The Hutterites are adamant that they must split their communities once they get above 150 in size because, they say, if a community gets larger than that you cannot manage it by peer pressure alone. You need laws and a police force, and that would be against their whole communalistic ethos. When the community splits, one half moves out to start a new community farm nearby. An analysis of community fissions over the last century that I carried out with the American anthropologist Rich Sosis yielded an average size at fission of 167 in two separate community lineages.

There are a few examples where Dunbar's Number turns up in the contemporary world. The best-known, though it long predates the discovery of the Social Brain Hypothesis, is the company Gore-Tex that makes the waterproof material. When Willard Gore set the company up in the 1970s, he realised that one of the constraints on the efficiency of large companies was simply their size: people cease to pass on information and are less willing to trust each other. To circumvent this problem, he insisted that all his company's factories should number fewer than 200 people. That ensured that everyone knew each other, and would cooperate with each other. The Swedish government tax-collecting agency apparently restructured itself so that each tax officer dealt with just 150 clients and only these individuals, so that they knew the individuals personally. Another recent example is the purpose-built IJburg College in Amsterdam which, while having a total student body of 800 pupils, is structured into self-contained '*deelscholen*' (learning communities) of about 175 pupils.

In other words, natural human communities *and* personal social networks seem to have a typical size of about 150. These might seem to be two different kinds of thing, but remember that until the advent of cheap, fast transport a century or so ago your personal social world *was* your village. You might know a few people from the next village, and a cousin or an uncle might have gone to work in the big city, but beyond these your entire social world was the world of your village, and you shared that world with everyone else in the village.

Friends online

One of the commonest responses to any mention of Dunbar's Number has usually been: 'It can't be right because I have five hundred ... a thousand ... two thousand friends on Facebook.' It is true that, since the growth of Facebook and its strategy of recommending friends to you because they are friends of friends ... of friends, some people have notched up large numbers of 'friends' online. But the real question is how many of these are *meaningful* friends. Some years ago I was interviewed by a well-known Swedish TV host who had decided to put this to the test on his programme. As with all media people, he had built up a very large Facebook following as part of his media presence and he had the idea of visiting every single one of the several thousand people on his list to see whether or not Dunbar's Number actually held up. So he spent several months traipsing round northern Europe, complete with camera crew in tow, tracking down all the people on his list. On one occasion, he told me, he even turned up uninvited at someone's wedding. When he later reported back on one of his shows, he had to admit that I was probably right. The people that had welcomed him were the ones he already knew and who were part of his personal social circle. Most of the rest had expressed surprise, some had indicated that it really wasn't very convenient, and a few had slammed the door on him for his impertinence. After all that effort, it seemed that most of them couldn't be counted as friends at all. Well, I had warned him when he interviewed me for the programme ...

So how many friends *do* people have on Facebook?

One of our forays into this world was initiated by an accidental collaboration with the boutique Dorset bakers and biscuit-makers Thomas J. Fudge. Since they were interested in what people did with friends as an advertising pitch and I was interested in finding out about people's online friendship networks, our interests converged. As part of the project, they ran two separate national polling samples totalling nearly three and a half thousand people across the British Isles in which the participants were asked how many friends they had on their social media account. The average was 169, with most people listing between 50 and 300, much as we have found in the offline samples. So it looked like people really don't have more friends online than they do in the offline world.

Tom Pollet and Sam Roberts sampled a population of Dutch university students to see how their use of social media affected their social network size. The average number of friends they had, online and offline combined, was 180. We were not surprised to find that those who spent more time active on social media had a larger circle of online friends: with more time spent online, it's inevitable that you have more time to contact more people. But the amount of time they spent online did not correlate with the size of their social network in the offline face-to-face world – or, for that matter, with higher levels of emotional closeness to their offline friends and family. It seemed, at least from this sample, that being active on social media does not necessarily enable you to have more friends.

An even more comprehensive – and impressive – analysis was carried out by Stephen Wolfram, an innovative software engineer and businessman who has undertaken extensive analyses of how people use the internet. He sampled the number of friends listed on one million Facebook pages and published a graph of the distribution on his blog. His graph allows us to make two key observations: first, the vast bulk of people list somewhere between about 150 and 250 friends, and, second, there is a long tail to the right with a very small number of people having a very large number of friends. As in our much smaller Fudge-the-Bakers sample, only a very small proportion of these people listed more than 400 friends, and only a very tiny number had more than 1,000. Nonetheless, given the number of people on Facebook, even a tiny proportion of a very, very large number is enough to allow almost everyone to know someone who has more than a thousand friends.

Meanwhile, inspired by reading about Dunbar's Number, two different groups of physicists had the idea of looking at traffic in the online world. Jan Haerter and his colleagues from the University of Copenhagen examined 23 million emails sent by 5,600 staff members and 30,000 students at the University of Oslo, Norway, over a three-month period, both amongst themselves and to some 10 million people outside the university. They looked at the patterns with which contacts joined and were lost over time, as well as whether or not messages were reciprocated (replies were received to emails sent, implying there was a real relationship), and they concluded that the number of contacts had a steady state somewhere between 150 and 250 individuals.

The other group, Bruno Gonçalves and Alessandro Vespignani,* chose to look at conversations on Twitter (i.e. those between members of the follower communities of Twitter accounts). They examined some 380 million tweets over a six-month period, from which they extracted some 25 million conversations for detailed analysis. Rather than just looking simply at the absolute number of different contacts someone had, they took account of the strength of the relationship (indexed by the number of tweets exchanged). This allowed them to discount casual conversations that lasted only one or two exchanges so as to focus on the more important relationships that each person had. They concluded that the number of contacts any one individual had, taking into account their strength, was typically in the order of 100–200 individuals.

---

* So far as I can ascertain, they were the first people to use the term 'Dunbar's Number' in print in an academic journal.

So, contrary to repeated claims, most people don't in fact seem to have very large numbers of friends on Facebook. Yes, a handful do, but the bulk of us have numbers that are in the same range as those we find in the everyday face-to-face world. In fact, it seems likely that most of the people we sign up as friends on Facebook really are just our everyday friends, with perhaps a handful of extra people we have met online. A few of us are more enthusiastic 'frienders' and are willing to sign up people we don't really know, but the number is actually pretty small. Most of us, it seems, are just too cautious to want random strangers peering into our private world.

The differences amongst us

Every study we have looked at has consistently suggested that people vary in the number of friends they have, and that the range of variation is typically between 100 and 250 individuals. This obviously raises the question as to why some people have more friends than others. There are a number of possibilities, including personality, sex and age.

In one of our first studies, 250 British and Belgian women completed a long and very tedious questionnaire about their personal social networks. There was a distinct ∩-shaped relationship between the number of friends people listed and the women's age. Network size increased up to the age of about thirty, stabilised, and then began to decline again from the age of about sixty. In the sample obtained for us by the polling agency in the Fudge-the-Bakers study, there was a steady linear decline in network size (in this case, indexed by the number of friends on Facebook) from around 250 in eighteen- to twenty-four-year-olds to seventy-three in the fifty-five-plus age group, with the thirty- and forty-year-olds group having almost exactly 150.

One explanation for the fact that younger people have more

friends is that they are less discriminating in whom they sign up. We know this is true for young children, who tend to see as a friend anyone they would like to befriend even though the other child has no interest in them at all. As we age, we learn whom to trust and whom to beware of, and start to be more selective in our choice of friends. It probably takes longer than we think to figure out the fine details of the difference between your view of the world and how other people see it – but of that, more in chapter 15. The point is simply that younger people might simply be more casual in their definition of friendship.

An alternative, though not necessarily mutually exclusive, explanation is that this age trend reflects shifts in social priorities. In effect, younger adults behave like careful shoppers: they are trying to sample as widely as they can among the pool of potential friends available to them in order to find the best set of life partners and friends. As a result, they distribute their time more widely – after all, they have much more time available in which to do so than older adults – and they ought to be happy to sacrifice relationship quality for quantity if it means they can sample a larger proportion of the available population. Into their thirties, people become more selective as they identify the best choices. In part, this is probably forced on them by the demands of parenthood. As every new parent knows, free time is decimated by the early years of childcare, and this in turn impacts on the time (and energy!) available for socialising. We shed our more casual friendships and concentrate what time and mental effort we have on the handful of really important friends. Hence, social network size stabilises for a few decades at around 150, as casual friendships are relinquished.

Interestingly, we documented exactly the same effect in gelada baboons when we were working on this species in Ethiopia during the 1970s. The energetic demands of lactation are so high for female monkeys and apes that they are forced to increase steadily the time devoted to feeding as their infant gets older and demands more milk; to provide the extra time needed for feeding, they withdraw progressively from interactions with all but their core social partners. Once the baby is weaned (at about a year old), the pressure is off and they reinstate social interactions with casual friends . . . until the cycle begins again with the next baby, of course. It's a universal problem, it seems.

The final phase in the human life cycle seems to kick in around the sixties, when we start to lose friends through death. If we lose friends when we are younger, perhaps because they moved away, we simply make a renewed social effort and replace them with new friends. In older age, however, we lack the energy and the motivation (and are less mobile as well) to seek and build new friendships. Moreover, the kinds of places where we found friends when we were younger are now no longer quite so appropriate as places to go. We don't quite know the right codes of behaviour for the context, are not even sure how to start a conversation with a stranger any more. So we become less inclined to go out in order to replace old friends. As a result, we gradually shed friends – and family – until in very old age we are confined to our house and seldom see anyone from one day's end to the next. The fact is that we start life with one or two close carers and, if we live long enough, we end life that way too.

Within each age class, however, there is still a wide range of variation in the number of friends people have, so other factors besides age are clearly at work. The most likely of these is personality, with the difference between extraverts and introverts being the obvious culprit. I have to say that I am not a great fan of personality as a psychological construct, mainly because it's the first thing – sometimes the only thing – that psychologists ever look at. Nonetheless, Thomas Pollet had a look at personality in a Dutch sample and found that extraverts typically did have larger networks than introverts, and this was true of both sexes. We knew from our previous analyses of the British and Belgian women's network sample that people with larger networks tend to have less emotionally close relationships, on average, with their network members than those with smaller networks. And this turned out to be true of Tom's extraverts and introverts. In effect, extraverts behave like social butterflies, flitting from one person to another and not devoting a great deal of time to any of them.

It is as though we all have the same amount of emotional capital (think of this as the time you have for spending with people), but introverts choose to spread this thickly among just a few people whereas extraverts choose to spread it thinly among many people. As a result, extraverts have friendships that, on average, are much weaker than those of introverts. Given that someone's willingness to support you is directly related to the time you spend socialising with them (and hence their perceived emotional closeness to you), one consequence of this may be that extraverts are less likely to be supported by their friends. It's as though introverts feel less secure about the social world, so they prefer to invest more heavily in a few people whom they know really well and whom they can really rely on. One strategy is not better than the other – they are just two different ways of ensuring that your social network provides you with the kinds of support you want. It may be that introverts prefer that to be emotional support (shoulders to cry on, as it were), while extraverts prefer it to be information about the wider world out there. In other words, it all depends on what you consider is the more valuable kind of resource.

The kith and the kin of it

So far, I have faithfully followed Facebook in calling anyone you have a relationship with a 'friend'. However, there is one important aspect of our social networks that we (and Facebook) have quietly ignored: family. In reality, it turns out that our social world consists of two quite distinct sets of people, namely friends and family – or, as the old expression has it, kith* and kin. We are, I suppose, apt to treat family as part of the social furniture, making much more of our friends, which is perhaps why Facebook and other networking sites typically emphasise friends. Nonetheless, even though we often make much more effort to see our friends than we do our extended family members, family members are an important component of our social networks. In our British and Belgian women's social networks, members of the extended family made up half of people's social networks on average.

When we began to look more closely at the family component of people's social networks, we soon realised that these two halves of our social networks in fact behave very differently. It is as though we really have two quite separate social worlds that interdigitate, yet mostly remain quite separate. For one thing, we seem to give preference to family. One example of this is that, in our women's network data, people who came from large extended families actually had fewer friends. Many years before we did this study, Matt Spoors and I had sampled people's inner-core networks (the number of people that they contacted at least once a month) and found exactly the same effect: people who had few kin listed in their network had more non-kin friends, and vice versa. I remember someone telling me after a lecture I had given at a science festival that she and her husband were the archetypal examples of just this. She came from a very big family, and all her time was taken up with her many cousins, aunts and uncles, so she actually had very few real friends; in

---

*   In case you were wondering what the expression 'kith' refers to, it's an archaic Anglo-Saxon term meaning friends. 'Kith' originally meant 'the things well known' (the things that are *couth*), and referred to the neighbourhood you lived in and hence the people who live within it. Kith came to refer to that part of your neighbourhood that wasn't part of your family as such but was nonetheless well known to you. Its opposite is the more familiar word 'uncouth' (*unkith*), which originally meant the things that aren't familiar and 'proper' – hence the drift into its modern meaning of 'uncivilised' (which is, obviously, true of all people who don't belong to your particular tribe because they don't know your ways and so behave in ways you consider outrageous, inappropriate or just plain odd).

contrast, her husband, who came from a very small family, had a large number of friends.

This seems to be a consequence of the fact that our networks are limited to around 150 slots, and we first slot all our family members in and then, if we have any spare slots left, we set about filling them with unrelated friends. It seems likely that friends in this sense are a relatively recent phenomenon, and are a consequence of the dramatic reduction in family size that has occurred over the last two centuries, especially in Europe and North America. In a population that does not practise contraception (or at least, contraception as efficient as that provided by modern medicine in the form of little pills), a community of about 150 people is exactly what you end up with in the three living generations (offspring, parents, grandparents) from an ancestral pair of great-great-grandparents in a population that practised exogamy (marrying outside the immediate group, as is characteristic of almost all known human populations). That is interesting in itself, because that is about as far back as the oldest members of the community are able to remember who is who from personal experience (the grandparents' grandparents) and so be able to specify exactly how everyone is related by marriage and birth. Everyone in a community of this size is related to everyone else as a third cousin at the furthest, and most will be much closer. As anthropologists continue to remind us, in small-scale societies kinship is the single most important factor regulating social life: it determines how respectfully we speak to someone, whether we are allowed to joke with them, what obligations we are under, and even whom we can marry. Its reach is all-pervasive, and it provides society – at least at the village level – with its fabric and texture.

A particularly intriguing fact that bears this out is that none of the six main kinship-naming systems in the world have terms for anyone who is less closely related than cousins. It is as though this is the natural limit for human communities, and everyone beyond that magic circle of cousins is a stranger of no particular importance. In most traditional ethnographic societies, anyone joining the community has to be assigned some kind of fictive (or fictional) kinship, usually by being adopted as a son, or perhaps a brother, by someone; until that happens, they have no place in the community. All their adopter's kin then become their kin, with the same rights and obligations as real kin. We do much the same with adopted children, and of course we do it with very close friends when we teach our children to address them as 'Aunty Mary' or 'Uncle Jim' even though they are not biological aunts and uncles. Kinship is so central to small-scale societies that it might legitimately be regarded as one of the main organising principles of the human social world.

One reflection of this is that, all things being equal, we are much more willing to help relatives than we are friends. This is sometimes known as the *kinship premium*. Think about what happens if someone contacts you out of the blue and explains that they are your long-lost third cousin, and that you share a great-great-grandmother. You might just ask a few questions to check that this really is so, but once you accept the evidence, you'll offer them a bed for the night – and would they like to stay longer? But if the person says that they are a friend of a friend of a friend, your response is likely to be very different: after the usual pleasantries, you might suggest they try the Day's Inn down the road to see if there's a room available – and perhaps they might like to pop round some time for a cup of tea . . .

The kinship premium seems to derive from one of the most fundamental principles in evolutionary biology, the theory of kin selection – that we are more likely to behave altruistically, and less likely to behave selfishly, towards close relatives than distant relatives, and towards distant relatives than to unrelated folk. This is sometimes known as Hamilton's Rule, after the New Zealand evolutionary biologist Bill Hamilton who worked it all out while he was a lowly graduate student. It is a general organising principle in all species of animals (and even plants, in fact). Thomas Pollet showed this very nicely in a study of German and Dutch students. He asked them about the last time they had visited a relative, how they were related to them and how far away they lived. He was interested in whether they were willing to make more effort to visit a close relative than a distant relative, just as Hamilton's Rule predicts they should. He found that they had indeed travelled much further to see someone who was more closely related than someone less closely related. Being willing to go that extra mile is more worthwhile for a close relative than for a less close one.

Rick O'Gorman and Ruth Roberts used a well known social psychological test (the Implicit Association Test, or IAT) to explore the differences between family and friends. The test is designed to detect the strength of a person's subconscious association between mental representations of objects or people, and is commonly used to study implicit biases and stereotypes. They found that people hold more positive attitudes toward friends, view their friends as having more similar attitudes to them, but consider family (but not distant kin) as being more representative of their 'real community' than their friends are.

Another respect in which family and friend relationships differ is that friendships are more costly to maintain than family relationships. Our women's network data illustrate the general principle: people typically devoted more time to their close family than to their close friends, but they devoted much more time to their less close friends than to their less close family. Distant family relationships need only the occasional reminder to be kept ticking over, but friendships die fast if they are not maintained at the appropriate level of contact for any length of time. The consequences of this were evident in our longitudinal study of high-schoolers going away to university. We found that friends very quickly (within months) slipped down through the list of friends once they weren't being seen so regularly. It takes only a couple of years for a friend to become just an acquaintance – someone I once knew. Family members, in contrast, required much less work to maintain, and emotional closeness to them hardly budged an inch over the eighteen months of the study. If anything, it actually increased a little – absence really does make the heart grow fonder (but only for family). We can go many years without seeing them, and they still welcome us with open arms, will still come to our aid like the cavalry coming over the hill when we really need it.

One category of people who sit uncomfortably between family and friends are in-laws (otherwise known technically in anthropology as affines, or relatives by marriage). They are not biological kin, but at the same time they are not really unrelated friends either. They share with family the fact that they turn up in our lives whether we like it or not. Max Burton looked at the differences in how we interact with biological family, in-laws and friends in our British and Belgian women's social networks database. He found that the friends and family have very distinct signatures in the frequencies with which we contact them, and that in-laws look identical to biological family members in this respect. Of course, we almost never include the entire in-law extended family in our personal networks. Typically, we only include immediate in-laws (the parents, grandparents and siblings of our spouse); we rarely include our siblings' in-laws, for example. Moreover, it seems that we tend to view our in-laws as though they were one step less closely related to us than the equivalent member of our biological family – a sister-in-law as more like a cousin, for example. Close but not too close. The point is that we still treat them as family rather than friends. They have suddenly been catapulted into a different category as a result of a social ritual (marriage). But, and herein lies the crucial difference, even though they are unrelated, *your* in-laws share with you and your immediate family a common interest in your children, and so, in biological terms, they rank as kin, as the late Austin Hughes showed in a brilliant but mathematically difficult little book entitled *Evolution and Human Kinship*.

It is worth reminding ourselves that friends and family are not the only people we can have in our networks. There is nothing in all this to say that our social networks can only contain living humans. Our social networks are, after all, about *relationships*, not about specific kinds of beings. So it is quite appropriate for people to include recently dead ancestors in their networks. We visit their graves, we remember their birthdays and the anniversaries of their deaths. In fact, in some societies people attend to their long-dead ancestors every year. On the Day of the Dead (31 October, or All Hallows' Eve as we know it), the 9,000 members of the Pomuch community in Mexico visit their local cemetery and lovingly remove the bones of grandparents and great-grandparents from their niches, carefully clean them and dress them in new clothes before replacing them until next year. It's a way, the Pomuch say, of staying in touch with your ancestors. In New Guinea, some tribes used to carry around the skulls of their ancestors in a sling.

In fact, you can include anyone in your social network who is important to you – a favourite saint, the Virgin Mary, God himself. You can even have your favourite soap opera characters if you are especially hooked on these. And you can certainly include your favourite pet – cats, dogs, horses, your favourite chicken. You might even put them in your innermost-five circle if you felt they were especially emotionally close. With real human friendships, we expect a degree of reciprocation in the relationship for it to count as a real relationship, but it seems that you may only need to *think* that these other beings talk to you for you to include them in your network. This is obviously true of pet owners (most of whom *know* that their pets talk to them) and probably true of many intensely religious people (who commonly engage in direct conversations with saints or even God through prayer). Dogs, of course, milk this for all they are worth – partly because, being descended from monogamous wolves, they are naturally demonstrative and partly, no doubt, because, in the millennia since we first welcomed their wolfcub ancestors into our homes, we have bred them to exhibit all those behaviours that make them seem so affectionate. One measure of this emotional closeness is the way people invariably apply moral partiality to their pets. The dog that has just savaged an innocent stranger can, in its owner's eyes, do no wrong and must have been the innocent party.

3

Making friends with your brain

The value of 150 as the limit on the number of friends we can have did not appear from nowhere. In fact, I had predicted it from an analysis of the relationship between social group size and brain size in monkeys and apes. Even that had come about by accident while I was trying to solve what, at the time, I thought was rather a trivial problem that had nothing to do with the limits on group size. Behavioural scientists don't often get the chance to make serious predictions in the way that the hard sciences like physics and chemistry do. Such predictions as behavioural and social scientists make are usually rather trivial, and often simply obvious. Predicting that humans had a natural group size as small as 150 really was a step into the wild blue yonder. No one would seriously have expected it to be true. Let me explain how it came about.

Brainstorming

In the early 1990s, I turned my attention to what I thought at the time was a very trivial, albeit rather irritating, problem, namely why primates spend so much time grooming each other. The conventional view at the time was that grooming was simply about hygiene – removing burrs and other bits of vegetation from the fur and generally keeping the skin clean and healthy. Grooming certainly does that, but after many years watching monkeys in the wild I had been deeply impressed by the fact that they groomed far more than they ever needed to for purely hygienic purposes. It seemed obvious that grooming was intensely social and pleasurable.

Of course, grooming helps to keep the fur clean, and surely evolved originally for this reason. But somehow it seemed to have been co-opted during the course of primate evolution (as well as by some other intensely social species, such as the horse family and even some birds) to subserve a more explicitly social function. Some of the most social monkeys spend as much as a fifth of their entire day grooming each other, and it simply didn't make sense to suggest that all of this was needed for hygiene – especially when other species of similar body size spend only 1–2 per cent of their time grooming socially. The problem was how to test between these two alternative explanations.

It occurred to me that one way of doing so was to see whether time spent grooming in different species correlated better with their social group size (implying a social function for grooming) or with their body size (essentially, a measure of how much fur they had to be cleaned). It turned out that grooming time did correlate with group size, and not at all with body size. I felt vindicated. Just a year or two earlier, Andy Whiten and Dick Byrne at St Andrews University in Scotland had proposed that monkeys and apes had larger brains than other mammals because they lived in socially much more complex groups, a suggestion they termed the 'Machiavellian Intelligence Hypothesis' after the medieval Italian political philosopher Niccolò Machiavelli. It occurred to me that, if this was true, then grooming time, group size and brain size should all correlate with each other: large groups have more dyadic relationships (more possible friendship pairs) than small groups, so species that live in large groups would need bigger brains to manage these *and* have to devote more time to grooming so as to bond the group together. And, indeed, so it proved to be: both brain size and time spent grooming increase in proportion to group size across the primates as a whole.

Having discovered this relationship, I was prompted to ask the obvious question: what did the relationship between brain size and group size imply about the natural size of human groups? There were brain data for humans in the same database that provided the brain data for the primates, so it was just a matter of plugging the human brain size (or more correctly, neocortex size) into the equation for the social brain. There was a catch, however. As Figure 1 shows, the Social Brain Hypothesis turns out to consist of a series of four distinct grades in the relationship between group size and brain size (indexed here as relative neocortex size), with the grades corresponding to groups of progressively increasing size as well as correspondingly smarter cognitive abilities. Since the apes form one of these grades in their own right (grade 4), it is this relationship we need to use, not the overall relationship. When we plug human neocortex size into the ape social brain equation, the answer we get is 148 – or, to the nearest round number, 150, give or take a bit.

Could this possibly be right? Did humans *really* live in groups of this size? After all, we live in huge cities and conurbations of many millions of people! But cities, even towns, are of very recent origin. Before 5,000 years ago, there were hardly any towns with more than a few thousand people. Indeed, the earliest settlements with houses for even a few hundred people only date back 10,000 years. Prior to that, stretching back several million years into the distant evolutionary mists, we lived as hunter–gatherers, as some tribal peoples still do. Hunter–gatherer societies all around the world have a very characteristic form: they consist of a community that is scattered across its territory in three or four camp groups or bands. Several communities are in turn gathered together into what is sometimes known as a mega-band, and several mega-bands are gathered together into a tribe. People generally only live with members of

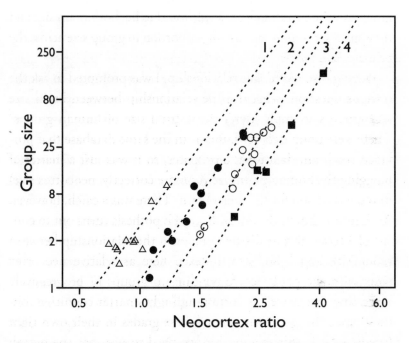

Figure 1. The Social Brain Hypothesis. Mean group size for individual primate species plotted against neocortex ratio (neocortex volume divided by the volume of the rest of the brain). The neocortex is the part of the brain that does all the smart thinking for you: it forms a large thin sheet wrapped around the inner ancient vertebrate brain (the part that is mainly responsible for keeping body and soul together). Statistical analyses reveal that there are in fact four distinct grades in the social brain relationship: semi-solitary prosimians (triangles); less social monkeys and social prosimians (filled circles), highly social monkeys (unfilled circles) and apes (squares). Humans are the square in the top right corner. The grades are numbered 1–4.

their own community, but within that they can switch from camp group to camp group pretty much as they feel inclined; they may occasionally visit other camp groups in their mega-band (but probably won't settle there on a permanent basis), and they will trade or give presents to other members of their tribe. In other words, each layer of society has its own characteristic set of relationships.

At the time, I had no idea which of these many layers was the right one to use as the natural grouping size for humans, and no anthropologist I discussed this with was willing to say. In fact, if anything, they would have plumped for the camp group or band. But the camp group is an ecological grouping. It is the group that people spend the night in, mainly for protection, and its size depends on season, latitude and ecology. It is not a social grouping as such. So, instead, I turned the question on its head and asked whether any of these layers, each with its characteristic size, was close to 150. I found data on twenty-one societies from all around the world, ranging from Inuit in the Arctic to Australian Aboriginals, and the Yanomamo of Venezuela to the pygmies of the Central African forests. It turned out that, of the four grouping levels, it was the size of the community that was nearest to 150. The terms used to describe groupings in ethnographic societies are somewhat elastic, but the community, or clan as it is known in some cases, is the group of people that share a common hunting territory and come together every year or two for ceremonies like puberty and marriage rituals. When these have the more formal status of clans (as they do among Australian Aboriginals and some North American Indian tribes), they are usually bound together by descent from a common ancestor and are exogamous (marriages are normally contracted outside the community). The size of this grouping varied from roughly 100 to 200 in size, with an average of 148.4. It could hardly have been closer to the predicted value of 147.8.

The social brain is for everyone

When I originally came up with the Social Brain Hypothesis, I had assumed that it would apply to all mammals, and I did run some analyses for insectivores (the rather ragbag grouping of the most primitive mammals like shrews and voles) and for carnivores. There was a sort of relationship in both cases, but it was a bit messy to say the least and nowhere near as clear as for the primates. Many years later, Susanne Shultz had another more serious go at this. She looked at the ungulates (animals with hooves), the carnivores, the bats and the birds, and found that while there was a linear relationship between group size and brain size in primates, as we had previously found, this did not hold in any of the other groups. Instead, the birds, bats, carnivores and ungulates all exhibited a distinct qualitative version of the social brain effect: species that lived in monogamous pairs had larger brains than species that lived on their own, or in small harem-like groups or large amorphous herds. Moreover, within the birds, there was a distinct difference between the species that paired for life (the parrots, crows, and the birds of prey) and those that paired only for a single breeding season and found a new mate the following year (most of our familiar garden birds). The former had significantly larger brains than the latter, who in turn had larger brains than the species that mated promiscuously (most of the other species). Think of the pair-bonded crow's heavy, dumpy head on its small body compared with the promiscuous peacock's tiny head on its massive body.

Later, Susanne was able to show that the increase in brain size over geological time within different mammalian orders correlated with the proportion of their living species that have bonded social groups. The families whose brains had increased most dramatically in size included the anthropoid primates (the monkeys and apes), the camel family (the South American guanaco and vicuña, and the more conventional Asian camel), the dolphins, the elephants and the horse family (the horses, asses and zebras), all of whose living members typically have bonded social relationships. The prosimian primates (the lemurs, galagos and their allies) brought up a distant rear in this group, not too far ahead of the dogs whose brain sizes have increased only modestly (all the dog family are monogamous), with the cats and the deer and antelope, whose brains have hardly increased at all over the last 20 million or so years (most of them are either solitary or live in anonymous herds), bringing up the rear. Later still, she and Kieran Fox at the University of British

Columbia analysed data for the whales and dolphins and showed that, in this group, brain size correlates with both social group size (as reflected in pod size), as befits species with bonded groups, and with foraging style.

It was these data that made us realise that the real issue is not group size as such but bonded social relationships. The overarching principle that bound anthropoid primate social groups with monogamous pair-bonds of the carnivore, ungulate, bat and bird families was that all these groups depended on personalised relationships in which individuals are mutually committed to each other by a form of trust, reciprocity and obligation. In other words, friendships to you and me.

There did, nonetheless, appear to be a difference between anthropoid primate sociality and that of the carnivores and ungulates, at least. When Susanne, Javier Pérez-Barbería and I examined the correlation between the switch from non-sociality to sociality and the switch from small to large brains across the phylogenetic history of these three groups, primates stood out, because the switches in these two variables seemed to happen simultaneously: if one changed, the other changed at the same time in a very tight co-evolutionary relationship. In contrast, in both ungulates and carnivores, the changes were much more sloppy: one might change, but the other might stay the same for a while. In addition, there were often reversals in the ungulate and carnivore sequences: they might switch from solitary, small-brained to social, large-brained, and later switch back again. This never ever happened in primates. It suggested that primate sociality and brain size were in a much tighter co-evolutionary relationship than was the case in these other mammals. That is because all primates have bonded social relationships, whereas only a few ungulates and carnivores have these kinds of relationships – and those are mostly associated with pair-bonded monogamy.

Taken together, all this suggests that there is something very different about primate social relationships that only a very small number of other mammals seem able to match. This is the intensity of the bonded relationships they have and the fact that they can have these relationships with several individuals, not just a reproductive mate. While monogamous reproductive relationships represent the high point of sociality and bondedness in many mammal and bird lineages (90 per cent of bird species have this kind of social system), this seems to represent the least demanding form of social system in primates.

There have been a surprising number of misunderstandings as to what this relationship is all about, so let me just clarify a few points before we go any further. The Social Brain Hypothesis has sometimes been viewed as an alternative to ecological explanations for why primates evolved large brains – with the ecological version usually couched in terms of clever food-finding. In fact, the Social Brain Hypothesis *is* an ecological hypothesis. The alternative hypotheses are not social versus foraging, but whether animals solve their ecological problems on their own by individual trial-and-error learning (and social groups form only because animals converge on rich food patches) or do so socially and live in groups in order to make this possible. The problem with living in stable, permanent groups is that considerable diplomatic and social skills are needed to prevent the stresses and niggles of living in close proximity with others from overwhelming us (and who doesn't know *that* from everyday experience?). If we cannot defuse these stresses, they can have serious consequences for mammals, including us, by having terrible effects on our immune system and even switching off females' fertility by shutting down their menstrual endocrinology system. If this continues unabated, individuals will eventually leave the group to find a smaller one that is less stressful. In the end, we will all end up living on our own.

Bonded relationships, and the sophisticated cognition that underpins these, are the key solution that primates, in particular, evolved to maintain social groups. One example of this is that, in bonded social groups, your friends keep an eye on you and make sure they stay with you even if you decide to wander off. We found that primates and pair-bonded antelope are constantly checking on the whereabouts of their closest friends, whereas herd-forming species (such as the wild goats I studied) hardly ever do. So the Social Brain Hypothesis is a two-step explanation: ecological problems are solved by living in a group, and living in a group is solved by having a large enough brain to manage the stresses involved.

The other important distinction between these two views lies in what we assume the ecological driver is. Those who favour a one-step ecological explanation for large brains think only in terms of food-finding; those who favour the Social Brain Hypothesis emphasise protection from predators. This is really a question of which factor most limits primates' ability to prosper in particular habitats. The reality is that food is rarely a big problem, at least for vegetarians; being eaten by predators is always a much more serious problem and demonstrably prevents primate species occupying some otherwise suitable habitats. Part of the problem in this respect is, I suspect, that many researchers seem not to appreciate just how complex social relationships in bonded societies (including our own) actually are. By comparison, deciding whether to eat this berry rather than that root is a cognitive walk in the park. The bottom line is that our social world is by far the most complex thing in the universe precisely because it is so dynamic and in constant flux, and keeping track of that and managing it is very demanding in information processing terms.

Friends in your brain

So to the big question: if the social brain hypothesis applies between species, does it also apply *within* species – does the size of *your* brain predict the size of *your* personal friendship circle? Evolutionary biology suggests that this ought to be so, because it is variation in a trait that makes it possible for evolution into new forms to occur.

You wouldn't end up with differences between species if there hadn't been differences between individuals in the first place.

In the past, we wouldn't have been able to test this possibility until people had died and we could extract their brains from their skulls. But by then we might not have been able to determine the number of friends they had had – we want to know how many they had in the prime of life, not how many they had in their lonely old age. The advent of brain-imaging technology in the last couple of decades has changed all this. Now we can scan people's brains and measure the size and structure relatively painlessly while they are still alive. The most commonly used technology is known as magnetic resonance imaging (MRI for short), which is now widely used in diagnostic medicine. It works by using super-strong magnets to track the location of hydrogen or oxygen molecules in the brain, and this allows a very detailed picture of the brain to be produced.

So around 2006, I began to discuss the possibility of doing this with several people. Penny Lewis, then a young lecturer at Liverpool University (where I then was as well) and now a professor in her own right at Cardiff University, was keen to give it a go. The idea was to get a group of people to make a list of their friends and family, and then put them in the brain scanner and measure the size of relevant bits of their brains. Since we knew from our earlier studies that asking people to list out their entire network was frustrating and boring, we asked them to provide just the number of friends and family they had contacted in the last month. For reasons that we will discover in the next chapter, this turns out to be closely correlated with total network size.

Brain-scanning experiments are very time-consuming, as you can only put one person in the scanner at a time and each scan takes the better part of an hour by the time they have filled in all the questionnaires you give them to find out about their social networks. Nonetheless, after many hours of hard work, we had a set of brain scans and matching network questionnaires. It was just a matter of seeing which bits of the brain increased in size most with the number of friends. Penny opted to do this by partitioning the brain into tiny volumes a few millimetres in diameter, and then adding together all those that were part of the same cognitive system. In addition, Joanne Powell (now a lecturer at Liverpool Hope University) ran some more laborious analyses to measure the volume of the prefrontal cortex and its parts – the part of the brain right at the front of your brain just behind your forehead where most of the clever thinking gets done. These two very different approaches – one broad but very fine-grained, the other focused but very coarse-grained – showed pretty much the same thing. The more friends you had, the bigger were the bits of the brain known to be involved in social skills – the prefrontal cortex (roughly the front quarter of the brain), the temporal lobe (that runs alongside your ear) and the area known as the temporo-parietal junction (TPJ for short) where the temporal lobe joins the parietal lobe just behind the ear (Figure 2). All of these areas were bigger in people who listed more friends, but the prefrontal cortex regions seemed to have the strongest relationship of all. As we shall see in chapter 6, these are the parts of the brain that are most closely involved in processing social relationships. For now, however, it is enough to know that the

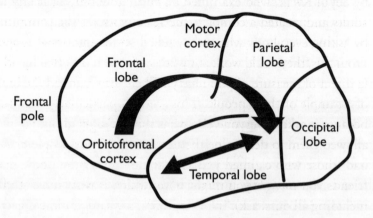

Figure 2. The main regions of the brain, with the mentalising network indicated by the arrows.

number of friends we have is correlated with the size of the key parts of the brain that we use in social situations.

In science, a new discovery usually prompts other laboratories to repeat the experiment to make sure it wasn't just an accident. So over the next few years, more than a dozen other studies tested this hypothesis, using different measures of friendship as well as different imaging techniques. Some asked people to list out all 150+ of their friends and family, others have used the number of Facebook friends, a few have used the numbers of supportive relationships participants have, while yet others used measures of how social they are rather than the actual number of friends. All of these studies found relationships between social network size (however measured) and brain-region volumes. Some have placed more emphasis on the role of the amygdala and the limbic system, others have emphasised the frontal and temporal lobes (a group of brain units known as the theory of mind network, or more recently the default mode neural network). The main point is that all of them broadly confirm what we found in our original study: the number of friends you have correlates with the size of those bits of the brain known to be involved in managing the social world.

In many ways, however, the prize goes to a Korean group led by Seyul Kwak, who examined an entire township of nearly 600 adults and created a complete social network for the community by asking everybody whom they relied on for emotional support. From this, they could work out who was listed most often by others (a direct of measure of popularity). Then they scanned the brains of a sample of these people. This study is particularly important because it asked everyone else what they thought about you: this allowed them to determine the number of friends people *actually* had (those who claimed you as a friend), rather than how many friends you *thought* you might have (which is what most studies, including all ours, ask). In other words, it was a bit more objective than most previous studies. They found that the number of friends was best predicted by the orbitofrontal cortex, the dorsomedial prefrontal cortex and the lingual gyrus (an area just above the orbitofrontal cortex sometimes associated with high-level visual processing, but also with the logical structure of events).

Ryota Kanai had been responsible for one of the brain-scan studies that confirmed that people with fewer friends (in his case, indexed as the number of friends on Facebook) have smaller brains. In following this up, he had the idea of looking to see if people who described themselves as being lonely differed in brain organisation from those who were not lonely. He found that lonely individuals have less grey matter in the superior temporal sulcus, or STS (part of the temporal lobe that runs along either side of the brain just by your ears). This is one of the areas that invariably feature in all the brain-scan studies of theory of mind and mentalising. Since the temporal lobe is also strongly associated with memory storage (including such things as the meanings of words), its role in mentalising is probably in allowing us to compare different event memories in the vignettes used in these kinds of studies. His study also confirmed that loneliness was associated with difficulty in processing social cues, as might be expected, as well as confirming that other psychological factors such as a small social network size, high anxiety and low empathy independently contribute to loneliness. However, only social perception skills seemed to explain the association between the temporal lobe volume and loneliness.

The fact that the amygdala has been flagged up in several of the studies is interesting. The amygdala is part of the limbic system, and is involved in processing fear and other emotional cues that allow us to avoid dangerous situations. Although it lies outside the neocortex in the older parts of the brain, it has a direct link into the orbitofrontal neocortex right at the front of the brain. The orbitofrontal neocortex is involved in interpreting emotional cues, and it seems that it can act to suppress the amygdala's panicky responses when it thinks these are misplaced. Since all relationships, and especially those with strangers, are potentially risky (we don't know *quite* how they are going to behave), the initial instinct will always be to run away. The orbitofrontal cortex is able to dampen down this tendency when there isn't any need to run away – something that may be especially important during court-ship and mating, for example. This is an important reminder that the different brain regions interact to create a fine-tuned balance that allows us to function effectively in complex situations.

Another important reminder of this was provided by a study carried out by MaryAnne Noonan, one of my colleagues at Oxford University. She looked at the brain's white matter and showed that its volume was also correlated with the size of the friendship circle. The brain consists of two ostensibly different types of cell: white matter and grey matter. Grey matter is really just unadorned nerve cells and it is the stuff that does all the hard computational work – the brain's computational engines. White matter is essentially the wiring that links different grey-matter units, some of which may be in different locations within the brain. These are white because they are covered in a fatty sheath called myelin that acts like the plastic insulation on electrical wires. The myelin sheath does two related things. First, it prevents the nerve sparking over onto another nerve (which would cause messages to end up in the wrong place). Second, it speeds up the rate at which the nerve can transmit an electrical signal, and hence the efficiency with which different bits of the brain talk to each other. MaryAnne found that white-matter volume correlates particularly well with the size of your social network. This is probably why treating the neocortex as a whole unit (including both grey and white matter) as we did in all the original social brain analyses actually works as well as it does. Particular functions, such as figuring out if Jim has misbe-haved, do not happen in one small corner of the brain, but rather involve messages being shunted backwards and forwards between a number of brain units.

Almost all these analyses were done on right-handed people. This is standard practice in brain-scanning studies: it avoids the complication created by the fact that most (but, inconveniently, not all) left-handed people have brains that are reversed to those of right-handers. For right-handers, the part of the brain that best predicted number of friends in our experiments was the very front part of the brain (technically, the orbitofrontal cortex immediately above your eyes, or the adjacent part known as the medial frontal cortex). This area is associated with experiencing emotions and the control of emotions, and seems to suggest that processing knowledge about relationships is being done in a semi-automated way – or, rather, in a way that is below the consciousness horizon. Joanne Powell ran some additional imaging studies on left-handers. The results were essentially the same, except that the part of the frontal lobe that best predicted number of friends in left-handers was the dorso-frontal cortex, one step back from the orbitofrontal cortex on the upper surface of the brain. This brain region is usually associated with rational thought and reasoning. It looked suspiciously to me as though left-handers were thinking more consciously about their relationships than right-handers did. In other words, right- and left-handers might process their relationships in different ways: one more emotionally, the other more rationally.

Subsequent studies have indicated that the way the brain processes social information can be quite complex and may depend on exactly what social context is involved. Sylvia Morelli and her collaborators mapped the social networks among students in two undergraduate dormitories by asking everyone to nominate the socially most valuable individuals as sources of friendship, empathy and support. This allowed them to see who acted as hubs (i.e. who was especially popular) in these networks. When they scanned the brains of a subset of these people as they viewed pictures of the other individuals, they found increased activity in those brain regions known to be involved in mentalising (specifically the medial prefrontal cortex, parts of the temporal lobe and the precuneus) and regions associated with value processing (the ventral striatum) when they were viewing photographs of hub individuals, even when controlling for the individual's personal relationship with the hub.

Similar results were found by Noam Zerubavel and Kevin Ochsner in a study of two small student clubs, each of which had fourteen members. They asked everyone to rate all the other members of their club for likeability and then scanned their brains as they watched photographs of each club member in turn. As in the Morelli study, looking at pictures of more popular individuals resulted in more brain activity in the mentalising and valuation regions, with the latter including the orbital prefrontal cortex and the amygdala as well as the ventral striatum. However, what was particularly interesting in their case was that activation of the valuation region only occurred in viewers who themselves had been rated highly. Those who had been rated as less attractive showed no differences in activity as a function of whose photograph they were looking at. They did, however, exhibit much higher activity levels in these brain regions overall. In other words, the less popular individuals seemed to be paying much closer attention to everyone, whereas the more popular ones were only interested in the most popular individuals (the community leaders).

In a third study, Carolyn Parkinson and her collaborators found similar patterns of activity in these same regions in a class of graduate MBA students. Everyone in the class first rated everybody else in terms of how much leisure time they spent with them. Then twenty volunteers were asked to watch videos of the other class members while their brains were being scanned. Once again, popular individuals whose friends were also rated as popular triggered the strongest responses in the brain regions associated with valuation and mentalising. In other words, the mentalising and valuation networks were responding not just to the viewer's own relationship to the person in the video, but also to these people's relationships with the other members of the group – or to put it another way, friends of friends are as important as friends are, just as the Framingham Heart Study suggested.

More interesting, however, is the fact that two recent studies of especially social Old World monkey species (macaques and baboons) have shown that the number of animals an individual is housed with correlates with the size of units in the temporal lobe, the prefrontal cortex and the amygdala, just as it does in humans. So it seems that the Social Brain Hypothesis applies not just between species but also within species at the level of the individual in both monkeys and humans. That is impressive. It also speaks to the evolutionary basis of the social brain.

Of course, everything I have said so far is based on snapshots of brain size. What we don't know is whether the size of your brain determines how many friends you can have or whether the number of friends you have determines the size of your brain. There are good grounds for thinking that the latter must be at least partly true. We now know that the brain is much more flexible in its responses to circumstance than we had previously ever imagined. We will see later that the social skills that mediate the social brain effect are so complex that they take more than two decades to learn in humans, and that may very well influence how the brain grows. It is possible that your prefrontal cortex and other social brain areas grow in size as a result of how much they are used, though this probably doesn't continue much after the mid-twenties. Be that as it may, by the time you reach adulthood it seems that your brain is probably pretty much fixed. Anything after that is just tinkering round the edges.

Sex and the social brain

One of the things we had noticed in our various studies of social networks was that women always had slightly more friends than men. Even when the difference was not significant, it was consistently in this direction. Did this mean there were brain differences between the sexes that were relevant to friendship? It has been known for a long time that the two sexes differ not just in overall brain volume (men, being larger in body size, have bigger brains) but also in the sizes of some brain regions (women typically have more white matter and prefrontal cortex than men).

In a roundabout way, these findings dovetail neatly with an earlier finding by the eminent Cambridge neuroscientist Barry Keverne. In the 1980s, he had become interested in a newly emerging topic that went under the name of genomic imprinting. Very briefly, this refers to a phenomenon whereby the genes we inherit from our parents seem to know which side they came from and, as a result, one set may be actively suppressed so that they do not influence how we develop. Most of these genes seem to be involved in the development of the brain, and it was two aspects of this that had caught his attention. One was the fact that our father's neocortex genes seem to be suppressed during development so that the neocortex we have is determined by our mother's genes; the other was the fact that the genes for our limbic system (the emotional machinery of the brain) are inherited from our fathers (with those from our mothers suppressed).

This rather weird process makes a certain sense in terms of the main drivers of male and female reproductive strategies. For most female mammals, and primates in particular, being able to work effectively in a social environment is much more important for their reproductive success than anything else. For most male mammals, reproductive success is mainly a consequence of how effectively they compete against each other. For males, the red mist rising in competition with other males tends to be the most effective way of doing this. Male mammals that politely say 'After you! Do help yourself!' are unlikely to leave many descendants. Conversely, in primates at least, sociality is the key to female reproductive success: females that have more friends are less stressed by events such as rampaging males, have more offspring who in turn are more likely to make it to adulthood, *and* live longer themselves. (Similar findings have been reported for wild horses, by the way.) So the social skills needed to engineer friendships are likely to be selected for, and hence those parts of the brain that support these skills will be prioritised by evolution. And these parts, as we have seen, are the frontal lobes of the neocortex in particular.

Aside from these hints, however, the question of sex differences in brains, and especially brain size, has remained on everybody's backburner, mainly because in certain quarters the topic became rather toxic. Then, in 2018, I received an intriguing email out of the blue. It came from Danilo Bzdok, who turned out to be a quietly spoken young neuroscientist from the University of Aachen in Germany. With almost British understatement, he indicated that he had some results that he thought I might find interesting because they seemed to support the social brain hypothesis. Would I be interested in meeting him to discuss them? Intrigued, I naturally said yes. Our paths happened to cross in London a few months later when he was passing through on his way back to Aachen and I happened to be at a conference there. We met in the hotel bar where I was staying while he was on his way to Heathrow airport. Over a beer, he showed me some of his data.

He and his research group had been analysing data from the UK Biobank database. The database had been built up in the early 2000s by asking half a million British people to contribute their health data as well as being assessed for some specific psychological and physiological measurements. More interestingly, the Biobank provided an enormous sample of over 10,000 scanned brains, linked to their associated physiological, psychological and sociological measurements. This had allowed Danilo and his group to look in minute detail at how the volumes of different parts of the brain correlate with individual social measures in the two sexes. There were particularly strong sex differences in how the limbic system (the amygdala) and parts of the prefrontal cortex correlate with the frequency and intensity of social contacts. He found that women who lived in households with more people had a larger amygdala than women who lived with fewer individuals, whereas there was no effect of household size on amygdala size for males. In contrast, men in larger households had larger orbitofrontal cortices, whereas women exhibited no consistent pattern. The reverse was the case for those who had more opportunity to engage with emotionally close relationships. Women who expressed greater satisfaction with their relationships and who said they had more opportunities to confide in others had larger volumes in these two areas than women who did not.

I'll come back to the thorny question of sex differences again in chapter 13, but in the meantime there are several take-home messages here. First, social, and hence brain, evolution may have been driven mainly by female interests. Second, this seems to have knock-on consequences for how the neurological systems that underpin sociality are organised. They may not be the same in the two sexes. Third, differences in the way our neurobiological machinery is organised are likely to have subtle but important effects on how we think and behave.

*

So far, I have tended to speak of our social networks as though they are homogeneous – a friend is a friend is a friend, much as social media would have us believe. Yet, at the same time, I have hinted that friendships come in different kinds – some more intimate, others less so. I mentioned at the outset that we typically have five close friends. I have even mentioned that we have acquaintances who are less close than people we would consider to be friends. In the next chapter, I want to unpack this a bit more.

4

Friendship in circles

What do the following have in common: juries, most team sports, the inner cabinets of most governments, the Apostles, the smallest unit in most modern armies (usually known as a section), the number of people whose death tomorrow would really upset you? The answer is that they are all of about the same size: 12, 11–15, 12–15, 12, 11–16, 11–15, respectively. It seems there is something very odd about the number twelve in human psychology. It keeps reappearing in a variety of contexts where people have to work closely with each other. I first came across this when I was searching for evidence on the natural size of human groups in the early 1990s. I chanced upon a paper by a couple of American social psychologists, Christian Buys and Kenneth Larsen, who named this grouping the *sympathy group* and were the first scientists to collect data on its size by asking people to make a list of all the people whose death would upset them. There is, they suggested, a limit on the number of people we can feel sympathy for, and this seems to set a limit on other groupings where close psychological interaction is required.

A football team offers an obvious example. A successful team is not one that consists of eleven individual players who rush about the field trying to score as many individual goals as they can, if necessary by stealing the ball from other members of their own side. Rather, it consists of a *team* of eleven players who coordinate their actions in order to score goals.* The forwards and backs have different jobs to do, and they need to stick to their tasks rather than rush about the field in a frenzy chasing the ball. In really successful teams, each player is so attuned to how everyone else in the team plays that they know exactly where everyone will be on the field at any given moment; they know exactly where the one with the ball is likely to kick it to so that they are waiting in the right position even before the ball arrives there. That requires them to know how the others think, inside and out.

Our very first attempt to look at the size of sympathy groups in the early 1990s was a survey carried out by one of our graduate students, Matt Spoors (he went on to become a biology teacher). It confirmed the existence of the sympathy group. But it also threw up a smaller grouping of around five people within the sympathy group that we named the *support clique* because it consisted of all the people who would unstintingly give you support or help if you needed it. There was clearly more structure to social networks than we had previously imagined, and there was a striking consistency to this structure between individuals – everyone seemed to have the same pattern. It was the first hint that the typical social circle of 150 that surrounds us is in fact made up of a series of layers.

The circles of friendship

I had noticed when I analysed the data on the sizes of small-scale societies that the different social layers seemed to form a rather distinct series that took the form of a hierarchically inclusive set

---

*   You might rightly point out that rugby football has fifteen a side, while its variants, such as rugby league, have thirteen (or even eighteen in the case of Australian Rules football). Notice, however, that these games divide the 'team' into two subgroups (three in the case of Australian Rules) that play completely different games and engage mainly with other members of their own subgroup.

of groupings at roughly 50, 150, 500 and 1,500 individuals. Later, we noticed that our Christmas-card data had a similar pattern of 5, 15 and 150 (with the hint of another possible layer in between) that tucked neatly into the lower end of this series. We had been wondering how we could explore the significance of this when I received an email out of the blue from the French physicist Didier Sornette, who had begun life trying to predict earthquakes and then become interested in those other equally unpredictable phenomena, the stock market and financial bubbles. Having come across my papers with the hunter–gatherer grouping sizes, he asked whether I had noticed the pattern in the data, and could he analyse the data to see what the pattern was. So I sent him our data, and he persuaded a young Chinese researcher named Wei-Xing Zhou (now a professor at Shanghai's East China University of Technology) to run the data through some sophisticated mathematical analyses. The analysis used the mathematics of fractals to look for recurring patterns in the data. He found a very consistent pattern in both datasets: relationships were structured into a series of inclusive circles, or layers,* with each layer three times the size of the layer immediately inside it. Figure 3 illustrates the pattern. (You will have noticed another layer at 1.5. I'll come back to that in a minute.) These layers are successively inclusive, so that the 15 circle includes everyone in the 5 circle, and the 50 circle includes everyone in the 5 and 15 circles, and so on. In other words, the people in the 15-layer consist of five close friends whom you see often and what look like two more groups of five friends whom you see somewhat less often.

To give these circles a bit more of an everyday feel, we might think of them as, respectively, our close friends (five), best friends (fifteen), good friends (fifty) and just friends (150). The inner layers make intuitive sense in terms of our everyday experience. But the two outer layers beyond 150 were a bit less obvious. I had

---

* I will refer to these interchangeably as layers or circles.

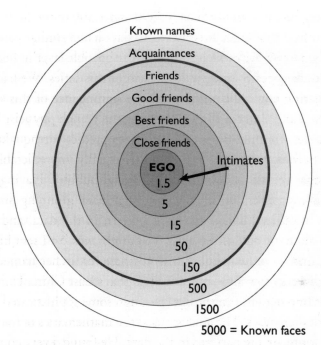

Figure 3. The circles of friendship. The approximate numerical size of each layer is inclusive of the layers within it. In each case, the layers are inclusive and their sizes form a regular fractal pattern with a scaling ratio of approximately three (each layer is three times the size of the layer immediately inside it).

thought that they might represent something like acquaintances (people you are familiar with, many of whom you probably work with, at around 500) and what seems to be something like the number of people you know by name (1,500). This last suggestion came from a study done in the early 1970s which had estimated that there was an upper limit at around 2,000 on the number of faces we could put names to. But we could say no more than that.

However, a recent study by Rob Jenkins at the University of York has allowed us to define these outer layers a bit more explicitly. He used a face-recognition task to determine how many faces people recognise (even if they couldn't put a name to the face). Subjects were shown a large number of photographs of faces, and subsequently asked which ones they knew and which ones they had seen before. These data suggest that we know personally around 500 people (defined in this study as consisting mainly of friends, family and colleagues) and can recognise by sight (but without necessarily being able to name) a total of around 5,000. So, putting these different insights together, my best guess is that the 1,500-layer is the number of faces you can put names to (which, for most people, would include people like the Queen and Donald Trump, or Mo Farah), and the 5,000-layer identified by Rob Jenkins is the number of faces you can recognise as someone you have (or have not) seen before, even if you don't know their name. In neither case do you have a *personalised* relationship with anyone in these outermost layers: you might recognise them in the street if you saw them, but they would have no idea at all who you are. Those in the 500-layer are best described as acquaintances, and many of these are people you work with or perhaps know casually through some social group or perhaps buy your morning coffee from on the way to work. Unlike the celebrities and semi-strangers that people our 1,500-layer, those in the 500-layer know who we are. They are the sort of people you know well enough to have a beer with after work, but you wouldn't think of inviting to your big celebration party – and they are unlikely to bother turning up to your funeral. By the way, Rob Jenkins was not interested in proving the existence of these layers: he is a vision scientist who studies the mechanisms of face recognition, and was simply interested in the question of how many faces we can recognise. That his results fit so neatly with ours is very encouraging.

What surprised all of us was that the ratio between successive layers (known as the 'scaling ratio') is very close to three. There is no obvious reason why the ratio should be three, rather than, say, two or four. This prompted us to see if we could find a similar pattern in other datasets. One of those we looked at was our large sample of 250 women's social networks. And sure enough, there they were. In this case, the layers seemed to be defined by the frequencies with which people contacted their friends, as well as how emotionally close they felt themselves to be to each of the people. The 5-layer corresponded to people that we contact at least once a week and feel very emotionally close to, the 15-layer to people contacted at least once a month but felt a little less close to, the 50-layer to those contacted at least once every six months, and the 150-layer to those we make an effort to contact at least once a year and feel least close to.

When Alistair Sutcliffe and Jens Binder sampled network size and structure among the academics and students at Manchester University, they found a support clique size that averaged 6, a sympathy group that averaged 21 and a total network size of 175, figures that are close enough to our values to 5, 15 and 150 to be encouraging. Later, Padraig MacCarron, a mandolin-playing Irish postdoc in my research group, had a look at the giant European mobile-phone dataset that we had access to through our collaborators in Finland. If truth be told, he was rather sceptical as to whether the layers existed at all – or, more correctly, if they did exist that the scaling ratio was three rather than any other number (or, indeed, different numbers for different individuals or different layers). But when he analysed who called whom how often, there the layers were, with cumulative mean sizes of 4, 11, 31 and 130 – slightly smaller than the layers we had found in face-to-face networks, but there nonetheless, and with a scaling ratio of 3.3. He found a very similar pattern when he analysed the durations of calls made to these numbers, as opposed to just how often people called. Subsequently, Wei-Xing Zhou and Didier Sornette analysed over a trillion phone-call records from 4 million subscribers to one Chinese mobile-phone network and found layers with cumulative mean values of 2, 7, 20, 54 and 141, and a scaling ratio of 2.9. It really doesn't come any better.

Meanwhile, some delightful Italian computer scientists from Pisa that I had struck up a collaboration with on a previous project started looking for these patterns in other datasets. In between a lot of fine meals and good Italian wine, Valerio Arnabaldi (then a graduate student) and his two supervisors, Andrea Passarella and Marco Conti, located two Facebook datasets, one small and one large (and, no, they didn't get either of them from Cambridge Analytica ... both are publicly available), and downloaded a large sample of Twitter traffic (if you know how to do this, it is easy to do and, because Twitter is publicly accessible, it is perfectly legal). These datasets all consisted just of named postings: as with the mobile-phone data, we only knew who posted to whom, and not what was actually said. Analysing the patterns in these digital-world datasets yielded circles that were virtually identical in size to those we had seen in the face-to-face social networks and the phone-call dataset. Even more remarkable was that the frequencies with which people in each circle contacted each other were virtually the same in all four of the datasets (face-to-face, phone calls, Facebook posts and Twitter tweets).

Personally, I found the Twitter data quite alarming. I can understand why Facebook networks should look like face-to-face networks – most of the people in our Facebook list of friends *are* our real-life friends, and we see most of them face to face during the normal course of everyday life as well as sending them posts and updates online. But the people we interact with on Twitter are likely to be strangers – yet the patterns we found in Twitter networks were indistinguishable from those of real-world face-to-face networks, except that they only had the first three layers (the 5, 15 and 50 circles)! Do these people really live their *entire* social lives online, with few face-to-face contacts in the real world? That is, of course, completely possible, and might be characteristic of the younger online generation. It might even be characteristic of older males, who, with plenty of time on their hands and a limited social life, seem to be among the most active inhabitants of the Twitter world. But if so, it implies a degree of social isolation that I had never really anticipated. It raises worrying questions.

Valerio also analysed the co-authorship networks of over 300,000 scientists. Writing papers together is the regular outcome of collaborations among academics, so the number of co-authors on a paper is a very simple measure of whom you have collaborated with. The average number of co-authors per paper was six (in other words, you and five friends), though the exact number did vary from one discipline to another. The most successful authors (indexed as those whose papers were cited most – widely regarded as a measure of how influential a paper is) typically had more co-authors than those who were less successful. Analysis of the frequencies with which papers were co-authored with different individuals revealed an underlying layered structure. Across six fields of science from physics and computer science to biology, the layers averaged 2, 6, 15, 38 and 117, with an average scaling ratio between adjacent layers of 2.8 – pretty close, in other words, to what we see in Figure 3 for everyday face-to-face and online social networks. Even the frequencies of co-authorship declined across the layers in just the same way relationship quality did in real social networks. You may be relieved to see that the numbers for the outer layers are somewhat smaller than we might expect – making just a little room for friends and family, but only a little!

You will have noticed that in all these series there is a value of 1–2 at the start of each sequence. The consistency in this pattern caught us by surprise, because we hadn't anticipated anything inside the 5-circle layer. Well, I say that we hadn't anticipated it, but in a way I had, though I had thought of it only as a joke. When I gave lectures on this topic, I would often point to the 5, 15, 50, 150, 500 and 1,500 circles in Figure 3, with their very distinct scaling ratio of three, and ask: isn't there a circle missing? Just work backwards from the 1,500-layer, I would say, and what should you find? Well, a layer of 1.5 individuals, of course! Perhaps these are what we would think of as intimate friends – really intense relationships like romantic partners, for example. The usual response would be: but how can anyone have half a romantic partner? Well, the answer is surely obvious: half the people have two of these special friends and half only have one. And isn't it obvious who these are? Women have two (a romantic partner and a Best Friend Forever, who is usually another girl), but men only have one (either a romantic partner *or* a drinking buddy, who is obviously male) because they can't manage both at the same time. And just in case you think that these might be wife-and-mistress or husband-and-lover combinations, I'll anticipate a finding from chapter 12 which rather strongly suggests that, when people do have an extra romantic interest of this kind, the original partner is rarely included even in the 5-layer, never mind the 2-layer.

It hadn't really occurred to me that this might actually be true. I had simply assumed that these special friends were really just part of the innermost 5-circle friendship layer. But when the Pisa group produced their analyses of the digital databases, there it was, and glaringly obvious. A layer of 1.5 really does exist. It exists precisely because some people (mainly men) have only one special friendship at the centre of their social universe, and some (mainly women) have two. So who is this extra person? In most cases, they turn out to be what I had thought they might be – a Best Friend Forever. This is almost always someone of the same sex as you. It is, however, a phenomenon almost entirely confined to women, and rather alien to men. In a sample of intimate friends obtained by Anna Machin, 98 per cent of women said they had a BFF, 85 per cent of whom were female. Although 85 per cent of the men in the sample also named *someone* as a best friend (76 per cent of whom were male) simply because we forced them to, these did not seem to be in the same league as women's BFFs. A woman's best friend is an intimate, someone to confide in and seek advice from; a man's best friend is just someone to spend an evening in the pub with. It is a very different kind of friendship. This is suggested by the fact that men were four times more likely to have a best friend (someone to go drinking with) if they were single than if they were married (63 per cent versus 15 per cent, respectively).

In fact, it seems that this pattern of numbers with their scaling ratio of three may be a universal feature of all complex societies, animal as well as human. We first noticed this in the structure of hunter–gatherer societies. These typically have a hierarchically nested structure in which each layer consists of several groupings from the layer below – several families form a camp group or band, several camp groups form a community, several communities a mega-band and several mega-bands a tribe. Two separate databases for hunter–gatherer societies, an ethnographic dataset that I had collated and the one obtained by Marcus Hamilton and Rob Walker at the University of New Mexico, yielded very similar results. The mean sizes of the various grouping layers in our sample were 42, 127, 567 and 1,728, with a scaling ratio of 3.5; those for Marcus's sample were 15, 54, 165 and 839, with a scaling ratio of 3.9. The 839 looks suspiciously as though they had combined the two outer levels at 500 and 1,500: if so, then their scaling ratio is actually 3.3, all but identical to one we got.

Two other examples of the existence of these layers came from rather left-field sources. Matt Grove looked at the size of Bronze Age stone circles in Ireland dating from about 3000 BC to around 1200 BC. Although none of these is quite as grand as the better-known Stonehenge in southern England, there are a hundred and forty of them, and they vary considerably in size from the tiny to the very large. Archaeologists have always assumed that these are ritual spaces of some kind – a communal centre where the community met for religious or even political ceremonies. On the assumption that everyone in the local community has to be able to cram into its local stone circle, Matt reasoned that we could estimate the size of the community from the size of its circle. Using a figure of three square yards ($2.6m^2$) per person for comfortable standing room and assuming that the community only occupied half the circle while a handful of officiants performed the religious rituals in the other half, Matt estimated total community sizes that varied between 1 and 156 people. Some careful statistical analysis suggested that the range of community sizes was really made up out of four separate distributions (in effect, layers) with means at 4, 11, 38 and 148, and a mean scaling ratio of 3.4. The middle layers are a bit on the low side, but only the 38 is actually significantly smaller than the 50 we might have expected. Given the nature of the data, however, this is a surprisingly good fit to the 5–15–50–150 pattern that we found for the layers of personal social networks.

A few years after we had discovered this pattern, a young German student by the name of Tobias Kordsmeyer contacted me with the suggestion that we could look at the sizes of German residential campsites. A new fashion had emerged in Germany over the previous decade or two whereby older people sold up their city homes and moved out to live in caravans on trailer parks in the countryside, perhaps next to a nice lake with views of the mountains. Sometimes these were special areas set apart for permanent residents within more conventional touring campsites, sometimes the whole campsite was for permanent residents only. Either way, they had by now been accepted as official residences for tax purposes and people lived there in small permanent communities. Tobias thought these might show the same fractal pattern. I was, I have to say, a bit sceptical: it was not obvious to me why campsite owners should deliberately design their properties with my numbers in mind. It seemed unlikely that they were the kind of people who regularly read the scientific literature and so would know about Dunbar's Number and its circles. But, to my astonishment, it turned out that the sizes of these campsites did exhibit a very clear pattern, with the number of residents peaking at 16, 56, 140, 350 and 677, for a scaling ratio of 2.6 – again, close to the network layer sizes, especially given the way the two larger numbers bridge the 500-layer. The campsite designers certainly weren't doing this deliberately, and there was no obvious financial or architectural reason for using these numbers. They just seemed to be natural grouping sizes in the back of the owners' minds when they were laying out the pitches for the caravans. That's little short of remarkable.

It seems that this pattern is not just something peculiar about humans. The grouping patterns of other socially complex species follow the same sequence. When Russell Hill (who did the original Christmas-card study) and Alex Bentley (a physicist-turned-archaeologist) looked at grouping patterns in some of the most socially complex mammals – chimpanzees, baboons, elephants and killer whales – they found exactly the same pattern (though the groupings didn't go beyond the 50 circle). There were the same numbers, and the same scaling ratio with each circle three times the size of the circle within it. In fact, nearly a decade earlier, the Japanese primatologist Hiroko Kudo and I had shown that the structure of grooming networks in a number of Old World monkey and ape species also had a scaling ratio of three, but at the time we hadn't appreciated the significance of this finding. Scaling ratios of about three have since been reported in the social organisation of giant noctule bats, Galapagos sealions and Columbian ground squirrels. They appear to be ubiquitous.

Later, when Padraig MacCarron, Susanne Shultz and I looked at the distribution of species' average group sizes across primates as a whole, we found exactly the same fractal pattern, with peaks at 1.5. (semi-solitary species), 5 (mainly monogamous species whose groups consist of a breeding pair and their dependent young), 15 (mainly harem-forming species whose groups typically consist of a single breeding male and several females and their young) and 50 (species that lived in large social groups with several adult males and several adult females). (Primates don't have groups of 150 as a regular feature, so this layer didn't feature in the data.) Once again, the same scaling ratio of three, the same magic numbers. What seems to be happening is that as species are forced to increase the size of their groups to cope with the particular demands of their environment, they create larger groups by, in effect, combining groups. The way they do this seems to be by preventing groups from subdividing and undergoing fission so that the subgroups remain together rather than separating off. It seems that when they do this, only certain group sizes are stable.

Once again, the layer sizes that are given in Figure 3 for humans are averages. There is some variation around the figures in each layer, though less in the innermost layers, of course, than in the outermost layers simply because of their sizes. Again, there are slight differences between the sexes in the layers (women consistently tend to have more '5-layer' friends than men), and both inner layers tend to increase initially with age and then decline. There are also consistent differences in the size of the layers as a function of personality, just as we found in chapter 2 for the total number of friends. Tom Pollet and Sam Roberts looked at the influence of extraversion on network size in a sample of Dutch students and found that extraverts have more friends in every layer than introverts do, as well as more friends overall. As we might anticipate, they also had emotionally less close relationships with each individual in each layer, even when we control for network size. Extraverts have been reported to have better social skills than introverts, so it seems that it is not their skills that lead to poorer-quality relationships but simply the fact that they are dividing their time (and hence emotional capital) among more individuals. On a finer analysis of a separate dataset, Catherine Molho found that extraverts who had larger support networks scored higher on openness to experience (in other words, people who like new challenges) and emotionality (those able to express more emotion, and who perhaps were less uptight). Sympathy-group size, on the other hand, was correlated with your honesty and humility.

A life in threes

In our research, we have always looked at social networks as a series of layers, or concentric circles, with you in the centre – the world as seen from your personal perspective. However, there is a longstanding tradition in social psychology of viewing social relationships as sets of triads – sets of three people bound together in different combinations by relationships of different quality. This is known as *Heider's Structural Balance Theory* after Fritz Heider, the Austrian psychologist who first proposed it in a 1958 book, *The Psychology of Interpersonal Relations*. The basic idea is that there can be a variety of different ways that any three individuals could relate to each other: we can all like each other, two of us can like each other but both hate the third person, A can like B who can like C but not the other way around, we can all hate each other, and so on. This became very influential after two American mathematicians, Dorwin Cartright and Frank Harary, formulated a mathematical theory of social networks based on triads. In fact, the concept is so embedded in the fabric of social-network research now that when one very eminent researcher who works for a very well known internet company first heard about our circles of friendship, he is said to have declared (so I was told, anyway) that it simply couldn't be true because everyone knows that the social world consists of triads. So, we had better pause here to consider Balance Theory and ask how it might relate to our world of circles.

It's important to remember that triads are not friendships: they are simply sets of three connections in a network graph (the spider's web of interconnections, friendly or otherwise, among a community of individuals). What Balance Theory does is make some very clear predictions about which kinds of triad will be stable and which not. Those where all three possible relationships are of the same sign (we all like each other or we all hate each other) are more likely to be stable than ones where the signs are inconsistent (I like you and Jim, but you and Jim hate each other). The latter is obviously not likely to be a great recipe for a fun dinner party. It will also impose a level of stress on the relationships and you may well be forced to choose between me and Jim. Some other triads (for example, where you and I like each other and both of us hate Jim) can also be stable, but most of the other possible ways a triad can be formed are likely to be unstable.

We can view a network as consisting of an extended series of these triads, where each person may be part of several neighbouring triads. The bottom line is that the network as a whole can really only be stable if all the links are positive. However, the integrity or cohesiveness of the network may depend not on everyone liking everyone else but simply on some individuals forming links (known as bridges) between adjacent triads – in other words, two triads are linked together to form a network because one member of each triad like each other, creating a kind of figure-of-eight shape. The assumption is that social communities (your network of 150 friends, for example) consist of a large number of triads (50 of them, presumably!) linked together in this way. The triads that make up the innermost layers are likely to be stable ones, otherwise the whole structure will come crashing down. However, it may be less necessary that the links to members of the outermost 150-layer are all positive: you may not really like Jemina, but she is your second cousin and you really can't exclude her for fear of what grandma might say.

Given this, one obvious explanation for the scaling ratio of three is that it emerges naturally out of the fact that social relationships are organised in triads. Fritz Heider had argued that having too many close friends was a disadvantage because it increases the risk of conflict between them, and this would then set a limit on the number of close friends you could have. In addition, friends incur obligations, and too many obligations can weigh you down – and especially so if obligations towards different close friends come into conflict with each other. You can't be a friend to your friend's enemy. So his claim was, in essence, that you could afford to have only a few high-obligation friendships, but you could have many more low-obligation ones. The latter are rather like hangers-on whom you don't feel so obligated to, but they are there in your friendship network because they are friends-of-a-friend. In other words, something that sounds a bit like our circles. Some years ago, Joseph Whitmeyer, of the University of North Carolina, developed a mathematical model of this on the basis of Heider's triads, and concluded that five was the upper limit for the number of close friends. He examined a number of datasets that broadly confirmed this. So there is some support for the 5-layer as a kind of base unit off which the superstructure of our extended networks might be scaffolded in a Heider-like way.

Returning to Heider's original triads, there are four main ways that three people could be linked up with positive and negative relationships that are likely to be stable, and hence at all common. Two of these are considered balanced, and so likely to be very stable, and two are unbalanced and hence less stable. Peter Klimek and Stefan Thurner sampled some 78,000 triads in the Austrian online gaming world *Pardus* over a four-month period and showed that only two of these types were at all common: these were triads composed of three positive friendships (which were nearly three times more frequent than expected had triads formed at random) and a friendship dyad with a common enemy (about a third more common than would be expected). The two less stable triads (three common enemies and two positive dyads whose arms hate each other) were rare (a mere 5–10 per cent of all triads). In other words, triads of three friends are not only more stable but are unusually common; combined with simple dyads (two friends with a common enemy), these seem to form the basis of social networks.

The same logic might explain the scaling ratio of three that we find at higher levels of grouping within human networks as well as in animal networks: sets of three subgroups who all 'like' each other give the social group structural stability and resilience in the face of external attack. Five does seem to be pretty consistent as the value for primary social partners across a very wide range of monkey and ape species, including, obviously, humans. At least in the case of monkeys, it also seems to be the limit set by how much time they have available for social interaction to create friendships and the minimum time that needs to be invested in any one friendship to ensure that the individual concerned does come to our aid when we need their help. Which brings us neatly to the question of time and its role in creating friendships.

The strictures of time

Time is a limited commodity, and the time we have available for social interaction is very much a zero-sum affair – the time we give to one friend is time that cannot be given to another. We know from our studies of both monkeys and humans that the quality of a friendship depends directly on the time we invest in it. In the gelada baboons we studied in Ethiopia during the 1970s, the likelihood that an adult female would come to the aid of another female was directly proportional to how much time they spent grooming each other. In humans, Max Burton showed that our expectation of someone helping us out is directly related to how much time we devote to them. In effect, we decide who is important to us and then we allocate time to them in ways that reflect their value to us.

This is perhaps obvious from Figure 4, which shows the average frequencies with which the women in our British and Belgian dataset contacted each person in the various circles of their social networks. The differences between layers are dramatic. Indeed, they correspond to very specific frequencies of interaction. If you multiply the average time by the number of people in the layer, it seems that we devote about 40 per cent of our total social time to the five people in the innermost layer, and a further 20 per cent to the 10 people that make up the rest of the next layer, the 15-layer. That is, 60 per cent of our total social effort is devoted to just 15 people. The remaining 135 people have to make do with what's left over, getting less than a third of a per cent of our time each. That's about half a minute a day.

That time really is limited in this respect was shown in a series of analyses by Giovanna Miritello and Estaban Moro who, at the time, were involved with Telefonica's research division in Barcelona. We had developed a somewhat accidental collaboration with them after Sam Roberts met one of their group at a conference. They looked at the patterns of phone calling in 20 million customers of Telefonica's Spanish network (some 9 billion phone calls over a seven-month period). They were able to show that subscribers who called more people did not spend more time on the phone; they just spent less time phoning each of their friends compared with those who phoned fewer people, suggesting that

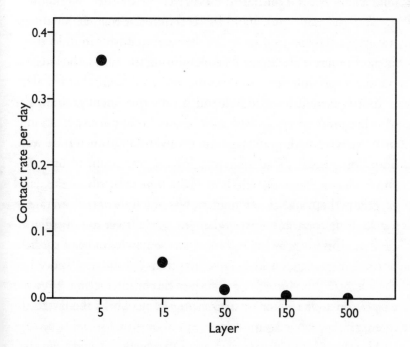

Figure 4. Average frequencies per day with which we contact individual members in each additional layer of our social networks. The data come from 250 women's social networks.

everyone faced the same time constraint. The optimal number of friends was almost exactly 150. If you want to phone more people, you have to sacrifice your time investment in at least some of the others in order to be able to do so.

Masanori Takano and Ichiro Fukuda analysed data from six, mainly Japanese, social-networking sites and found that the more contacts someone had, the fewer posts they devoted to each contact, and hence the average strength of the tie with each contact declined – again suggesting that time is acting as a constraint on their ability to invest in each contact, even in the online world. They also detected a difference in investment among the contacts, with a small number of more intense relationships and a larger number of less intense ones. So this suggests that the layers and their basis in time allocations are not just a European effect: they hold across two very different cultures.

We have made two attempts to try to understand how time structures the layering in social networks. Both required some fairly complex mathematical modelling, so let me simply summarise the main findings rather than explain in detail.

The first model was developed by Alistair Sutcliffe from the Manchester University Business School. I had known Alistair since we were both graduate students in the 1970s when we were both doing perfectly sensible research on primate behaviour. We had both completed our PhDs at a time when the job market, and especially the academic job market, was in a state of tailspin due to a collapsing economy. I struggled on, but he took the decision to capitalise on his growing expertise in the newly burgeoning field of computer science and disappeared from my radar. Twenty-five years later, he re-entered my life when he came to see me with the suggestion that this layer structuring in networks would be an interesting problem to model.

Alistair and his collaborator Diane Wang approached this question using a form of computer modelling known as agent-based models. These models involve a number of virtual agents who are allowed to interact randomly with each other according to a set of rules that determine their behaviour. The aim is to see what happens when very large numbers of agents with different rules for how they should behave interact. It is a widely used technique when a problem is just too complicated to solve analytically, as is often the case when many things (or individuals) are interacting with each other simultaneously. Of course, you really do need to understand how the world you are trying to model actually works. If you don't, you inevitably get what is known in the trade as a GIGO outcome – garbage in, garbage out. Because you have no idea what is actually happening inside the model (it is, after all, going on inside a computer), you have no real idea why the model is behaving the way it does. In such cases, it is dangerous to assume that the model bears any relationship at all to what happens in the real world. Less competent folk commonly ignore this sage advice, confusing complexity for understanding. The solution to this is to have some very clear real-world benchmarks against which to compare the predictions of the model. In other words, can the model predict *exactly* what we see in the real world, and if so what set of model parameter values gives exactly those results – *and no others*? This is known as reverse engineering: we know what happens in the real world, so how much do we have to tweak the operating rules and the parameter values in the model to get exactly what we see in the real world? And what do these particular values tell us about the mechanics of how the real world works?

We decided to focus on the trade-off between the efficiency with which organisms forage for food and investment in social relationships as a function of the time costs these incur and the benefits that accrue from them. They are, after all, the two main activities that monkeys and apes devote their time to. In essence, the model allowed large numbers of individuals to go about their daily business of finding food and socialising, with different sets of rules governing their social preferences when food and social relationships had different impacts on their biological fitness (which, in the biological world, is always defined as the ability to reproduce successfully). What we were looking for was the combination of behavioural rules and parameter values that produced a community with a layered structure of the exact layer sizes that we had found in all our studies of human social networks and social groupings. To simplify our lives a bit, we focused on the 5-, 15- and 150-layers, which we defined as strong, medium and weak relationships. Our model had to reproduce exactly those numbers.

We found that the layered network structure that we find in humans, with numerical values close to 5, 15, and 150, occurs only under very specific circumstances, implying that it should be extremely rare in nature – which, of course, it is (we find these kinds of social systems in only a handful of mammal species, including, obviously, humans). It emerges only when there are significant benefits in terms of wellbeing and alliance formation and high levels of social interaction. Most choices for foraging and social preferences lead either to unstructured herd-like outcomes (large groupings with little internal structure) or to small harem-like arrangements with a large, loose community but no intermediate layer. In other words, unless there are significant benefits to forming social cliques, we get exactly the kinds of social organisation that we find in most mammals and birds: harems or anonymous herds. The specialised, highly structured forms with distinct layers occur only when there is intense selection pressure in terms of the benefits that accrue from social relationships.

By the time we had developed this model and published it, I had become involved in a large project on social and economic models being run by the Spanish statistical physicist Anxo Sánchez in Madrid. One of the people involved in this project was a graduate student named Ignacio Tamarit. Ignacio was one of those people that put us all to shame by managing to combine being a professional physicist with being a professional classical guitarist. He suggested that we might be able to explain why we get these layers analytically using equations from classical statistical physics. In effect, he was suggesting that we do in pure mathematical theory what Alistair Sutcliffe, Di Wang and I had done as a complicated agent-based model that took a lot of time and effort to program. We had originally thought the problem too complicated to solve by maths alone, so had used the more clunky computer-modelling approach to try to do so. Being a physicist, Ignacio had a much bigger mathematical toolkit at his disposal than we did. The model he developed viewed the individual as having to decide how to allocate effort, or time, to different kinds of relationships in order to gain different kinds of benefits, subject to the constraint that the time available for doing so was limited and a minimum time had to be invested in each relationship to gain a given benefit. When that's the case, you do indeed get a layered structure with exactly the values we observe in human social networks.

What made this model unexpectedly interesting was the fact that the maths told us there were *two* optimal solutions – one with the layered structure we observe (a few very close friendships and many weak relationships) and the other with the reverse structure (more close friendships and fewer weak relationships). Under certain conditions, it seems that the world inverts itself. We thought this a bit strange at first, and wondered whether we had done something wrong with the mathematics. But we eventually realised that what the maths was actually telling us was something about the size of the population from which you could draw your relationships. If your community is a large one, you get the standard pattern; but if it is small, you have fewer opportunities for weak relationships and so invest your unused time in creating more close friendships. It occurred to us that these were exactly the circumstances that immigrants might find themselves in: as outsiders, they don't have access to the wider community as a potential source of weak friendships. Their choice of friends is limited to the small community of migrants that they belong to, and this is very often a community that is very limited in size.

This kind of balkanisation or ghettoisation of communities

seems to be very common in real life. For present purposes, however, the important point is that the model made this surprising counter-prediction, and it prompted us to look for data to test it. Ignacio managed to find data on network structures in several immigrant communities in Spain, and, sure enough, there were the reversed networks. More importantly, when we looked closer at both the immigrant network data and network data from conventional members of Spanish society, we found both patterns represented, but the frequencies differed: a few members of the immigrant communities had conventional networks with a classic scaling ratio of three, and they turned out to be people with larger-than-average networks, while a few members of the Spanish community had reversed networks and they turned out to have smaller-than-average networks. Because we had always previously focused on the average pattern, we hadn't noticed that some people were exceptions to the rule. In fact, even if we had noticed it, it is very likely that we would simply have viewed it as part of the natural variability that is always present in real-world data, and thought no more about it. The model had drawn our attention to it and made us ask why these differences existed.

Different strokes from different folks

The existence of these layers in our social networks raises one last important question: do the layers offer different benefits? The way we had conceived both Alistair Sutcliffe's agent-based model and Ignacio's mathematical model certainly implied that there were different benefits, but we didn't really know much about these benefits, or whether different layers were associated with different benefits – and especially benefits that differed in their investment requirements. As it happened, way back in 1990 Barry Wellman, the leading Canadian researcher on social networks, published a paper with the title 'Different strokes from different folks'. He had spent many years studying the community of East York, a residential town of about 100,000 people just outside Canada's most populous city, Toronto. Having explored in considerable detail the structure of social networks within the community, he turned his attention to the functions that different kinds of relationships provide. He came to the conclusion that there are many very different benefits and they are rarely all provided by the same type of relationship – which, of course, may be one reason why we need so many different kinds of friends. Strong ties, he suggested, provide emotional aid, loans of household items, the occasional help with household chores, and companionship. Parents and adult children exchange financial aid, emotional aid, a variety of important services including help with repairs, regular childcare or health care. Weak ties provide more casual benefits, including information exchange.

When we discovered the layered structure of networks many years later, we began to wonder how his idea might translate into our layers. After all, the layers seemed to define relationships of very different quality, and it seemed plausible to suggest that friendships in the different layers provide different kinds of benefits. The 15-layer was already spoken for, of course, in its capacity as the sympathy group. The 5-layer seemed to function as the *support clique* – the small group of people willing to provide unstinting emotional, physical and financial help and advice. I often refer to this layer as the shoulders-to-cry-on friends. The 15-layer is probably where you draw most of your everyday social companions from – the people you invite round for a quiet dinner or an evening out at the pub or theatre. I am inclined to think of the 50-layer as your party friends: the people you would invite round for a weekend BBQ or a celebratory birthday or anniversary party. The 150-layer is what you might call the wedding/bar mitzvah/funeral group – the people that would turn up to your once-in-a-lifetime events. It also probably contains most of the children of your closer friends. Otherwise, our women's network data suggest that this layer is mainly populated by members of your extended family – people whose friendship does not need much regular reinforcement because it is held in place by the ties of kinship.

Evidence for the functions of the innermost layers came from a study by Jens Binder and Sam Roberts. They asked just over 300 people to list everyone in their support cliques and sympathy groups. They found values for the sizes of the two layers (just under 6 for the support clique and just under 16 for the sympathy group) that were very close to the 5 and 15 values we had found in other samples, providing yet more confirmation for groupings with these particular sizes. They then asked the people to select one person in each of the two layers and rate them on a list of twenty things they might have done with them. These twenty items reduced to four key dimensions in terms of maintenance activities: positivity (laughing together, expressing thanks), supportiveness (support during a difficult time, accepting the other for who they are), openness (having intellectually challenging conversations, sharing of private thoughts) and joint activity (making an effort to spend time together, visiting each other's homes). In addition, they rated them for the provision of eight social benefits (companionship, affection, guidance/advice, reassurance of worth, intimate disclosure, instrumental aid, emotional support and reliable allies). They found that all four of the maintenance activities and all eight social benefits were rated as higher or more common in the support clique than the sympathy group. In effect, socialising needs were satisfied by the sympathy group (best friends), whereas intimacy needs were satisfied by the support group (close friends).

They had also asked everyone to rate how lonely they felt. Loneliness turned out to be negatively correlated with both the number of friends and the number of family members that people had in the two layers – the more friends and family they had, the less lonely they felt. So, as well as providing more explicitly positive benefits, these layers also buffer us against feelings of isolation and all the adverse consequences that follow from this.

I mentioned Oliver Curry's altruism experiment in chapter 1, and its results are very relevant here. He had asked people to identify specific individuals in each of the three main layers (5-, 15- and 150-layers) and to rate how likely they would be to act altruistically towards these individuals either by lending them some money or donating a kidney to them if they needed one in emergency. Both these indices of altruism declined steadily with each layer. We are much more likely to act altruistically towards our innermost friendship circle, but we do so with much less enthusiasm to those in the layers further out. It seems that the 150-layer, however, marks an abrupt transition point in our willingness to be altruistic. That circle at 150 seems to demarcate a real phase shift in our willingness to act prosocially, as though it divides the world very firmly into Us versus Them.

*

There are several lessons to be drawn from the last three chapters. One is that the number of meaningful friends is surprisingly limited, and, on the whole, seems to vary only to a limited extent across individuals, and even cultures. A second is that this social world of ours is highly structured into a series of circles, or layers, that also have very distinct sizes, each of which is associated with very specific frequencies of contact, a specific sense of emotional closeness and willingness to provide help. These layers seem to extend outwards by three more layers of much weaker-quality relationships that represent a sea change in the willingness to act altruistically: we are much less motivated to help them, and if we do so it is usually on a strictly reciprocated basis – I'll help you out now, but I expect you to return the favour later. When we help our 150 friends, we do so without necessarily expecting to be paid back (but it's nice if you do). For close friends, we don't even expect to be paid back at all. The third point is the way that kinship structures our networks – even in the developed West where we no longer think of family as being quite as important as more traditional cultures do. Apparently, despite what we sometimes say, family is still very important for us.

The regularity in the structuring of the social network circles begs the question of what causes it to happen. Our models have given us some hints, but models are essentially high-level descriptions. We need to relate these findings to the psychological and behavioural mechanisms that underpin them. The next four chapters examine the mechanisms involved and explain just why we cannot have social circles of limitless size.

5

Your social fingerprint

It's surprising what you can learn from telephone calls. We first realised this when looking at our high-school sample. We were struck by the fact that three of the students sent an average of over *one hundred* texts a day, and they kept this up for the whole of the eighteen months of the study. And no, you didn't misread that: a *hundred* texts a day, and that was the average, not the maximum! That is one text sent every eleven minutes throughout the school day, the meals at home with Mum and Dad, and the evening – when presumably they were supposed to be revising for the exams that were about to engulf them. Extraordinary. We could tell exactly what time they got up in the morning and what time they went to bed at night from their first and last texts. And, by the way, two of the three were boys. We regretted not having asked for everyone's exam results to see if there was a (negative!) correlation with the frequency of texting. It might have been very illuminating.

The pull of friendships can sometimes be overwhelming. I remember a colleague commenting that his family had had a South American au pair when their children were small and he had been astonished by the fact that, instead of getting out and enjoying the cultural experiences of London and meeting new people, she had spent all her free time in her room on the internet 'talking' to her friends back in Brazil. He had never ceased to marvel at this: why had she bothered to come all the way to London? Of course, there is the perennial problem of how you get to meet new people when you don't know the local culture and the places to go. But even so . . .

In fact, these two examples raise some important questions about both the patterns of our friendships and the effort we put into maintaining them through time. This is particularly important for friendships (as opposed to family relationships), since these seem to be especially fragile and very sensitive to the time we invest in them. Until the internet, social media and the mobile phone became widely available a mere decade ago, friendships would have died naturally if someone moved away. Before that, it was very much a face-to-face world in which you bumped into friends and family in the street or the pub. The phone on the hall stand might be useful for family and making social arrangements, but it wasn't the medium of choice for maintaining friendships in the way it is now. Post-Facebook, Skype and Zoom, it seems that we would rather stay in and chat with our old friends back home. Is that a good idea? Is it more important to keep old friendships going or to make new ones?

The uniqueness of me

When Sam Roberts and I set up our longitudinal study of a group of high-school students, we hadn't anticipated quite how much we would learn from it. The aim of the study had been to see how moving away from home affected the quality of friendships and social networks, and how the mobile phone in turn influenced this. We picked them up as eighteen-year-olds at Easter in their final year at school, and monitored them through the following eighteen months to the end of their first year at university. The deal was that we gave them a free mobile-phone subscription for eighteen months in return for being able to download their monthly bills so we could see who they phoned and texted. They also had to fill in a questionnaire at the beginning, middle and end of the study telling us about their relationships with everyone in their network – who everyone was (parent or sibling, friend, romantic partner, acquaintance, and so on), how emotionally close they felt to them, when they had last contacted them and how (face-to-face, phone, text, email, social media, etc.), and what they had done with them when they had met up face-to-face. It was a laborious task for them, so we remain ever grateful for their diligence.

Between them, they gave us huge quantities of data. As it happened, I was collaborating at the time with a group of physicists on a project about online networks, so we were able to talk a couple of them into helping with the complicated task of analysing these data. One of these was Jari Saramäki from Aalto University in Finland, and the other a young Mexican postdoc named Eduardo Lópes. Eduardo undertook the tricky task of converting large numbers of paper itemised bills into a digitised database so that they could be analysed statistically, and Jari was responsible, with Elizabeth Leicht (another of the postdocs), for carrying out the analyses that followed.

Probably the single most astonishing finding that came out of these analyses was that each individual had a distinct pattern in the way they distributed their phone calling among their friends, and that this pattern remained remarkably stable across the eighteen months. While we could see the 5, 15 and 50 layers of their relationships very nicely, what we hadn't expected was that the fine detail in how often they called their first, second, third ... etc. most frequently called friends would be quite so distinctive. It is like a social fingerprint. I call James thirty times a month, and Jemima ten times a month, but you call your two most important friends twenty times a month each. This pattern remained remarkably constant over the whole eighteen months. It really does seem that your social fingerprint is characteristic of you as a person, though we have no idea why this might be so.

There was, however, one more finding that was even more surprising. The patterns of phone calling revealed that there was around a 40 per cent turnover in network membership (technically known as 'churn') over the eighteen months that we had been tracking them. This was much higher than we had expected, though we later discovered that it is in fact fairly characteristic of eighteen- to twenty-year-olds. In this particular case, it resulted from the almost wholesale replacement of one set of friends by another after moving away from home to university. This isn't too surprising, perhaps: after all, going away to university thrusts you into a whole new social environment, with large numbers of new people with whom you are forced to live, eat and (occasionally) sleep. You see them every day, and they have the inevitable habit of suggesting you go out for a drink, or to a club, a film, a party . . . You just see a lot of them, whether you like it or not.

In fact, it wasn't just those who went away to university that underwent this dramatic turnover in friendships. Even those who didn't go to university but instead stayed in their home city to work exhibited the same turnover in friends in that first six months after leaving school. Of course, part of that was due to the fact that many of their school friends had gone away to university. But most of it seemed to be due simply to a change of social environment. They met new people at work or in the local clubs and started to go out with them. In contrast, the turnover in family members in the network was quite modest. Family members might drift up or down through a layer in the network, but by and large they were more stable, at least in so far as they remained within the network.

The big surprise was that when we looked at the patterns of contact before and after a change in friendships, they were almost identical. It seems that when we replace someone in our social network with a new friend, we slot the new friend into exactly the same position as that previously occupied by the old friend in terms of the frequency we contact them. You see or phone the new friend with the same frequency as you used to see the previous occupant of that position in your network. This seems to reflect your natural social style.

Time is of the essence

How much time do we actually spend engaged in social interaction with our friends and family? Some years ago, I collated data on time budgets in different cultures and economies to try and find out. I found around half a dozen studies where researchers had recorded the amount of time in the day that people had devoted to different activities – sleeping, collecting and processing food, cooking and eating, working on plots or making tools and clothing, relaxing and in social interaction. In some cases, researchers had laboriously checked on the people concerned every ten or fifteen minutes (sometimes even through the night!) and recorded what they had been doing. In other cases, they had asked people to fill in time diaries that did much the same thing, if only during waking hours: exactly what were you doing at 10 a.m., 10:15, 10:30, and so on. I managed to find samples for housewives in Dundee, Maasai pastoralists in East Africa, Nepalese hill farmers, New Guinea horticulturalists, various agricultural tribes in sub-Saharan Africa, and !Kung San hunter–gatherers from southern Africa.

Averaging across these various studies, it seems that we spend around 20 per cent of our eighteen-hour waking day engaged in social interaction. That's about three and a half hours a day, averaged across the week. That is *not* party time, by the way! It is time spent eating with people, sitting with people in a social context, talking to people. That may seem like a lot, but distributed among your 150 friends and family, it works out at just one minute and forty-five seconds each per day – barely time to say

'Hello and how are you?', never mind waiting for the reply. In fact, as we saw in chapter 4, that is not what we do. Something like 40 per cent of this social time is devoted to the five people in our innermost social circle, the support clique, with another 20 per cent devoted to the ten additional people that make up the fifteen members of the next layer, the sympathy group. On average, we devote seventeen and a half minutes each day to each of the five people in the support clique, and about four and a half minutes a day to each of the ten people that make up the rest of the sympathy-group layer. Of course, we don't see all of these people every day. Remember that the definition of the support clique is the people you see at least once a week, while the sympathy group consists of the people you see at least once a month. Over the course of a month, you would devote around 520 minutes (about eight and a half hours, in effect an entire working day) to *each* support-clique member (more for some and less for others, no doubt), probably in half a dozen or more sessions. And you would devote 130 minutes (a bit more than two hours, or a whole evening every other month) to each of the ten additional sympathy-group members. The remaining 135 people in the two outer circles get an average of just thirty-seven *seconds* a day each – less than twenty minutes a month.

There is an unwritten law in the study of social networks known as the 'Thirty-Minute Rule': you will make the effort to see someone, and view them as important to you, if they live within thirty minutes' travel time of where you live. It doesn't seem to matter much whether this is thirty minutes on foot, by bicycle or by car. It's the psychological significance of the time it takes you to get there. That being so, you might suppose that you would be more inclined to phone or text those who live beyond the thirty-minute limit to make up for the fact that you can't get round to see them in person. In fact, it seems that you don't. You are more likely to phone the friends that live near you, as Hang-Hyun Jo was able to show from an analysis of phone-call patterns in the

Aalto mobile-phone database. Contrary to what you might suppose, you phone most often the people you see most often.

In the study that Barry Wellman did on the East York community in Canada, he and Diane Mok looked at how distance apart influenced the frequency with which members met up in person with their friends and family. They found that there was a clear break-point for face-to-face contacts when two people lived more than five miles apart, with a further drop off at about fifty miles (about an hour's drive) and another at 100 miles (the limit for a comfortable day trip – well, in Canada anyway!). Phone calls showed a broadly similar pattern, albeit at a slower rate of decline, with a particularly sharp decline at around 100 miles. John Levi Martin and King-To Yeung found a similar effect when they analysed contact frequencies among former members of American 1960s hippy communes. The frequency with which former friends contacted each other correlated negatively with how far apart they now lived: the further away they were, the less they saw of each other.

When people move away and don't have the opportunity to meet up so often, friendships seem to flag surprisingly quickly. Bob Kraut, at Pittsburg's Carnegie Mellon University, estimated from his studies that the quality of a friendship declines by about one standard deviation for each year that two former friends spend apart (e.g. in different cities). In statistics, three standard deviations either side of the mean accounts for more than 99 per cent of the data. In effect, three standard deviations' change is equivalent to saying that a friendship of high strength will decline to no more than a mere acquaintanceship in just three years.

The first year apart seems to have a much bigger effect on the quality of the relationship than the subsequent years. At least, this is what we observed in the British high-schoolers' mobile-phone sample. In terms of their ratings of emotional closeness to their former friends, it took at most six months' separation for a friend to drop down a layer in the friendship circles when people

moved away. But that first drop in relationship quality was by far
the biggest: the drops in the following two six-month periods got
progressively lower, as though the relationship was quietly levelling
out into the lowest common denominator of being 'just an old
acquaintance'.

This wasn't true for family relationships, by the way. These
remained remarkably stable across time. By comparison, friendships were much more fragile. They depended on constant
reinforcement to maintain their strength. I guess we all know this.
When, after many years, we meet up again with people we had
been with at school or university many years before – people with
whom we had once spent a great deal of time partying, drinking,
playing sports and games – we suddenly find we have surprisingly
little in common. We are interested enough to spend half an hour
catching up with what they've done in life, but then we are glad to
move on. Yes, yes, what fun it has been to catch up and we must
meet up again . . . but we never quite get around to it. Sometimes,
we are just left wondering what on earth we saw in these people
all those years ago . . .

To be fair, there is a very small handful of friendships that do
seem to stand the test of time and absence. In their analyses of
the American hippy communes data, John Martin and King-To
Yeung found that people who spent a lot of time together while in
a commune were more likely to still be in regular contact twelve
years after they had left. Lars Backstrom and his colleagues found
something similar in an analysis of a very large Facebook dataset:
people who exchanged more posts were more likely still to be
friends six months later than people who exchanged few posts.
But these special friendships are very few in number – maybe just
three or four. They tend to be the friends that we were particularly
close to and spent most of our time with, the ones with whom we
shared the ups and downs and traumas of early adult life, whose
advice we sought in those moments of deep crisis, the ones we sat
up with late into the night discussing deep philosophical issues,

the ones we most regularly went out drinking or partying with. It's as though this small number of special friendships are carved in stone into our psyches precisely because we engaged in such intense, emotionally passionate interactions. We can pick up these relationships years later exactly where we left them off. But for the rest, friendships are fickle things, here today and gone tomorrow. In many cases, they are just matters of convenience – someone to party with or go on day trips with, who will do for the moment in the absence of anyone better.

Many of our more casual friends are friends of convenience of this kind. They just happen to be accessible (and presumably willing to give us some of their time), or they are people whose value to us in other contexts besides the purely social makes it worth our while investing in them. The archetypal example of these friendships is what I call 'school-gate friends'. They are the parents you meet at the school gate when collecting your children from school, and with whom you eventually start casual conversations out of boredom while waiting for the children to come out. If your respective children strike up a friendship, you begin to see more of the parents socially outside school – briefly when picking your children up after a birthday party or a sleepover, then perhaps for a Sunday BBQ, or an evening social, perhaps eventually even taking holidays together. Then something very weird happens. The children fall out or go off to different universities, and suddenly you stop seeing the parents. The children have found new friends and have lost track of each other, never look each other up when they come home for a visit. And, ever so quietly, the parents drift apart. No one says anything. It is just that no one makes the effort to keep in touch. Once in a while, you bump into each other in a supermarket aisle. There will be a moment of enthusiastic 'How lovely to see you! What have you been up to? You *must* come round some time!' and then you part. The same little ritual will be repeated a year or two later in the same supermarket aisle – but you still don't get to meet up. These were friendships of convenience, driven mainly by the children's friendship with each other. When their friendship ends, there is too little social cement to hold the parents' friendship together. First, you stop seeing each other, and then you stop sending Christmas cards. Only rarely will your friendship have grown close enough to survive the test of time.

Friendships depend on you investing enough time and effort in each other to keep the relationship well-oiled and functional. See someone less often, whether deliberately or by force of circumstance, and that relationship will inexorably fade away. Indeed, so conscious are we of the fact that failure to contact someone will weaken a relationship that, when you next contact them, you do so for longer – as though to smooth over the cracks that might have opened up in the relationship. When Kunal Bhattacharya and Asim Ghosh analysed the duration of successive phone calls in the Aalto mobile-phone dataset, they found that there was a correlation between the length of the gap since the last call and the duration of the next call for special friends – though not for weaker friendships (as judged by the baseline frequency of calling). A gap of ten to fifteen days without a call resulted in a dramatic increase in the length of the next call for people that were normally called every day or two.

We saw something analogous to this in the gelada baboons we were studying in Ethiopia. Mothers gradually withdrew from casual social interaction as the milk demand for their growing infant increased and forced them to spend more time feeding. But they also tended to spend less time grooming their main social partners – their Best Friends Forever. Instead, they relied on the friend to do all the work to keep the relationship going, so saving the time that they should have spent grooming the friend. However, once the infant had started to wean, and the pressure on the mother was reduced, they would pay back the debt, devoting much more time to grooming the BFF than the BFF groomed them.

In our high-schoolers dataset, some friendships held up better than others over the course of the study, and we wondered what the difference was between those that did and those that did not. Besides rating everyone in their contact list for emotional closeness, they had told us when they had last contacted them and how (face-to-face, phone, email text, etc.), and whether they had done any of a list of twenty activities with them. The list included things like spending time hanging out with them, going out together, going partying or clubbing with them, helping them to move, going shopping with them, going on holiday with them, etc. It turned out that, for both sexes, the friendships that survived were the ones they had devoted more effort to than they had during that last term at school before going their separate ways. Those whose friendships had declined in quality had spent less time with the friend after leaving school than they had done before.

But there was a surprising sex difference here. For the girls, the activity that had most effect in preserving a friendship was talking together, whether in person or by phone. For the boys, talking together had *absolutely* no effect at all – and I mean no effect *at all* – on how likely the friendship was to survive. What made the difference for the boys was making the effort to 'do stuff' together more often than they had done before – going to the pub, playing five-a-side football, climbing mountains, or whatever it was that they used to do. Of course, 'doing stuff' together also had a positive effect on the girls' friendships, but the effect was nowhere near as great as it was for the boys. Investing more time in activities than they had done before would just about maintain a girl's friendship at its original level, but it didn't improve it in the way just *talking* together did, or the way doing stuff together did for boys. What is important for maintaining boys' friendships (with either sex of friend, it seems) is doing, not talking. Joking, joshing, bragging maybe, yes – but not in the kinds of intimate discussions that girls have. Constitutionally, that's foreign territory for boys. In my mind's eye, I have a picture of two elderly Greek men sitting on either side of a table in the sunshine outside a café. Occasionally, they sip their coffee or a pastis, but not a word passes between them. That is men bonding.

This seems to reflect a difference between the two sexes in the way they maintain, or service (to borrow a motoring metaphor), their relationships. The one does it by talking, the other by action. This is clearly one reason why boys' phone calls are invariably so much shorter than girls'. Girls, notoriously, will spend an hour on the phone to each other – having just spent all day together at school. You'll be lucky if you can get a five-minute call out of a boy even if you haven't seen him since last month. But then, all he's really got to say is: I'll see you down the pub at seven o'clock. In our high-school sample, the boys' calls averaged around one hundred seconds no matter what time of day or night they phoned someone. The girls' morning calls averaged about a hundred and fifty seconds, and then increased steadily through the day, reaching an average of *five hundred* seconds during the late evening and early hours just after midnight. Boys at that time were still averaging only a hundred seconds.

When we checked this on the full Aalto mobile-phone database with its 33 million adult users and 1.9 billion phone calls, men's calls were significantly shorter, averaged over all ages, than women's phone calls, although the difference wasn't as extreme as it was for the adolescents. Similar results have been reported from other studies: when Zbigniew Smoreda and Christian Licoppe analysed the phone calls from a sample of 317 French homes, they found that the women accounted for two-thirds of the time on the phone (whether or not they worked part-time or full-time, or were at home all day). Simply looking at the number of calls rather than their duration, the woman in the household made between two and three times more phone calls than the man, especially to family members, irrespective of their age and whether or not they had children.

Early birds and night owls

Like all monkeys and apes, we are a diurnal species: we are awake in the day and sleep at night. In fact, we are so influenced by the day–night cycle (our circadian rhythm) that even the way we interact with others is affected in subtle ways by the way our patterns of getting up and going to bed map onto the sun's daily cycle. When Talayeh Aledavood looked at the diurnal patterns of calling in our high-school dataset, she found a very clear difference between those who were most active on their phones during the day and those who phoned most at night. What's more, this pattern persisted across the eighteen months of the study in a way very reminiscent of the social fingerprint story. The early birds (or 'larks') at the start were still the early birds a year and a half later, and the night owls at the start were still the night owls at the end, and this despite the turnover in their friends.

Later, Talayeh analysed another mobile-phone dataset that had been collected by the Danish computer scientist Sune Lehmann on a thousand Danish university students. Once again, she found the same difference between larks and owls. This much larger sample allowed her to look at the relative frequencies of these two types in more detail. Around 20 per cent of the students were committed larks who were active mainly in the morning and died socially by the evening, and 20 per cent were committed owls who hardly stirred before midday but came into full social mode in the evening and into the night, with the rest being neither one nor the other. Owls had larger social networks than larks (thirty-five as against twenty-eight people, at least as measured in terms of whom they phoned most often). However, owls spent much less time on the phone to each friend than larks did (94 seconds as against 112 seconds, on average), so that their networks were less well integrated and reinforced. Looking at the community formed by these students, owls were more central to the social activities of the network as a whole. Their butterfly patterns of interaction

helped to keep the community integrated, allowing social information to flow from one side to the other. Remove them from the
network, and it would fragment into a number of small communities between whom there was little communication. Although
larks did not show any particular preferences, owls also tended to
associate more with owls, exhibiting a strong homophily effect in
this respect. That no doubt reflects the kind of busy social world
that owls live in: the best parties are the ones that consist mostly
of owls – and take place at night.

This discussion of the differences in how and when we choose
to live our social lives reminds me of some rather mischievous
analyses carried out by Daniel Monsivais (a Mexican physics PhD
student in the Aalto group). He had the idea of using the Aalto
mobile-phone database to look at the influence of diurnal and
seasonal patterns of calling activity. He was curious to know what
was responsible for the national habit of the country concerned of
taking a siesta in the early afternoon. Because of the huge amount
of data involved, this required some very heavy computing – both
to filter out the non-social calls (or at least as many as possible)
and to identify, on an individual-by-individual basis, the timings
of when people went to bed and woke up *each day*. In essence,
we are looking for the times at which first and last calls are made
either side of a long gap of inactivity, when the phone owner is
presumably asleep. Given that we were dealing with some 10 million people in this sample, there is no way this could be done by
hand – at least, not if you wanted any kind of social life. It had to
be automated, which is why you need a physicist with the statistical skills to develop a computer program that can sift through
terrabytes of data searching for the right kinds of patterns. There
will be a few errors here and there, and occasionally you will think
the phone is down when in fact the owner is in a private meeting
or the battery ran out. But these instances disappear into the statistical mush when you have a large enough sample.

There turned out to be two such periods of sleep, one at night and one in the early afternoon (the traditional siesta). Since the database gives us the postcode where the phone account is held, we can allocate everyone to a city where they officially lived. Daniel was able to show that, over a 5½ degree north-to-south latitudinal range (that's about 380 miles, or 600 km), people in the south of this Mediterranean country took longer siestas at midday than people in the north. Within each latitudinal band, the length of the siesta across the year varied with temperature, being longest at the hottest time of the year (in the most southerly city, around two hours) than during the coolest time of the year (when they dozed only for about an hour).

Resting in the early afternoon when ambient temperatures are at their highest and it is too hot to be out in the sun is a common practice among hunter–gatherers in the tropics. Indeed, it is pretty much characteristic of all primates in the tropics, as well as a lot of other mammals. Those in the more southerly part of our sample who were closest to the northern edge of the tropics (the Tropic of Cancer) were simply following this pattern more closely. Better to sleep during the heat of the day and switch the rest of your working day to the cooler early evening. And that is exactly what they do.

Another intriguing finding was that the length of the night was inversely correlated with the length of the siesta in any given city. People in the north were sleeping longer at night, whereas people in the south were sleeping longer during the afternoon, and so stayed up much later at night, only going to sleep around midnight when it became cooler. Both northerners and southerners were sleeping for the same number of hours each day; they were just distributing it differently across the day in response to the heat.

Just how sensitive we are to the ebb and flux of daylight was illustrated by another of Daniel's analyses. Because the sun rises in the east, the day obviously starts slightly earlier in the east than it does in the west within any given time zone. The country our mobile-phone dataset comes from has only one time zone, but has quite a long east–west span (10 degrees of longitude, roughly 600 miles or 900 km), so that the difference in the time of sunrise between its easternmost and westernmost cities is actually around forty-three minutes. Daniel looked at five cities lying east to west along the same latitudinal axis, and found that people in the east got up and started phoning half an hour earlier than the people in the west *even though* they were living in the same time zone – and despite all the cultural factors that help to standardise our lifestyles!

*

This chapter has introduced two key findings about how we make friendships, and the consequences these have. One is that each of us seems to have a natural social fingerprint in the way we allocate our social effort. In part, that is likely to reflect aspects of our personality such as how extraverted we are and how anxious we are about our relationships. These aspects of social style can affect how and when we prefer to socialise, and hence offer one factor that guides our choice of friends – if we are night owls, we are more likely to end up socialising with other night owls because they will be the only ones still around at 2 a.m. in the morning. The other is that these patterns seem to be remarkably stable, and quite impervious to who is actually in our friendship circle at any given moment. It is as though exactly who our friends are doesn't really matter, so long as we have friends. Of course, we opt for people who are as congenial as possible, but so long as these boxes are ticked more or less anyone will do. That way the processes of *maintaining* the relationship over time are made easier. This probably helps to impose some stability on the size and structure of our social networks as well as our communities, because once a community has been established, its framework won't change that much compared with what would happen if our social preferences changed by the week.

6

Friends in mind

There is a poignant moment in a BBC television documentary on autism where an eleven-year-old boy with Asperger syndrome* turns to his mother and asks: 'What is a friend, mummy? Can I have one?' and then, after a pause playing with his toys: 'How do I get a friend?' He understood that the children he mixed with called each other friends. But there seemed to be some mysterious process involved that he did not quite fully understand. Just how do you set about getting a friend? He has already tried asking other children to be his friend, but it didn't seem to work, and he doesn't really know why. And now he is genuinely stumped.

His perplexity is a reminder that we all have moments of puzzlement when our overtures of friendship are rejected, or a friend lets us down and we don't understand why. These moments of social anguish are a reminder of an important aspect of friendship: friends are not, in reality, all that easy to acquire and maintain.

---

* Asperger syndrome is a form of autism. Autism is characterised by some key deficits, the most important of which is a lack of the cognitive skills that underpin fully functional sociality (sometimes known as mentalising or mindreading – the ability to understand what someone else is thinking). In more severe cases, individuals may lack language, may have poor behavioural control and find loud noise and crowds, even physical touch, extremely stressful. Autism is really a spectrum of conditions rather than a single condition. Asperger individuals usually have normal (in many cases, above-normal) intelligence and normal language; they often have very good mathematical and computer programming skills.

We have to work at them, and it can take months, sometimes even years, for a real friendship to blossom. More importantly, we all vary in our ability to manage the social world. At one end is the young boy who is completely defeated by the very concept of friendship; at the other is the perfect host who seems to know by effortless intuition what to say to enliven a social occasion, how to bring the best out in everyone, who would hit it off with whom. Most of us lie somewhere in between these two extremes, lurching from one social minefield to another relationship catastrophe, while just about managing to keep ourselves afloat. And then there are the times when circumstances leave us stranded on a social desert island, watching enviously as everyone else seems to be having the social time of their lives.

The human social world is possibly the most complex phenomenon in the observed universe – far more complex than the mysterious processes that create stars and engineer the orbits of the planets. The social skills that make this world possible are astonishingly sophisticated, and the cognitive mechanisms that underpin these skills are a miracle of evolutionary engineering. Yet we take them for granted and hardly ever give them a second thought. We struggle with the simple mathematics of Pythagoras and Archimedes, yet we unerringly execute much more complex calculations about the social world without giving it even a second thought. That's because our minds have been designed by evolution to be social computers. By contrast, the calculations we need to do to get by in the everyday physical world are elementary and astonishingly simple. It only gets complicated when we want to design major architectural structures or jet engines, or send a mission to Mars – circumstances that have been way outside the normal run of everyday experience for all but the last few millennia of our evolutionary history.

To handle this complexity, we need a special skill – the ability to read and understand other people's minds. Sometimes known as mindreading or mentalising, it's a skill that is all but unique to humans. Although some of the smarter monkeys and apes exhibit elements of it, and share with us the neural circuits in the brain that underpin it, only humans can aspire to the levels of mindreading that allow us to have language, produce fiction and cope with the complexities of religion and science. It is mindreading that determines our social skills, and hence, in the end, our risk of being autistic (or its milder version, Asperger syndrome).

Sally versus Ann

Here's something to try with young children. Psychologists call it the *Sally and Ann Test*. Sally and Ann are two dolls who are playing with a ball together on the sofa. Sally hides the ball under the cushion on one side of the sofa, and then leaves the room. While Sally is out of the room, Ann takes the ball from where Sally hid it and hides it under the cushion at the other end of the sofa. You can act all this out with the two dolls, explaining it to the child as you do. Now Sally comes back into the room. And you ask the child: Where does Sally think her ball is? Where will Sally *look* for her ball?

A four-year-old will typically point to where Ann put the ball, because they know that this is where the ball is. A five-year-old will point to where Sally put the ball before she left the room. It is a very striking difference, and really quite consistent. At around the age of five (sometimes a bit earlier, sometimes a bit later), the child seems to go through a major transition known as *theory of mind*. At four, it cannot distinguish between its own knowledge of the world and someone else's. Whatever it thinks is the case it supposes everyone else thinks too. But from five onwards, it can distinguish between its own knowledge of the world (where the ball actually is because it saw Ann hide it there) and someone else's knowledge (where Sally *thinks* the ball is because she hid it there and didn't see Ann move it). The key to this is the ability to understand a 'false belief' – that someone else believes something about the world that you *know* is not true. As the philosophers have it, this is to have, or acquire, a 'theory of mind'. More colloquially, it is known as mindreading or mentalising – the ability to understand what someone else is thinking, how *they* see the world as opposed to how *you* see the world.

Theory of mind is the key to human sociality. It is what allows us to empathise with others and it is what allows us to manage the interminably complex network of relationships, friendships, enmities etc. that make up our social world. Making friends with someone isn't just a matter of having a slot for them in your brain, however important it might actually be to remember who they are and how they behaved towards you when you last met (the economist's view of friendships). It is a much more complicated process. In fact, how we do it goes back to the way monkeys and apes create and maintain friendships. This is quite different from how other species of mammals and birds manage their relationships. Monkey and ape (and human) friendships have a permanent quality to them that is very different to the rather casual, here-today-and-gone-tomorrow relationships we typically find in mammals and birds – with the exception, of course, of the pair-bonds that characterise monogamous species and the few other species like horses and elephants that have bonded relationships. It's the difference between autistic individuals and what psychologists rather coyly refer to as neurotypical people – meaning the rest of us.

Primates manage their relationships by what psychologists would call a dual-process mechanism – two separate mechanisms that work in tandem. One has to do with the deep emotional content of relationships, much of which acts below the radar of consciousness. This mainly involves endorphins. Triggering their release allows primates to build up a sense of warmth and positivity towards each other. It provides a deep psychopharmacological platform off which the second, more explicitly cognitive, mechanism allows them to build relationships of trust, obligation and reciprocity through a process of psychological reflection. It is this second process that really underlies the social brain hypothesis, since it is computationally expensive and requires a brain with sufficient spare capacity over and above that needed to keep the body alive. This second (cognitive) mechanism forms the basis of this chapter. I will postpone discussion of the first (the endorphin-based pharmacological mechanism) to the following chapter.

While it is true that the size of your brain limits the number of friends you can have, it is an oversimplification to say that this is just because the brain imposes some kind of limit. In many respects, the brain is like a computer, and, yes, the size of your computer does limit what it can do, but in the end it is the software that goes into the computer that really does the work. For brains, the equivalent of the software is the cognitive processes that allow the brain to think through what is going on in a social situation and to make predictions about how people will react if you behave in different ways. We actually have to learn much of that.

I have always been puzzled by the fact that many people seem to think that the social brain is simply about remembering who is who, that the whole issue is simply a memory game. Aside from suggesting that you haven't read the papers we have published on the social brain, it speaks of a very limited understanding of social relationships. Of course, you do need to remember who is who in your social world, but that alone wouldn't make it possible to hold a large network of friends and family together. It wouldn't even allow you to hold a conversation. Speaking in turns without interrupting each other, adding meaningfully to what the other person has just said, judging when it's appropriate to start a new thread – all these depend crucially on being able to read the other person's mind correctly, to anticipate what might interest them, to know what would follow logically on from what the speaker has just said rather than chipping in with something completely tangential and irrelevant, knowing how to say what you want to say without causing offence. We seem to do this effortlessly, but – as we have all discovered at some point in our lives – it is something that is all too easy to get wrong. It can lead to the abrupt end of a conversation, or the rupture of a friendship.

The real work comes in the way you think through the relationships you have with others *and* the relationships that these in turn have with each other: it is being able to ask how would Ann respond if I said this to her, or, more important perhaps, how would Sally react if I said this to Ann? Or even: what would Sally's mother say if Sally was upset by what Ann said after I had spoken to her? That is what mentalising is all about.

Having theory of mind is to know that someone else believes something. It is important because it seems that only humans, and perhaps the great apes (the chimpanzees, gorilla and orang-utan), have this ability. All other sentient animals cannot get beyond the 'I know ...' statement. They act like four-year-old humans and don't appreciate that Sally can have an understanding of a situation that is different from their own. Great apes seem to be just about able to solve Sally–Ann tasks, and in this respect seem to be on the same cognitive ladder as five- or six-year-old humans. But neither they nor five-year-olds are in the same league as adult humans. Apes and five-year-olds stand only on the second rung somewhere far below what any competent human adult can do. In fact, without these advanced mentalising abilities, you wouldn't even be able to read this book, because you wouldn't be able to parse these long complicated sentences with many clauses ...

Another aspect of language for which mentalising is crucial is that we almost never say exactly what we mean, but instead rely on the listener to interpret what we say correctly – and even to be amused by the particularly witty way we have used ordinary words out of context. The metaphorical use of words – making allusions to novel contexts, drawing an analogy between two completely unrelated things or contexts – is what makes conversations rich and rewarding. We give time a spatial dimension (before and after four o'clock), we speak of the sea or the sky being angry, we speak of people being cold (when we really mean unfriendly), we say that someone slapped our wrist when all we mean is that they told us off, or that someone lit up our life when we mean they made us happy, of life as a journey even though we might never leave our house. We fish for compliments, we drown in a sea of grief, we feel blue (when we really mean depressed); we speak of someone having a bubbly personality, of being the apple of our eye, that something is the icing on the cake ... the list goes on and on.

What is truly remarkable is that we seldom make mistakes, even when we hear a novel metaphor. In most cases, we instantly grasp its meaning. This is so much a part of everyday language, so much second-nature for us, that we forget just how complicated this verbal juggling really is. So imagine how difficult the social world must be for someone who cannot read either the conversational or the social signals, never mind the metaphors – how confusingly unpredictable it must seem, how difficult it must be to engage with someone in a sufficiently intimate way to create what most of us would instantly recognise as a friendship. That is the world in which individuals on the autism spectrum live, and it is extremely stressful.

Last but not least, theory of mind allows us to lie convincingly. To be able to lie in a way that will influence your behaviour, we have to understand how you see, or might see, the world. If I can manage that, I can feed you false information knowing that you will believe it. Animals do occasionally deceive each other, but it is because they have learned by experience that if you do X, other people will do Y. But they don't really understand *why* other animals do what they do, only that it works most of the time. With theory of mind, we can understand the mind behind the behaviour and understand why they are more likely to believe X than Y. That ramps up the sophistication and scale of the deception to new heights.

Theory of mind is what makes it possible to have a rich and engaging literature of fiction, as well as poetry – to be able to imagine another world quite distinct from the one in which we actually live. It is also what makes science possible, because it allows us to imagine that the world could be other than as we directly experience it. The problem for most animals is that they have their noses thrust so close up against the grindstone of life-as-they-experience-it that they cannot step back far enough mentally to wonder why it has to be the way it is, or whether there might be worlds which are organised in some other way – which is what we need to do when we give explanations for our experienced world in terms of the physiology or genetics or the invisible chemistry or physics that lie beneath it.

When Sally met Harry met Marie ...

In the 1989 Meg Ryan/Billy Crystal film *When Harry Met Sally . . .*, the two main characters spend a lot of time discussing not only their past relationship with each other but also their relationships with their respective current romantic partners, Jess and Marie – not to mention the fact that they were responsible for Marie and Jess, at the time their own respective best friends, meeting up and subsequently marrying. It all gets very complicated. The central theme of the story is friendship, but the undercutting theme is the question as to whether a boy and a girl can be friends without sex intervening. Sally thinks it's perfectly possible, but Harry disagrees. The film ends with them getting married, which perhaps suggests that Harry was right.

Be that as it may, our interest lies in the fact that Sally and Harry are deeply embroiled not just in trying to understand each other, but also in seeing their relationship against a background of their friendships with other people – their respective romantic partners of the moment, Jess and Marie. Life does not consist of a set of unrelated dyadic relationships (you and your mum, you and your daughter, you and your best friend). Rather, these dyadic

relationships are all embedded within a complex network of relationships where what happens in one dyad spills over and affects
what happens in another. What is more, like the relationships in
the film, the relationships in networks are constantly changing.
Two people fall out of friendship over some minor dispute, and
that affects their relationships with the other friends they have in
common. It changes the signs on the relationships in the triad,
so that what had once been a stable triad with three positive relationships now becomes an unstable one with two positives and
a negative. Everyone is in a state of kerfuffle about it because a
breakdown in a relationship ramifies through the social network
affecting everyone else. We live in a complex, interwoven, constantly changing social world that requires immense skill and
mental effort to steer a manageable course through.

In the previous section, we looked at mentalising as simply
being able to understand someone else's mind. But, as the philosophers who invented the term pointed out, theory of mind
is a naturally recursive phenomenon. If I can understand what
you are thinking, then there is nothing in principle to prevent
me understanding what you are thinking about what is on Jim's
mind, and so on for as many different minds as you care to add.
In fact, we don't really need to have other people here: the recur-
siveness works just as well between you and me. I *think* that you
believe that I am *wondering* why you *suppose* that I *intend* to do
the opposite of whatever you *want* me to do. That's at least six
recursions, each marked by the italicised verb denoting a separate
mindstate. Philosophers use the term *intentionality* to refer to
these mindstate terms as they are typically all loosely associated
with having intentions. They use the phrase the *orders* (or *levels*)
of intentionality to index the number of recursions or mindstates
involved in a particular utterance. A sentence with six recursions
like the one above is a sixth-order intentional statement, and so
someone who can unpack such a sentence successfully can be said
to have sixth-order intentionality, or to be sixth-order intentional.

Although philosophers pointed this out many decades ago, in fact no psychologists have ever questioned whether there are any limits to this kind of recursion. That's mainly because the people who have been most interested in this topic have either been developmental psychologists interested in when children first understand other people's minds or clinical psychologists with an interest in autism. They have no reason to be interested in higher-order recursions since none of the people they are concerned with ever get beyond simple theory of mind (second-order intentionality: I *think* that you *believe* [some fact about the world]). That does not, however, mean that the rest of us don't (although that doesn't stop some psychologists speaking as though there was only basic theory of mind and nothing else). We can and regularly do manage to think about the mindstates of several people simultaneously. If we couldn't, we wouldn't be able to worry about the consequences of our behaviour for our other friendships. There would be no such thing as guilt – not just because we feel guilty about breaking some abstract law, but because we worry that our actions may hurt or upset someone, or that others will think badly of us.

It is one thing for philosophers to claim that people can handle more than two mindstates at a time, but what *are* the actual limits on this? The clinical psychologists Rich Bentall and Peter Kinderman and I set about trying to find out. I wrote some simple vignette stories of everyday social life similar to the Sally–Ann story but involving more people, together with questions about who was thinking what about whom among the characters in the story. The vignettes were around 200 words and described someone trying to do something, always with some kind of social component to them – find out how to get somewhere such as the nearest post office, engineer a date with someone, make some social arrangement, negotiate a pay rise with the boss. There were usually several people involved in a story, each of whom was thinking something about what the others were thinking. In the original set of stories, there were up to nine mindstates in some stories. Eventually, with some revisions and standardising, these stories became our standard method for assessing mentalising competences, and we have used them in all our studies of mentalising ever since. Our first study, however, was simply intended to determine the natural limit on the mentalising capacities of normal adults. The answer turned out to be five mindstates on average. Five mindstates would be the equivalent of being able to think your way through a sentence like this: I *believe* that you *wonder* whether Jim *expects* that Jemina *intends* to ask Sally whether she is *in love* with Fred. Only 20 per cent of people can do better than that. We have since confirmed these results in around half a dozen subsequent studies.

Because mentalising underpins our ability to handle metaphor in conversations, and because jokes depend heavily on metaphorical use of language, we had wondered how mentalising ability affected our appreciation of jokes. Jacques Launay, Oliver Curry and I analysed the number of mindstates in a compilation of The Hundred Best Jokes Ever. We found that most jokes consisted of either three or five mindstates (counting the mindstates of the audience member and the comedian as two of these), with only a handful having six or seven mindstates. To give you a flavour of these, here are two examples, one a second order joke (there are no mindstates in it other than the comedian's and the audience's – you) from the American comedian George Wallace, the other a fifth order joke that has been recycled so often no one seems to know who originally created it. The second order joke: *At the airport they asked me if anybody I didn't know gave me anything. Even the people I know don't give me anything.* And here's a fifth order joke: *A young boy enters a barber shop and the barber whispers to his customer, 'This is the dumbest kid in the world. Watch while I prove it to you.' The barber puts a dollar bill in one hand and two quarters in the other, then calls the boy over and asks, 'Which do you want, son?' The boy takes the quarters and leaves. 'What did I tell you?' said the barber. 'That kid never learns!' Later, when the customer leaves, he sees the same young boy coming out of the ice cream store. 'Hey, son! May I ask you a question? Why did you take the quarters instead of the dollar bill?' The boy licked his cone and replied, 'Because the day I take the dollar, the game is over!'*

When we asked people to rate these jokes for funniness, the ratings increased with the number of mindstates (jokes that involve several protagonists are funnier than those that involve only one) up to five mindstates, but after that they quickly became less and less funny. It seems that when there are more than five minds involved people just cannot get their head around (yet another metaphor) the point of the joke (another metaphor, of course).

So far, then, what we have learned is that there is a typical upper limit at five on the number of mindstates people can handle at any one time (with some variability round that). But what determines that limit? And how does it relate to the number of friends we can have?

Keeping your friends in mind

We saw in chapter 3 that the number of friends you have correlates with the size of certain key parts of the brain. The brain regions involved form a distributed network that has come to be known as the 'theory of mind network' because it always seems to be involved when people are solving standard two-person theory-of-mind tasks. When we ran our brainscan studies to see which bits of the brain correlated with the number of friends you have, we also asked everyone to take our mentalising vignette task so that we could see how the brain responded as the number of minds involved increased.

In her analyses of the large-scale structural components of the prefrontal cortex for these data, Joanne Powell had shown that it was the orbitofrontal cortex that seemed to increase in size in proportion to the number of mindstates someone can manage. This, in itself, is interesting because this part of the brain is involved in managing emotions, and it has direct links down to the amygdala which is responsible for processing emotional cues. The dorsal prefrontal cortex, which lies above it just behind your forehead, is generally thought to be responsible for rational thought. Although it does feature in some studies of theory of mind, it didn't come up as of special significance in our multi-mind studies, which tended to emphasise the importance of those parts of the brain that seemed to deal with emotional responses – the 'raw feels' that characterise friendships that go on well below the radar of consciousness. We know what we are feeling, but somehow we can't quite express it in words.

What is clear, however, is that mentalising when thinking about the social world is a great deal harder work for the brain than thinking about physical-world relationships such as understanding causal relationships between, for example, clouds building up and rain, or between striking a match and its tip bursting into flames. To investigate this, Amy Birch (then one of our students, and now a brain researcher at Imperial College London) compared how much work the brain was doing when it was working out mentalising questions with different numbers of mindstates compared with when it was working out just the physical elements of the story (that someone did something rather than *intended* to do something). When we matched the number of propositions involved (each mindstate is, after all, a proposition: 'Jim *thinks* something' has the same grammatical structure as 'Jim *does* something'), mentalising tasks were much harder than working out causal relationships in the physical world, and became disproportionately harder the more mindstates involved.

In my view, this is because, when we think about other people's minds, we are actually modelling their mindstate in the virtual space of our own mind, whereas physical relationships (something causes something else) are simply there in front of you in the sense of being simple factual memories. A mindstate is one step further removed from reality than a physical event because you have to use indirect cues to figure out what someone else is thinking. One is about the evidence for something, the other is about inferring something that you can't see when the evidence (what you say or how you look) and the mindstate behind the evidence are qualitatively different. The second will inevitably be computationally more difficult. Your grimace is not the same thing as the pain you are experiencing; it certainly reflects your state of mind, but I have to make that inference and I do that on a balance of probabilities because grimaces can in fact imply many different mindstates from pain to irony to 'Oh, for heaven's sake, that really was a bad joke . . .'

In chapter 3, I mentioned that Penny Lewis, Joanne Powell and I had been able to show that the size of the theory-of-mind network in the brain (and especially the size of the prefrontal cortex) correlated with the number of friends you have. In this chapter, we have seen that your mentalising abilities correlate with both the number of friends you have and these same brain regions. But what are the causal relationships that underlie this three-way relationship? Does brain size affect mentalising ability, or does the number of friends influence brain size? Joanne Powell was able to show, using a statistical technique known as path analysis, that the causal chain has to be: brain size determines mentalising ability, and mentalising ability determines the number of friends you have. This both provides an explanation for the Social Brain Hypothesis (why you need a bigger brain if you live in a bigger group) and tells us that the cognitive processes involved in mentalising are key to understanding how we manage to keep so many friendships going at the same time – or not, as the case may be.

Geoff Bird, one of my colleagues at Oxford, exploited a relatively new technique known as Transcranial Magnetic Stimulation, or TMS, that uses a very small electric current passed through electrodes attached to the skull to switch on or switch off the regions of the brain immediately below the electrode. He showed that positive stimulation of the temporo-parietal junction, or TPJ, enhanced the accuracy with which subjects performed on a perspective-taking task, while inhibitory stimulation (which shut the area down) had the opposite effect, though it did not affect the ability to assign mental states to self or others. The TPJ's role in mentalising seems to be concerned with representations of the self and other people, which is not quite the same thing as processing mental states (which may be more the function of the areas in the prefrontal cortex), but it is certainly a part of the story.

The importance of these mentalising abilities is reinforced by studies of the neural circuits involved in managing social relationships in monkeys. Jerome Salet and Rogier Mars have shown that key neural circuits involved in social processing in humans are already present in Old World monkeys. They showed, from detailed neuroimaging of brains, that the way connections in the frontal cortex are organised in the macaque monkey is very similar to that in humans, and especially so in respect of those connections associated with social skills (such as mentalising). They argued that, although monkeys may not have full mentalising skills, nonetheless the similarity in the organisational structure of the prefrontal cortex suggest that they have cognitive skills that are of the same generic kind – the kind that appear to us as mentalising when humans can do them on a large enough scale. In effect, the cognitive differences are a consequence of *quantitative* differences in the volumes of particular brain regimes rather than qualitative differences in brain regimes. More importantly, in a truly inspired series of experiments, Marie Devaine and her colleagues in Paris and Rome tested seven species of monkeys and apes on a specially devised mentalising-like task in which the animals interacted with a human operating at different mentalising levels and showed that a species' ability to solve these tasks correlated with its brain volume. As is so often the case with imaginative, ground-breaking research, they had enormous difficulty getting their paper published in the more conventional journals, and ended up having it published in a computer-science journal of all places! It's but one of too many examples where science advances knowledge despite, not because of, scientists and the peer-review system that is supposed to guarantee the quality and importance of published research.

On knowing when to say 'No'

The central significance of mentalising for our social world emphasises the importance of being able to see how our actions might affect someone else, or being able to see why a friend might have acted in the way they did and so make allowances for their behaviour rather than immediately cutting them off in a fit of high dudgeon. It is this that allows us to teach children, and to explain to adults why something has happened – why we behaved so badly last week, or why their behaviour has upset us. There is, however, a second mechanism that is equally important in allowing us to regulate our friendships, namely the phenomenon known to psychologists as the *inhibition of prepotent responses* – or what, in everyday language, we might refer to simply as willpower. Prepotent responses refer to your natural tendency to grab the biggest slice of cake on the plate before anyone else gets it. Or your tendency to fly off the handle when someone annoys you without stopping to think – the 'act first, think after' principle. The problem with this kind of behaviour is that relationships will only work if the benefits are fairly equally balanced. If you try to grab more than your fair share of the cake or trash someone every time they get in your way, it will destabilise the relationship; do that too often, and friends will stop spending time with you.

Of course, we are prepared to bend over backwards for certain kinds of relationships by forgiving all manner of misdemeanours (parents for their children, lovers for their beloved, inferiors for their superiors – at least sometimes). But there is always some limit to how much we are prepared to put up with. If you keep taking most of the cake every time we meet, or you keep allowing me to pay for *all* the drinks we have together, or you keep shouting at me, even the dearest of relationships will crack. There is a world of difference between someone being just a bit in your debt (which will encourage them to want to go out with you so as to repay the debt) and being someone's economic slave (because they expect you to do all the work in the relationship).

What prevents us acting in too greedy a fashion, or deters us from responding with unnecessary violence when someone upsets us, is the capacity to inhibit our behaviour. It is not entirely clear how natural or instinctive this is. We spend a lot of time when children are young trying to teach them not to be greedy, to share their toys with visitors, not to throw tantrums if their desires are thwarted, to be tolerant of other people's invariably annoying habits. In most cases, they learn these skills, though some are clearly better at it than others – and some never seem to learn (more about them in a later chapter). It is the basis of diplomacy, of democracy, of being able to survive a difficult situation and live to fight another day – especially when failure to manage this might have led to the break-up of a relationship or an escalating conflict that ends in a fight with fatal consequences. These skills are not to be dismissed. Without them, our friendships wouldn't survive the weekend in most cases. Human society as we know it – indeed, even primate society – would be impossible without it.

In large part, this is because primate social groups, and hence the relationships that make these up, are implicit social contracts. We agree to live together, or to be friends, so that we can both benefit by solving the problems of daily survival and reproduction more efficiently than we each of us could do on our own. The problem is that there is always the temptation for you to steal a march on me either by not paying your share of the costs, or by taking too big a share of the benefits. It is the problem that gives rise to what is known as the *tragedy of the commons*. In medieval and early modern Britain, commons, as their name suggests, were the public land where everyone could graze their horses, cows and other domestic stock. Of course, if too many animals were grazed there, it would inevitably exhaust the food supply, resulting in the death by starvation of all the animals. So the villagers normally came to an arrangement about how many sheep, cows or horses each household was allowed to graze on the commons. It was a very delicate balance, because there was a perpetual temptation to graze one more animal than you were supposed to. Doing so meant that you did better, but at the expense of your fellow villagers who had less forage available for their animals. If only one person does this, we can probably cope; but if everyone does it, the only possible outcome is that we destroy the very resource on which we all depend. It is a problem that has bedevilled social life since time immemorial – from the level of friendships right up to the conservation of fisheries and forests. Some mechanism is needed to prevail on people to stick to the informal agreements and expectations that we have about our relationships with each other and our access to shared resources.

In effect, it is all about the ability to forgo a small benefit now in order to gain a much larger benefit in the future. This will inevitably be a trade-off: there will always be a point at which the value of the resource now exceeds its possible value in the future, and at that point we will opt for harvesting now. Economists call this *discounting the future*, and on the whole we are very bad at it (at least judging by our willingness to cut forests down, where it is also known as *the poacher's dilemma*). That's because taking the short-term view is actually a rational attitude sometimes: the future is unpredictable and may never happen (not least because I might die), so I need to be sure that the benefit in the future outweighs the risk I run of not actually making it through to tomorrow if I decide to wait and forgo the cake-on-the-plate now.

Stephanie Carlson and Louis Moses, among others, have shown

that the ability to delay gratification or inhibit inappropriate responses is linked to better social skills, in particular theory of mind, in children. Similar results were reported in a study of adults by Jacques Launay, Ellie Pearce, Rafael Wlodarski and James Carney from my research group. B. J. Casey, at Cornell's Sackler Institute, and her collaborators found that your ability to inhibit prepotent responses as a child remains remarkably stable well into adulthood. They compared forty-year-olds on a standard behavioural inhibition task with their ability to delay gratification when they had been aged four years (with the latter usually indexed as the capacity to resist eating a cookie when left alone with one on the table and told not to touch while the experimenter was out of the room). The task they used for the adults is known as a go/no-go task: you have to press a button or not depending on whether the visual stimulus you are shown matches a criterion. When the task involved explicit social cues (press for a happy face, but not for a fearful one), the adults' performance on this task correlated with their ability to delay gratification four decades earlier, but not when there were no associated social cues (neutral faces). When they scanned the brains of the adults while they were doing these tasks, the low and high delayers differed significantly in neural activity in the right frontal lobe, especially when correctly inhibiting the response.

The capacity to inhibit our behaviour may also depend critically on the part of the brain known as the frontal pole. It is the bit right on the front just above the eyebrows (see Figure 2). This brain region (known technically as Brodmann Area 10) is found only in monkeys, apes and humans. Other mammals, including prosimian primates, do not possess it. It is also involved in a number of other important cognitive abilities known generically as executive functions. Besides inhibition, these include causal reasoning, one-trial learning (inferring a general rule from a single observation, in contrast to the kinds of rote learning from many repeated examples that underpin learning in most animals), and the ability to compare multiple outcomes in order to choose the best. These kinds of more sophisticated forms of cognition have a significant effect on the speed and efficiency with which animals can make inferences or decide what to do. Individuals who have a smaller frontal pole are likely to be less able to control their behaviour, less able to take the long view, less able to forgive friends who offend them, less able to distinguish accidental from intentional actions. It is the ability to inhibit immediate actions combined with theory of mind allowing us to predict the future that makes social life, as well as friendships, possible. Being able to decide what to do fast is much more important in social contexts, where the action often proceeds at lightning speed, than in food-finding contexts – at least for primates, most of whom only eat vegetable matter which is usually happy to sit there and wait while you take your time deciding whether or not to eat it.

Molly Crocket and Tobias Kalenscher ran a series of functional imaging (fMRI) studies that looked at which brain regions were especially active when making decisions between a small reward now versus a larger reward later when they were exercising either willpower to inhibit impulses or a behavioural strategy known as pre-commitment whereby we anticipate failures of willpower and deliberately restrict our access to temptation ahead of time. (In everyday terms, examples of pre-commitment would include making public promises to behave in a certain way or avoiding places where we would be exposed to temptation.) They found that when subjects were using willpower to inhibit an undesirable choice (a small reward now), the dorsal prefrontal cortex was heavily involved along with other areas in the parietal cortex. But when pre-commitment was being exercised, parts of the frontal pole were more active and had increased connectivity with the dorsal prefrontal and the parietal regions involved in willpower. They argued that this implies a hierarchical arrangement for this kind of decision-making: if the decision is fairly simple, we use rational willpower and the dorsolateral prefrontal cortex, but if it is more tricky we bring pre-commitment and the frontal pole into play, since this allows us to suppress activity in the dorsal cortex. Later, they confirmed this using transcranial stimulation: they found that positively stimulating the frontal-pole area improved pre-commitment decisions, but had no effect on tasks that involved non-binding decisions, willpower or preference for particular rewards, none of which are known to involve the frontal pole.

*

In this chapter, I've tried to set out the two key psychological mechanisms that are important for social life, and hence in particular our friendships. One – mentalising – allows us to see the consequences of our actions and to figure out why others behave in the way they do. This allows us to see how the consequences of our actions are likely to reverberate through the members of our social network. Most of the time, of course, we probably think no further than how what we do will affect the friend it is directed at. But every time that action has consequences for the friends of friends, then we need our high-order mentalising skills to be able to see that. The other mechanism – inhibition – allows us to suppress our natural inclination to do something that would destabilise relationships. Not surprisingly, the mentalising neural network in the brain that is crucial for both of these also turns out to predict the number of friends we have. It's like a cognitive juggling act: the better we are at it, the more mindstates we can keep in the air at the same time without dropping one, and hence the more friends we will have.

7

Time and the magic of touch

I f you want to know what someone really thinks of you, check out how they touch you. There is an honesty about touch that cannot be matched by any other sense, and certainly a great deal more honesty than can be inferred from the words they may speak to you. A touch is worth a thousand words. That's because touch is intensely intimate in a way that no other sense is. Words are slippery things. Not only are we good at saying one thing when we really mean another, but even the words we use change their meaning according to how we say them. We are extraordinarily skilled at lying when it suits us, sometimes with the best of intentions (as when we don't want to offend someone with a brutally honest opinion) and sometimes deliberately for personal gain. In contrast, the way someone puts their hand on your shoulder or strokes your arm says a great deal more about how they view their relationship with you than anything else ever could. In part, that is because there is an intimacy to touch that the other senses lack. Taste and smell, the other two intimate senses, can tell me *who* you are, but they cannot tell me how you feel about *me*.

Touch is what makes the world of relationships go round. The very intimacy of touch means that we are very sensitive to who touches us, and how they do it. Being stroked or rocked is calming, creating a sense of both pleasure and relaxation. The cares of the world drop slowly from your shoulders. It's the business of the masseur in the everyday world. It is why we rock babies, and why rocking calms them. But at the same time, there is an ambivalence about touch, perhaps precisely because it is so intimate. We want to be touched by some people, but shrink from being touched by others. This ambivalence is the bane of our lives, not least because it sometimes makes it difficult for those with whom we interact to know which category they belong to. I am willing to stroke you affectionately, but you are not willing to allow me to do it. So we have to develop rules that help smooth that particular pathway. A handshake is fine between strangers, a stroke on the back or a kiss is not. Learning these rules takes most of our childhood and adolescence, and even then we make mistakes. A yearning to be touched goes unfulfilled; or we blunder in where we are not welcome.

The intimacies of touch

It seems there are universal rules of touch that apply broadly across cultures. In a study coordinated by one of my Finnish collaborators, Juulia Suvilehto, we asked people in five European countries (Finland, Russia, France, Italy and the UK) where they felt comfortable touching others and, conversely, where they felt comfortable being touched by them. They did this for a specific named individual of each sex ranging from a close intimate (parent, sibling, romantic partner, best friend) to a less close family member (uncles, aunts, cousins) to non-intimates (unrelated acquaintances, complete strangers). They were shown a body outline on a computer screen and asked to paint in those parts of the body where they were content to touch or be touched. Just over 1,300 people took part. The results were very consistent, even across cultures. The more intimate the relationship, the more of the body it was permissible to touch. Strangers were restricted to the hands, with the abdomen and upper legs being complete no-go zones – which is why we shake people's hands on first being introduced rather than enthusiastically hugging them, and why we feel uncomfortable if a complete stranger does try to hug us overly enthusiastically on first meeting. Close family have much wider freedom, but only romantic partners have uninhibited access to the whole body in both directions. Interestingly, women were allowed to touch a wider range of body areas, and similarly tolerated a wider range of touching, than men. More importantly, on a finer scale, these patterns correlated closely with how emotionally close the subject felt to the person concerned, irrespective of sex.

There were, of course, some national variations, with the Finns, surprisingly, being the most touchy-feely (probably all those naked saunas?) and the British (not too surprisingly) the least. But the general pattern was the same across Europe. Later, when Juulia collaborated with some Japanese scientists, we found that the Japanese behaved rather like the British, except that Japanese romantic partners had much less freedom of touch – certainly more than close relatives, but a great deal less, it seems, than in the less inhibited post-hippy West. The main difference between the two cultures was that the Japanese were less tolerant of touching their very close relative's bottoms and lower legs than the British were. Most surprising, however, was the fact that feet were a no-go area for the Japanese. Now explain that to me if you can.

The fact that touch conveys a sense of intimacy even found its way into management advice at one point. In the 1980s, when British companies were falling like ninepins and managers were having to dole out the bad news of redundancy to staff on an increasingly regular basis, they were advised never to sit across their desk from the victim. Always go round to them and put your hand on their shoulder as you gave them the bad news was the advice given by the management gurus. That casual stroke of the arm or hand on the shoulder took the sting out of the situation, and the victim was less likely to respond aggressively.

The reason why touch is so important in the context of relationships is that it forms the basis of how primates build and service their friendships: their social life revolves around social grooming. Animals that groom each other regularly are more likely to support each other when one of them is threatened or attacked. In a seminal experiment on wild vervet monkeys in East Africa, the American primatologists Robert Seyfarth and Dorothy Cheney played the distress calls of a monkey under attack through a hidden loudspeaker placed near a target subject while this individual was feeding. If the caller was the target animal's main grooming partner, it would stop feeding and peer into the bushes, trying to check out what was happening. But if it was someone else's grooming partner, they were likely to ignore it and carry on feeding, perhaps just giving a quick glance in the direction of the speaker. This was also true of the gelada I studied in Ethiopia: the more two females groomed each other, the more likely one would come to the other's aid if she was threatened by animals from the harem next door. It's true of humans, too. Not only are we more willing to be altruistic to someone if we spend more time interacting with them, but, as we showed in the study carried out by Max Burton, we *expect* them to be more willing to help us out.

All this is underpinned by the intimacies of grooming. Being groomed by someone implies an element of trust – trust that they won't take a bite out of you when your guard is down. This is especially so because the areas that are most often groomed during social grooming are the parts of the body that animals cannot groom for themselves – the head, shoulders, back, haunches, bottom. Those parts of the body like the hands and feet, the fronts of one's limbs, and stomach that are easily groomed for oneself are rarely the target of grooming by others.

Primatologists have often insisted that monkeys are engaged in a simple exchange of grooming (a service) for social support (a more risky benefit). If that really is the case, it must be a very bad bargain because grooming, at least between friends, is almost always reciprocal: friends take it in turns to groom each other during a morning or evening social session, swapping roles every five or so minutes. So the debt is neutralised before it is even needed. Those cases where animals do have a grooming debt because one did most of the grooming are precisely the ones where animals are least likely to support each other in a conflict. They usually involve a low-ranking animal trying to curry favour with a dominant one, or someone apologising for some social infringement. Another case, I'm afraid, of science being hindered by a lack of attention to what animals are actually doing.

In fact, grooming in monkeys and apes has a completely different purpose. Bonded relationships created through grooming have two important consequences for the animals. First, they ensure that the two of you stay together when one of you moves. That happens dozens of times a day, and would soon result in friends becoming separated in the dense forest or undergrowth. If contact is lost, you quickly lose the benefit of having the group as a source of protection against predators. Second, it also creates a passive defence alliance against attacks by other members of your group. This passive form of defence is much more important than active coalitionary support. Merely seeing that you have a friend makes the rest of us cautious about harassing you in case we end up in trouble with your friend as well. Active coalitionary support only becomes necessary on the infrequent occasions when passive protection fails to do its job (or I fail to inhibit my behaviour and attack you in a blind rage).

Grooming creates a relationship of trust and obligation, and is underpinned by a desire to be always with your partner and in physical contact with them. We see that illustrated very clearly in the differences between monkeys and ungulates. Using data from our field studies, we compared the frequencies with which individuals looked at other adult members of their group while feeding in the highly bonded gelada monkey, the intensely monogamous klipspringer antelope and the much less social feral goats with their more casual form of sociality typical of most of the herd-forming deer and antelope. The two bonded species averaged a look at another member of their immediate group every six to eight minutes, compared to once every forty minutes in the much less social goats. In other words, in the two bonded species, animals constantly check on their social partners – not because they are frightened of them but because they are anxious not to lose sight of them. It is that same sense of yearning to be near the other person that characterises human romantic relationships and best friendships.

In other words, what grooming actually does is build up a sense of psychological yearning for the individual you groom with. You crave to be with them, to huddle and cuddle with them. And because of that very targeted psychological predisposition, you will come to their aid when they need it, whether that is rushing to defend them when someone else attacks them, giving them the £50 loan they've asked for, or helping them out with their shopping or gardening. But how does grooming do this?

The soporifics of friendship

So far, I have talked about the brain's role in friendship in a way that implies that the limits are imposed by our ability to think about our friends and evaluate their relationships to us. But there is a deeper, more emotional side to the brain story that is not so widely appreciated. It concerns the brain's own painkillers, a set of molecules that go under the generic name of endorphins. In fact, there are three families of endorphins: enkephalins, dynorphins and endorphins. It is the latter, and within this family the beta-endorphins in particular, that are of particular interest to our story. Endorphins are neuropeptides that often function as neurotransmitters. Their main role, however, seems to be in the context of pain. Chemically similar to morphine (the psychoactive substance in the latex of the opium poppy), they act as painkillers. Weight for weight, endorphins are thirty times more effective as a painkiller than is morphine.

Endorphins are activated in response to pain and stress of any kind. Both psychological as well as physiological stress activates the endorphin system. It is because endorphins are chemically very similar to morphine that we become addicted to morphine and heroin so easily. It is also the reason why we get addicted to the new opioid drugs like oxycodone, hydrocodone and fentanyl that have become such a disastrous feature of American life in the twenty-first century. In 2017, around 1.7 million people were addicted to commercially produced, prescription-only opioid drugs in the USA (more than three times the number addicted to heroin), and more than 47,000 deaths were attributed to overdoses of these drugs that year. The difference in chemical structure between endorphins and these artificial opioids is tiny, but it is enough to cause us to become addicted to the one but not the other. To be sure, we can become *psychologically* addicted to endorphins – it is one of the reasons we get addicted to alcohol and to sex, since both are very effective triggers of the endorphin system. But this is not the same kind of destructive *physiological* addiction that we have to synthetic opioids and opiates like morphine and opium.

Nonetheless, there is now growing clinical and pharmacological evidence that abnormal endorphin levels may be responsible for a number of psychiatric conditions, including schizophrenia, some forms of depression and some autistic spectrum disorders, especially those that have been labelled as 'immunophenotypes' – conditions that seem to be associated with immune system abnormalities, and often involve the production of inflammatory cytokines (proteins that are part of the immune system's response to infections). It has been suggested, for example, that, through their effect on the body's immune response, endorphins may be involved in the 'neuroinflammation' responses that may be responsible for the dysphoria often seen in these conditions, as well as in opiate addicts. This suggestion is reinforced by the fact that some of the symptoms of these conditions, especially those related to withdrawal from social interaction such as occurs in depression, seem to be very similar to the behaviour of opiate addicts.

Why is all this important?

The endorphin system, aided and abetted by the dopamine system, is central to the process of social bonding in primates. In mammals in general, and primates in particular, the endorphin system is activated by social grooming. Indeed, there is a highly specialised peripheral neural system, the afferent c-tactile (or CT) neurons, that enables this. The uptake of endorphins in the brain creates an opiate-like sense of relaxation, analgesia, general bonhomie and all's-well-with-the-world that seems to create an intense sense of bonding and trust between those involved.

The stroking motion that is so central a part of grooming stimulates the CT nerve receptors at the base of each hair follicle. CT fibres are unlike all other peripheral sensory nerves: they are unmyelinated (and so very slow in their speed of conductance), they have no return motor loop (the one that, in normal pain neurons, causes you to pull your hand away from the fire when you accidentally touch it), and they respond to one, and only one, stimulus – light, slow stroking at a speed of exactly two and a half centimetres a second . . . precisely the speed of hand movements in grooming. Francis McGlone and his colleagues showed this rather dramatically in a study of babies' responses to pain (a pinprick): stroking at three centimetres a second quickly calmed them down, but stroking at 30 centimetres a second did not. If stimulated in the right way, the CT fibres trigger the endorphin system directly, precipitating a flood of endorphins into the brain that is picked up by a specialised set of receptors (the μ-receptors) that are found throughout most of the brain.

That grooming does this and that it is explicitly endorphins that are involved was demonstrated thirty years ago by the Cambridge neurobiologist Barry Keverne. Socially housed monkeys were given either a very small dose of morphine or an endorphin blocker (naloxone) that locks onto the endorphin receptor sites in the brain but is pharmacologically neutral so that you don't get the opiate effect. Monkeys that received naloxone couldn't get enough grooming and kept soliciting grooming from the other animals. Those who received the opiate – a dose so small, by the way, that you wouldn't have been able to pick it up in a blood sample – soon lost interest in being groomed because they were getting their opiate hit without needing to groom. (By the way, this probably explains why opiate addicts lose interest in the social world and their social relationships: they are getting their hit artificially and don't need human contact to do it for them.)

We humans have this same system. We activate it day in, day out in our interactions with each other. We experience the uptake of endorphins in the brain as that feeling of warmth that we associate with physical contact with intimates, a mild sense of analgesia, a blunting of the everyday mental and physical pains that we all occasionally suffer from, and a distinct sense of euphoria (from the associated dopamine activation). If you want to know what it feels like, just go for a jog. Most people experience something known as 'second wind' or the 'runner's high' around ten minutes in. Quite suddenly, the stresses of running drop away and you feel you could run for ever. In a social context, it makes us feel relaxed, and well disposed towards the other person, and increases our sense of trust in them. Tristen Inagaki and Naomi Eisenberger used brain scanning to show that the feelings of social warmth we get from our friends are actually the same feelings we get of physical warmth when we hold a warm object: both sensations are processed in the same part of the brain – the ventral striatum and insula that are invariably activated during both pain and stroking. Their subjects even felt more 'connected' after picking up a warm object than after picking up a cool one.

If you want to see real primatelike grooming in humans, just watch mothers with young children relaxing in the park or at the seaside. Watch them leaf through their toddler's hair (the only patch of fur we still have) with exactly the same movements as any monkey would use. The loss of most of our fur (probably around 2 million years ago – but that's another story that I discuss in my book *Human Evolution*) meant that our capacity for conventional grooming became limited. Nonetheless, even though we are a bit thin on body hair, the mechanism is still there and working just as it always has. In case you don't believe me, think of the way your skin puckers up when you get goosebumps. These are the same tiny muscles round the base of each hair follicle that every dog, cat and monkey uses when they raise their hackles to make themselves look bigger when under threat. Our body hair, such as it is, may no longer stand on end the way a dog's does, but the anatomical mechanism in the skin that would make it do so still works as well as it ever did. So much so that we still speak of experiences that 'make your hair stand on end'. We have lost the fur, but not what's below the skin. So it is with the CT receptors. Lacking the hair to groom on most of our body, we have simply replaced the grooming actions with stroking, patting and cuddling that have the same effect: rubbing the skin triggers the CT fibres and sends a signal racing off to the endorphin-producing neurons in the brain. It is the stroking and skin-rubbing that we do in the lead-up to sex that relaxes our partner and makes them more willing to take part.

We were, naturally, anxious to confirm that stroking the skin really does cause the endorphin system in our brains to go wild. The problem is that endorphins don't cross the blood–brain barrier, so you cannot assay for endorphins in the brain by taking blood samples in the way you would do for most of the body's other chemicals. There are only two ways to assay for endorphins. One is by lumbar puncture – a painful procedure whereby you puncture a hole into the spinal column so as to draw out a sample of the fluid that circulates round the brain and its neural extension down the spinal cord. The problem is you have to do this twice, because you need to first establish a baseline level in order to know whether the experimental manipulation has changed the amount of circulating endorphin. Aside from being quite painful and something you really wouldn't want to inflict on a volunteer twice in the space of a half-hour experiment, lumbar puncture often has unpleasant consequences in the form of headaches or even infection – you are, after all, knocking a hole into the brain's deliberately self-contained circulatory system and letting who knows what in from outside.

The alternative is a form of brain imaging known as PET, or Positron Emission Tomography. The clue is in the positron – this subatomic particle is emitted from an atom in some forms of radioactive decay. Already you know this doesn't sound good. It's used in certain forms of medical imaging when they want to observe metabolic processes at work because it allows you to see chemical reactions in the body in real time. PET is probably the least pleasant of the brain-imaging techniques because it involves injecting radioactive tracers into the bloodstream and then seeing where these get taken up in the brain as the nerves gobble up the blood and its oxygen fuel when they are busy doing some cognitive task. Even so, you still need to give two doses because you need to see if the activity you ask them to do results in an increase or decrease in endorphin activation. Aside from the fact that you cannot give people successive doses of radioactive substances too close together, you also have to allow enough time for the first dose to clear from the body before you can run your experiment, otherwise you won't be able to see if endorphins have been taken up by the brain receptors. That means volunteers have to spend most of the day in the laboratory so that they can have one scan mid-morning and a second mid-afternoon. That's a lot to ask of them. And, as if that isn't enough, the whole process is very expensive. The radioactive tracers are expensive to produce and the fact that you are injecting radioactive substances into people means that you need a full medical crash team on standby in case anyone responds adversely (even though that is, in actual fact, *extremely* rare). It's not ideal, but, realistically, it is the only option.

We tried several times to get funding for a PET experiment to confirm that stroking triggered endorphins in humans, but it proved impossible to get this done in Britain. The research-funding agencies weren't interested, mainly, I suspect, because the reviewers and committees really didn't understand the point of the experiment and preferred to fund the mostly rather dull run-of-the-mill neuroscience studies they normally fund. We tried a hospital that did clinical PET scanning. They were very enthusiastic, but didn't have the kit to make up the specific radioactive tracer we needed. Instead, we would have had to courier the tracers up from London, a journey that would have taken an hour and a half on a good day with no traffic on the roads – for a chemical that has a half-life of just two-and-a-half hours. In other words, if there were any holdups on the motorway or in London's increasingly congested streets, the tracers would have arrived with most of their radioactive properties so decayed as to be useless. It was frustrating. Then, by chance, when I was bemoaning this impasse to my Finnish collaborators during one of my periodic visits to Aalto University, the neuroscientist Lauri Nummenmaa casually suggested that he could run the study in Finland, and at a fraction of the cost we would have had to pay in Britain. And so he did.

We had decided to run the experiment just on men on the principle that if we could show this mechanism worked in the less social sex, then we could show that it worked in anyone. So he had a group of male volunteers come into the scanner where they were stroked gently on the torso by their female partners. The partners were very carefully instructed not to go above the shoulders or below the belt. In any case, the volunteers completed questionnaires after the scanner session that checked their psychological and emotional responses to the experiment, and none reported any kind of sexual response or arousal. But the brain-scan images showed that, after being stroked, their brains fired up as endorphins were spewed out and the receptors all over the brain greedily gobbled them up.

Finally, in what is, in effect, a replication of Barry Keverne's experiment on monkeys, Tristen Inagaki and Naomi Eisenberger showed that, when humans took naltrexone (another endorphin blocker) for four days, they rated themselves as less well socially bonded than after they had taken a placebo (these are usually a pharmacologically neutral sugar pill) for four days. In short, endorphins really do directly influence our sense of social bonding.

A neurochemical spider's web

The last decade or so has witnessed a plethora of studies and media reports on the role of a dozen different brain chemicals in our social lives. Of these, oxytocin has received far more attention – and especially media attention – than any of the others. Sometimes known as the 'love hormone' or, worse still, 'liquid trust', oxytocin is part of the hormonal armoury of all the vertebrates. It seems to have evolved originally in fishes as part of the mechanism for maintaining the body's water balance – in this case, ensuring that too much water doesn't find its way into the fish's cells from the surrounding sea. After the early fishes had successfully invaded the land to give rise to the ancestors of the amphibians and reptiles, and eventually the birds and mammals, they had the reverse problem: in the dry air, they risked losing water and drying out. Oxytocin was co-opted to make sure the body didn't dry out, and that is how it still functions for all us mammals. However, it came to have an additional important function in mammals as a result of their novel strategy of lactation: part of oxytocin's role came to be ensuring that lactation didn't throw the mother's water balance into complete disarray. From here, it seems to have been co-opted into facilitating the mother–infant bond that was essential to ensure that the mother kept coming back to suckle her young.

And in due course, when pair-bonding evolved, it was a very short step from mother–infant bonding to adapting oxytocin to play a role in pair-bonding.

Then, during the 1990s, came the news, initially from Sue Carter's neuroscience lab and later from Larry Young and his lab, that oxytocin seemed to differentiate between monogamous and promiscuous voles. These mainly herbivorous mouse-like mammals scurry about in the ground-level vegetation, providing one of the main sources of food for owls and other birds of prey as well as coyotes and foxes. They rear their young in burrows. Like most species of their size and habits, gestation is short (about three weeks) and lactation even shorter (two weeks).

It so happened that the two species that the two teams studied, the montane vole and the prairie vole, differed radically in their mating systems. The one is promiscuous and the other monogamous (at least during the reproductive season). Paralleling this is a difference in the oxytocin genes they carry. In an elegant series of studies over many years, these labs were able to show that, for example, injecting oxytocin or inserting the monogamous prairie vole's genes for oxytocin into the promiscuous montane vole transformed the montane vole into a pair-bonded species by making them more tolerant of each other.

This spawned a veritable media scrum, followed inevitably by many attempts to extend these findings to humans. Since oxytocin seemed to be one of those neurochemicals that cross the blood–brain barrier, it could be conveniently delivered as a nasal spray, making it easy to use with humans. Many experiments were run to test whether oxytocin squirted up the noses of ever-patient human subjects turned them into more trusting, more generous or better-behaved individuals – with, I think it fair to say, modest rather than convincing success. A recent review by Gideon Nave of the role of oxytocin in human social behaviour concluded that the evidence was, not to put too fine a point on it, questionable. Not only did the technical aspects of many of the studies leave a great deal to be desired, but replications by different research groups often produced conflicting results. In respect of the influence of oxytocin on trust, in particular, he concluded that, while there did appear to be a small positive effect, it was actually barely distinguishable from zero. Subsequent evidence that oxytocin might not, after all, cross the blood–brain barrier might go some way to explaining the patchiness of the results from these kinds of experiments.

However, there are more fundamental problems with the oxytocin story. Voles are rodents whose level of sociality is best described as transitory – at most a few weeks during the breeding season even in the most social species. They can hardly be said to be in the same social league as primates with their lifelong social bonds and their deep commitment to each other. They do not even vie with the monogamous klipspringer whose male is so assiduous in his attachment to his partner that he never lets her out of his sight and is rarely more than a few metres from her. Worse still for the oxytocin story, the effects of oxytocin seem to be rather transient. Studies of hamsters indicate that the animals habituate to its effects after just a few weeks – long enough to satisfy the requirements of the reproductive needs of voles and hamsters, but not exactly a recipe for the lifelong bonds of primates. Worse was to come: comparative analyses across all the many vole species showed that, in fact, monogamy did not correlate with oxytocin genes as neatly as the original studies had assumed. Indeed, it has since turned out that the monogamy versus promiscuity of the two original vole species can be predicted just as well by the endorphin genes they have. Oh dear!

There are other problems too. Most of the experiments that tried to manipulate oxytocin have not controlled for other neurochemicals that might have been activated by the manipulation. In one study, for example, people were given a stressful task to do (such as giving a public speech); some of them were allowed to have a hug from their partner before doing so, and others weren't.

Those who had a hug were less stressed when they gave the talk, whereas those who didn't were not. But, as we saw earlier, hugging will also activate the endorphin system. So how can we be sure that the lowered stress levels weren't due to the relaxing effects of endorphins? We can't, because no one thought to control for them.

Perhaps the most serious problem for the oxytocin story is that oxytocin seems to be something that acts only endogenously. Having the right genes for oxytocin may well make you a warmer, more friendly and more trusting person, but not everyone you meet will be like you. Some will have the variants of the oxytocin gene that make them less trusting. Every time you bump into a social shark, they will laugh while they fleece you, thanks to your boundless generosity. This is precisely where endorphins come into their own. Endorphins have the distinct merit that you can trigger their activation in other people by grooming them. That way, you can turn the sharks into well behaved puppies – something you can't do with oxytocin. The evidence that endorphins seemed to be involved in social grooming prompted Barry Keverne to suggest that while oxytocin might well be the social neurohormone of choice for the wider mammal world, it will not be anything like effective enough for maintaining the more intense, lifelong forms of social bonding characteristic of primates. Something stronger was needed, and this was, he suggested, the endorphin system. At some point during their evolution, primates co-opted the endorphin system to provide a more powerful platform for maintaining social bonds.

In my experience, the world seems to be divided into two camps who never talk to each other, never mind read each other's publications: these are the oxytociphilics (those who love oxytocin and think it is the explanation for everything) and endorphophilics (those who love endorphins and think they are the explanation for everything), with the latter in a distinct minority and seemingly causing much sighing and eyebrow-raising among the former. In fact, the endorphin story is much older, having first been suggested as the bonding agent by the Estonian neuroscientist Jaak Panksepp, who had come to this conclusion from studies on mice. Psychiatrists working on addiction and marital relationships in humans had also suggested something similar. However, since this tended to be on the basis of casual observations in the consulting room rather than on any experimental evidence, it rather tended to be ignored. The real problem was that endorphins are hard to work with and horribly difficult to test, whereas oxytocin is easy to use in experiments. And as the new kid on the block (and, regrettably, science is as prone to fashion as haute couture), oxytocin attracted rather more attention than it probably deserved, to the rapid exclusion of anything else. Sometimes scientists' behaviour can get in the way of science.

Having become frustrated by all this, we eventually set up a large-scale study that tried to sort out what was going on in an attempt to impose a bit more rigour on the field. We identified two main problems with the previous research. One was a failure to control for the impact of other social neurochemicals. There were at least six of these that we could identify: besides oxytocin and endorphins, there were plausible claims on behalf of testosterone, vasopressin, serotonin and dopamine. Second, we were mystified by the fact that almost all the research on oxytocin had focused on dyadic relationships, often in the context of romantic relationships. That came about, of course, partly because this was the context in which oxytocin had emerged in the vole studies. But it also partly reflected the rather impoverished view of sociality that seems to be remarkably widespread among behavioural scientists.

Part of the problem here has been the stranglehold that microeconomics has had on the field of human behaviour more generally in the last couple of decades. Economists' view of social life seems to be limited to versions of the secondhand car salesman: you want to buy a car, and I have a very dodgy old banger that I want to get rid of for as high a price as I can get away with because you are too stupid to know its real value. The thing about secondhand car sales is that, like most trading arrangements in the modern world, they involve strangers. The secondhand car salesman is someone we are unlikely ever to meet again. But our social world isn't like that: it mainly involves exchanges between people who know each other well and who, for many and various reasons, have deep obligations towards each other, most of which are a consequence of being embedded in a network of relationships. The secondhand car salesman problem is a problem precisely because it happens only once in a very long while. More conventional purchases and trades happen on a near-daily basis and involve people we know well – well, at least in the days before eBay.

In many ways, this point had been made a few years earlier by a celebrated large-scale study in which a number of anthropologists and economists ran some classic economic games in small-scale ethnographic societies in various parts of the world, as well as on the usual workhorses for economic experiments (namely American economics students). Mathematically, there is an optimal way to play such games, but it assumes that players are strangers who will never meet again (i.e. you and that secondhand car salesman). Dutifully, the students produced the optimal solution. But most of the players in the ethnographic societies did not. They either accepted offers that were far too low or insisted on much higher offers. The problem, of course, was that the students were playing against strangers and the people in ethnographic societies were playing against folk with whom they had well developed relation-ships. Many of them, for example, were playing the game in social contexts where accepting a gift from someone incurred an obliga-tion that would have to be repaid later. For obvious reasons, they were very reluctant to do that for too low a price. In other words, people living in the real world are embedded in social networks that incur obligations that have long-term consequences.

What this should remind us of is that, while many social transactions certainly do take place in dyads (I lend you my lawn-mower, you come and help harvest my apples), those dyads almost always involve people who have an existing relationship, and furthermore these relationships are embedded in a much larger community. Those community relationships impose obligations and involve policing mechanisms (Granny gets to hear about your bad behaviour) that impose discipline on the individual members by making it costly for them to infringe on the community's social mores.

Given all this, we came to the conclusion that we needed to look at three different levels of sociality: social disposition (how nice you are to people in general – your natural social style), dyadic relationships (with a chief focus on romantic partners) and social networks (how well embedded you are in your social community). So we ended up with six neurochemicals that could act in any or all of three very different social domains. Ellie Pearce, Anna Machin and Rafael Wlodarski spent weeks at various science festivals and museums around Britain persuading people to 'spit for science' so as to provide us with samples of their saliva for DNA analysis, as well as to fill in questionnaires about their social lives. It was the largest and most expensive study I have ever undertaken. More than a thousand people contributed and had their DNA assayed for thirty-five genes for the receptors of the six social neurochemicals. Just the tubes for them to spit into cost us over £20,000.

The results were very clear. By far the best predictor of the quality of people's romantic relationships (and, in particular, their degree of promiscuity) was their oxytocin-receptor genes. However, the strength of this relationship did fall away in some of these cases if we controlled for endorphin-receptor genes: in other words, it seemed that at least some of these oxytocin effects were probably due to endorphins rather than to oxytocin. The endorphin-receptor genes, on the other hand, had by far their strongest effect on measures of social predisposition, including such psychological parameters as attachment style (how warm or cold you are in your relationships) and how empathetic you are with others, as well as a significant effect on romantic relationships. Dopamine had its strongest effect at the network level (indexed by measures such as how many close friends you have, and how engaged you are with your local community), with a lesser supporting contribution from the endorphin system. The other three neurochemicals (testosterone, vasopressin and serotonin) had no significant effects at any level. In other words, the endorphin–dopamine system seemed to be central to how we interface with the social world, and oxytocin is relevant only to romantic relationships.

The pain of friendship

The fact that pain tolerance is underpinned by the endorphin system and endorphins are involved in creating and maintaining friendships made me wonder whether people who have higher pain thresholds (indicating a greater density of endorphin receptors in the brain) have more friends. Could the connection between the two be so direct? Katerina Johnson decided to test this suggestion. As a test of pain tolerance, we used the infamous Roman Chair. This involves sitting with your back against a wall with your thighs at right angles to the wall and your feet flat on the floor, as though you were sitting on a chair. Because the entire weight of your body is supported only by the muscles of your thighs, it quickly becomes excruciatingly painful. Most people can hold this position for only about a minute; few can manage more than two minutes. Katerina found that people who could hold this pose for longer (and hence had a higher pain threshold, presumably because they had more endorphin receptors) did indeed have more friends in their sympathy group (or 15-layer of the social network).

Before undertaking the PET study of stroking, Lauri Nummenmaa had been running a series of studies on the role of endorphins in other social contexts. One of the questionnaires he always included (mainly just to give volunteers something to

do while waiting for their second scan) was the standard psychological Attachment Scale that measures your social style – how
warm or cool you are in the way you interact with people. It has
several subscales, but in essence if you score high on it you have
that demonstrative, Italian kind of social style – all hugs and
air-kisses – and if you score low you have a rather cool don't-
touch-me-I'm-British style. It turned out that warm, socially
effusive people have a very high density of endorphin receptors
in the brain, and especially in the prefrontal cortex – the brain
region that seems to be especially important in managing your
friendships. Conversely, those at the cool attachment end had a
much lower density of endorphin receptors. It is as though they
have fewer slots to fill with the endorphins triggered by physical
contact, and so lose interest or don't want any more contact sooner
than more effusively social people.

This bears some similarity to what happens in autistic people.
As we saw in chapter 6, they lack the core cognitive skills involved
in social relationships and, as a result, they typically have few or
no friends. Some, however, find physical touch very unpleasant,
even distressing. It is as though they sit at the ultra-cool end of the
attachment scale with an ultra-low density of endorphin receptors,
especially perhaps in the frontal lobes. The suggestion that autism
might be related to the endorphin system was originally proposed
by Jaak Panksepp. The suggestion was not viewed with enthusiasm at the time by autism professionals, but the evidence of a role
for endorphins in autism does seem to be growing.

Lucie Pellisier and her colleagues have recently argued that
autism does seem be underpinned by poor responsiveness in the
endorphin system, just as Jaak Panksepp suggested. Mice that have
been bred so that they have no endorphin receptors don't vocalise
as pups when they are separated from their mothers (something
that mouse pups will normally always do); as adults, they will not
respond to females' vocalisations (which males will always do), and
show reduced interest in social interaction. They also exhibit many

of the ancillary features that autistic individuals display: increased aggressiveness, greater anxiety, motor clumsiness, susceptibility to seizures, impaired spatial learning, lowered pain thresholds and disturbed gut activity. It's always risky to place too much weight on similarities between human and rat behaviour, but this looks very much like autistic behaviour in humans. Recent brain-imaging studies indicated that, in response to social stimuli, autistic individuals have significantly reduced activity in the orbitofrontal, ventral and dorsal regions of the prefrontal cortex, the nucleus accumbens and the insula (all regions that, as we saw in chapter 3, are normally active in managing social relationships), as well as an overactive response in the amygdala (indicating high responsiveness to social threat). Jaak Panksepp may have the last laugh yet.

How time creates emotional closeness

The fact that grooming underpins social bonding in primates points us to what is perhaps the second-most important aspect of this part of the story, namely the fact that animals have to invest a great deal of time in mutual grooming in order to produce a strong enough endorphin effect to create friendships bonded enough to do the job they are needed to do for them. In both our Christmas-card survey and our survey of women's networks, we asked everyone to say both when they last saw each person they listed as a friend and how emotionally close they felt to them on a very simple 1 to 10 scale, where 1 is pretty neutral (neither here nor there) and 10 is you love them dearly – with no negative component (after all, if you disliked someone, why would you include them in your list of friends?). This emotional-closeness scale is really simple and intuitively easy to use. More important, it turns out to correlate extremely well with all of the more complex rating scales for relationship quality that social psychologists and sociologists have invented over the years. Our two measures turned out to be very highly correlated: the more emotionally close you feel to someone, the more often you see them. Our data showed that this is as true of family as it is of friends.

What this tells us is that how emotionally close we feel to someone is directly related to how much time we invest in them. We'll explore some of the consequences of this in more detail in chapter 8. For the moment, it is enough to notice that, as we discovered in chapter 4 (see Figure 4), friendships draw heavily on time. Perhaps the best evidence on how important that is comes from a study by Jeffrey Hall, one of the leading authorities on the psychology of friendship. He sampled a group of college students as they developed friendships and determined the time investments they had made in them. He found that it took about forty-five hours spent in each other's company after first meeting for someone to progress from being an acquaintance to becoming a casual friend. People who averaged only thirty hours together over nine weeks (the equivalent of just 15 minutes a day) remained acquaintances. To move from being a casual friend to a meaningful friend called for another fifty hours spent together over the course of three months, while those who advanced to be best friends took another 100 hours to be spent together. In effect, to make it into the most intimate category of friendship required something close to two hours a day to be devoted to the friend, day after day, for some considerable time. Friendship does not come cheap.

If you don't believe me when I say that time is the basis of friendship and the problem is that time is in very short supply, perhaps the fact that falling in love will cost you two friendships might convince you. As you'll be well aware by now, we typically have five intimate friends in that inner social circle of ours. In one of our studies of this inner circle, we happened to include a question as to whether or not the respondent was in a romantic relationship at the time. As in all our other samples of this grouping layer, the average number of people in the layer was exactly five. But it turned out that people in an active romantic relationship in fact averaged only four. Think about it this way. You never fall in love with someone in your inner 5-layer, and very rarely even with someone in your 15-layer – not least because half of them will be very close family. Your new romantic interest almost always comes in from the outer layers of your social network or from way outside your social circle. That means you have just added an extra person to your existing 5-layer, bringing it up to six. To have reduced this to four means that you must have sacrificed *two* close friendships. That's not too surprising, of course, because a romantic relation-ship is usually *very* time-consuming: you devote a great deal of your mental effort and attention to this lucky person, much much more than you ever do to anyone else in that circle.

The interesting question, then, is whom you sacrifice, given that this inner layer typically consists of two close family members and two friends (plus an odd one to make up the difference). There is a trade-off here, because your family provide you with the only really secure source of long-term support – they are the only ones who will stand by you through thick and thin, no matter what. But when you come home in tears after you have been jilted, they are invariably less than helpful. They are inclined to come out with such encouraging observations as: 'Don't worry – there are plenty more fish in the sea' or, worse still: 'Well, we never really liked him anyway . . .' That is not what you really want to hear at that particular moment. What you want is an unconditional hug, and the only people who will give that are your friends. So there are costs and benefits to sacrificing both of the individuals in either of these two key categories. The fact that, in these circumstances, we sacrifice one of each rather than both of one is a tribute to the subtlety of human behaviour: we do our best to hedge our bets.

*

Time determines the number of endorphin hits we get from a relationship in a very simple way. In primates, this is obvious because most of that time is spent grooming or being groomed, and every minute spent being groomed gives an extra endorphin hit. We humans get that from stroking and patting, and all the other forms of physical contact that we engage in when we are with friends. In fact, this is all so spontaneous and below the radar of consciousness that most of the time we aren't even aware that we are doing it. In fact, we actually do it a great deal – much more than we imagine. However, there are a number of other social behaviours that we engage in that turn out to be remarkably effective at triggering the endorphin system. These include laughter, singing and dancing, storytelling and feasting. How these enable us to manage our friendships is the subject of the next chapter.

Binding the bonds of friendship

About fifteen years ago, I experienced a musical epiphany. I was at a workshop on the evolution of music, organised by the cognitive archaeologist Steven Mithen and the composer, conductor and musicologist Nick Bannan. One evening after dinner, they had organised a special lecture by Pedro Espi-Sanchis, a Spanish musician then working with disadvantaged communities in South Africa. No one can now remember what he actually talked about, but all of us there that evening can remember vividly the demonstration he put on to illustrate the main point of his lecture. He got us all to come up to the space at the front of the lecture hall, gave each of us a short section of plastic plumber's tubing, cut to different lengths, and invited us to blow across the tops of these in whatever rhythm we liked while we walked around in a circle. The different lengths of tube would, of course, have different pitches, so between the twenty or so of us we had a veritable orchestra of sounds that we could produce. We would, he assured us, find that after a mere five minutes doing this we would all be in synchrony and producing a genuine piece of polyphonic music. As we walked around in a circle, he orchestrated our movements, asking us every few minutes to add something new into our movements, such as stamping with the right foot, swaying a little from side to side or speeding up a bit. He was absolutely right. Somehow, spontaneously and as if by magic, we evolved a natural rhythm, coordinating our whistling on the plastic piping to produce an integrated soundscape. And all without intending to do so. Extraordinary.

But it was what he hadn't told us, and may only have dimly appreciated himself, that turned out to be the really electric moment in this experience. It took perhaps ten minutes to emerge, but emerge it did – a feeling of oneness, of being melded into the group as a single coordinated organism, each of us a part of a greater whole. It bonded this group of semi-strangers like nothing else could have done. And it did so almost instantaneously. None of us have ever forgotten it. It made me realise what an important role music must have played in the evolution of human communities during the course of our evolution – not for some esoteric musical reason, but because it triggered, deep inside us, psychological and physiological experiences that are central to community bonding and friendship.

It is this issue of bonding that is central to how we have managed to create our extended networks of friendship and, through these, our large communities. Primates, as we have seen, use grooming for bonding their groups. The problem with grooming is that it is very time-consuming and animals do not have infinite time available to devote to it. Even the most social of all the monkey and ape species only devote 20 per cent of their day to social grooming, and that sets an upper limit on social-group size at around fifty individuals. This is because, as we saw in chapter 7, each friendship requires the investment of a minimum amount of time and because it is only possible to groom one individual at a time. This might not be such a problem if we could groom with several individuals simultaneously. But we can't. Physical touch creates an intimacy that makes it all but impossible for three individuals to groom simultaneously with each other. If you don't believe me, try sitting in the back row of the cinema cuddling with two other people simultaneously. I guarantee it won't work for long: one of them will soon take umbrage because you are paying too much attention to the other person, and is very likely to storm off in high dudgeon.

When we needed to increase the size of our social groups during the course of later human evolution, we had to find some way of extending our grooming circle proportionately. Increasing the time devoted to grooming was no more an option for our ancestors (or us, if it comes to that) than it is for any other monkeys and apes. The only realistic alternative was to use what time we had available more efficiently, and the only way this could be done was to groom with several people simultaneously. It seems that we discovered several ways of triggering the endorphin system using behaviours that allowed us engage in virtual grooming at a distance such that we could, in effect, groom several people at the same time. These include laughter, singing and dancing, feasting, storytelling and the rituals of religion, probably in that order.

Laughter – the first medicine

I first realised that laughter plays a central role in social bonding when I was asked to contribute to a management workshop run by a firm of well-known accountants in London. We had all turned up at some excessively early hour on the promise of a fruit-and-croissants breakfast. We duly had our croissants and coffee, mostly standing around awkwardly in ones and twos wondering who to talk to, but never quite managing it. Then, at 9 a.m., everyone was herded into a room and asked to sit down. We sat waiting expectantly, but nothing happened. People began to shuffle their feet and look surreptitiously around at everyone else. We were a mixed bag, some dressed casually, some London cool, a couple of older men in pinstriped suits who looked as though they had stepped out of a government ministry just down the road and accidentally taken the wrong turning. Everyone was perplexed.

Then suddenly someone at the front of the room stood up and announced that they believed something – I can't remember what, but something very innocuous like that the sky is blue – and then immediately sat down. Silence. A minute later, someone else did the same thing – they believed the world was round, or something equally silly. The puzzlement in the room was palpable. The Men-from-the-Ministry were looking decidedly uncomfortable. A third person stood up and declared that they believed something else. This was altogether *very* odd. Everyone looked at their feet. Then some wit at the back of the room announced loudly: 'I believe everyone here is completely baffled as to what is going on.' For all I know, he may have been a stooge, just as the others had obviously been, but the room collapsed in laughter. From that moment on, we were bonded as a group and the rest of the day went swim-mingly because we all felt we had known each other for years. It was the perfect icebreaker. Infinitely better than the usual formal introductions round the room saying who we were and why we were there, none of which anyone can ever remember afterwards. We didn't need to know who we were, or even who we worked for; we only needed to know that we *belonged*.

Laughter is a human universal. Every tribe and culture laughs, and they laugh at pretty much the same kinds of things – other people's embarrassments, minor accidents like slipping on a banana skin, and, of course, jokes. Or just because someone else is laughing. Laughter is involuntary, and very visceral. It's also extraordinarily contagious. If somebody in your conversation group laughs, it's impossible not to laugh as well, even if you didn't hear the joke. The late Robert Provine, one of the stalwarts of research on laughter who did more than anyone else to revitalise scientific interest in this behaviour, pointed out many years ago that we are more likely to laugh at something when we are in a group than when we are alone. We confirmed this in a series of experiments in which we asked people to watch a video of stand-up comedy either alone or in groups of three or four. Subjects were four times more likely to laugh when they were in a group than when watching the *same* video alone. It is *very* weird stuff. The nearest thing to it in the natural world that I can think of are the raucous dawn choruses of South American howler monkeys. One will start up, and then others gradually join in – almost like a slow-motion group laugh.

Laughter involves the rapid pumping of the lungs with the mouth open and the teeth covered by the lips in a very characteristic facial expression known as the round open mouth (or ROM) face. In fact, the ROM face and our pant-like laugh derive from the play face and play vocalisation of Old World monkeys and apes. They use these both to invite someone to play and to comment on the fact that they are playing – in effect, to say: 'Whatever I do next [such as mouth or bite you], don't take it seriously! Don't panic and bite back!' Great apes, however, seem to use laughter in a slightly more human way, and, at least so it has been claimed, seem to have a sense of humour. The difference is that, as with play pants, they laugh on their own, whereas we laugh in a chorus.

The difference between ape and human laughter is that we have changed the form of the vocalisation slightly. In monkeys and apes, laughter is a simple exhalation–inhalation sequence: huh-uh ... huh-uh ... huh-uh ... We have adapted this so that it becomes a series of exhalations with no intervening inhalations: huh ... huh ... huh ... The result is that we rapidly empty the lungs when we laugh, leading to that sense of 'dying with laughter' when we can't get our breath back after a vigorous full-throttle belly laugh. That doesn't happen in monkeys and apes, where it is a much more genteel business – more like one of our polite laughs. Emptying the lungs in the way we do places enormous stress on the muscles of the diaphragm and chest wall, never mind the vigorous pumping action these do when expelling the air from our lungs. Between them, the pumping action and the oxygen starvation trigger the endorphin system.

There is an important distinction between involuntary laughter and voluntary (or polite) laughter. The first kind is known as Duchenne laughter, after the great nineteenth-century French neuroanatomist Guillaume Duchenne, who first described it. Voluntary laughter is usually referred to as non-Duchenne laughter. Non-Duchenne laughter is the kind of forced or polite laughter that people give when someone makes a rather feeble joke and you don't want to offend them by not laughing – especially if they are your boss. This kind of laughter may not be vigorous enough to trigger the endorphin system. Duchenne, or involuntary, laughter is distinguished by the fact that crow's-feet creases appear at the outer corners of the eye. It's what causes the twinkle in the eyes when you laugh. The muscles responsible are not under voluntary control: we cannot make this happen. It only happens when we laugh involuntarily. They do not appear in non-Duchenne laughter. So if you want to know whether someone really thinks your joke is funny, check for the crow's feet.

We've run more than half a dozen different experiments in which we tested subjects' pain thresholds before and after watching a short video. Half of them watched stand-up comedy, half watched rather more boring documentaries or instruction videos. In one case, Rebecca Baron even took the experiment to the Edinburgh Festival Fringe and tested people watching live stand-up and live drama. In each case, people who watched comedy *and laughed* exhibited an increase in pain threshold, implying activation of the endorphin system. Those who watched neutral clips and didn't laugh exhibited a negative change in pain threshold – they had a lower pain threshold afterwards, almost as though the skin remembered the pain from before. Subsequently, Sandra Manninen and Lauri Nummenmaa ran a PET brain-imaging study to check that laughter really did trigger the endorphin system. It did. Laughing floods the brain with endorphins.

If endorphins triggered by laughter make you more relaxed and at ease, then we might expect people who laughed together to feel more bonded to each other, and so be more willing to disclose intimate information, as well as being more generous to each other. We tested this is a series of experiments. Alan Gray asked people to watch a comedy video (such that they laughed) and then determined whether they were more willing to disclose personal information to a stranger. Although the subjects themselves did not think they were being more intimate in their disclosures after laughing in the comedy condition, independent raters did in fact think they were. The likely reason for this is that the endorphins released by laughter make you *feel* more relaxed and intimate with those with whom you laugh – and so more willing to let your hair down. In another series of experiments, Anna Frangou, Ellie Pearce and Felix Grainger showed that people were more willing to give money to each other (though not to strangers), and they felt more bonded to each other, after laughing at a comedy video than when they watched a non-comedy video and didn't laugh.

Come dance with me

Though we now often do them separately, singing and dancing always go together in traditional societies. That's because in these societies, men often do the dancing and the women provide the music in the form of clapping and singing. Both almost certainly pre-date language by some considerable margin, since we don't need words in order to sing. We can hum and chant in perfect musical formation, as is obvious from the many forms of singing like jazz scat singing and Gaelic mouth music (*puirt à beul*) that involve nonsense rather than actual words. To explore the role of singing and dancing as mechanisms for social bonding, we ran a parallel series of experiments using our by-now standard format: a test for pain threshold, an activity (singing or dancing) for fifteen minutes, and then a retest of the pain threshold. We also threw in some simple pencil-and-paper rating scales of bondedness. The bondedness index we used is known as the

Inclusion-of-Other-in-Self (or IOS) index and consists of seven pairs of circles which vary from completely separated to almost completely overlapping; you select the one which best reflects how bonded you feel to another person or group. It was originally developed to describe romantic relationships (how immersed in the other person do you feel), but it works extremely well with reference to a group of people (how immersed in the group do you feel). The dance projects were mainly carried out by Bronwyn Tarr (herself a dancer and dance teacher, as well as being a Namibian Rhodes Scholar in our research group). The singing projects were done by two of my postdocs, Ellie Pearce and Jacques Launay.

One of the key features of both singing and dancing is that everyone is highly synchronised in their actions. We had been alerted to the importance of behavioural synchrony a few years earlier when we had run some experiments on rowing crews. We did this on Oxford University's men's boat crews – the eight-oared racing hulls that compete every Easter in the annual Oxford–Cambridge University Boat Race on the River Thames in London, perhaps the most famous boat race in the world and incubator for future Olympic rowers from all over the world (many of whom go to Oxford or Cambridge for the year just for the chance of being selected for the crews). The study was originally suggested by Robin Ejsmond-Frey, at the time one of our graduate students. He asked whether he might test the idea that synchrony in rowing triggered a heightened endorphin release, thereby elevating pain thresholds. The obvious place to do it, he suggested, was on the university boat crew. I remember telling him there was absolutely *no* chance – the very idea that the coaches would allow some random student to have access to the two boat crews in the month before the most famous boat race in the world ... well, it just wasn't going to happen. And, in any case, I didn't fancy being on the end of the telephone when the irate coaches rang me up and gave me an earful for having the audacity to send our students in their direction with daft ideas. Robin looked me up and down, and then quietly observed that it wouldn't be a problem: he was the President of the University Boat Club and they would do whatever he told them to do. And, of course, they did. In fact, not only was he President of the Boat Club that year, he was already a double Blue (meaning he had already rowed for the Oxford crew in the two previous years' Boat Races).

In between his own exhausting twice-daily training regimes, Robin recorded the athletes' pain thresholds before and after their regular morning workout on the rowing machines when training on their own, and then repeated this a week later when they worked out as a crew with the rowing machines linked up as a virtual boat. And then he repeated all this again a week later. In both series, the physical effort produced the expected increase in pain threshold when rowing alone on the machine, indicating endorphin activation due to the stress being placed on their muscles. But rowing in synchrony as a virtual boat doubled this – despite the fact that the rowers were not putting in more effort (as we could tell from the gauges on the rowing machines). Somehow, acting in synchrony ramps up the endorphin effect to much higher levels, though we still have no idea why.

The dance experiments were done using a 'silent disco' format so that we could look at how important synchrony was when people were dancing together in small groups (usually four people facing each other in a square). In a silent disco, everyone hears the music through earphones, as well as instructions on which simple dance moves they should do next. This way, we could sometimes have people doing exactly the same dance moves and sometimes doing different moves out of synchrony with each other but in time to the same music. We ran some of these in the lab in Oxford and some in Brazil. The more energetic the dance moves and the more synchronised the members of the group were, the greater the change in pain threshold and the more bonded they felt to the group. In the Brazil study, we asked them to say how bonded they felt both to the people they were dancing with (mostly people they knew, but weren't friends with) and to their best friends who weren't present on the day. The increase in bondedness applied *only* to the people they were dancing with. There was no effect at all on how bonded they felt to their absent best friends. In other words, the effect seems to be very specific to those you are actually doing the activity with.

Later, to check whether this effect really was due to endorphins, Bronwyn ran the experiment giving half the subjects a dose of naltrexone. The result is you don't get the endorphin hit. Subjects who had been given naltrexone exhibited a reduced pain threshold and somewhat reduced bonding, suggesting that the active ingredient is, indeed, endorphins.

The obvious question at this point is whether dancing increases the size of your 'grooming' group, allowing you to reach more people and so increase community size. Cole Robertson and Bronwyn Tarr carried out an observational study in nightclubs. They found that, in free dancing, you can dance with about eight people during the course of the average record, but always subject to the limit that at any one time you can't have more than four people dancing together as a group. We thought this was probably because of the need for dancers (many of whom are strangers) to pay attention to and coordinate their movements with each other as an explicit sign of social engagement. Eye contact is an important component of this and, like grooming, you cannot hold eye contact with more than one person at a time. What dancing does allow you to do, however, is to switch between partners faster than you can during a conversation, so you get to 'talk' to more people. In a conversation, you have to integrate into an existing conversation topic, whereas in dancing you simply need to be there and be in time. The fact that the upper limit on the number of people you can dance with is eight may explain why many 'set' dances are designed explicitly for four couples (i.e. eight people). Examples include many English and Scottish country dances, as well as American square dances (the clue is in the word 'square', since they usually involve four couples forming a square).

Our studies of singing came about almost by accident. There had been a lot of interest, at least in some corners of the medical profession, in the benefits of singing for mental and physical health. A chance meeting put us in contact with the Workers' Educational Association, WEA, who were keen to promote singing classes both for their own sake and as a means of improving people's health. The WEA put on four series of weekly novice singing classes for us, along with three series of hobby classes as controls, each to run for seven months. The singers showed a nice increase in pain threshold and a correspondingly increased sense of bonding with the class compared to the hobby classes. Not only did they form more new individual friendships within the class, but they also felt more bonded to the group as a whole. This much was clear both from their own ratings of their bondedness to the group and from the more dense structure to the group's social network. In fact, this effect was so instantaneous that we christened it the *Icebreaker Effect*. Both the singing and the hobby classes also showed significant improvements in physical and mental health, as well as in satisfaction with life; the effect seemed to be driven by a sense of bonding to the group as a whole rather than being anything to do with individual friendships established within the groups.

We ran other singing projects elsewhere (one in London with the musicologist Lauren Stewart and her student Daniel Weinstein, another in Leiden with Anna Rotkirch and Max van Duijn), with very similar results, so these effects are obviously robust. In the Leiden study, we found that synchronised singing with a rival group enhances the sense of bonding with the rivals, whereas singing in competition with them reduces the sense of bonding. The London study, run by Daniel Weinstein, allowed us to test whether the effects of singing are scale-free. We exploited the fact that a large amateur London choir of about 230 singers, the Popchoir, practised in smaller groups of around 20, and then came together as a single large choir for a performance at the end of the year. Singing in a large choir of two hundred people produced a stronger sense of bonding than singing in small choirs. In other words, there was an extra added bonus due to group size, and this seemed to be unique to singing. We have never found anything similar in any of the other bonding behaviours.

My suspicion is that singing and dancing first appeared around 500,000 years ago with the appearance of archaic humans (the Heidelberg folk and their European descendants, the Neanderthals), and it allowed them to increase community size from a value of around 75 in their predecessors to the 120 that seems to be typical of these early humans. At this stage, singing may well have been without words – humming or chorusing. One reason for thinking this is that although the anatomical markers for speech (as opposed to language) appear for the first time in archaic humans, fully modern language (as we would now recognise it) is unlikely to have evolved before the appearance of our own species, *Homo sapiens*, around 200,000 years ago. The mechanisms of speech (breath control, articulation) are the same as those that make both laughter and singing (without words), as well as speech, possible and these all appear with archaic humans. However, the mindreading capacities required for language as we know it do not appear until the arrival of our own species 300,000 years later. If Neanderthals had language, it was much less sophisticated than ours. (There is a great deal more on this in my book *Human Evolution*.)

That music-making (and specifically singing) might indeed be older than language was suggested by an imaginative study carried out in Taiwan by Steven Brown, Mark Stoneking and their collaborators in Taiwan. The island has nine indigenous populations that occupy different parts of the island, each with its own dialect and song traditions. Combining this information with data on the genetics of these populations, they found significant correlations between all three variables. But the correlation was strongest between music and the genes, suggesting that the musical differences had much deeper historical origins than the language differences.

I can't resist one final observation on singing and bonding. The *haka* is a traditional Maori war dance, originally performed to taunt and terrorise opponents, but now staged at the start of every international rugby match by the New Zealand All Blacks national team. The team chant assertively in unison, adopt stressed body poses (including exaggerated facial expressions), and perform in synchrony what are, in effect, vigorous dance moves involving much stamping. It has all the hallmarks of a good ritual, every element of which triggers the endorphin system. It's an impressive sight to watch at the best of times. But the key is surely that, under the influence of raised endorphin levels, the team enters the fray in a heightened state of alertness, with a sense of calmness and elevated pain thresholds that allow them to absorb far more punishment and exhaustion during the game that follows than would otherwise be the case. I cannot help wondering whether this extraordinary performance explains why this team, from one of the smallest countries that plays top-flight international rugby, has dominated the international rugby scene for the better part of a century.

Friendship, feasting and community spirit

We had devoted a great deal of time to looking at the different bonding behaviours one at a time. But there was still one aspect of our social bonding that eluded me: feasting. It is such a major feature of human social life that I could not believe endorphins weren't involved somehow. I became even more persuaded when one of my Finnish neuroscience collaborators assured me that alcohol definitely hit the endorphin system, which was why alcohol addiction clinics often use an endorphin blocker such as naloxone as part of their treatment regime. Later, Barry Keverne, whose experimental work on the role of endorphins in primate grooming had been instrumental in setting me down the road that led to this book, suggested that the same was almost certainly true of eating: the heat generated by food consumption and digestion, combined with that distended feeling after a big celebratory meal, almost certainly trigger the endorphin system. Subsequently, Jetro Tuulari and Lauri Nummenmaa ran a PET-scan study which showed that eating a meal did, in fact, trigger the release of endorphins in the brain, and did so irrespective of how pleasurable the food actually was.

It seemed increasingly obvious to me that both eating and the consumption of alcohol, with their intensely social nature and subject to so much ritual in formal feasts, must be part of the armoury for activating the endorphin system for bonding our communities. After all, major feasts to which neighbouring communities are invited are the very stuff of anthropological studies the world over. But how could we study this? I couldn't imagine the university's ethics committee viewing with much enthusiasm a proposal to fill undergraduates with drink that they already consumed far too much of anyway. Then, in one of those serendipitous moments when science collides with the real world, the venerable campaigning organisation CAMRA (the Campaign for Real Ale that campaigns to promote the old British ales and old-fashioned pubs) contacted me to ask if I would help them with an upcoming campaign.

CAMRA planned to undertake a large national UK tele-survey on pub use as part of their campaign to stem the tide of pub closures. After discussing possibilities, they agreed to fund a separate study to be done in the pubs themselves at the same time as the national survey. I was interested in how several standard social measures interacted with each other – and, of course, how this related to the frequency with which people visited pubs. Then, shortly afterwards, the Big Lunch Project (a derivative of the famous Eden Project) contacted me about doing something similar for social eating. The Big Lunch was born out of the recognition that we increasingly live in communities where we no longer know who our neighbours are. We live among strangers. In part, that is because, instead of our friends and family being clustered around us in the village as they once were, they are now dispersed all over the country, sometimes a whole continent. One consequence of this is that we are less engaged with the people we actually live among, and, as a result, we behave less well towards them than we might otherwise do. We are less courteous, less kind, less willing to pass the time of day with them. The Big Lunch project was launched to persuade everyone to down tools one day each summer and have lunch with their neighbours in the middle of the street where they lived so as to get to know them better. In the last couple of years, around 6 million people (10 per cent of the entire population of Great Britain) have arranged for their street to be closed off to traffic, set out trestle tables and sat down to lunch with their neighbours. A wonderful idea. The Big Lunch organisers wanted to launch an advertising campaign to encourage people to do this again in the following summer. As part of this, they intended to do a national survey to find out how often people normally ate socially. I persuaded them to include the same questions as we had used in the CAMRA study, but with the questions about how often you went to the pub replaced by how often you had your midday and evening meals with other people.

So, between these two projects, we ended up with two large surveys of around 2,000 people each, carefully structured to reflect the age and sex structure of the UK population and the way it was distributed around the British Isles. And carried out professionally by leading polling agencies. Aside from the questions about the frequency of the social activities of particular interest to each, both surveys provided data on exactly the same questions.

What these two studies revealed is that the number of close friends you have is closely correlated with how engaged you are with your local community, the level of trust you have in those among whom you live, your sense of how worthwhile your life is and how happy you feel. Most of the relationships between these variables work both ways: increase the sense of community engagement and it increases your sense that life is worthwhile; but, equally, increase your sense that life is worthwhile, and it increases how engaged you become with the rest of the community. These are, however, influenced in slightly different ways by whether we eat or drink with other people. Social eating tends to influence the number of close friends we have and our sense of life satisfaction most directly, and then through these the other components, whereas drinking socially influences our sense of engagement with the community and our trust in its members most directly, and then through these the other components. The net outcome, however, is much the same in either case: engaging in these activities with others strengthens our membership of the wider community and elevates our general sense of wellbeing and satisfaction with life – and, through these, our health for the reasons suggested in chapter 1.

In the CAMRA study, we were also able to ask people actually drinking in pubs the same kinds of questions in person – as well as breathalyse them to check on their levels of sobriety. (I should, for the record, point out that only a couple of the people we sampled came even close to exceeding the very modest UK drink-drive limit. So they were all pretty sober.) Needless to say, there was much bemusement among the punters, and not a few had to be persuaded to take the very modest payment we were offering those who completed our survey. However, this close-up study did allow us to probe some additional aspects of friendship. One of these was whether being a regular in the pub or just a casual visitor made a difference. On all our measures (having more close friends, being more satisfied with life, happiness, feeling that life was worthwhile and trusting members of the local community), people who were drinking in their 'local' (i.e. were regular drinkers in that pub) scored higher than people who were casual visitors, who in turn scored higher than those who were non-drinkers (i.e. might have visited that pub regularly with their friends or partner, but did not drink alcohol).

Interestingly, our tolerance of alcohol is something we share with the African great apes (the gorilla and chimpanzee), and only with the African great apes. Its origins go back to some mutations in the enzymes that allow us to detoxify alcohol and convert it back into usable sugars – something that was probably an adaptation to allow our common ancestors to exploit rotting fruits on the forest floor. Rotting fruits contain up to 4 per cent alcohol by volume, about the same strength as beer. (More on this fascinating story can be found in the volume *Alcohol and Humans: A Long and Social Affair* that I co-edited with Kim Hockings.)

Feasting, in other words, provides an important mechanism for bonding. And it works at two separate levels. Casual eating and drinking with close family and friends reinforces these close bonds, while the occasional large, more formal feast involving many people creates bonds within the wider community. Both are important in their different ways. The first strengthens the close alliances that protect us both from the stresses of living in large communities by providing us with those reliable shoulders to cry on. That's why eating and drinking with close friends needs to be done regularly. The second embeds us within the wider community. These bonds are weaker, so they need only the occasional reminder to keep them up to scratch.

In the Big Lunch study, we had asked the people to think back to the last time they had dinner with a close friend or relative, and tell us what had been involved besides eating. Four things emerged as common factors predicting how satisfied they were with the occasion: the number of diners (more is better), the occurrence of laughter, reminiscing about the past, and the consumption of alcohol. The occurrence of laughter and reminiscing both resulted in an elevated sense of bonding to the other people than was the case where neither happened.

*

It seems that, in order to live in our much larger communities, we discovered a series of novel behavioural and cultural processes that trigger the same neuropharmacological and cognitive mechanisms that underpin primate sociality. We have not, however, thrown away the old primate grooming mechanism. This is still very much in evidence. We use these old, more intimate touch-based primate processes for our closest relationships – the ones that require more intense bonding – perhaps with the addition of some more deeply biological phenomena like laughter, singing and dancing. The novel, cultural processes like feasting and storytelling (about which more in the next chapter) are used to create the weaker bonds that hold together the outer layers of our communities. Because these are based on weaker relationships, we only need to do them occasionally.

9

The languages of friendship

However much friendships are about the 'raw feels', or emotional experiences, of relationships, we spend a great deal of our social time engaged in conversation. Language obviously plays a central role in this, and language, in the true meaning of the term, is unique to humans. Much has been made of the language abilities of animals from honeybees to chimpanzees, but the reality is that, however clever the 'languages' of dolphins and apes might be, their forms of language pale into insignificance beside what we humans can do. At the very best, they do about as well as three-year-old humans – which is exactly what you would expect for species just on the edge of having theory of mind. There is one very big difference between animals' exchanges and human conversations, however. From the honeybee's 'There's nectar in the third patch of flowers to the right' to the monkey's 'Watch out – there's an eagle about to launch itself at us', animals are limited to comments on factual matters. Our conversations are mostly about the social world we live in, a mental world that doesn't exist in material form because it only exists in people's minds. And however intense animals' exchanges may be, they never involve the animated group conversations that we have about this world on so regular a basis.

That said, our conversations are so dominated by language that we often forget just how much communication actually goes on below the language radar. How we say something is often just as important as what we say. So given this, just what does language add? Why do we even have this extraordinary faculty? Why don't we do all our communing by touch in the tried and tested way that monkeys do it? This chapter, and the three that follow, bring in a shift of focus from the hard-wired side of our social world to how we use our extraordinary communication abilities to create and service our relationships.

The miracle of language

The key to modern human-like language lies in our mentalising competences. A conversation is not a shouting match. Well, OK, sometimes it is, but even when these don't involve a dispute they tend to involve rather unsatisfactory exchanges in terms of the relationships they create, precisely because shouting (however good-tempered) does not usually allow the respective parties to *engage* with each other. Normal conversations involve enormously complex exchanges in which the speaker tries to make the listener understand what it is that he or she wants to say. And the listener in turn has to work very hard to try to grasp just what the speaker has in mind. Moreover, maintaining the thread of a conversation is much more taxing cognitively than most people imagine, because you have to know what might interest the other people in the conversation and figure out how your next contribution will facilitate the conversation rather than stop it dead by an inappropriate remark. Obvious as this might be when you stop to think about it, it is something we know very little about: no one has researched this aspect of conversational behaviour.

A successful conversation requires us to use very high-level mentalising skills because, in effect, we need to try and get inside each other's minds. When I fail to do that and launch into a completely new topic that is off tangent, it breaks the flow of the conversation and frustrates everyone else – especially someone who was halfway through trying to explain something complicated or, even worse, emotionally upsetting. Do that too many times, and you may find that people avoid you: conversations with you become too difficult and unsatisfying. What makes a successful conversation is one that has 'flow' – the alternate contributions follow naturally on from each other, building the story step by successive step. Mentalising abilities allow us to recognise when we can take the floor and what would slot well into the development of the topic. Now, add to that the fact that social conversations often involve discussions about other people's behaviour, intentions or mind-states, and very quickly you escalate the mentalising demands.

The bottom line is that without these very high-level cognitive skills, we wouldn't have language *as we know it*. We can certainly have language of a kind if we have more modest mentalising abilities, but it would lack the sophistication and expressive subtlety that we can achieve with our five, or occasionally six, orders of intentionality. On the basis of their brain size, we estimate that the now extinct Neanderthals of Europe and the other archaic humans that dominated the half-million years of our evolutionary history before modern humans appeared could only have managed fourth-order intentionality. That one order of intentionality difference would have had a dramatic effect on the complexity of the stories they could tell and the number of people they could hold in a conversation.

I won't say more about this here other than to reinforce the point that the richness in the way we use language in conversation is entirely dependent on our mentalising abilities, and that these in turn are cognitively costly and required the evolution of a much larger executive function brain than any of the Neanderthals and their allies ever achieved. Conversation is hard cognitive work and it doesn't come for free, though you would be surprised at how little attention has been paid to this rather fundamental point either by archaeologists or by evolutionary anthropologists – or psychologists, if it comes to that. That's probably because, as adults, we do it without thinking – a tribute to how highly skilled we become at this during the course of development from toddler to fully functional adult. That it involves a great deal of skill-learning is evidenced by the length of time it takes to reach real adult proficiency in language, especially in boys. It takes the better part of the first two decades of life.

We know from experiments that Nate Oesch and I ran that the ability to unpack complex sentences with many clauses depends critically on an individual's mentalising abilities. Those with limited mentalising abilities (below the normal range for human adults) cannot fully understand sentences with many subordinate clauses. Just how important this is in everyday life is illustrated by storytelling. Storytelling would not be possible without the capacity to process several mindstates at the same time. This was highlighted in a study by James Carney, one of the research fellows in my group. The question at issue is how our enjoyment of a story is determined by the mentalising level at which the story is written. James composed some short stories written at two different mentalising levels – one with nothing higher than third order (including the reader's mindstate) and the other running up to fifth order. These were then rated for enjoyment and engagement by subjects whose mentalising competences we ascertained using our standard vignette tasks (see chapter 6). He found that people whose natural performance was at third-order mentalising preferred the three-mindstate stories, whereas those whose natural function was at fifth order or above found these versions rather boring and much preferred the five-mindstate versions.

Increasing communication complexity is central to being able to handle larger groups. Across primates as a whole, both vocal complexity and gestural complexity increase with the size of the social group that characterises the species. In fact, this was first demonstrated in a clever set of studies on wild Carolina chickadees (a small North American bird related to European tits) by Todd Freeberg: even within the same species, their vocalisations become more complex when they live in larger groups – the more individuals you need to 'speak' to, the richer your language has to be to ensure that communication is unequivocally directed at, and received by, the individual it is meant for. Similar claims have been made in respect of the complexity of gestural communication in wild chimpanzees by Anna and Sam Roberts based on their field studies of wild chimpanzees in Uganda. As Tamas Dàvid-Barrett showed from one of his computer models, communication and group size is likely to go through a ratchet effect in which the two feed off each other, each allowing small increases in the other until they go through a threshold after which everything takes off very fast.

With much larger groups to bond, formal language might have evolved in the human lineage for one of two reasons. One is to allow information about the state of the network to be passed on. In other words, with so many people to keep track of, it may be difficult for us to check up on everybody – especially if they are distributed in different camp groups that don't meet up all that often. When we happen to meet up, you can fill me in on what Jim and Penny have been up to. That way, I can update my information on their relationship by proxy so that when I do bump into them I don't commit some terrible faux pas by asking them if they have been having a wonderful time when in fact they have just been going through an acrimonious separation. This was the basis of the gossip theory of language evolution, outlined in my book *Grooming, Gossip and the Evolution of Language* (1996). A second and equally important possibility is that language is used for storytelling. Stories and folktales are what bind us together as a community. They tell us who we are and why we have obligations towards each other. Folk tales and other stories form an important basis for bonding the wider community: we belong together because we all know the same folktales, we find the same things amusing, we share the same moral values, we have the same history expressed in the origin tales of our tribe. As we shall see in chapter 10, these serve to bind us into a single community that facilitates cooperation.

Irrespective of which of these came first, our conversations are clearly dominated by the social world, as we have found in a number of studies. In one of our earliest studies, Neil Duncan, Anna Marriott and I sampled natural conversations in cafés and other venues, categorising the general topic of the conversation into ten broad types (personal relationships, personal experiences, culture/art/music, religion/morals/ethics, politics, work, etc.) every fifteen seconds. Social topics occupied around two-thirds of conversation time for both sexes. There were really only two obvious differences between the sexes: men tended to talk much less about personal experiences in all-male groups than when they were in mixed-sex groups, and they talked much more about other people and technical topics when women were present. In contrast, women showed much less variation between all-female and mixed-sex groups, tending to maintain a much more consistent pattern of topics. Many years later, I collaborated with the Iranian linguist Mahdi Dahmardeh on a similar study of native Farsi speakers in Iran. Because these conversations were recorded, we could measure the exact number of words devoted to each topic. Once again, social topics dominated, with around 83 per cent of the speaking time devoted to social topics in women's conversations and 70 per cent in men's. As in the UK samples, women's topics remained much more consistent between all-female and mixed-sex groups than was the case for men.

In a technically more sophisticated version of our experiments, Matthias Mehl, Simine Vazire and others at the University of Arizona persuaded seventy-nine students to wear an automated recording device that, eight times an hour, recorded their speech for half a minute. The students wore these for four days, allowing the researchers to determine whether or not the wearer was having a conversation, and whether the conversation was casual (small talk) or more engaged and intense. They found that students who spent less time alone and more of their conversation time in meaningful (as opposed to 'small') talk reported having much higher wellbeing. Matthias has since shown that these results extend to adults. He and his assistants also sampled patients attending hospital, volunteers attending an adult wellbeing clinic, and a group of divorcees. Although the amount of time in small talk didn't correlate with how content they were with their lives, the time spent in *meaningful* conversations did predict life satisfaction.

We followed up these observational studies with a couple of experimental studies that used memory for the content of a story to provide insights into the design of the language faculty. The idea was that if language was designed to transmit factual knowledge, then we should remember factual details best; conversely, if it was designed with social functions in mind, then we should be more likely to remember the social content of a story, and especially the mentalising content. Two series of experiments explored this, one run by Alex Mesoudi (now a professor at the University of Exeter) and the other by Gina Redhead. Both studies showed that we were much more likely to remember the social content of stories, and in particular that related to the mental states of the actors, than a purely factual account. In other words, I am more likely to remember why you intended to do something than simply that you did it. I can reconstruct what you did if I know why you did it, but I certainly can't reconstruct your motives simply from knowing what you did.

Once again, it is all about understanding mindstates and what motivated your behaviour. In fact, this process seems to underpin the very processes of remembering. Studies by psychologists suggest that when a witness at a criminal trial recalls what happened, they don't replay a video of what happened; rather, they remember general principles such as likely motivations, and reconstruct the events to fit their understanding of the underlying motivations – which explains why witnesses often disagree even though they saw the same event.

In our observational studies of the content of natural conversations, critical comments (negative gossip) were relatively rare (no more than 5 per cent of conversation time). That might be because we sampled the conversations in rather public places such as cafeteria, and people may prefer to keep their criticisms of other people to more private occasions where they cannot be overheard. However, it is clear that negative gossip can have social benefits: it reduces the risk of members of our social group exploiting us. Even infrequent complaints about others may help to reduce the frequency of bad behaviour. Kevin Kniffin and David Sloan Wilson of Binghamton University in up-state New York listened in to the conversations of rowing crews and found that complaints by other crew members about those who were not pulling their weight often did have the desired effect of making backsliders pick up their game.

Similarly, in an experimental study, Bianca Beersma and Gerban van Kleef of the University of Amsterdam found that people were much more likely to contribute to a group effort if they were told that the group passed on information about who contributed and who did not. The grapevine really did seem to keep group members in line. Lisa Feldman Barrett, one of the doyennes of social neuroscience, paired pictures of neutral faces with negative, neutral or positive gossip statements purportedly describing the person behind the face. When the same photographs were later shown with a neutral stimulus, her subjects were more likely to attend to faces that had been paired with negative gossip ('threw a chair at a classmate') than those paired with neutral ('passed a man on the street') or positive ('helped an elderly women with her groceries') gossip. Being cheated or attacked is always a much more costly mistake to make than overlooking a good person, so we are more likely to sit up and pay attention when someone has a bad reputation. We remember who they are for future reference.

However often we may criticise others, it seems that the great bulk of our conversations involves the exchange of social information about ourselves (our likes and dislikes), discussions about our relationships and those of third parties, arrangements for future social events and reminiscences about past ones. This is just as true in small-scale traditional societies, even though they often use social gossip to police people's behaviour. Polly Wiessner, an anthropologist at the University of Utah who has spent a lifetime working with the !Kung Bushmen of Botswana in southern Africa, sampled the conversations that !Kung had around the campfire in the evening as well as those they had during the day. There was a stark contrast between the two. Daytime conversations were typically more factual and economics-related, and often involved complaints about the behaviour of other people, whereas those round the campfire at night were mainly stories and folktales. During the day, 34 per cent of conversations involved complaints and just 6 per cent involved stories; in the evening, 85 per cent involved stories and myths, while just 7 per cent involved complaints.

It's not what you say but the way that you say it

When all is said and done, however, the words we use are only a small part of the equation, especially in respect of the transmission of information about the social world. We gain a surprising amount of information from the nonverbal cues that we wrap around our words when we speak. Some of these are facial cues (grimaces, smiles), some are vocal (the pitch of the voice, the rise and fall of intonation), some are gestures (the shrug of the shoulder, a hand sign). *How* you say something can totally change the meaning of the words you utter. It's the difference in intonation between 'That's really *nice*!' (meaning: thanks a million) and '*That's* really nice!' (meaning: why did you treat me so badly?).

In the 1970s, the Iranian-born American social linguist Albert Mehrabian attracted considerable attention when he claimed, on the basis of some elegantly simple experiments, that around 93 per cent of the information in what we say is actually conveyed by nonverbal cues (38 per cent from the tone of voice, 55 per cent from facial cues) and only 7 per cent by the actual meaning of the words. Many psychologists later doubted his claim and subsequent experiments claimed to disprove his view. However, these experiments were not without their own problems. One was that the researchers used actors to model the different emotional contents of utterances, and they almost always used only a single word or a short phrase as the utterance. These stimuli were about as relevant to real conversations as a Mickey Mouse cartoon is to real life. When we speak, we normally do so in lengthy conversational exchanges that involve two or more people, and this provides much more complex contextual and linguistic information. Moreover, these experiments usually involved stimuli in which the verbal content expressed one emotion ('I am sad') but the nonverbal cues expressed the opposite ('I am happy'). I remain frankly sceptical as to how well the 'actors' involved could actually manage this rather sophisticated level of acting. I also have doubts about the design of such experiments given the level of confusion that mixed messages would have created for subjects.

Two recent experiments, however, offer some grounds for thinking that Mehrabian might have been right. Gregory Bryant coordinated a large-scale study that asked people from twenty-four different cultures scattered all over the world, some tribal, some Westernised, to listen to audio clips of two white Americans laughing together. They simply had to decide whether they were friends or strangers. Overall, people did slightly better (55–65 per cent correct) than they would if they had chosen at random (when we would have expected fifty-fifty). Interestingly, everyone was much better (75–85 per cent correct) at identifying friends if the two people laughing were both female. In the other experiment, Alan Cowen and his collaborators asked a sample of Americans and Indians to decide what emotion was being expressed by actors speaking emotion words or phrases in a number of different languages. They found that both cultures were equally good at identifying a set of fourteen basic emotions. Again, while they did better than if they simply guessed, they were very far from perfect.

Clever though both these experiments are, they leave a lot to be desired, both in terms of their design and in the fact that they still do not involve conversations. So to explore this question in a more realistic setting, I collaborated with the Cambridge-based artist Emma Smith and the musicologist Ian Cross in a study where we presented listeners with a set of eight audio clips of real-life natural conversations from YouTube clips. Each of the eight was chosen to represent a different kind of relationship (four negative and four positive). Half the subjects heard clips in English and half in Spanish. In addition to hearing the original clip, they also heard the same clips after they had been passed through filters that either obscured the actual words (but left all the intonations and pitch) or, more extreme still, converted the audio signal to pure tones (pitch only). These were produced in some fancy software by a Chilean student, Juan-Pablo Robledo del Canto. In each case, we asked subjects to identify the relationship involved from the list of eight that we gave them. As a final complication, we ran the experiment twice, once with native English speakers based in Britain and once with native Spanish speakers living in Spain (the Spanish version being run by our multi-talented Madrid work-horse, Ignacio Tamarit).

Matching Mehrabian's original task (which required subjects to classify the relationship only as positive or negative), our subjects were almost as good as his: they were 75–90 per cent as accurate on the clips where the verbal content had been obscured as they were on the full audio clip. Even when they were asked to identify which of the eight relationships they had heard, they were still 45–55 per cent as accurate on the obscured clips as on the full audio, which is four times better than chance (approximately 12 per cent). More important, both English- and Spanish-speakers were as accurate on each other's languages as they were on their own, even though most of them declared that they had little understanding of the other language. We really do get a lot of information about relationship quality just by hearing how someone says something, and how people interact in a conversation. In short, grunts would do almost as well as words.

Smile and the world smiles with you

If there is one behaviour without which both a conversation and a relationship would be deathly dull it is surely a smile. Everyone smiles in the same language, as the saying goes. Smiles express interest, grant permission to continue a conversation, provide encouragement that the interaction is welcome, express apology and sympathy, and a dozen other emotions. Most people assume that smiles and laughter are one and the same thing, that a smile is a laugh that never quite got out. In fact, there is an important difference between laughing and smiling. While laughter, as we have seen, derives from the monkey play face, smiling derives from the monkey submission face. In monkeys, the 'bared teeth face' (or snarl) is associated with submission or appeasement. In contrast to the ROM face of a laugh, a smile, like a snarl, has the teeth firmly clamped together and the lips drawn apart to show the teeth. Even though both are about friendship, one is about bonding, the other about subordination. That's why we smile so much when we are nervous or embarrassed, or when we are introduced to people whom we don't know or perceive as being superior. In other words, although laughter and smiling become somewhat confused in humans, they have very different origins, and signal motivations that are actually polar opposites. As with laughs, there are two types of smile: involuntary Duchenne smiles that signal appeasement (extended to include approval) and voluntary non-Duchenne smiles that signal polite acquiescence. A Duchenne smile is encouraging of further interaction, whereas a non-Duchenne smile is indicative of uncertainty and nervousness.

In a series of observational and experimental studies, Marc Mehu (then one of my research students, and now an associate professor at Webster Vienna University in Austria) found that Duchenne smiles were more often associated with generosity when sharing during dyadic interactions. Indeed, smiles were more likely to be rated as indicative of generosity and extraversion, and particularly so in male faces. These effects did, however, exhibit a strong sexual dimorphism: smiling faces were most likely to be rated as generous when the faces were female and the rater was male. He also found that, in freely forming social contexts such as dance clubs, younger males gave a higher frequency of non-Duchenne (forced) smiles when in groups of mixed age than more mature males did, whereas older women gave more forced smiles than younger women.

Somewhat similar results were found by Robert Provine in his extensive observational studies of laughter under naturalistic conditions. He noticed that women were much more likely to laugh at something men said than they were at anything a woman said; and men were less likely to smile at either sex than women. He interpreted the women's behaviour as a form of appeasement to men in particular, but also to other women. As an act of submission, smiling may encourage us to be less critical or suspicious of others. Lawrence Reed found that people were more likely to believe a statement purporting to describe the behaviour of a person in a photograph if the person in the photograph was giving a Duchenne smile, and least likely to believe it if they were giving a non-Duchenne smile or a controlled smile (the kind of smile where you are trying to stop a full Duchenne smile breaking out).

Just as an aside, let me make a casual observation. Over the years I have spent watching people, I've noticed that not only do women smile more often than men but they seem to do so much more naturally than men. Men's smiles seem to *look* more forced than women's smiles. I suspect this has to do with a sex difference in the structure of the jaw, in particular the size of what is known as the mental eminence (the point at the front where the two halves of the jaw join). This is larger in males, and their jaws are typically squarer with a more acute angle which makes their jaws jut more. The shape of the male jaw somehow seems to make it more difficult for the smile muscles to pull the lips apart. Take a look next time you see people engaged in conversation and see if you agree.

Why we tell stories

So why bother to have language at all when we could do most of what we need to do by way of a grunt? The answer is that language allows us to specify time and place, to make statements about events that happened elsewhere or in the past, or might happen in the future. I can tell you what Jim did or didn't do last week while you were out hunting. Or what he is planning to do next week. More interestingly, I can tell you what might happen in an imaginary world. In other words, we can tell fictional stories.

Every culture throughout history has loved hearing stories, especially if they are told by skilled storytellers. These tales are always about people and their actions, even if those 'people' sometimes have the form of animals (as in Beatrix Potter's Peter Rabbit tales, for example). Even travelogues have a hero. By the same token, we are all of us captivated by gossip about others' activities. Storytelling has, however, always seemed a bit of an evolutionary anomaly. Why would we be so willing to spend hours around the campfire listening to stories and folktales when there is real-life work to be done in the fields or in the hunt? Or, for that matter, all kinds of useful technical information that you could teach me. Yet, adults and children alike will happily listen to the same old stories being told repeatedly over and over again. We will return again and again, paying good money that could be invested in something more useful, to see the same play or film, or read the same book, all with the same enthusiasm as we did the first time around.

It seems obvious why we should like comedy: comedy makes us laugh, and that triggers the endorphin system and makes us feel happy. But why come back again and again to have your heart tortured to the point of crying by a tragedy? It doesn't make any sense unless tragedy also triggers the endorphin system. One reason it might do so is that psychological pain is experienced in the same place in the brain as physical pain, and this might cause emotional storytelling to trigger the endorphin system. That we feel psychological pain and physical pain in the same part of the brain was established in a long series of brain-imaging studies by Naomi Eisenberger and her group at the University of California Los Angeles. Could we show that the psychological pain of watching tragedy triggers the endorphin system, and through that makes us feel more bonded with others in the audience?

An opportunity to study this came about through a project on the psychology of drama being run in the Calleva Research Centre of Oxford's Magdalen College. This was an unusual project, because it involved a collaboration between two experts on Shakespeare (Laurie Maguire and Sophie Duncan) and two experts on classical Greek drama (Felix Buddelman and Evert van Emde Boas), as well as Ben Teasdale, who, almost uniquely, straddled both English literature and neuroscience, and myself. It was a perfect context in which to test the hypothesis that tragedy triggers the endorphin system and makes us feel more bonded.

We had talked through how we might do this at great length, and eventually Ben came up with the perfect answer: the made-for-TV film *Stuart: A Life Backwards*, starring Benedict Cumberbatch and Tom Hardy (perhaps the best character actor of his generation). The film is based on the book by the Cambridge-based writer Alexander Masters, which in turn is based on a true-life story that recounts Alexander's growing friendship with the down-and-out Stuart Shorter. The story is built around Stuart's life and the question of how it could be that, physically disabled and abused as a child, he ended up on the streets, a drug addict, in and out of prison. As the film progresses, it becomes clear that this is all going to end very badly – and, indeed, it does when Stuart, unable to cope with the prospect of yet another jail sentence, throws himself under a train. It is a truly heart-wrenching story, and deeply affected everyone who watched it, especially the researchers who had to watch it many times over a period of just a few weeks.

As always, our subjects did the pain threshold assay before and after watching the film, and completed our bonding index with respect to the group of strangers with whom they watched the film. A control group watched some rather dull TV documentaries, and of course showed no responses on either count. But at first the results from the groups that had watched *Stuart* puzzled us because, although there was an effect in the right direction, it was nothing like as strong as we had anticipated. After puzzling about this for a few weeks, I realised that our subjects divided rather neatly into two groups – those who were completely unmoved by the film and showed little or no change in pain threshold or bonding and those who were moved by it, had elevated pain thresholds and felt more bonded to the audience members with whom they had watched the film.

This made us wonder whether there are genre specialists – some people like one kind of story, others prefer another. We tested this in a follow-up experiment in which we compared people's responses to two different film genres in the form of a poignantly sad extract from the cartoon *Up* (that follows a couple's life story from first meeting to death in old age) with a thrilling clip of the same length from a Bond action movie. Although most people enjoyed both, it was clear that there were genre-specialists much as our *Stuart* results had implied. Some of us like romantic comedies, some like tragedies, others like action movies. In a roundabout way, this perhaps suggests that having a good cry to clear the air only works for some of us, but it may not be a universal remedy. My guess is there is a strong sex difference here. It is not just that boys won't cry, it's that they don't and they can't.

Our results were confirmed by a similar experiment carried out quite independently by Miriam Rennung and Anja Göritz of the University of Freiburg, Germany. They had subjects watch a film as a group of four either together on a single screen or on separate screens with earphones so that they might watch the same or different films. In effect, they compared an emotional experience shared *with* a group (watching the same film but with earphones, so that you didn't hear everyone else's responses) with an emotional response that occurred *in* a group (watching the same film as a group together). They compared four different films: high arousal/negative emotional valence vs. high arousal/positive emotional valence vs. low arousal/negative emotional valence vs. low arousal/positive emotional valence. They found that experiencing intense negative arousal together as a group resulted in higher levels of group cohesion than experiencing the same level of negative arousal on your own despite being in a group setting. There is something about everyone being involved in the same emotion that is important.

It seems that shared emotional experiences are a very strong bonding mechanism. This explains some curious and seemingly unrelated phenomena. One is the fact that puberty rituals in small-scale traditional societies always involve inflicting pain (they are invariably associated with circumcision) and fear on groups of boys undergoing their initiation into manhood, often in frightening environments in the depths of the forest at night where people normally don't go. The emotions aroused by this shared experience create a bond between the boys that lasts right through manhood and beyond. They will for ever stand by each other, especially when they are in the warrior grade and have to defend the community against raiders (and, of course, when they go raiding themselves). Soldiers who have been under fire together often experience the same kind of bonding, and most military training regimes involve pain, exhaustion and fear for just this reason. It is said that firemen, and even wildlife guides, find themselves at the mercy of the (sometimes unwanted) attentions of women whom they have rescued from burning buildings or from being trampled by rampaging buffalo.

Conversational boundaries

Although our ability to talk to each other is essential to the formation of friendships, there are surprising limits to what we can do with language. Aside from the fact that language seems to be a particularly poor medium for expressing feelings, its real limitations lie in our ability to communicate with large numbers of individuals. It is not that we can't speak to very large numbers of individuals; it is that we cannot have a *conversation* with them. Over the last two decades, we have carried out more than half a dozen studies on the natural size of conversation groups. Some of these have been done in cafés, some in pubs and bars, some in parks and public places, some during the day and some in the evening. Most of these studies have been done in Britain, but one was done in the USA and another in Iran. The picture is the same everywhere: few conversations that involve more than four people last for any length of time.

The limit of four for a conversation is a remarkably robust effect. If a fifth person joins, it will split into two separate conversations within as little as half a minute. In one of our studies, we sampled the size of the social group in which a conversation was embedded – in effect, the number of people sitting around the table at the pub – as well as the number of people actually engaged in each separate conversation. What these data show is that social groups fragment into another conversation every time their size hits a multiple of four. Up to four people, it will likely be a single conversation. Five or more and it will be two conversations, more than eight and it will be three, more than twelve and it will be four. This doesn't, of course, mean that you stay in the same conversation for ever as the group splits. Conversations are very dynamic as people switch from one conversation to a neighbouring one, or strike up a new subsidiary conversation with somebody else when they are bored with the main topic.

Occasionally, people have expressed doubts as to whether there can possibly be such a limit to conversation size. I remember one referee of a paper of mine asserting with complete confidence that a limit at four individuals on the size of conversation groups couldn't possibly be true because he regularly had conversations with more than a dozen people at the same time. Having rather more than an inkling as to who this 'anonymous' referee was, I was tempted to respond that this might well be true in his case because, in my experience, conversations with him were more akin to lectures dominated by his stentorian voice while the rest of us were never allowed to get a word in edgeways ... but I resisted the temptation. And that is really the point: the only way we can prevent a 'conversation' with more than four people breaking up into several smaller conversations is by turning it into a lecture with *socially* agreed rules that oblige the rest of us to maintain a respectful silence and not interrupt the speaker. Remove that rule, or remove the chair of the event, and chaos very quickly results – as happens, for example, if a heckler starts shouting at the speaker and won't sit down. If the chair leaves the room for a moment at a large committee meeting or a formal lecture, the audience will divide up into a series of small conversations, each of just two, three or four people, within at most a minute. Try watching next time you are at a public lecture or similar event.

Part of the problem is that, if speaking time is to be shared equally, every extra person who joins the conversation reduces the time that everyone else has available in which to speak. A conversation with ten people means that you only get to speak for one minute in every ten if you share the time equally, and so have to spend the other nine minutes listening in frustration before your turn comes round again. This is because of a very strict psychological rule whereby we allow only one person to have the floor at any given time. Failure to do so results in mayhem when too many people try to speak at once. That, after all, is why we have a chair at meetings, since, without someone to regulate the order of speaking, chaos would reign supreme and no one would be able to hear what anyone else was saying. This is probably one of those social rules we have to learn – we are forever having to tell groups of children to speak one at a time, after all. Because of this, it means that some people either have to be willing to take a back seat and become listeners (an early study of ours suggested that this would often be women in mixed-sex groups, probably because their lighter voices made it more difficult for them to be heard above the cacophony) or split off to form a separate conversation of their own (thereby creating sexually segregated conversations, as we shall see in chapter 13).

Perhaps the most important constraint on the size of conversations, however, is our limited mentalising capacities. Being able to keep a conversation flowing requires us to monitor each of the members and keep their respective desires to contribute in mind, so that we can judge when to speak and when to let someone else have the floor, as well as what is appropriate to say. Our ability to inhibit prepotent actions becomes critical in this context: this finely balanced turn-taking will only work if we can suppress our desire to monopolise the whole conversation.

The importance of mentalising as a constraint was illustrated very nicely in a study by Jaimie Krems (originally one of our graduate students and now a lecturer at Oklahoma State University). She monitored conversation groups on an American college campus, counted the number of people involved and then had the insight (or was it effrontery?) to rush up to them and ask them who or what they had been talking about. It turned out that if they were talking about the mindstate of someone not present, there were never more than three people involved in the conversation; if they were talking about the mindstate of a member of the conversation group, or some factual issue like where to go for lunch or the lecture they had just been to, then four was the limit. It seems that we adjust the number of mindstates we have to deal with in the conversation in response to what we want to talk about.

It turned out, to our surprise, that laughter has a similar intimacy. Guillaume Dezecache, who spent a year with us while he was doing his PhD at the École Nationale in Paris, sampled conversation and laughter groups in pubs around Oxford and in France. No matter how many people were in the *social* group sitting round the table, there was an upper limit at four on the number of people actually engaged with each other in a conversation and an upper limit at around three on the number of people who laughed together during a conversation. On reflection, this is not too surprising, of course, because we use language in the form of jokes to trigger laughter. But it does suggest an explanation for one curious observation: while we cannot help laughing if those we are talking to laugh, we find it positively irritating if another conversation across the room bursts into uproarious laughter. It feels like an intrusion into our private social space. Laughter as a social device and a bonding mechanism is very specific to the little group actually interacting with each other.

In addition to our studies of real-life conversations, Jamie Stiller and Jaimie Krems undertook detailed analyses of Shakespeare's plays and modern films using the number of characters who appear in a scene together as a measure of conversation group size.

They found that there is a very strict limit at four characters, and this is as true of Shakespeare's plays from the sixteenth century as it is of Hollywood films from the twentieth century. Jaimie even looked at two very different film genres: women's-interest films (such as *Pride and Prejudice*, *The First Wives Club*, *A League of Their Own*) and what are known as hyperlink films (examples include *Crash* and *Babel*) in which a deliberate attempt is made to break through the constraints of everyday interaction so that people in different parts of the world, or the same place at different times, can interact. They did not differ in scene size. Dramatists, it seems, are constrained by the fact that their audience can only cope with four people in a conversation, and successful dramatists are very mindful of this.

Jaimie also analysed the mindstates of the characters in scenes from Shakespeare's plays as she had done for real conversations. She found that when the characters were discussing the mindstate of someone else not present, there would usually be a maximum of three of them present, whereas if they were discussing the mindstate of someone in the conversation or facts about some event that had happened offstage, there could be up to four of them – just as she found in natural, real-life conversations. We clearly don't think about this in real-life conversations, but somehow do it naturally. And a good observer of human behaviour like Shakespeare picks up on this and structures their stories in the same way so as not to overtax their audience.

These natural limits on the size of conversation groups are largely responsible for the traditional size of dinner parties and even the size of dining tables. Four people is perfect because they can form a single conversation. Six or eight are OK because they add variety of opinions and a single table can accommodate two or perhaps three separate conversations – with the table still small enough for people to switch from one conversation to another when they feel inclined. But more people than that means that the table has to be so large that conversations across it become impossible (you just cannot hear what someone the other side is saying), and you end up being stuck with just the people either side of you. Moreover, it is very easy for someone to get stuck between two conversations and end up with no one to talk to. Check this out next time you are at a wedding or a formal dinner where tables often seat ten or twelve. Of course, one reason for larger tables at these kinds of events – and the reason they can get away with this arrangement – is that you aren't really expected to spend the *whole* time deep in conversation: you are supposed to listen quietly to the speeches.

Dark magic

Buried beneath all these studies on human conversational behaviour is an interesting question – the fact that there seems to be something very special about doing all these things at night when it is dark. There is something magical about telling stories in the dark by the flickering half-light of a fire: it seems to give stories an added edge, ramping up the sense of anticipation and thrill to make them more exciting and more meaningful. In fact, all our social activities are more exciting when we do them at night. Parties, dinners, feasts, the theatre, storytelling, singalongs, dances, even bingo, all seem to acquire a much more magical quality in the half-dark.

The same seems to be true of almost everything else we do in the social domain. In our Big Lunch study, women preferred a lunchtime meal for meeting someone new but an evening meal for meeting up with an old friend or family member, while men tended to prefer evening meals for both. An evening show at the theatre is more magical than a matinee. A drink in the pub with friends in the evening is somehow more enjoyable than one at lunchtime. A candle-lit dinner for two in the evening has a more intimate quality than a candle-lit dinner for two in broad daylight.

Social activities that happen at night seem to hold special significance for us. There seems to be something truly magical about the dark. We don't get anything like the same frisson of excitement if we do these social activities in daylight – or non-social activities like model-making or crossword puzzles in the dark.

When Talayeh Aledavood looked at the pattern of calls across the day in our high-school telephone dataset, she found that the late-evening calls (those after midnight) were much more likely to be directed at a particular person than daytime calls. Although there was quite a lot of individual variation, as many as half of these late-night calls (especially those after midnight) were to just two specific individuals. Because we had also asked the volunteers in this study to complete lengthy questionnaires telling us about their relationships with everyone they phoned, we know that these late-night calls were to individuals to whom they had strong emotional attachments. They are also the people they called most often overall.

Predominantly, the recipients of the late-evening calls were friends rather than family: boys' calls to friends at this time were eleven times longer than late-evening calls to family members, while the girls' late-night calls to friends were three times longer than those to family during the daytime. For girls, these late-night calls were more likely to be calls to boys than to close girlfriends. Not only were these calls to a boy more frequent, they were also much longer: late-evening calls to boys averaged nearly 700 seconds, whereas similar calls to girlfriends averaged a mere 400 seconds. The picture was quite the reverse in the morning: calls to girlfriends were twice as long as calls to boys, averaging 200 versus 100 seconds – so much to discuss after the long call to the boy the evening before, perhaps? Well, you don't need to be a genius to figure out what is going on here. The message for the boys, however, is very clear: if she calls you late at night, she's interested . . . If she doesn't, well, maybe you had better check out someone else.

Why should the dark make such a difference? Rather oddly,

no one has ever commented on this odd behaviour or thought to ask why this should be. My guess is that its origins lie deep in our ancestry when our ancestors, the archaic humans, first learned to control fire – around 500,000 years ago, according to the archaeological record. Doing so gained us an extra four hours or so of 'daylight', though it was daylight that confined us to the space of a camp. We could not travel and hunt, but we could use that time for eating and for socialising. In fact, the time we gained in this way seems to be exactly the time we still devote to social interaction – around three and a half hours a day. I explain how all this works out in my book *Human Evolution*, so I won't elaborate on it any further here. The important point for now is simply to notice that the evening seems to enhance our social interactions in a very special way, and that the origins of this are probably very ancient.

*

As much as our friendships are dependent on the half-conscious raw feels that are underpinned by the endorphin and dopamine systems, conversation and language clearly play an important part. We talk *with*, rather than just *to*, each other. So what is it that we talk about? This brings us to the last piece of our jigsaw puzzle, the Seven Pillars of Friendship. This is the subject of the next chapter.

Homophily and the seven pillars of friendship

Here are two facts that might surprise you. You are twice as likely to share genes with a friend as you are with any random person from your local neighbourhood. This is what Benjamin Domingue and his colleagues found when they compared the genes of 5,000 pairs of teenage school friends with the genes of the rest of their school class. Similarly, using data from the US National Longitudinal Study of Adolescent Health, James Fowler and Nick Christakis found that friends were more likely to share the same DRD2 dopamine receptor gene (one of the two neurochemicals that allow you to maintain your friendships), and less likely to share the same CYP2A6 gene (a gene that regulates the enzyme responsible for the oxidation of nicotine – an enzyme that, useful as it might be in other contexts, is of no real use for maintaining friendships). They were able to confirm both of these findings in the Framingham Heart Study dataset. The second surprising fact is that when Carolyn Parkinson and her collaborators scanned the brains of undergraduate students from the same class while watching the same movie, they found that those who had nominated each other as mutual friends had more similar neural responses to the same clip of film than they did with members of the class whom they didn't consider to be friends. This was especially the case in areas of the brain related to emotion processing (the amygdala), learning, integrating information into memory (the nucleus accumbens, the caudate nucleus) and some aspects of mentalising (areas in the parietal lobe). In other words, not only are you more likely to share genes with a friend, you are also more likely to *think* like your friends. That's not because being friends makes you think alike, but that you gravitate together *because* you think alike.

These two observations are so counter-intuitive that they should give us pause for thought. What is going on here? Can't I even choose my friends for myself? Well, actually, yes – that is, in fact, exactly what you do. But the friends you choose are people who are as similar to you as you can manage under the circumstances. This tendency for birds of a feather to flock together is known as *homophily* and is a dominating feature in our friendships. The criteria you use in evaluating someone's friendship potential are what I call the Seven Pillars of Friendship. They are a set of seven cultural dimensions that are rather like a supermarket barcode emblazoned on your forehead. Except, of course, that you speak them. Some are about the way you actually speak (your dialect), some about the things that interest you, others are about your attitudes to life and society in general. In essence, they are who you are culturally. They define you as a person, and they place you into a particular social context, a particular segment of society. In other words, they establish you both as a friend and as a member of a wider community.

The seven pillars of friendship

The Seven Pillars were discovered completely by accident. I was collaborating with a group of computer scientists on a project whose central question was whether we could do away with mobile-phone masts by using the phones themselves as way sta-tions so that your call to your Aunt Joan in Halifax is passed on from one phone to another that happen to be between you and Aunt Joan. In the digital tech world, this goes under the name of *pervasive technology*. It sounds obvious and, in principle, simple to arrange, but there is a problem. In fact, several problems. One is that it would drain your battery very fast – though the tech-nical people assured us that this minor difficulty would soon be solved by new battery technology. The more serious problem is why I should allow you (or at least your phone) to have access to my phone. That would enable you, if you were so minded, to download everything on my phone, use my phone for nefarious purposes or even send the most *interesting* photographs of me to my friends and family, or worse still the newspapers, that could get me into all sorts of trouble. It doesn't sound like a good idea at all.

The solution to this was, we thought, simple: exploit the fact that we trust some people *because* they are our friends. The more you trust someone, the more likely you are to look favourably on their request to use your phone as a way station. In most cases, that trust is based on past knowledge. You have known Jim since you were at kindergarten together and you know exactly how much you can trust him. But sometimes you can also make an instant judgment about a stranger. Probably not for the loan of your life savings or the pin-number to your bank account, but certainly for a drink at the bar or a bit of help at the roadside. So how do we make that judgment? If we knew, that would be the perfect solution to the pervasive-technology problem.

We wondered whether, if your likes and dislikes were registered on your phone, your phone could decide if it liked another phone enough to take the risk of allowing it to connect. (In fact, this was eventually implemented in the *Safebook* security software developed by our collaborators at the Institut Eurécom near Nice in southern France.) So my postdoc on the project, Oliver Curry, ran a survey in which a large number of people were given a long list of things you might share with someone – beliefs, attitudes, hobbies, interests – and asked which they shared with specific people in their social circles (a named family member and a friend of each sex in each layer of the social network), and, as a measure of altruism, how likely they were to lend this person a sum of money or donate a kidney if they were in desperate need of one.

When we analysed the data, it soon became clear that these questions clustered into a number of groups that were answered in the same way. Looking at the kinds of questions in these groupings suggested that they involved the following:

- having the same language (or dialect)
- growing up in the same location
- having had the same educational and career experiences (notoriously, medical people gravitate together, and lawyers do the same)
- having the same hobbies and interests
- having the same world view (an amalgam of moral views, religious views, and political views)
- having the same sense of humour

To this, in a later study with Jacques Launay, we subsequently added the seventh:

- having the same musical tastes

The more of these boxes you tick with someone, the more time you will be prepared to invest in them, the more emotionally close you will feel towards them, the closer they will lie to you in the layers of your social network, and the more willing you will be to help them out when they need it. And the more likely they are to help you. Birds of a feather really do flock together. You tend to gravitate towards people with whom you have more things in common. You tend to like the people who are most like you. In fact, each layer of your social network is equivalent to a particular number of 'pillars' shared – six or seven for the innermost 5-layer, just one or two for the outer 150-layer. It doesn't seem to matter which ones you actually share in common. These pillars are, as economists put it, substitutable – that is, any one is as good as another, there is no hierarchy of preference. A three-pillar friend is a three-pillar friend irrespective of which three pillars you have in common.

We had been surprised by the fact that sense of humour appeared in this list. Somehow, that seemed rather trivial compared with the other more weighty pillars like moral views or political convictions. Oliver Curry set about trying to unpack this a bit more. He selected a set of eighteen jokes from a 100-best-jokes-of-all-time compilation, choosing the ones on which people disagreed most, and asked people to rate how amusing they found each of them. Their ratings provided a kind of humour profile that was quite specific to them. Then, a week or so later, he contacted them again with a set of humour profiles that purported to come from other people and asked how well they thought they would get on with these people, and whether they thought they would like them as a friend if they met up. What they didn't know was that the humour profile they were being shown was actually their own, but modified to be 10 per cent, 33 per cent, 67 per cent or 90 per cent identical to theirs. The closer the humour profile was to their own, the more they thought the person concerned would make a good friend. You like people who share your sense of humour. They were also much more likely to help someone whose humour profile was more like their own.

My take on this is that the process of making a new friend follows a fairly set pattern. When you first meet someone new you invest a lot of time in them (in effect, catapult them into one of the innermost circles) so that you can evaluate where they lie on the Seven Pillars. That takes time, but once you know where they stand, you then reduce the time you devote to them to a level appropriate to the number of pillars you have in common. As a result, they quietly slide back down through the layers to settle out in the layer appropriate to that number. In other words, friendships are born and not made. You just have to find them. It may take several goes before you find the right person to be your best friend, or even in your top five friends list, but if you keep searching you will find them eventually.

In fact, homophily extends well beyond these kinds of cultural icons and interests. Not only do we like people who think more like us, we also tend to prefer people of the same sex, ethnicity, age and perhaps even personality. In our studies, most people's social networks of 150 or so individuals typically consist of around 70 per cent the same sex as themselves. Men prefer to have men friends, women prefer women friends. Many other studies have noted this pattern. In an analysis of a large Facebook dataset, Lars Backstrom and his colleagues from Facebook found that females sent 68 per cent of their directed messages to another female, though males were less discriminatory in this particular case. Rather similar findings were reported by David Laniado and his colleagues from data for nearly 5 million users of the Spanish networking site Tuenti (which operated from 2006–16 and was known as the 'Spanish Facebook'). When they analysed each person's postings, they found that half of all females had females as their first- and second-best friends and only 12 per cent had two males (we would expect a quarter in each case if they chose these friends at random). Males were, again, much less choosy, with a third having two males and a quarter two females. For women, the likelihood that a friend was female declined from 72 per cent for the most frequently contacted friend to just 40 per cent for the thousandth friend (for those who listed this many). Males exhibited the reverse pattern, but with the likelihood of a friend being male declining with position much less steeply. In fact, while the probability that a female's friend would be female did not fall below 50 per cent (random) until around the 110th friend, the probability that a male's friend was male did not fall below 50 per cent until around the 300th friend.

One reason for this might be that women share more interests in common with other women than they do with men, and vice versa, making the flow of the conversation easier to maintain with fewer pregnant pauses while people try and think of something to say. Another explanation might be that mixed-sex conversations become too much of a mating market and cause women, in particular, to feel they need to put themselves on display when they would rather just relax. Yet another might be that men and women's natural conversational styles are just *so* different that mixed-sex conversations are too stressful. In these contexts, men tend to dominate conversations, and, with their lighter voices, women find it increasingly difficult to get a word in edgeways. While these might be costs women are prepared to pay when there is an ulterior romantic interest at stake (such as mate-finding), they might just prefer to avoid paying that cost altogether when this is not the case.

Signals of belonging

In trying to make sense of all this, it dawned on me that the Seven Pillars are actually cues that identify the small community where we spent our formative years and learned how to be members of a community. Knowing how to recognise a member of your community cuts through the long-winded process of getting to know someone by having to spend half a lifetime with them. I know you are a member of my community because I instantly recognise your dialect the moment you speak. You know the same streets and pubs that I know. You know the same jokes that we used to tell over a pint of beer. You belong to the same religion as I do. Any one of these is a rough and ready guide to a shared history, and any one of them will do to mark you out as someone I can trust – because I know how you think. They point to the fact that we grew up in the same place, we absorbed the same mores, the same attitudes to life and the wider world. I don't have to explain my joke to you because you get it straight away. In fact, I don't even have to finish the punch line because you know the same jokes as me, or even just the way a joke is constructed. This harking back to the community we grew up in seems to explain the extraordinary attachment many people feel to 'home' – the place where they grew up – even decades after they moved away.

In small-scale societies of the kind in which we have spent all but the last few thousand years of our history, that small community would have been the hunter–gatherer community of around 150 people. In these kinds of societies, the members of the community are all related to each other, directly or by marriage. A community is, in fact, an extended family. So the Seven Pillars in effect identify an extended family group where family loyalty will be a strong force for social bonding, underpinning that sense of obligation that we always have towards family members. In effect, the 'pillars' function like a totem pole in the centre of the village – something on which we can all hang our hats as a sign of belonging. We are committed to the community and its wellbeing because we are members of the community.

In fact, we can tell a massive amount about a person from just the first sentence they say. We can identify where they come from, and, at least in Britain, which social class they belong to. Social linguists reckoned that, in the 1970s, you could place a native English-speaker to within 35 km (20 miles) of their birthplace just by their accent and the words they used, so fine-scale were these differences in dialect. In a hunter–gatherer society, that would just about be the area occupied by a tribe of 1,500 people. Scousers from Liverpool all sound the same to people from other parts of Britain. But Liverpool is divided into north and south through the middle of the city centre, with very different accents and a long-standing mutual dislike. If you are a Liverpudlian, you know straight away which side of the city someone is from. (Just in case you didn't know, all four of the Beatles came from the more upmarket south side.)

Sensitivity to dialect seems to emerge naturally at a very young age, and long before we have had a chance to be socialised about these things. In a series of studies, Katherine Kinzler and Elizabeth Spelke (one of the leading developmental psychologists of the last three decades) studied responses of six-month-old infants from English-speaking American families to video clips of women speaking to them in English (the language they were used to hearing), Spanish, or the same English clips played backwards. When subsequently shown pictures of the women side by side, they spent much longer looking at the woman who had spoken in the language they were familiar with. In a study of seven-year-olds, Caroline Floccia from the University of Plymouth and her collaborators at the University of Rheims in France played audio clips to five- and seven-year-old children. The clips were of people reading the same English text in three very different accents: native English-speakers from the southwest of England (the local accent for the Plymouth children) and native Irish and French nationals with their natural accents when speaking English. The task required the children to indicate when the accent they heard was a foreign one. Although the five-year-olds didn't seem to differentiate quite so clearly between the accents, the seven-year-olds were significantly better at detecting foreign accents than they were at identifying that the regional one was not foreign. A parallel experiment with five-year-old French children in the Rheims area produced similar results: these children could recognise an accent as being foreign better than they could their own regional accent. We clearly learn these fine differences in how speech is articulated very early in life and become focused on them.

It is perhaps not too surprising that language, or dialect, looms so large in making these judgments. If you don't speak the same language, you won't be able to understand my jokes, and the flow of conversation will inevitably be stilted and inhibited. The other six Pillars are important too. Just as you can never learn to speak a new language like a native when you learn it later in life (you just can't quite get the accent right on some words, or you don't use quite the right word), so you can never be fully immersed in another culture if you haven't grown up in it. You can only do these things if you spent your childhood sitting around the metaphorical campfire, absorbing the tales of the adults, listening to their explanations of how the particular community came to be. I have always considered myself very privileged to have grown up in East Africa where I was immersed in the local Swahili and Indian cultures even before I became fully competent in English. It provided me with insights into, and understanding of, these cultures in a way that would never have been possible had I gone there as an adult.

Some years ago, my then PhD student Daniel Nettle (now a professor of psychology at Newcastle University) developed a computer model to look at the role of dialect as a mechanism for controlling freeloaders. In societies that are essentially social contracts (as all human societies are), freeloaders who take the benefits of the contract but avoid paying all the costs erode trust in other members of the community and quickly lead to the collapse of society. When that happens, it causes communities to fragment, and we retreat into the little clusters of people we really trust. The question that motivated this model was whether dialect might provide a quick-and-dirty guide to membership of your community, and hence of whether you could trust someone.

We can think of a dialect as a supermarket barcode exhibited on your forehead. Each individual checks out the barcodes of the people they meet, but only agrees to form relationships if their respective barcodes match. Over time, freeloaders can learn to mimic the local dialect, pretending to be good citizens but all the time exploiting those with whom they interact. Left to their own devices, freeloaders will very quickly overwhelm the population, driving the collaborators to extinction in as few as a dozen generations. The interesting finding was that if the population changed its dialect regularly from one generation to the next, it held freeloaders in check because they couldn't track the changes fast enough. As a result, they were never able to take over the population. In this particular case, the population had to change about 50 per cent of its barcode (or dialect) each generation to stay one step ahead of the freeloaders. Less than that meant that freeloaders got out of control.

This perhaps explains why dialects change so fast, decade by decade and generation by generation. People do not speak exactly like their parents. New words come into fashion, old ones die out of use; new ways of saying the same thing appear; the pronunciation of old words drifts – and the older generation perpetually complain of the lazy ways in which the youth of the day speak. Which is odd, if you think about it. If dialects are meant to identify who is in your community, you might expect them to be stable across generations. However, over time as the population grows, that would result in more and more people having the same dialect, and eventually the whole world would sound much the same and speak the same language. You would no longer be able to identify your small home community of 100–200 people. The only way you can ensure that is for dialects to change through time as each generation develops its own speaking styles and the words it likes to use. In effect, you are identifying your personal cohort in your community, not the community as a whole.

And so it is that languages and dialects spawn endless numbers of descendants that, over the generations, begin to sound so different that they eventually end up as new languages. Modern English evolved out of Anglo-Saxon (itself a variant of the Friesian dialect of Dutch), and in turn eventually gave birth to six official English languages. In addition to English itself (including, by the way, American English), these include Lowland Scots, Caribbean patois, Black Urban Vernacular (BUV, as spoken by African Americans in the major US cities), Krio (or Sierra Leone creole) and Tok Pisin (or 'Talk Pidjin',* the version of English spoken in New Guinea).

Making friends with strangers

Meeting people we don't know – strangers – is a fact of life. That is how we make new friends. But we don't really want to waste time checking out how they sit on each of the Seven Pillars of Friendship. If we did that for every new person we met, there wouldn't be enough time in the day. Ideally, we want some simple rubric for deciding whether it is worth investing further time and effort in getting to know them better. So what's the best criterion to use when deciding whether someone might be worth investing time in so as to check them out in more detail? Jacques Launay explored this by examining how strangers are judged on the Seven Pillars. The traits that people selected significantly more often than expected were ethnicity, religion, political views, moral views and, strongest of all, musical tastes. Music was the surprise here. It seems that if a stranger has the same musical tastes as you, you are much more likely to see them as a promising prospect for being a friend.

Intrigued by this, Jacques wondered whether rarity might play a role in selecting friends. Subjects were told that a particular trait that they held in common with a fictitious stranger was one that was held by 1,632 other participants in the experiment, by fourteen participants or by just four participants – numbers essentially chosen to represent the two innermost social layers (the 5- and 15-) and the outermost one (the 1,500-layer) without making it

---

* The word 'pidgin' is an eighteenth-century Chinese corruption of the English word 'business' – the language English traders used when trading in mainland China. It was transposed to New Guinea for the language used to communicate with the local tribes by English-speaking administrators, missionaries and traders.

too obvious that it was these numbers we had in mind. When they were asked to rate the stranger for likeability, they much preferred strangers who shared a rare trait and least preferred those who possessed a common trait. Again, it seems that being able to identify that someone comes from the same small community as you is more important than anything else.

The fact that, indirectly, ethnicity appears in the list of favoured traits merits a comment. In our ancestral past, this points back to a common origin in a small local community. As members of an ethnic community, you share a whole suite of cultural and behavioural traits that facilitate the process of social interaction and offer cues of trustworthiness (how likely you are to stick to our informal agreements on how to behave). In most parts of the world, that community is likely to have explicitly ethnic origins. Even if the historical depth is not especially great, many of the people in small communities will be related by marriage or descent. Indeed, that seems to define hunter–gatherer communities. In other words, the Seven Pillars are really cues of membership of a small kinship community. In our ancestral past (the circumstances in which this trait evolved), these would have identified members of the same ethnic group. But like many effects in evolutionary biology, there is an important difference between cues and reality. These cues scale up well, allowing us to use them, individually or collectively, to identify communities to which we belong, but now they needn't refer to people who are especially closely related. Religion is clearly a very powerful marker in this context.

Most societies in history and around the world have been suspicious of those who do not look or sound like them. So deep-rooted is this in the human psyche that, in most languages, the name for the tribe that speaks your language simply means 'people', and serves to distinguish us (as 'proper people') from all the rest of the humans we occasionally bump into (who may often be classified with all the other animals). The word English, after all, is simply a corruption of Angle, the name of one of the Germanic tribes that invaded Britain after the Romans had retreated in the fifth century AD, who gave rise to the language and dominated the political and social landscape of Britain. Similarly, the linguistic group known as the Bantu (the largest and most widely dispersed super-tribe in Africa, accounting for about half the population of the continent, and the generic name for the languages they speak) comes from the roots *Ba-* (meaning 'people') and *ntu* (meaning 'human being') – literally, the human people – and versions of this appear in most of the 600-odd languages in the Bantu family as the word for 'person'. The word *Māori*, for example, literally means 'normal people' – us, as opposed to them out there, the *pākehā*.

Visual appearance often provides a rough-and-ready cue to whether or not someone belongs to your ethno-cultural group. Their physical appearance, the way they style their hair, the clothes and jewellery they wear – all these identify the community they come from, and still do even in our own Western cultures. During the nineteenth century, it became customary (building on earlier informal attitudes that in fact date back to biblical days) to distinguish between several major races purely on the basis of appearance – Caucasoids (whites) from Europe, Negroes (from the Spanish word for 'black') from Africa, Mongoloids from East Asia and the Americas, and later the Australoids from Australia and its nearby islands.

The problem is that skin colour is not actually a particularly good criterion for choosing those with whom one shares either culture or a biological ancestry. Skin colour simply reflects how long your particular ancestors have lived in low-latitude (tropical) or high-altitude habitats. Dark skin colour (due to dense melanocytes in the surface layers of the skin) protects the underlying skin and organs from harmful cosmic rays, and so predominates in the Tropics and at high altitudes where exposure to the sun is at its greatest. Light skin colour reflects a history of living at high latitudes (both north and south of the equator) where a weak sun means that the dark skin cannot synthesise enough vitamin D.

Vitamin D is essential to allow the intestines to absorb calcium (for bones), as well as magnesium and phosphate. Low calcium intake results in rickets (softening of the bones, often associated with bowed legs and stunted growth). Bowed legs obviously do you no favours when trying to escape predators, human or otherwise. Dark-skinned people living at high latitudes are at much greater risk of vitamin D deficiency, so the populations that invaded these habitats very quickly lost the genes for melanocytes – hence developing lighter skin and fairer, straighter hair.*

Because modern humans evolved in Africa, our ancestors were all dark-skinned, or at least copper-coloured. Evolving light skin colour was part of the suite of adaptations that made it possible for those populations that migrated out of Africa to colonise the high-latitude habitats in Europe and Asia, displacing as they did so the light-skinned archaic humans (Neanderthals in Europe and the Denisovan peoples in Asia) that had been there for several hundred thousand years. We modern Europeans and Asians are actually very recent arrivistes in our respective homelands: modern humans left Africa only 70,000 years ago to colonise southern Asia, reaching Australia some 20,000 years later. They did not enter Europe (the homeland of the Neanderthals) until around 40,000 years ago. The Neanderthals, who had occupied Europe as far as the Urals for some 300,000 years by then, went extinct within just a few thousand years of our arrival, probably with a little help from their new neighbours.

The problem with the nineteenth-century racial classifications is that Africans are not a biologically (or linguistically) homogeneous group: in fact, modern sub-Saharan Africans consist of four distinct genetic (and linguistic) groups, to one of which also belong all the Europeans, Asians and Amerindians and Australian Aboriginals. If you really want to have four

---

* The genes for melanocytes that give rise to dark skin also influence hair colour and the tendency of hair to curl tightly.

human races you certainly can, but one of them has to include Europeans, Asians, Amerindians, Australians *and* the Bantu (by far the darkest-skinned of the African tribes) and their allied tribal groups – perhaps three-quarters of the population of the world.

By the same token, you could, if you wanted, have an ethnic subcategory called Europeans (*not* the same thing as Caucasians), a group that would be united by a common language family (the Indo-European languages), as well as a common genetic ancestry. While it would include most, *but not all*, modern Europeans, it would also include most (but not all) of the Iranians, Afghans, and the peoples of the great north Indian plain from modern Pakistan east as far as Bengal. It would *not* include the Hungarians, Estonians or Finns, whose languages are descendants of historical Mongolian invasions (though to be fair, only some of their genes are Mongolian) or the Lapps of northern Scandinavia (who are Siberian Mongoloid peoples in origin), and it most definitely wouldn't include the Basques from Spain and southern France.

The Basques are the remnants of the original inhabitants of Europe from before the arrival of the Indo-Europeans some 6,000 years ago, and their language (*and* genes) are unrelated to anything else nearer than the southern borders of eastern Siberia (and maybe some North American Indians). Having been the sole occupants of Europe since the demise of the Neanderthals 38,000 years ago, the Basques' ancestors were squeezed out by Indo-European invaders that swept into Europe from the Russian steppes around 6,000 years ago. The Basques were the only population to have survived because their ancestors were able to retreat into their remote Pyrenean mountain fastness and were left alone there because it wasn't worth fighting over. The absence of their genes elsewhere in Europe suggests that the rest were either driven out or, more likely, exterminated on a very grand scale.

There are other groups living within the geographical range of the Indo-Europeans, such as the Untouchables (or Dalits) of northern India, who are the descendants of the original inhabitants before the arrival of the Indo-Europeans. The Dalits fared rather better than the Basques' ancestors: they at least survived, albeit at the cost of being confined to the margins of a society ruled over very firmly by the Indo-European invaders, whose social subgroups became the four official castes of modern Hindu society. There have been attempts to claim that these castes are purely cultural in origin, but recent genetic studies of north Indians indicate that the proportion of European (or, to be strict, Indo-European) genes a person has correlates with their rank in the Hindu caste system, with the very exclusive Brahmin caste as not only the social pinnacle but also the most European, and the Untouchables at the bottom as the least. And this is after more than 4,000 years of cohabitation. Even surnames are enough to identify which caste you belong to, with certain surnames being held only by the members of a specific caste, sometimes even a specific sub-caste. What has kept the caste system relatively pure has been the very strict practice of endogamy (marrying only within one's caste) over a very, very long time – notwithstanding some degree of casual intermarriage round the edges. In general, the caste you are born into is the caste you and your children and grandchildren die in. Sheel Jagani, then one of our students, undertook an analysis of Indian marriage websites, and we were both really surprised to find how overwhelmingly important caste is even now as a criterion in marriage choice in India (and still is among the Hindu diaspora even in places like Britain).

Just how pervasive these effects are is well illustrated closer to home by the history of the British Isles. Across southern England, for example, women's mitochondrial DNA (inherited only through the female line) is mainly of ancient Celtic (or Romano-British) origin, but men's Y-chromosomes (inherited only down the male line) exhibit a distinct east to west cline with Anglo-Saxon genes predominating in the east (the point of entry of the Angle and Saxon invaders from the continent after the Romans left in 410 AD) and Celtic ones predominating in the west. It seems that the invading Anglo-Saxons imposed a form of radical apartheid in which they excluded the native Celtic men while appropriating their women. This was apartheid reinforced by laws introduced by the Saxon invaders who, for several centuries, treated the local British inhabitants as having no rights before the law, putting them at an economic as well as a legal disadvantage (much as was the case for blacks in South Africa under apartheid during the second half of the twentieth century). This form of oppression was only alleviated 300 years later when King Alfred the Great introduced new laws that gave equal rights to all inhabitants – in part, no doubt, because by then intermarriage combined with cultural and linguistic domination had made it difficult to distinguish one ethnic group from the other. Old cultural habits die hard, however. One curious hangover from this period is the use of the word 'Welsh' for the people of modern Wales at the western end of this cline: it derives from the Saxon word *wealas* meaning a 'foreigner' or 'slave', the two concepts being more or less synonymous since anyone labelled a foreigner is up for grabs as a slave.

Ironically, of course, the Anglo-Saxons suffered the same fate five centuries later when the Normans conquered England in 1066 AD. The Normans systematically killed or banished the old Saxon nobility and senior clergy and replaced them with Normans, took over their estates and lands, and treated the rest of the Saxon peasantry as serfs who could be bought and sold by their new masters. (Serfdom was a form of institutionalised slavery introduced into Britain by the Normans from the continent – where it continued to be in use in the Austrian and Russian empires until well into the nineteenth century.) A thousand years later, the descendants of those Norman families still make up much of the upper echelons of English society, as we can tell from their French family names. Many still own the land originally given to them by William the Conqueror. None of the pre-industrial English nobility have Saxon, or even Norse, names. English still bears the scars of this in the words we use for meat: we use old Germanic Saxon names for the animals in the field (sheep, cow, pig) and Norman French names (mutton, beef, pork = French *mouton, boeuf, porc*) when we serve it on the table. The Saxon serfs tended and killed the animals in the field in their native Anglo-Saxon, but served it to their Norman masters in French.

It is important to appreciate that even in modern post-industrial societies a preference for ethnic origins does not of itself necessarily imply racism, in the sense that we currently understand this term (i.e. differentiation based on skin colour). What you seem to be looking for is someone with the same *cultural* background because that makes it possible to create friendships and community bonding. Someone whose skin colour is similar to yours is more likely to come from the same community as you (or at least was in the not so distant past), so they are likely to share your culture. When race and cultural traits such as language are pitted against each other in experiments, cultural similarity takes precedence over race or ethnic origin in friendship preferences, as one study of children by Elizabeth Spelke showed.

It seems that people of similar racial origins are just as likely to be on the receiving end of exclusion and abuse if they come from a different community. After the Union of the Crowns of England and Scotland in 1603, the English Parliament was asked to consider granting English citizenship to the Scots. However, pointing to Poland's experience of influxes of large numbers of rather troublesome Scots traders and hawkers over the previous two centuries, it concluded that 'we shall be over-run with them' and declined to do so. A century and a half later, the London magazine *Punch* was full of excoriatingly abusive articles about the influx of Scots into the capital city following the Union of Parliaments in 1707, sniffily alluding to their roughness and tendency to live in enclaves. The Scots would complain that nothing has changed since, but in fact England is full of Scots who have become so fully assimilated over the generations that you would never know their origins if some of them didn't have Gaelic *Mac*- surnames.

What's in a name?

Because family names are inherited, they are often quite a good guide to common ancestry – though, like all these cues, they are not perfect, as people can adopt names in much the same way they can adopt new languages. In addition, some names simply refer to occupations – Butcher, Baker, Smith [blacksmith], Fisher, Reeve, Cooper, Dyer, Farmer, Thatcher, Mason, Wright (or Carpenter) among many others in English, not to mention their equivalents in many other languages. These tend to be very common names, with quite independent origins all over the country. You may well be related to the Bakers of your local community (families did, after all, monopolise particular trades), but you are very unlikely to be related to the Bakers from the other end of the country. In contrast, some names are very rare, either because they are place names or because they are obscure local family names.

Some years ago, the Canadian evolutionary psychologist Margot Wilson ran an ingenious study of this. She emailed a set of randomly selected people with a request from a stranger asking whether they would help out with a particular project. In fact, she was simply interested in whether the recipient said yes or no and whether that depended on how similar the sender's name was to the recipient's. She concocted fictitious senders by combining the ten rarest and ten most common first names and surnames as listed in the US census. So some of these 'people' had a rare first name but a common surname, others a common first name and a rare surname, while others had both names common or both rare. Recipients were much more likely to respond 'yes' if they shared a rare surname with the sender, and even more likely to respond if both names were rare. In the latter case, they often commented on the spooky fact that they shared both names, and wondered whether they were related.

I confess to responding in exactly this way when I come across my two family names. Dunbar is an extremely rare surname, even in Scotland, and my ears prick up the moment I hear or see it: if we share the surname, we are almost certainly related, and probably by fewer than twenty-five generations because the name became at all common (relatively speaking) only after the Earls of March (meaning the Scottish borders) and Dunbar (the location of their castle) had their lands sequestered for the second and decidedly final time by the Scottish crown in 1434 for switching sides once too often. In contrast, my second family name, MacDonald (or, more correctly, McDonald), which has been inherited through three generations from my great-grandmother, is by far the most common Scots name of all time and I barely even notice if it is mentioned.

The adoption of local names by immigrants has been a common strategy for fitting in for this reason. We find it in the English census returns during the early nineteenth century where Irish immigrant parents with obviously Gaelic names like Seamus (James) and Padraig (Patrick) had their children christened with the English equivalents. We see it in the use of English first names by Italian and German immigrants to the United States during the second half of the nineteenth century. We find it in the adoption of Spanish first names by descendants of the Welsh emigrants to Patagonia during the middle of the nineteenth century: it is not uncommon to see names like Juan Thomas or Ignacio Jones on tombstones in southern Argentina. It seems to be an important strategy designed to allow your children to blend in rather than stand out as strangers or immigrants, allowing them to make friends and find mates.

However, where there is a powerful group of invaders, we often find the reverse pattern: the adoption of *their* names. In Norman England, there was a rapid adoption of French first names (William, Henry, Alice, Mathilda, Adela) by the subservient Anglo-Saxons and the complete disappearance within a century of almost all the old Saxon names. How often do you come across an Ethelbert, an Ælfgifu or an Æthelred now? Blending in with a new all-powerful elite can be both a matter of survival and a passport to economic success.

The challenges of blending in to a new community when you are an immigrant are considerable, not for racial reasons as such but for cultural reasons. The cultural obstacles to multi-ethnic friendship are well demonstrated by the social networks of immigrant communities. Initially, immigrants embed themselves on the edges of the local community because they have no other choice. As a result, their social networks are almost always smaller because their accessible community is small: they are outsiders. And because their networks are smaller, the structure of their networks looks very different. As we saw in chapter 4, instead of having a few close friends, and then layers of increasing numbers of less and less intimate friends, they tend to have a network structure with more closer friends (especially in the middle layers) and few casual friends. This may have little to do with the attitudes of the native community: it is simply easier to form friendships within your own community because you have more things in common with people from your own culture, as well as having similar concerns about how to survive and get on, all of which facilitate the exchange of useful information about where to go or how to get something done. More important, conversations are just so much easier in your own language or dialect. Of course, any tendency by the host community to look suspiciously on strangers of any origin will simply exaggerate this. The problem is that, as more immigrants join the community, the less incentive there is to look outside for friendship. Ghettoes and social isolation become a self-fulfilling prophecy. It takes a couple of generations for the children to become sufficiently embedded in the host community (and less than enthusiastic about adhering to their own cultural traditions) to be fully integrated into the wider community. After all, who in England now knows whether their ancestors were Romano-Celts, Anglo-Saxons, Viking or Norman? Or, if it comes to that, a descendant of the Protestant French Huguenots that poured into

London in their tens of thousands in the aftermath of the Edict of
Nantes that outlawed the Protestant religion in 1685?

So the lesson here is: our choice of friends is heavily dictated
by trying to find like-minded people, people we feel comfortable
with in casual company, people we don't have to explain the joke
to every time, people who think like us and whose behaviour
we don't have to work hard at trying to understand, people with
whom conversations have a natural and effortless flow that we
don't have to work at. In short, people we can trust because we
think we know how they think. We use cues that provide short
cuts to identifying like-minded people that work plausibly most
of the time, but not always.

Friendships in newly forming communities

Intrigued by both this form of community groupishness and by
the speed at which friendships can be made even among strangers,
we were keen to explore how this happened. We toyed with many
different ways to do this, but the difficulty was always how to
find groups of strangers coming together to make a community.
We had thought about studying the way new recruits become
embedded into the army, but never had any reply to our enquir-
ies from the military. Eventually, two projects came our way by
accident. One involved a fraternity house at an old and venerable
Dutch university. It developed out of two quite separate existing
collaborations with a Dutch graduate student, Max van Duijn,
and with Anna Rotkirch in Finland. Having been an undergraduate member of this particular fraternity house, Max was keen
to see how the new cohorts each year bonded. The other project
came about through Mary Kempnich, an especially enthusiastic
and hard-working new graduate student in my research group,
who was very keen to see how social networks developed among

strangers forced to live together. She suggested looking at the new intake of students at one of the Oxford colleges, few, if any, of whom will have known each other before coming up to university.

The fraternity houses of Leiden University are student-run housing and social associations with about 1,700 members and a long historical tradition. In Max's fraternity house, 300–400 new members join each year, and as part of the joining process they are encouraged to form single-sex friendship groups. These eat together regularly, take part in singing competitions and highly ritualised contests in the fraternity bar at weekends, and develop their own uniform, songs and traditions, all of which help to create a sense of camaraderie and bonding. Friendship groups form naturally because groups either work (and so stick together) or they don't (in which case they break up and disperse when members switch to other groups). After three years of regular, intense social engagement in this highly competitive environment, the members of these friendship groups often become so strongly bonded that their relationships as a group continue long after they have left university, with many of the groups continuing to meet up every few years well into later life. Indeed, so strong is the bond that it is not unusual for them to become godparents to each other's children and, many years later still, even to attend the funerals of members.

We followed one cohort through the whole of its first year, during which members completed several waves of a questionnaire about their activities and relationships with each other, as well as taking part in a day of tests at the end of the year. We wanted to know what factors contributed to the success of these groups, and whether they exhibited any form of homophily – especially in terms of intrinsic psychological dimensions like personality and mentalising ability. Psychologists have traditionally described personality in terms of what they call the Five Factor Model – five dimensions that are usually labelled Openness, Conscientiousness,

Extraversion/Introversion, Agreeableness and Neuroticism, or OCEAN for short. Conscientiousness refers to people who tend to be diligent and reliable, Openness to those who are curious and open to new experiences, Neuroticism to people who tend to be rather anxious and sensitive, and Agreeableness to those who are friendly and compassionate.

The average size of the friendship groups in our cohort was fourteen – remarkably close to the 15-layer in the social brain circles. We used two measures of group success: the number of group badges and practices (e.g. special group songs, uniforms, or extra-curricular activities) they developed over the year and a simple self-rated measure of how bonded they each felt to the others. These indices seemed to tap into different aspects of group bonding, but there were strong correlations for both with how similar the group was on the Conscientiousness personality dimension in male groups and the Neuroticism dimension in female groups. In other words, the more similar the group members were in terms of certain personality dimensions, the more successful the friendship group was and the more bonded its members felt. The difference between the two sexes is especially striking as, once again, it suggests that the friendships of the two sexes may have very different dynamics.

At the end of the year, we asked four members of each friendship group to sing some of the fraternity songs that everyone was familiar with, and to do so either competitively (facing each other in two lines) or cooperatively (all standing in a circle together) with another group of four, either from their own friendship group or from another friendship group. After the singing task, they completed our standard Roman Chair pain-threshold test and rated their sense of bonding to the two foursomes. Pain threshold was higher when they were singing competitively than if they were singing cooperatively, and especially if the two groups came from different friendship groups. In both conditions, singers felt more bonded to their own foursome than to the members of the other foursome, but they felt closer to the other foursome if they had sung cooperatively with them as opposed to competitively.

Mary Kempnich's study focused on the new incoming cohort of about 100 students at a particular Oxford college. Oxford (and Cambridge) colleges differ from the Dutch fraternities in that they are not student-run, are much smaller (typically around 400 undergraduate students), and include graduate students (typically around 200) as well as academics (typically around 50), with the latter responsible for teaching the college's undergraduates on a very personalised basis. They are similar in that they involve communal dining (though often in a more formal setting) and college-based social, cultural and sporting activities, and, because they function more like a family, result in lifelong attachment to the college and the members of one's cohort. They differ in that friendship formation is more casual and open-ended, but some of these can become lifelong relationships.

Mary found that, having come in as complete strangers, friendships developed quickly between the students. Of particular interest is the fact that, by the end of the third month, there was already very strong gender homophily: the girls made friends with significantly more girls, and the boys made friends with significantly more boys. At mid-year, this gender effect had reduced, but was still very strong, and continued to be so beyond that. Overall, she found that the main factors promoting friendships initially were gender, ethnicity and the personality dimensions Extraversion and Agreeableness. Over the longer term, homophily increased for gender and degree subject (in other words, common interest in this hot-house academic community), but ethnicity and personality continued to be as important as they had been at the start.

The capacity to form bonded relationships on the basis of what are, in effect, arbitrary criteria was demonstrated in an iconic social psychology study that became known as the Robbers Cave Experiment (or sometimes as the *Lord of the Flies* experiment).

In 1954, Muzafer and Carolyn Sherif took a group of twenty-two eleven- and twelve-year-old boys who were all strangers to each other to a summer camp in the Robbers Cave State Park in Oklahoma. The boys were divided into two equal groups that were, for the first week of the study, housed in separate cabins some miles apart where they didn't know of each other's existence. After each group had bonded, the two groups were brought together to play a set of competitive games against each other. During this competitive phase, the boys developed markedly negative attitudes and behaviour towards the boys of the opposing group. In the third week, the two groups were brought back together again in a series of cooperative games in which the groups were mixed. During this final phase, most of the animosity of the previous week disappeared and was replaced by cross-group friendships. Many years later, Lutfy Diab repeated the experiment with ten- and eleven-year-old Lebanese boys in groups that mixed Muslims and Christians.* The results were very similar, and remind us how even the potent forces of religion can be at least temporarily overcome in contexts where other cross-cutting loyalties are allowed to build up – no matter how arbitrary those loyalties might be.

In the years since, these studies have attracted criticism on the grounds that it was unethical to force children into groups that became antagonistic towards each other. Superficially, that might seem to be the case, but that would be to ignore the fact we do this all the time when classes, schools, clubs and churches compete against each other in sports, spelling and maths competitions, and all manner of other activities. I am reminded of my own experiences at about the same age in the 1950s when we boys divided ourselves, with no outside encouragement (in fact, it would have been discouraged by the adults), into two roughly even sides (Protestants versus Catholics) and held major battles between the

---

*   This study has never been published, but is referred to by David Berreby in his book
     Us and Them (2006, Hutchinson).

two factions in which boys were occasionally injured. I am not at all certain that any of us really knew about, let alone understood (or even cared about), the theological or ritual differences between these two branches of Christianity, never mind their political origins, but we certainly knew which side our families belonged to and we joined in with relish in the weekly battles. Yet we would sit down together afterwards in perfect harmony, happily forming cross-religion groups for the leisure activities that filled the rest of the day. It seems to reflect boys' natural groupishness, a capacity to form groups or clubs irrespective of who the other members actually are – something we will return to in chapter 13.

*

Looking back over these studies allows us to see not only how important homophily is in engineering our relationships, but also how important are activities like singing, eating together and developing group-specific cultural traditions (such as special uniforms and songs) in creating a sense of belonging to a community of friends. For better or for worse, they build the psychological foundations on which trust is based. And trust, as we shall see in the next chapter, is what underpins both our friendships and our communities.

Trust and friendship

Alistair Sutcliffe, whom we met in chapter 4, had long been interested in the role of trust in managing social relationships. We had arranged to meet about developing the model of social networks that I discussed in chapter 4. It was midday of 11 September 2001. We were halfway through what was intended to be an all-afternoon session when one of my colleagues burst into my office in a state of shock and asked if we had heard the news that two planes had crashed into the Twin Towers of the World Trade Center in New York. Of course we had not, and looked rather blankly at him, shaking our heads in puzzlement. He rushed out again, muttering something that we didn't quite catch. We looked at each other, shrugged and went back, without a hint of irony, to the problem of trust. Every time we board a plane, cross a road, walk into a shopping mall, greet someone, or buy someone a drink, we do so on trust – trust that those involved will behave honestly and civilly, that they will not stab us in the back, metaphorically or literally. On this particular occasion, 2,977 people were going about their everyday business and had the misfortune to assume that nineteen other people wouldn't hijack some planes and fly them into their building.

Yet without trusting our fellow citizens, friendships would not be possible. Society itself would not be possible. That 9/11 happened is simply a reminder that we are caught on the horns of a dilemma. Without trust, we cannot forge friendships; but if we trust everyone unconditionally, we will in the end fall prey to freeloaders who exploit our trust for their own ends. Yet refusal to trust those we meet means we have to devote a great deal of effort to testing out everyone's credentials to ensure that we don't fall prey to cheats. How we solve that dilemma is the subject of this chapter.

Trust and deceit

What emerged out of that 9/11 afternoon with Alistair Sutcliffe was a second agent-based computer model of society with trust at its centre. We envisaged trust as a psychological quantity that is built up one step at a time as a result of each successful interaction between two people, but which could also be lost one step at a time every time one of them behaved badly towards the other – or precipitously by many steps at a time if either of them behaved extremely badly. We thought the level of trust required for a relationship might be proportional to the social layer that the relationship occupied. Only a modest level of trust was required for the relationship to occupy the outer 150-layer, but a much higher level would be required for it to be in the 15-layer and an even higher level for the 5-layer. A relationship's resistance to breaches of trust was viewed as a function of the level of trust: the more trusting the relationship, the bigger or more frequent the breaches had to be to destabilise it. I'll defriend a casual acquaintance for a minor breach of trust (but restore you equally quickly if you apologise or make up for it), but will only sever a close friendship after many repeated breaches of trust or for some positively dreadful failure on your part. But when that happens, the defriending may well be catastrophic and terminal. In this way, we tried to model our computer world on the way relationships actually seem to work in real life, with something of their subtlety and complexity. Once again, the computer programming for the model was in Di Wang's very capable hands.

The results suggest that if the effect of a defection on the trust in a relationship is asymmetric (only the trustor's level of trust is reduced, and the defector's level of trust is unaffected), then a frequency of defections on up to 10 per cent of interactions will have little or no effect on the average number of friends an individual will have; frequencies greater than 10 per cent will have a small effect on the overall number of friends, but will mainly reduce the number of strong and medium ties, with the effect being greater the higher the defection rate. Eventually, the frequency of defections will become so high that it won't be possible for the strongest 5-layer friendships to develop at all, because every time a potential friendship starts to get close to the level of trust required for a relationship, it gets knocked back by a defection before it has really had time to form. In some cases, the consequences of a defection or breach of trust might be symmetric, with trust breaking down on both sides. In such cases, the effect will be stronger than when the effect is asymmetric, with a defection rate of just 5 per cent being sufficient to reduce the number of close relationships.

In effect, relationships are like a game of snakes and ladders. Trust builds up over time as we have more and more positive experiences with someone. Then they do something that upsets us, and the relationship slides down a snake to land a row or two lower on the trust stakes. It is clear from this that defection is a serious problem for relationships, because if the level gets too high, it will prevent close relationships ever forming. We simply won't be willing to put that much trust in anyone, and instead will settle for weaker relationships where we run less risk of being cheated – or, at least, will suffer less damage if we are cheated.

So just how often does cheating or defection actually occur? It's hard to say. Because it isn't completely clear what should or should not count as a defection, there isn't a great deal of data on this.

However, there is one source of data that bears directly on relationships (as opposed to the economic transactions so beloved of economists), and that is lying. A sample of a thousand American adults found that on average people claimed to tell around 550 lies a year – equivalent to slightly more than one and a half lies a day! But not everyone behaved the same. Nearly a quarter of all the lies were told by just 1 per cent of the people sampled. In other words, the 1 per cent of habitual liars were telling nearly forty lies a day – though most are likely to be of a rather minor nature. This at least suggests that habitual liars are fairly rare, with most people telling the truth most of the time. In other studies, 92 per cent of people sampled admitted to lying at some point to their romantic partner, while 60 per cent of women and 34 per cent of men said they had lied to obtain sex. Of course, that might have been only once over a period of many years, so that the average frequency could be quite low. Nonetheless, it is clear that the temptation is there. Even in experimental games run in the laboratory, people were two or three times more likely to lie if the game was designed so that there was a benefit to be gained from lying. It seems that while most people are fairly honest, a small number of people can't help themselves, and probably become such habitual liars that they actually come to believe their own lies.

Lying brought me into another collaboration, this time with a pair of physicists from the National Autonomous University of Mexico. I had been introduced to Gerardo Iñiguez and his supervisor Rafael Barrio by Kimmo Kaski as yet another consequence of the Kaski Katapult. Kimmo and Rafael had been graduate students together in Oxford in the late 1970s and had remained friends and collaborators for over forty years. Friendships forged in the white-hot heat of science and student life can evidently last a lifetime. One of the things that had long bothered Rafael was the problem of deception, or lying. If you are repeatedly deceived and exploited, you will cease to trust everyone you meet, and confine yourself to the handful of people that you trust most. Instead of being a single large community in which favours are exchanged and mutual support given to all, the village becomes subdivided into small factions who don't trust each other, don't talk to each other, won't go to the same parties, and certainly won't go out of their way to help each other. Rafael argued that, given the destructiveness of lying for community cohesion, deception ought not to be common, because evolution would actively legislate against it in our relationships. Yet honesty and truthfulness is something we have to *teach* young children: they do not seem to act in this way of their own accord. And that seems odd from an evolutionary point of view: if something is such a problem, natural selection should have acted to neutralise it. (For more on the role that natural selection plays in the evolution of human behaviour, see my book *Evolution: What Everyone Needs to Know*.)

Rafael was particularly intrigued by the difference between selfish and prosocial lies (or, as we might call them, 'white lies'). Selfish lies are the kind where the liar benefits from their lie. White lies, in contrast, are the kind where the liar doesn't benefit directly because the lie is intended to preserve the target's personal wellbeing or to preserve the relationship between them. Examples might include 'liking' something someone said on Facebook when you really didn't think it was that interesting, but you thought it would upset them if you said that. Or saying how nice someone looks when you know they have tried very hard but it hasn't quite worked, and they would be devastated if you told them so. Or even failing to tell them something – massaging the truth – because you felt it might be better for them if they didn't know the gory details. In a very innocent way, we actually do a lot of this in the metaphors we use in everyday speech – as when the Victorians spoke of someone who had died as having 'fallen asleep' or, in more recent parlance, as having 'passed'.

The mathematical model that Gerardo Iñiguez and Rafael Barrio developed looked at how social networks evolved when people were scrupulously honest in their interactions with someone who was a member of a triad (a set of three close friends), told white lies when interacting with someone that had only indirect links with their triad, and lied selfishly in interactions with those with whom they had no previous links, direct or even indirect. Two interesting findings emerged. First, if there are only selfish liars and honest people in the population, the community very quickly breaks up into small subsets of very close friends who interact only with each other, whereas they form a single large, interconnected community if everyone is scrupulously honest. The more selfish liars there are in the population, the more fragmented the community becomes. Everyone circles the wagons and limits their social exchanges to their closest friends. Second, allowing white lies to be introduced into this social world helps to heal these divisions and makes it possible for the community to remain relatively well integrated despite the presence of selfish liars. Interestingly, the number of white liars in the population seems to make no difference to this: even a small proportion of white liars is enough to maintain the integrity of the community. It seems we are right to draw a distinction between selfish and white lies: they have very different effects on the quality of relationships – and, more generally, on community cohesion. In fact, white lies might actually be beneficial in smoothing over potential misunderstandings that would otherwise rock the community boat by causing rifts between some of its members.

In this model, honest people and liars were regarded as fixed types. In a dynamic version of the model, agents were allowed to learn these behaviours in the light of experience. In this case, the system evolved towards a stable state in which the vast majority of people are basically honest, but tell white lies occasionally, with just a very small number of selfish lies. Honesty generally pays off. Inveterately selfish liars are rare, mainly because they are ostracised by everyone else and can only get away with their deceptions now and again. This is what seemed to be the case in the finding that only 1 per cent of the population were serial liars. Interestingly, in the dynamic version of the Mexican model in which individuals learned how to behave rather than being of a fixed type, the community divided into small clusters of honest people and it was the liars who provided the links between these cliques that maintained the community as an integrated whole. Note, by the way, that the community size in these models was similar in size to typical hunter–gatherer and other small-scale societies. It won't necessarily apply on the scale of modern urban societies, though it will apply at the level of your personal network.

So while lying is frowned on, some forms of lying seem to serve a beneficial function for everyone by keeping the wheels of communication within the community well oiled. Society works on trust as much as friendships and family relationships do. The trust that has built up between us buffers our relationship against these mild transgressions because we can see why someone behaved in this way (something we can only do, of course, because of our high-level mentalising skills). The rule of law and moral codes help to set the benchmark for that: these provide a set of standards for behaviour that have been agreed by the community.

A spanner in the moral works

There is, however, one aspect of all this that invariably gets overlooked in all the discussions and all the models, as well as how we behave in our everyday relationships: it seems that we are more tolerant even of serious transgressions when we have a strong relationship with the person concerned than if they are strangers. It is a problem known to moral philosophers as *moral partiality*. If a stranger breaks a moral rule, we want to throw the book at them. But if a friend or family member does so, we'll make excuses for them and even try to protect them. What is surprising, given our usually intense moral stance, is that we are surprisingly unfazed by this inconsistency and often don't even comment on it. It seems to be a perfectly normal thing to do.

Anna Machin and I were much intrigued with this and set about exploring these differences in attitude in more detail. Anna devised a series of experiments on how we might discriminate between family and friends. The essence of the test she set her subjects was to think of two specific people in each of the social layers, one family member and one friend: would you report them to the authorities if you heard that they had been breaking some serious social rule like peddling drugs or pressurising under-age girls for sex. We even ran one of these experiments on native Samoan students at the University of Auckland in New Zealand in collaboration with one of my former postdocs Quentin Atkinson in order to see whether we got the same results from a very different cultural group – specifically one whose society was matrilineal rather than patrilineal like ours.

We were interested in whether people made moral decisions faster with kin than with friends because kinship acts as a simple schema that effectively makes the decision for you. Every decision you make is always a balance of interests. For family, it is simply a matter of 'My brother is guilty, but I don't want to see him in prison.' Family considerations just overrule everything else, because there is much more at stake. In contrast, you are more likely to trawl through the past details of the relationship with a friend before deciding how to act in the case of a casual friend. How often did Jim let me down? Did he ever pay me back that money I lent him? That takes time, so responses should be much slower.

As is often the case in science, the results weren't quite as straightforward as we had anticipated. It seemed that there was no difference in the speed of decisions between friends and family in the innermost circle of intimate relationships, suggesting that very close friends matter as much to us as very close family. For people in the 50-layer, the decision was made much more quickly for family members than for friends, just as we had predicted. In the outer 150-layer beyond that, however, things were more ambivalent, with decisions about friends being made faster than decisions about distant family, especially when the decision was not to help them out of a difficult situation. This suggests that these outer-layer relationships have less to do with personalised relationships and more with the social demands of kinship: we don't really feel distant family members deserve to be protected for what they've done any more than distant friends deserve it, but we agonise about the reverberations round the family network of a decision to let them hang. Failure to support kin is more likely to come back to haunt us later. Grandma will be upset that we let one of her cousins down. Friends in the outer circle, however, aren't so important to us, so we act on moral principle without giving it a second thought.

Later, we persuaded our Australian postdoc, Rafael Wlodarski, to run an experiment in the brainscanner to see if the difference in processing speed happened because these decisions were being made in different regions of the brain. As usual with brain-scan studies, we had to simplify the task. We decided to focus on mindreading, and used simple statements like: 'I think that Jim generally feels others' emotions' or, for a non-mindreading task: 'I think that Joe is not generally interested in abstract ideas', and asked subjects to say whether they agreed or not on a four-point scale (strongly disagree, disagree, agree, or strongly agree) with respect to specific family versus friend members of their social network, matched for network layer and sex. On the mentalising tasks, they consistently exhibited much more activity in the prefrontal cortex when making this judgment over friends than they did for a family member in the same social layer. What's interesting about this result is that the region where this activity was greatest was the part of the prefrontal cortex particularly associated with active rational thinking. In other words, they were laboriously cranking it out when doing the task for friends, whereas when it involved family members the decision seemed to be more automated – an instant response with very little conscious or even semi-conscious thought, just as we had suspected.

Trust, of course, is the solution to this dilemma: we learn to trust someone, and then use that as a short-cut guide to their future behaviour – 'He wouldn't do that to me!' But trust takes time to build up. When we really need to get close and personal, as with that handful of close relationships in the 5- and 15-layers that we really depend on, we have to do it by devoting a great deal of time to those concerned. That allows us to get to know them really well, and at the same time helps create the endorphin-based emotional bond between us that helps to persuade both of us to behave honestly. But time, as we saw in chapters 7 and 8, is in extremely short supply relative to the investment that needs to be made in order to achieve that kind of guarantee. That is why we end up with a layered structure to our networks, peopled by friends of different quality with only a very few of these being of the highest intensity (the five in the 5-layer).

But what about all the other people that aren't already in our closest social circles? Somehow, we need some short cuts that provide us with reliable cues of trustworthiness for those in the outer layers of our networks whom we don't see too often, and especially to provide us with a first-pass guide to trustworthiness for the many strangers we meet every day. It seems we rely on two main strategies. One is sanctions when people step out of line – something we may be willing to apply in person to people we know personally, but expect society to apply on our behalf to the people with whom we don't have close relationships. That allows us some leeway in which to assume, as a first pass, that so long as they belong to our society they will adhere to the rules and mores that society has established. The other strategy is being able to recognise scoundrels before we interact with them, for which we often use behavioural and physical cues of trustworthiness.

Sturm with a touch of *Drang*

Being cheated by someone is, as we all know, enough to make the blood boil. *Sturm und Drang* (storm and stress), as the nineteenth-century romantics might have put it. Not only do we seem to be very sensitive to the fact that we have been cheated, but we are also highly likely to remember who it was that cheated us. The evolutionary psychologist Linda Mealey showed photos of white males to students, with each photo tagged with a vignette about the person that reflected either trustworthiness (he found a wallet and returned it to the owner), cheating (he was caught embezzling money) or neutral information. When showed the same photos again a week later, people were much more likely to say that they recognised the faces of the men described as cheats, irrespective of the face. Reputations often go before us and colour how others see us – and, of course, allow us to engineer through gossip how other people see someone of whom we disapprove. Such behaviour can be both a warning to others and a form of social punishment. Social criticism, either directly to the individual concerned or to other members of the community, is one of the main ways we do this.

Polly Wiessner found that, in the !Kung San hunter–gatherers of Namibia, there was a striking difference in the reasons why the two sexes initiate criticism. Men initiated 95 per cent of discussions concerning land rights and politics, and two-thirds of cases involving troublemakers, whereas women initiated 95 per cent of conversations about jealousy over possessions, three-quarters of those over stinginess or failure to share, and two-thirds of those over inappropriate sexual behaviour and the failure to fulfil obligations towards kin. Only the young were criticised for not doing their share of communal activities, but that was probably because adult backsliders could be punished in other ways – for example, by not being given a share of meat from kills or by fewer offers of marriage. Men avoided criticising women, probably because doing so might lead to conflicts with the woman's spouse or – without being too cynical, because this did feature large in their lives – because it might result in fewer offers of casual sex in the future.

Punishment might involve mockery (especially in the case of pretentious behaviour, something most hunter–gatherer societies are appalled by), direct criticism or, in rare cases, physical violence. Even so, moral partiality was evident: people were circumspect about joining in with criticism if it was targeted against a close family member or a good hunter who made valuable contributions of meat to the community (in this case, for fear that they might lose a significant benefit if a good hunter took offence and left the camp to go and live somewhere else). As with everything in life, decisions about whether or not to put up with the foibles of other individuals are always a trade-off between the costs and benefits of doing so.

The ultimate punishment in hunter–gatherer societies the world over is banishment. In these societies, banishment is effectively death by a thousand cuts because people cannot survive without the support of a group. In Wiessner's !Kung community, one of the few cases of ostracism by the community involved a woman who had had frequent sexual relationships with Bantu men. Such relationships were not uncommon, but were viewed unsympathetically by the !Kung because of the Bantu's discriminatory, even abusive, attitudes towards the !Kung. Under pressure from criticism by other members of the community, she left the camp group and subsequently died. In another case, a man was suspected of incest, and, after a barrage of criticism, left the group; however, as he was a good hunter and took his family with him, he was able to join another community and prosper. A third case involved the expulsion of a family in which the wife was frequently drunk and had promiscuous sexual relations with Bantu men; and, to cap it all, the children were unruly. Eventually, after the entire community had ganged up against them, the family left to live elsewhere. They were allowed back only after the woman had died.

In an inspirational series of experiments carried out some years ago, Elinor Ostrom (the only woman ever to have been awarded a Nobel Prize for Economics) asked groups of people to play a classic economics game. In each case, people played in groups linked via a computer. They were asked to make monetary contributions to a common pot that would be shared out among them at the end of the game. Since the total amount in the pot was multiplied by the experimenters before it was shared out, the best strategy was for everyone to contribute all their money. That way, they would maximise the money in the pot and, hence, their individual shares. But the usual freeloader temptation to hold back invariably hovers in the wings: anyone who pays in less would keep the money they had held back *and* benefit from a share of everyone else's contributions. There was a consistent tendency for players to contribute less money to the pot with each successive round as people realised that they could benefit from freeloading – a very common finding in these kinds of public-good experiments, by the way. But when players were allowed to punish people who made low contributions by making a payment to deduct a fine from the backslider's share, the level of contributions was consistently higher. However, it seemed that monetary punishments weren't essential for keeping freeloaders in line. In another variant of the experiment, she allowed players to comment at the end of each round. Remarks like: 'Who's the schmuck that's not putting money in?' were enough to trigger a guilty response and improve behaviour. Punishment for backsliding when it impacts on others seems to be a human universal. The behavioural economists Benedikt Hermann and Simon Gächter at the University of Nottingham carried out a similar study in sixteen different countries in Europe and the Middle East with rather similar results: individuals were willing to pay a fee to punish players who contributed less than the average donation to the common pot.

Perhaps because adherence to the social contract is so important both for maintaining trust in our person-to-person relationships and for maintaining the integrity of the community as a whole, we often take pleasure in seeing others get their comeuppance when they've broken the rules – that delicious sense of pleasure described by the German word *schadenfreude* – enjoyment of someone else's sorrow. A few years ago, Tania Singer started a minor industry in the brain-imaging world by running a study that looked at people's responses to others being punished for their misbehaviour. Subjects played several rounds of an economic game in which they had to decide how much of their money to give to the other player, who, after the stake had been tripled in value, then decided how much money to give back. What the subject didn't know was that the other player was always a confederate who was instructed to respond fairly (by returning a similar amount) or unfairly (by returning a lot less, so that the original donor lost out). Subjects played against both types of confederate. After the game, the subject was put into the brain scanner with the fair and unfair confederate they had played against sitting on either side of them. Their brain was then scanned while they were watching a painful electrical stimulation being applied to each of the confederates' hands in turn.

For both sexes, the areas of the brain associated with empathy showed enhanced activation when pain was administered to the fair confederate, as one might expect. What was surprising was that the pleasure centres in the brain lit up when the unfair confederate suffered pain. Moreover, there was a very strong sex difference. Men seemed to take special pleasure in seeing those who had behaved badly getting punished in a way that women generally did not. More interestingly, Tania showed that the strength of the *schadenfreude* response correlated with the previously expressed desire for revenge. Other studies have since shown similar responses among sports fans in response to rival sports teams winning or losing derby matches and in response to the misfortunes experienced by members of rival political parties.

Tania Singer raised the possibility that her results might have reflected the fact that the punishment used in her experiment was physical, and that other kinds of punishment might have elicited stronger *schadenfreude* responses in women. This could be because there is a difference in the way the two sexes punish people: men tend to resort to physical forms of punishment, whereas women tend to rely more on psychological punishment – a strategy deployed to particular heights by adolescent girls. This has been highlighted both by Anne Campbell in her studies of girl gangs in New York and by Tania Reynolds and Roy Baumeister in a series of experimental studies of women's use of gossip. In both cases, romantic rivalry seemed to be much the most important trigger for such behaviour. Denigrating rivals and casting aspersions on their character was the standard mode of exacting revenge. This might be due to the fact that women are typically less physically strong than men and hence that physical retribution by women is likely to be less effective. It may equally be that, because they are socially more skilled than men, women are able to exert psychological pressure more effectively than men can.

Short cuts to trust

Punishment of backsliders is, of course, a bit like shutting the stable door after the horse has bolted. In many ways, it would be a lot better to be able to distinguish honest from dishonest people before risking your money. One way of doing this might be from cues present in someone's face or behaviour. There has been longstanding folk wisdom dating back as far as ancient Indian and Chinese times suggesting that people's personalities are etched onto their faces. The Taoist art of face-reading (*mian xiang*) dates back more than 3,000 years, but it became especially highly developed during the Northern Song period in the eleventh century AD. (For those interested, its instruction manuals are conveniently available on the internet.) Even Aristotle, by far the most acute observer of the natural world among the ancient philosophers, was much intrigued by the apparent relationship between physical appearance and character. In many ways, the claim reached its apogee in the West in the early nineteenth century in the form of phrenology, and the later work on physiognomy by the geneticist and polymath Sir Francis Galton (the person who discovered fingerprints, and who was, as it happens, a cousin of Charles Darwin). These had claimed to show that there was such a thing as a criminal face. By the second half of the twentieth century, however, the whole field had fallen into disrepute, mainly due to the excessive claims made by some of its more exotic early practitioners.

Since the 1990s, however, the topic has seen something of a revival, mainly thanks to advances in digital technology that have allowed us both to define facial characteristics more explicitly and to explore the dynamics of facial expressions. In one recent study, for example, Carmel Sofer and her Dutch colleagues used digital technology that allowed them to combine real faces to show that faces that were closer to the average of all faces were rated as the more trustworthy but less attractive. In another study, Tony Little asked a group of people to rate themselves either as natural cooperators or as non-cooperators and then used similar digital technology to combine their photographs to produce composite, or average, faces for cooperators and non-cooperators. Another group of people was then shown the composite face pictures and asked to rate how likely they were to be cooperators. The raters did rather better than expected at distinguishing cooperators from non-cooperators just on the basis of their faces, though the effect was quite modest (about 12 per cent better than chance). In a further analysis, he was able to show that men (but not women) who rated themselves as cooperators were more likely to have less masculine (i.e. more feminised) faces, and that cooperativeness was more likely to be associated with a more intense smile. These results seemed to confirm earlier findings that smiling and the facial expression of emotions are associated with low social dominance in men (but high social dominance in women) and that dominant men produce less broad smiles (probably because, as I suggested in chapter 9, they have a squarer, more prominent jaw). More masculine faces were generally seen as being less trustworthy.

Kinship probably remains the single best cue for trustworthiness because it is reinforced by the family community, especially in traditional small-scale societies. We see classic examples of this among the Scots during the eighteenth and nineteenth centuries. Wherever the Scots went in the world, they would, as often as not, send back to their home community if they needed someone to come and help out. The Manitoba fur trappers of the Canadian Hudson's Bay Company, in financial terms probably the most successful and longest-lived multinational company of all time (it is still going 350 years after its foundation in 1670), were heavily dominated by men from the Orkney Isles on the northern perimeter of Scotland precisely because they were regarded as hard-working and reliable in such difficult working conditions. My own grandfather went out to India in the 1890s because his cousin worked in Kanpur (or Cawnpore as it then was) as Secretary of the Cawnpore Woollen Mill (one of many Scots-owned factories in the town) and offered to arrange a job for him. The home communities were small, tightly knit, and most of the people were related to each other. Obligations of family, combined with great-grandmother sitting by her fireside in the windswept northeast of Scotland ready to wag her finger at miscreants, was enough to ensure that most people pulled on the ropes in the way they were expected to. That said, I have to confess that James MacDonald Dunbar, scion of an Inverness branch of the family, who was one of the under-managers of the Cawnpore factory at the time, had to be sent home for, shall we say, persistently failing to live up to expectations. But then, he wasn't on our side of the family (despite the shared middle surname) . . .

We just expect certain things from family in terms of loyalty and commitment, partly because of the kinship premium and Hamilton's theory of kin selection, but also partly because they are so socially embedded with each other. This was nicely shown in a rather complicated brain-scanning experiment of a moral dilemma run by Mareike Bacha-Trams at Aalto University in Finland. She had two subjects watch the same film at the same time while lying down in scanners so that she could correlate their respective brain-activity patterns in real time. The film was the 2009 feature film *My Sister's Keeper* and the subjects were shown a twenty-minute clip in which one of the sisters, Anna, is asked to donate a kidney to the other sister, Kate, who is dying of cancer; she refuses and Kate dies. The reasons why Anna refused were not disclosed in the clip, but half the subjects were told beforehand that the girls were full siblings and half that they were adopted sisters. The question was: would people be more shocked by Anna's behaviour in the first case than in the second?

Despite the fact that 90 per cent of the subjects reported that the genetic status of the sisters made no difference (sisters are sisters, after all), their brain scans told a very different story: the brain activity of the two subjects was significantly more correlated in parts of the prefrontal cortex, the parietal cortex and the anterior cingulate cortex (ACC) – all areas associated with mentalising and managing social relationships – in those pairs that had been told that the girls were genetic sisters than when they had been told that the sisters were genetically unrelated. Genetically unrelated adopted sisters will have no more incentive to help each other out than any two close friends, but the ties of biology should prevail on biological sisters to volunteer. The fact that biological sisters didn't help each other caused subjects to metaphorically sit bolt upright in an attempt to explain the surprising inconsistency implied by Anna's behaviour.

Of course, close kin don't always behave altruistically towards each other, though when they don't it is often the case that they are like chalk and cheese and have never got on. As we saw in chapter

2, however, family are much more likely to be willing to help each other out. In fact, when the chips are down and everyone else has deserted you, close family are the one group of people that will stand by you. Some years ago, Elainie Madsen (then one of our graduate students, and now at the University of Lund in Sweden) and Richard Tunney (then a young postdoc, and now head of psychology at Aston University) ran an experiment designed by the psychologist Henry Plotkin and myself that tested Hamilton's theory of kin selection. The idea for the experiment had been thought up by our collaborator George Fieldman many years before when he was himself a graduate student: it required the subject to adopt the Roman Chair position (see chapter 7) for as long as they could, with a cash reward determined by the length of time for which they held it. Since the position becomes exponentially more painful as time goes on, the simple measure of time was equivalent to the amount of pain they had been willing to bear. The crucial feature of the experiment was that each time they did the task (usually on different days), they did it for themselves or for a named relative or friend who was sent the money they had earned at the end of the experiment. We repeated this experiment five times (three times in the UK and twice on different Zulu populations in South Africa). In each case, the amount of pain they were willing to bear correlated with the relatedness of the person on whose behalf they were working. A best friend was treated roughly the equivalent to a cousin (in other words, much less well than parents, siblings and grandparents), but a children's charity consistently did worst of all. Instead, people worked hardest when they themselves were the beneficiaries. So much for altruism.

A closer look at the data from this experiment revealed two interesting facts. First, subjects' ratings of the pain they had experienced correlated with the duration for which they held the position. They *knew* what they were doing and that they weren't being as generous to some recipients as they were to others. Second, we asked them about the kinds of features they had in common with the recipient so as to look for homophily effects, but the best predictor of their relationship with the recipient was how much time they had spent with them during their second (teenage) decade of life. Once again, it seems that time is what counts in creating close social bonds.

Of sharks and berserks

So much for the rules that allow us to handle freeloaders and defectors. But how bad *is* the world out there? Is it really a case of dog eat dog, a world full of snake-oil salesmen and con artists waiting to fleece the very shirt off your back? Although most of us are protected from the worst of these disruptive effects by the communal rules laid down by civilised society, we are not entirely preserved from the fact that there is an incentive for some individuals to push the envelope of civil behaviour to gain an advantage. The clever ones are able to remain just on the right side of good behaviour when doing this, but inevitably some will overstep the boundary of the law. These are the individuals we view as antisocial – or, in the extreme cases, psychopaths and sociopaths. Nonetheless, the fact that this handful of individuals is so disruptive has motivated a great deal of research into the origins of antisocial behaviour, and provides us with a glimpse into why we should be so concerned with trusting others unconditionally.

In a study that followed some 400 London males from age eight to age sixty-one, the Cambridge criminologist David Farrington found that individuals who exhibited violent behaviour as teenagers continued to show such behaviour in each succeeding decade of life. He found that the most important childhood risk factors predicting convictions for violent behaviour later in life were: high risk-taking, lower than average IQ (especially verbal IQ), a broken family background, harsh parental discipline, hyperactivity (such as ADHD), and large family size. The more of these risk factors a child was exposed to, the more it was likely to end up in prison as a result of violent behaviour. Farrington is keen to point out that these predisposing factors alone do not suffice to tip a person into crime. The events that lead to violent behaviour usually require some precipitating factor like being bored, angry, drunk, frustrated, or being egged on by male peers. Such males may try hard to be rational and well behaved, but their ability to do so is invariably impaired by their inability to control their anger or by drink, or both. It is a reminder, once again, how important the capacity to inhibit prepotent actions is for a peaceful society. That said, of course, conviction for violent behaviour is not a one-off unlucky event: it is usually the outcome of a lifestyle dominated by constant poor behaviour and minor infringements that never quite get to court.

In another iconic study of antisocial behaviour, the husband-and-wife team Terrie Moffitt and Avshalom Caspi used data from the Dunedin Study* to explore the predisposing factors for anti-social behaviour in both sexes. They found that males were much more likely to exhibit such behaviour than females. Nonetheless, what seemed to characterise such behaviour in both sexes was the combination of an abusive childhood with a particular allele of the monoamine oxidase A (MAOA) gene responsible for the enzyme that breaks down the products of serotonin, dopamine and norepinephrine, three important neuroendocrines involved in modulating social behaviour. They found that antisocial behav-iour as well as diagnoses of conduct disorder were best explained by a combination of negative emotionality (a tendency to see everything negatively and to be suspicious of others' motives ... in other words, poor mentalising abilities) and poor self-control (i.e. inhibition). Between them, these two factors (both of which are genetically inherited) explained 98 per cent and 78 per cent,

---

* A longitudinal study of a thousand children born in the city of Dunedin, New Zealand, in 1972–3, who have been followed up and tested every few years ever since.

respectively, of the variance in two behavioural outcomes (anti-social behaviour and conduct-disorder diagnoses). That it should be these two cognitive abilities that emerge as the main factors shouldn't surprise us, given how crucial we found them to be in chapter 6 in the management of social relationships.

In a follow-up study, they scanned the brains of around two-thirds of the adults in the Dunedin sample, and were able to show that those whose childhood antisocial behaviour persisted into adulthood had smaller volumes in most parts of their cortex com-pared with those who had grown out of their childhood antisocial behaviour or who had never exhibited any antisocial behaviour. Importantly, many of the areas where they seemed to have less brain tissue were precisely those associated with managing social behaviour, including the mentalising network in the prefrontal cortex, the temporal lobe and the temporo-parietal junction. In particular, the frontal pole, with its association with the ability to inhibit behaviour, seemed to be especially small. This might reflect a genetic predisposition (unfortunately, they haven't yet compared these individuals with their siblings or other close family mem-bers) or it may be a consequence of reduced brain development during childhood following some developmental insult such as prolonged illness, starvation or just lack of social experience, all of which can inhibit brain growth.

Coping with the behaviour of antisocial individuals has long been a problem for human societies. Small-scale societies which lack law courts and a police force have always found these indi-viduals particularly disruptive and difficult to deal with. Like many small-scale societies throughout history, the early medieval Norse (Viking) society of Iceland struggled with violence within the community. Some individuals, known as *berserks* (from which we derive the English expression 'to go berserk') were a perpetual nuisance. A berserker was someone whose ferocity and prowess in battle was widely acknowledged, often associated with the ability to be a 'shape-changer' – someone who could turn into a ferocious animal like a wolf, sometimes with a little help from magic potions. These men were invariably feared, not least because they seem to have had many of the attributes of the sociopath – quick to anger, physically violent, deadly to tangle with and utterly self-obsessed. Egil Skallagrímsson, the eponymous anti-hero of the *Egilssaga* family history, was a case in point. He used what can only be described as terror tactics, unbridled violence and even murder to extract land and resources from other members of the community. Berserkers were much feared.

Some evidence of this was provided by an analysis of the many murders recorded in the Icelandic family sagas. Under Norse customary law, the family of a murder victim had the right to claim either a revenge murder by killing the perpetrator (or one of his family) or blood money from the perpetrator. In most cases, the families of victims preferred to opt for a revenge murder – unless the perpetrator was an acknowledged berserker, in which case they invariably settled for blood money. Berserkers were just too dangerous to risk attempting to murder, not least because murdering one of their family members simply invited retribution that rapidly developed into a vendetta that could rumble on for half a century or more and lead to the deaths of many innocent males. One such case is described in *Njalssaga*, which recounts the events that overtook one community in the second half of the tenth century and ultimately led to the death of over a third of all the adult males in the twenty-three families involved – with four families losing all their menfolk.

Along with the Swedish Viking Age historian Anna Wallette from Lund University, we analysed the pedigrees recorded in the family sagas to see whether berserkers benefited from their behaviour in terms of the numbers of descendants they left (the measure of biological fitness). We found that, on average, they had many more grandchildren than less violent individuals – even though they themselves sometimes ended up being murdered by an exasperated community. It seems that their reputation and the protection they provided during their lifetimes reduced the risk that their male relatives, in particular, ran of being killed by other members of the community. Paradoxically, even though their behaviour was utterly selfish, they gained through the fact that their behaviour benefited the reproduction of their close relatives. This process is known as kin selection in evolutionary biology, and reflects the fact that organisms can contribute copies of their genes to the next generation either by reproducing themselves or by facilitating the reproduction of relatives that carry the same gene(s).

What we learn from this is that people will resort to violence if they can get away with it when it provides them with benefits. Some may be predisposed to behaving in this way, others probably discover the effectiveness of such behaviour early in life and once they have done so continue to exploit it. We are all familiar with such individuals, the much-to-be-feared thugs and bullies. Though they rarely make good friends and we can never trust them, we often have to learn to live with them.

*

The burden of this chapter has been to emphasise the role of trust in making both our relationships and society function. We have to believe that most people will behave honestly because we really don't have the time to check them all out. For that reason, we use short cuts to trust that help reduce the burden. Occasionally, we get it wrong. In the next chapter, I consider a special case of this: romantic relationships. These offer some valuable insights into the dynamics of friendships precisely because they are so intense that everything about them is exaggerated.

The romance of friendship

No relationship we enter into ever has quite the intensity of romance. It is a weird and wonderful thing that has haunted poets, philosophers, kings and queens and the humblest citizens in every age. As though from nowhere, the whole body changes, the mind grows besotted and no longer the master of its own destiny. The signs are unmistakable: a dreaminess of demeanour, a constant desire to be with the beloved, a willingness to oblige their every whim, and a near-complete indifference to everyone and everything else. To be sure, not everyone suffers the full rigours of the condition, but it is general enough and (occasional denials notwithstanding) sufficiently cross-cultural to count among the handful of human universals in addition to laughter and tears. Peculiar as they are, romantic relationships share with friendships the same processes of evaluation and assessment, the same dependence on trust, the same fragility when exposed to being let down, the same risk of abandonment when someone better comes along. So let us see what romance can tell us about friendships.

Negotiating courtship

Karl Grammer, perhaps the leading human ethologist, has made a career out of studying human mate-choice behaviour. He suggested that courtship can best be understood as a process of punctuated evaluation: there are a series of decision points, separated by periods of stasis, where we pause to decide whether to move on to the next more intimate level or to pull out now before we have overcommitted ourselves. We begin with distance signals, and slowly but surely circle into ever closer and more intimate forms of evaluation. It begins with what does he/she look like? How well do they move ... dance ... play? If they pass this initial test, we arrange to spend more time with them, successively evaluating cues based on speech, smell and taste until, eventually, we commit ourselves to the full monty. At each stage, we pause to evaluate whether we should proceed to the next level.

What do we base these decisions on? In fact, the two sexes have very different interests, and so focus on quite different cues in a romantic partner – or, to be more precise, they are both interested in the same set of cues but weight them very differently. Rather than ask people to rate their preferences in the artificial vacuum of a laboratory, we used Lonely Hearts advertisements to explore this question because these provide a neat encapsulation of what someone is actually looking for when they are searching for a romantic partner. And they pay good money to do so, so are unlikely to be frivolous. Adverts typically consist of two clearly defined halves, usually separated by a word like 'seeks': the traits the advertiser has to offer about themselves are usually specified first, and the traits they are seeking in a prospective partner follow. A typical advertisement has the form: 'Fun-loving 30-year-old female who likes concerts and country walks *seeks* honest, reliable soul companion 30–45, no drink or drugs'. These advertisements are ideal because the number of words listed for a particular trait provides an index of the weighting the advertiser places on the trait.

Boguslaw Pawlowski (now a professor at the University of Wroclaw and the doyen of Polish evolutionary anthropology) was a visitor in our research group, and it did not take long to persuade him that an analysis of personal adverts held out the promise of a really interesting project. What his analyses showed was, first, that men and women are extremely well attuned to what the other sex is looking for: what the other side most commonly asks for in their adverts, advertisers most commonly offer. In fact, they were so well attuned to their relative standing in the marketplace at any given age that they were able to match their own demandingness pretty much exactly to their relative popularity – well, all except males aged forty to fifty who rather badly overestimated their standing in the marketplace. I say nothing.

Something else that is strikingly obvious about these adverts is the fact that women typically say less about themselves and much more about what they expect from a prospective partner. Men's ads tend to be the reverse. This demandingness by women advertisers harks back to some very basic biology. The decision at some very early stage in the evolution of placental mammals for one sex to take on the entire burden of gestation and lactation (the two defining features of this animal family) means that males can only ever play a very limited, indirect role in this process. The result is that the two sexes diverge in how they can best maximise their biological fitness (the number of descendants they leave) – the engine of the evolutionary process. Since, unlike the case in birds, extra matings don't lead to extra offspring for female mammals, they do best by ensuring that they have access to the best genes available and the best circumstances in which to rear their infants. In contrast, because (with the sole exception of the dog family) there is very little that male mammals can do to assist with the rearing process, the only way males can increase their fitness is by mating with more females. In effect, it's a trade-off between quality and quantity.

One consequence of this is that the variation in the number of offspring produced is much greater in male mammals than it is in females, even though both must produce the same *average* number of offspring. More males than females fail to reproduce, while more males produce very large numbers of offspring. The problem is that females have more to lose if a conception goes wrong. This has one important consequence for mate-searching strategies: female mammals will always be more choosy than males. This seems to be as true of humans as of any other species. What women ask for in prospective mates is cues of wealth and status (indexed by good jobs, preferably in the professions, or indicators of a solid bank balance), cues of commitment ('loving', 'romantic', 'tolerant', 'monogamous') and cultural interests (music, dancing, reading novels, travel, hobbies, and political and religious views) that can be matched to the Seven Pillars of Friendship that we met in chapter 10. Men tended to offer these but rarely to ask for them. About the only thing that men consistently specify, aside from the prospective partner's age (always young), is cues of physical attractiveness, and women invariably mentioned these in their ads ('petite', 'attractive', 'vivacious', 'pretty', 'wearing well'). Surprisingly, given that women often comment on this aspect of men, they rarely mention cues of physical attractiveness as a desired trait in their advertisements.

Wealth, and its partner in crime status, play an important role in human reproduction because these provide the resources that women use in the rearing process. In traditional societies the world over, women who have access to resources have higher offspring-survival rates and do better in the reproductive stakes than women who don't. We find this in societies that range from nineteenth-century European peasants to African agro-pastoralists. It is true even in contemporary Britain: childhood mortality declines and children's social and economic opportunities increase with socio-economic class. Because wealth is so important for the business of reproduction, men try to accumulate it so that they can use it as an advertising bid in mate choice. For this reason, conspic-uous display is an important feature of men's adverts as well as their behaviour. However, they rarely state their wealth directly; instead, they make casual allusion to cues of wealth – signals of what they can afford to buy such as expensive watches, handmade shoes and beautifully tailored suits, top-of-the-range cars – even tractors in one set of farmers' marriage offers we looked at.

There was a brief period when mobile phones were in this category. Having spent a lot of time travelling on trains in the early 1990s, I had noticed that men invariably put their mobile phones on the table in front of them as soon as they sat down. Women certainly had phones (as soon as they rang, they duly answered them), but they usually left them out of sight in their handbags. This was, by the way, a time when mobile phones were expensive and much rarer than they are now. Having one was a sign both of relative wealth and of being important enough to need to be on call no matter where you were. It was one of those casual observations that you tuck away in your mind with the intention of setting up a study on it one day. The opportunity to do so came a few years later when I was doing a study on mobile-phone use for Hewlett Packard. I persuaded John Lycett, then one of my postdocs, to spend several evenings observing people in a pub. He found that the men were indeed much more likely to place their phones on the table in front of them than women were. Moreover, they were much more likely to do so – *and* more likely to fiddle conspicuously with them or make calls on them – as the ratio of women to men at the table declined. In other words, as the implicit competition for the women hotted up (more men per woman present), so the men did their best to draw attention to their phones. They were behaving just like peacocks strutting their stuff as the peahens pass by.

Age is probably the single most important proxy for physical attractiveness in women, and men tended to seek women consistently in the same age range (mid-twenties), whereas women tended to seek males who were three to five years older than they were. Age and physical attractiveness are very straightforward cues of fertility in women; in contrast, men's fertility is unrelated to their age, but their wealth does increase steadily with age (according to the UK national statistics). Boguslaw Pawlowski and I were able to show that men's interest in women (as reflected in the ratio of the number of advertising women of a given age group to the number being sought in men's adverts) correlated almost linearly with women's natural fertility, with a peak in the mid-twenties and a steady decline thereafter. In contrast, women's preference for older men seems to be a trade-off between men's slowly accumulating wealth as they aged and their increasing risk of dying. Using the UK national demographic statistics, we could show that women really did seek to find an optimal balance between these two considerations, with a peak preference for men in their mid- to late thirties.

Another cue that women seem to emphasise, both in casual conversation and in the statistics, is stature: taller men are much preferred. Tall men are also more successful in everyday life. Timothy Judge and Daniel Cable reviewed a large number of studies on salary differentials, and concluded that, when other factors like age and employment type are held constant, every inch of stature is worth nearly $800 a year on your salary across a wide spectrum of jobs, especially in males. (The effect was *much* weaker in women.) Boguslaw and I were able to explore the consequences of this effect for mate attractiveness in a Polish medical database. Tall men were much more likely than short men to get married, and, if married, to have more children. When we published these results, to inevitable media attention, I had a man from somewhere in the eastern Mediterranean spend an hour on the phone berating me on the grounds that he was short but had never had any trouble at all having sex with as many women as he wanted. I really wanted to ask whether he (a) was married, (b) had any children, or (c) was rich. But he was so aggressive about his honour being impugned by our research that, for fear that he might appear at my office door wielding weapons of mass destruction, I merely nodded enthusiastically down the phone and said how delighted I was to hear of his success.

What was especially interesting about these Polish data was

that they started immediately after the Second World War. Poland lost huge numbers of men during the war, and emerged out of the conflict with a very badly skewed adult sex ratio: there were millions of women facing the prospect of not being able to find husbands. When we split the data decade by decade, it was apparent that the preference for tall men (as expressed in the likelihood of being married) progressively moved from near zero to a strong preference for taller men as each decade passed and the adult sex ratio gradually came back to normal. In the decade immediately after the war, the women had no choice and were forced to marry whoever they could lay their hands on – tall, short or in-between; by the 1970s, they had more choice and shorter men were actively being discriminated against. This does not seem to be true for women, by the way: in contrast, tall women are at a disadvantage in the marriage stakes. The fashion industry's apparent preference for tall, willowy models notwithstanding, men seem to prefer shorter women, and shorter women tend to be more fertile and have more children.

Risk-taking and sportiness are other cues to which women seem to pay more than just casual attention. Young males, in particular, are risk-takers: adolescent boys take so many risks (driving too fast, taking drugs, playing dangerous sports) that they have much higher mortality rates in their late teens than girls do. What risk-taking seems to be signalling is gene quality. In effect, they are saying: watch me – I can afford to take risks because my genes are so good I'll get away with it. This kind of dicing with death as a signal of mate quality is common in the animal kingdom, and is known as Zahavi's Handicap Principle after the Israeli ornithologist Amotz Zahavi who first identified it. Peacocks provide the most familiar example. Their long trains with the eyespots are not so much intended to say: 'Look how beautiful I am' as: 'Look how I can handicap myself and still manage to fly in order to escape predators.' Such cues are pointless if they don't involve real risks that some males fail. Some teenage boys pay that price.

Perhaps for that reason, 'bad lads' have a particular attractiveness as mates. This was highlighted in a study that Susan Kelly did. It was a very simple vignette study in which people were given a set of descriptions about a person and invited to rate them as desirable either for a one-night stand or as a lifetime romantic partner. She found that women much preferred brave, risk-prone males compared with altruistic, risk-averse ones as short-term mating partners. However, they preferred altruistic males as long-term partners. This is exactly what we would expect: get your genes from males who have proven quality and then rely on a safe pair of hands to see you through the long haul of childcare. The tricky bit, of course, is persuading the second kind of male to take the risk of being cuckolded.

The bottom line here is that women make much more complex decisions about a partner than men do. I won't go as far as suggesting that, from a man's point of view, anything will do (younger *is* better, after all), but it is clear that men make much simpler decisions because they seem to live in a more one-dimensional world. This may explain why, in all the societies that permit polygyny, men successively marry girls of about the same (young) age. Women, in contrast, are trying to balance many different, often conflicting, interests, and this makes their decisions both more complicated and, because of that, inevitably imperfect – they can never find the perfect spouse and are always obliged to make do.

There was, however, one factor on which both sexes seemed to agree, and that was the importance of commitment. In effect, the friendship bit. In our original study of personal ads, both sexes offered commitment in their ads equally frequently, although women were twice as likely to seek it as men were. Justin Mogilski and his collaborators asked subjects to rate vignettes of possible short- and long-term partners that differed along the main personality dimensions. They found that honesty–humility was rated higher than any of the other personality dimensions for both sexes, and especially so for long-term relationships. Honesty was here indexed as the individual's history of sexual fidelity, and interpreted as defining trustworthiness, and hence commitment.

As we saw in chapter 10, friendship relationships are dominated by homophily – the birds-of-a-feather effect. Yet it's often said that, in romantic relationships, opposites attract. In fact, it's not at all clear that the evidence supports this claim. In a study that looked at people who had been in a romantic relationship for at least a year, Patrick and Charlotte Markey found that similarity in personality was the best predictor of how satisfied they were with their existing relationship. The highest levels of relationship satisfaction occurred when both partners were similar in their degree of warmth. However, there was a suggestion that complementarity in dominance (one partner dominant and the other subordinate) also contributed to relationship satisfaction, indicating that there might be important nuances in terms of the fine details of relationship dynamics: when both were dominant personalities, things didn't work so well. Similarly, Kathleen Voh and Roy Baumeister compared friends, dating partners and married couples in both the USA and the Netherlands and found that relationship satisfaction (measured in terms of willingness to forgive, security of attachment, accommodation, healthy and committed styles of loving, smoothness of daily interactions, absence of conflict and absence of feeling rejected) was best predicted by having similarly high levels of self-control (in other words, inhibition). So it seems as though homophily underpins successful romantic relationships as much as it does successful friendships.

Real life is always a trade-off

Like finding friends, finding a romantic partner is a lottery and often requires us to compromise on our ideals. What each of us has to offer varies, and that inevitably affects how much we can afford to push our demands. You can hold out as long as you like for Mr Darcy and his ancestral pile, but Mr Darcy has the pick of the bunch and he will only choose one of you to be Mrs Darcy. The rest will join Jane Austen's other spinsters, waiting in vain on the village shelf. At some point, it is best to compromise and accept the curate's offer and be done with it. In the end, something, however meagre, is better than nothing – well, OK ... I grant you, there are some circumstances when nothing at all *is* better than the very meagre pickings that are sometimes on offer. But you get what I mean: you can't go on searching for Mr or Miss Right forever. Biology waits for no one.

Emily Stone and her colleagues surveyed the mating preferences of some 4,500 men and 5,300 women from thirty-six cultures round the world. They found that men dropped their standards of mate choice as the sex ratio became increasingly male-biased (more men than women, so creating more competition for women) and raised their standards (at least for long-term mates) when the sex ratio became more female-biased (i.e. when men were in short supply). More important, it seemed that men switched to more casual sex when they were in the minority – when women were forced to compete for men and, as a result, could exert less power over them. When there were fewer women available and men were forced to compete for women, men became more willing to accept committed relationships.

Although wealth and status tend to place men at an advantage compared with their competitors in the mating market, the decision on whom to choose actually lies with the women. Some surprising evidence of this came from our national mobile phone database. Vasyl Palchykov, a young Ukrainian graduate student in Kimmo Kaski's statistical physics group at Aalto University, looked at how the two sexes allocate their phone calls to the two people they called most often. He was interested in how likely the best 'friend' (the person they phoned most often) was to be male or female at any given age – in effect an index of the relative preference for one sex over the other. The data showed that, in early adolescence, a woman's best friend (the person she calls most often) is likely to be another female; but after about age eighteen, it switches to become increasingly male, reaching a peak in the early twenties that remains relatively stable until age forty, after which it falls rapidly to become female again at around age fifty-five, remaining consistently female-biased into old age. Males follow a reciprocal, but slightly different pattern: after a male-biased preference during adolescence, a male's main call partner becomes increasingly female-biased up to the age of thirty, after which it peaks briefly and then declines steadily towards a low level of female bias roughly similar to that exhibited by females.

Two things stood out in these data. One was the fact that the female curve hits its peak about seven years earlier than the male's does (at age twenty-three versus age thirty). The other was that it remains at this peak for much longer (until age forty-five versus age thirty-five in males). In other words, women maintain a focus on their partner/spouse for about three times longer than men do – for about twenty-one years compared to at most seven years for men. This tells us two things about romantic relationships. One is that women typically make a very early decision on which male to go for and they stick with it, constantly contacting him until even the dullest male finally realises and caves in. It looks like it takes the male around five years to wake up – or, at least, respond reciprocally – to this. This suggests that female choice is the norm in humans, as it is in many other mammals. Whatever men may do by way of display to attract the attention and interest of women, it is the women that ultimately decide whom to go with. Once a relationship has been established, it seems that the men lose interest long before the women do: their focus on the female partner lasts only a few years and then declines steadily down to a token level by middle age. The things you can learn about people from their phone calls . . .

The chemistry of romance

Romance is a particularly intense form of relationship, so it is perhaps not surprising that it involves some relatively specialised mechanisms designed to make this possible. Much fuss has been made, as we saw in chapter 7, of the role of oxytocin in pair-bonding and other close relationships. And indeed, our large-scale genetic study confirmed that oxytocin is indeed involved: the genes for the oxytocin receptors correlated strongly with indices of romantic relationship quality, including the Sociosexual Orientation Index that measures your predisposition to be promiscuous. There were important sex differences, with stronger effects in women, at least for some of the oxytocin genes. Having the right oxytocin genes makes you more affiliative towards and trusting of your partner (an attitude that is probably enhanced by oestrogen in women), but endorphins give you long-term bonding stability and dopamine creates that sense of excitement provided by the relationship, especially a newly formed one. Having the right oxytocin genes predisposes you to taking the risk of declaring your love, but the other two neurochemicals are what build the relationship once your offer has been accepted.

At the cognitive level, something else seems to be going on too. Some years ago, the neuroscientists Samir Zeki and Andreas Bartels showed that people who were deeply in love exhibited heightened activity in certain brain regions when looking at pictures of their beloved compared to pictures of other people. Aside from areas like the striatum that are associated with reward and the cingulate cortex and insula (which have associations with sexual activity, as well as endorphins and dopamine), there was *reduced* activity in the amygdala (the area associated, in particular, with fear and sadness responses) and in the temporal and prefrontal lobes (areas associated with mentalising and rational thinking, and in the latter case emotions). In a later study, they found similar responses in mothers looking at pictures of their babies, suggesting that maternal love and romantic love may share the same neurological underpinnings. The suppression of activity in the prefrontal cortex (essentially, the conscious-thinking part of the brain) is particularly interesting because it implies that something is switching off the ability to think too critically about the other person. It is reminiscent of an earlier study by Vinod Goel and Ray Dolan which showed that, when religious belief inhibits the ability to solve logical-reasoning tasks, there is reduced activity in the prefrontal cortex.

If you think about it, religious people, and especially those in the more ecstatic sects, have the same kind of dreamy, everything-in-the-world-is-wonderful demeanour that people in love do. In many such cases, of course, that is exactly what has happened: they have fallen in love with God. I have discussed a lot of this in more detail in an earlier book (*The Science of Love and Betrayal*), so I won't repeat it all here. Suffice it to say that falling in love, or just becoming besotted with anyone or anything (including your pet dog), seems to switch off the rational capacities of the brain that would normally allow us to evaluate other people and situations more critically and sceptically. Of course, this makes it possible for us to give ourselves wholly and unstintingly to the object of our affections without being too shy and retiring or too critical of their behaviour. In a word, your rational thinking centres are being deliberately switched off so that you don't ask too many questions and give up too early.

Sandra Murray has provided some behavioural evidence to support this. In a study of young married couples, she found that the more someone idealised their partner (i.e. switched off their reality check) at the outset of the relationship, the longer they continued to be satisfied with the relationship. And the more this was reciprocated, the more likely the relationship was to last. The moment reality strikes, and you begin to see your partner for what he or she really is, there is a slow but steady erosion in relationship satisfaction that can only ever have one outcome. Being unrealistic about your partner's shortcomings is not, it seems, a recipe for disaster in a relationship, but a recipe for success. Of course, in the end, it is all about trade-offs: how much disappointment can you put up with before you finally pull the plug? But if stability of relationship and a less disrupted life is what you want, then the longer the illusion lasts the better.

These inhibitory effects are probably important in enabling relationships to get off the ground in the first place. Somebody has to be willing to risk rejection by declaring their interest, otherwise nothing will ever get started. Something is needed to get us off the will-she/won't-she fence so as to initiate the process of relationship-building. It seems that women are more willing to do that than men, providing they have found someone that satisfies most of their requirements. These processes also apply to friendships, of course. Friendships have to be created, and that means someone has to take the plunge and make an opening bid to establish interest. You only know that I am interested in a friendship or a romantic relationship with you because I somehow make it obvious by turning up on your doorstep over and over and over again.

Pointing the finger of blame

There is one aspect of compatibility that is worth considering because a mismatch between two people at the outset of a relationship is likely to spell disaster later. There are a number of anatomical indices of mating systems that hold quite generally across the mammals. One is the relative size of the canines (larger in males than in females in species that mate promiscuously and males have to fight each other to monopolise matings with females; of similar size in species that mate monogamously). Another is the relative size of the male's testes (large relative to body size in promiscuous species, small in monogamous species). The reason for the latter is very simple: in species where males have to fight to mate with females, the more sperm he can inseminate a female with, the more chance he has that it will be his sperm rather than someone else's that fertilises her egg(s). In addition, males often only have a narrow window in which they are competitive enough to be able to mate, so they need a large reserve of sperm to ensure that they don't run out while mating with several females in rapid succession. Sperm being expensive to produce, the males in pair-bonded species can afford to reduce investment in sperm production and, as they say, take life easy.

A more surprising index, however, is the relative lengths of the index (second) and ring (fourth) fingers, otherwise known as the 2D4D (D for digit) ratio. In primates, monogamous species like gibbons have a ratio close to equality, whereas highly promiscuous species like chimpanzees have a ratio that is significantly less than one (index finger much shorter than ring finger). Evolutionary psychologists have conventionally held to the view that, on average, women tend to be more monogamous and men more predisposed to be promiscuous, and broadly speaking there is a lot of evidence to support this split. And this is reflected in the two sexes' 2D4D ratios: women tend to have ratios that approximate equality, whereas men tend to have ratios that are less than one (index finger shorter than ring finger).

Rafael Wlodarski had collected a lot of data on sexual behaviour and sexual attitudes as part of one of his projects. One of the questionnaires he had used was the Sociosexual Orientation Index, or SOI, part of which measures your predilection to mate monogamously or promiscuously. We were also able to get hold of a dataset on 2D4D ratios through the good offices of John Manning, a former colleague. As had been found before, overall men were more on the promiscuous side and women more on the monogamous side. But what struck us very quickly was that on both indices the two sexes actually seemed to consist of two distinct sub-populations – a more and a less promiscuous group. Overall, in both sexes, the frequency of these two types was close to 50:50 (a 57:43 split in favour of promiscuity in men, and 47:53 split in favour of monogamy in women).

This raises an obvious dilemma. If you choose partners at random, you have a roughly 25 per cent chance that both of you are monogamous (nirvana!), and a 25 per cent chance that both of you are promiscuous (presumably another kind of nirvana, providing you don't mind what your partner gets up to). But there is a 50 per cent chance that one of you is monogamous and the other promiscuous, which sounds like a perfect-storm disaster. One solution, of course, is to pick your partner very carefully, and that means having cues that identify people's sexual preferences. The differences in 2D4D ratio are far too small to recognise by eyesight (we are dealing with differences of a few millimetres), making it unlikely that this would ever be used as a cue. However, we do have plenty of behavioural cues.

The 2D4D ratio has long been known to be under the influence of fetal testosterone: the higher the maternal testosterone levels during pregnancy, the more extreme (i.e. promiscuous) the offspring's 2D4D ratio will be. In our big genetics sample, Rafael spent a great deal of time collecting scans of participants' hands so that he could measure their 2D4D ratios to compare with both SOI scores and gene patterns. What emerged from this analysis was that, in women in particular, there was a robust relationship between their 2D4D ratio and their testosterone, endorphin and vasopressin genes. Moreover, this effect influenced impulsivity (the willingness to act first and think about the consequences afterwards): more masculinised women (those with lower 2D4D ratios) were more impulsive and more impetuous, and more likely to discount the future. There was also some suggestion of a relationship with specific dopamine receptor genes, implying a thrill-seeking element to extrapair matings.

There is a residual question, especially given the current enthusiasm in some quarters for polyamory: is it possible to have two romantic relationships simultaneously? Might a couple who are both at the promiscuous end of the 2D4D ratio find they can manage a more open relationship without the risk of jealousy arising? History offers us many examples of semi-open marriages, including Friedrich Engels (Karl Marx's famous co-author), the philosopher Friedrich Nietzsche, the writers Aldous Huxley and Vita Sackville-West, and the physicist Erwin Schrödinger (he of Schrödinger's Cat fame) – although it isn't always clear how willing the third parties in these *ménages-à-trois* actually were. Famously, the wife of Joseph Smith, the founder of the Mormons, needed to be persuaded by Smith that God had ordered him to take on a second wife before she acquiesced – laying the foundations for polygamy in the Mormons that continue to this day, at least in some sects. By and large, the ethnographic evidence suggests that polygamous marriages are not as advantageous for women as monogamous marriages in the same culture, partly because the husband's resources and input are divided many ways and partly because of social and psychological stresses generated between the women.

By chance, Max Burton's survey of relationships gave us some unexpected insights into this question. The survey revealed that around 9 per cent of people admitted to having an extrapair romantic relationship, or lover, in addition to their official partner. That's very close to the estimated rate of genetic non-paternity in humans (estimated to range between 3–13 per cent). However, the extra demand imposed by this additional relationship did not lead to a further reduction in the size of the support clique, as it should have done if both relationships were emotionally draining. This suggests that the formal partner (the spouse) no longer carried the same emotional weight and had been sidelined. This seemed to be the case: only 15 per cent of the respondents who admitted to having a lover included their official spouse as well as their lover in their 5-layer. For the rest, the spouse had been demoted to a lower ranking layer. This strongly suggests that the emotional intensity of a romantic relationship makes it all but impossible to have two of these at the same time. One can, of course, have sexual relationships with two, maybe more, people simultaneously, but only providing these are not all equally emotionally demanding.

Lessons from the internet

Whether the internet does or does not make us happy or satisfied with life, there is one respect in which the balance sheet is definitely in the negative, and this by a sizeable margin. The internet has become the hunting ground for a community of individuals intent on fleecing the vulnerable and the desperate. Romantic scamming has become big business, with some victims persuaded to part with their entire life savings, not to mention their self-esteem and the fact that the whole experience leaves them psychologically crushed. It has been estimated that in 2011 around 230,000 individuals were scammed in the UK alone, at a financial cost running into several billion pounds sterling. Sad though all these cases are, understanding how these scams work provides us with some extremely valuable insights into how romantic relationships work and, in particular, the processes of courtship and relationship formation.

The Australian psychologist Monica Whitty is one of the leading authorities on romantic scams, and she was responsible for introducing me to this psychologically fascinating phenomenon. I came to appreciate how these hustles work as a result of being on a couple of panels with her at public meetings. Here is how they work.

You respond to an advertisement on a dating site of some kind because you are lonely, and the person seems nice enough from their profile. From the moment of that first nibble on the bait, the scammer starts to reel you in slowly but surely. After a few desultory email exchanges, they ask you about yourself while expressing interest in meeting someone like you who can reciprocate their need for intimacy. They court you assiduously, asking how you are, expressing their love, perhaps even sending small gifts or flowers or a daily poem (usually plagiarised). The scammers are remarkably skilled at persuading you to tell them about yourself while not giving much away about themselves. If they send a photo, it is usually one of a Greek god or goddess and you can't believe your luck – despite the fact that life's long experience has made it perfectly obvious to you that Greek gods and goddesses have never ever shown the slightest interest in you before. As likely as not, it's been photoshopped from a website for aspiring models.

Gradually, you come to believe it all. Then come the small requests – could you send a present of some expensive perfume, or perhaps a few hundred pounds to pay a debt. Or perhaps the money to buy a plane ticket to come and see you. Unfortunately, once you've sent the money, they were never able to make it owing to being hospitalised by a bad traffic accident or the diagnosis of some dread disease, which needs a bit more money to put them back on their feet. Then comes the sting. A big investment opportunity has come up, or the need for substantial funds to pay for the treatment necessitated by that awful diagnosis. By this stage, against all of your better instincts, you willingly pay up. Alas, the business goes bust despite your generous investment, or the cure doesn't work. But by then it is all too late.

In a recently published study, Monica Whitty examined the traits that make victims vulnerable. She found that around two-thirds of victims are women. They tend to be middle-aged, to score high on impulsivity and sensation-seeking, to be less kind but at the same time more trusting, and to have an addictive personality (which is likely to make them more clingy). Surprisingly, victims also tend to be better educated and better off than non-victims, showing that it wasn't lack of education or experience of the world that caused them to fall victim. Often the shame of having been taken in makes them unwilling to report the scam to the police.

And this points to two key characteristics that scammers target.

The first is that, since they want your money, they are not really interested if you aren't reasonably well off. Once they have established that you don't have any money in the bank or you don't own the house you live in (so it can't be put up as collateral for a loan), they vanish like the Cheshire cat. The second is that they target the lonely, and these are very likely to be people in later life who are divorced or widowed or who, having focused singlemindedly on their careers, have arrived at late middle age only to realise that life is about to pass them by. An air of desperation creeps into their dealings with the social world, and it is this that makes them vulnerable. In a word, it is Jane Austen's village-spinster dilemma: there is no Mr Darcy to sweep you off, the curate has moved on elsewhere, and anything is better than nothing.

Romantic relationships as well as friendships result from our deliberately putting reality on hold: we place a halo round the individual concerned. Not to put too fine a point on it, it is not another person that we fall in love with, but an avatar that we have created in our mind. In the normal course of life, the time we spend with the person concerned provides us with an element of ground-truthing: we learn that they are not as perfect as we first thought and we arrive at some kind of sensible compromise. Since scammers are very careful not to disclose who they really are, our minds run away with us and the avatar becomes more and more exaggerated. Eventually, we are so deeply in love with the avatar that we can no longer distinguish between avatar and reality.

At this point, victims become completely forgiving. If they eventually do get to meet the scammer and they turn out not to look remotely like the picture they sent, the dupe will simply make excuses for them. Their response is often that the scammer realised that the victim would be put off by a real photo, and their love for the victim was so great they didn't want that to happen. The extent of this head-over-heels immersion was so great, Monica Whitty once told me, that you could go round with the police and show them the evidence that they had been scammed and they would accept it and agree to terminate contact. Yet a few weeks later they would be back in contact with the scammer, being mugged by them again. And when you then asked them why, they were full of excuses about how the scammer really was *so* nice and confessed that they had behaved badly and that all they really wanted was a bit of help, but they just didn't know where to start getting that . . . So the victim had forgiven them and had restarted the relationship afresh. In short, the victim preferred to believe what they longed to be true, rather than the evidence that had been put in front of them. Friendships work in much the same way, but the stakes are usually lower and less emotionally damaging when we find we've made a mistake.

This is not to say that we cannot meet and make friends or romantic relationships on the internet. Monica Whitty has estimated that as many as 23 per cent of internet users in the UK have met someone online they didn't know, and that 6 per cent of married couples met their current partner online. A Pew Research Center survey in 2013 found that one in ten Americans had used online dating sites, around two-thirds of whom had dated someone they had met online and a quarter of whom went on to form a long-term relationship. Most of the people who advertise on dating websites are perfectly genuine: they too are looking for a companion or someone to love. It is just that the risks are greater. It is the 5 per cent of sharks that we need to beware of, and our problem is how to recognise them before they have swallowed us alive.

*

Romantic relationships are founded on the need for intensely intimate relationships in which sex provides both part of the glue (it triggers the release of oxytocins, endorphins and dopamine in large quantities) and part of the biological function (reproduction). The majority of these are, of course, heterosexual, but the principles if not the function apply equally to gay and lesbian romantic relationships. In both cases, the dynamics of the relationship are animated by sex differences in psychology and behaviour, and it is to this thorny topic that we turn in the next chapter.

13

The gendering of friendship

Here's something to check out next time you are at a reception or a party. Look for same-sex pairs who are engaged in conversation and make a note of how they are standing. You will notice that the women tend to stand facing each other, but men almost always stand at an angle of about 120 degrees so that they are looking across each other rather than staring directly into each other's eyes. It is not that men can't stand face to face, because if they are talking to a woman they often will. It seems to be that they find staring into other men's eyes discomfiting – probably because the only time men do stare straight into each other's eyes is when they are being threatening.

Current fashion has it that sex differences are only skin-deep, an artefact of upbringing and the patriarchy. Parenting is responsible for boys' antisocial behaviour as adults, as well as girls' nurturing attitudes. If we only set our minds to it, so the story runs, we could raise boys to be girls, and the world would be a better place. This has resulted in a conspicuous tendency to focus on the similarities between the sexes in order not to confront the differences. As John Archer, an authority on aggression and a leading evolutionary psychologist, humorously observed, this is a bit like saying that men and women have bodies that are identical because they have two legs and two arms, while studiously ignoring all the other ways in which they differ in between. Even if we ignore the reproductive components, women lack the physical upper-body strength of men and cannot run as fast. But these differences pale into insignificance by comparison with the differences in social style, whose origins ultimately lie in the conspicuous differences in reproductive biology.

This gendered (social) world

Most societies have encouraged women to dress modestly, often in rather uniform ways: examples include the demure, plain clothing of the Hutterite women and the burkas of the Middle East (which are not, incidentally, enjoined or required by Islam, even though modesty is). In some societies, women were shut away in women-only quarters – the harems and zenanas of the historical Islamic world – from puberty onwards. Many small-scale traditional societies physically separated boys and girls once they reached puberty, in some cases by insisting that they occupy separate men's and women's sleeping houses. You might think that, in the modern secular world, we have dispensed with all this enforced separation between the sexes. Superficially, we have. But it is still there, and glaringly obvious if you know where to look for it.

One of these contexts is whom we talk to. Social networks have a very strong degree of gender homophily. Around 70 per cent of women's personal social networks consist of women, and around 70 per cent of men's social networks consist of men (with most, but not all, of the cross-gender members being family members over whom we have little choice). When Clare Mehta and JoNell Strough asked a group of American adolescents to list their close friends from home and school, 72 per cent were same-sex. In a survey of American adults, Heidi Reeder found that 65 per cent of young men's friends and 80 per cent of young women's friends were same-sex. In a study of friendships in an American housing project for the elderly, 73 per cent of friends were same-sex.

In a study of young adults in their twenties, Suzanna Rose found that single women and married individuals of both sexes preferred same-sex friends because they provided more help and greater loyalty than cross-sex friends. Nearly half of all the married women and a third of the married men declared that they had no cross-sex friends at all other than their spouse. The women tended to see cross-sex friends as providing less intimacy, less acceptance and less companionship than same-sex friends. Same-sex friends scored higher than cross-sex friends on acceptance, effort, communication, common interests and affection. Ominously, cross-sex friendships scored higher on sexual attraction – raising that hoary old question yet again of whether it is ever possible to form friendships with members of the opposite sex without sex intervening. Importantly, women were not generally motivated by sexual attraction in forming cross-sex friendships, but men were. It's almost as though sex is a consequence of friendship for women, but a cause of friendship for men.

Remarkably, and rather unexpectedly, this segregation by sex even turns up in our conversations. We had, as I explained in chapter 9, been interested in the size of conversation groups, and had been sampling these in the streets, cafés, shopping centres, parties, pubs and parks of our cities, recording who was talking to whom. Looking at the data from these various studies, it was obvious that so long as there were no more than four people in the conversation, the composition was as likely to be mixed-sex as it was single-sex. But once the social group in which the conversation was embedded increased beyond four people, it was more and more likely to split into single-sex conversations. Even our samples of conversations in Iran showed the same effect, so this was a cross-cultural phenomenon. The surprise was how quickly conversations became segregated by sex. Have a look next time you are at a large reception or party. Once you know what to look for, it is obvious.

In fact, this tendency to segregate by sex appears even more strongly in respect of best friends. In Anna Machin's romantic partners sample, 85 per cent of the women who reported having a best friend stated that this friend was female, and 78 per cent of the men who reported having a best friend stated that the friend was male. Tamas Dàvid-Barrett analysed 20,000 randomly sampled Facebook profile photographs and found that if there were two people of similar age in the photo, it was likely to be a girl's account, with an evens likelihood that the other person was a male (the boyfriend or partner) or another girl (most of whom will be the best girlfriend, or Best Friend Forever). If the photograph contained more than three people, it was almost always a boy's account, and it would be a group of guys, usually engaged in some activity – the five-a-side Friday evening soccer team, a climbing or canoeing group, or just a bunch of guys at the pub. Girls seem to prefer the intimacy of dyadic relationships, whereas boys prefer the anonymity of groups.

These differences between the two sexes seem to reflect striking differences in the way men and women think about relationships and the processes they use to service them. In chapter 5, I mentioned that, in our longtitudinal study of young adults, girls' friendships were less likely to decay if they invested more time in talking to the friend, whereas this had absolutely no impact on how likely boys' friendships were to survive; what influenced the survival of boys' friendships was whether they invested more time in 'doing stuff' together (going out to the pub, playing football or other games, or engaging in some other physical activity). In the experimental study of Hamilton's Rule run by Elainie Madsen and Richard Tunney in which we asked subjects to incur pain for a monetary reward that would benefit someone else, women treated their same-sex best friend as though they were a sibling, whereas men treated their same-sex best friend as though they were a cousin. In other words, women's close friendships are much closer and hence more intense than men's are, more like the kind of relationship we typically have with romantic partners.

Jacob Vigil found a similar difference between the two sexes in the amount of time that young adults devoted to talking together (by phone or face-to-face): the women spent an average 17.5 hours talking to their best friend (much of it sharing intimacies), whereas the men spent only twelve hours doing so. As in our study, he found that males preferred to engage in physical activities rather than conversation. In the face of social stress, males preferred to avoid sympathy and comfort from others, responding with behaviours that promote distancing in order to be left alone; females, in contrast, were more likely to respond with behaviours such as crying that promote sympathy and comforting, and hence approach. There is a similar difference in the two sexes' responses to danger: women are likely to scream, whereas men freeze and are more likely to be silent or, if they vocalise at all, to swear. Check it out when you next go on a roller-coaster ride.

Shira Gabriel and Wendi Gardner asked adults to complete a large number of self-referential statements ('I am . . .') and found that women were more likely to give descriptions emphasising intimate relationships, while men focused on collective aspects of interdependence (e.g. group membership). When asked to read short vignettes describing an emotional experience and later recall the details, women were more likely to remember the relational aspects of the stories, whereas men were more likely to remember the collective aspects. In her study on the differences between how the two sexes view their romantic partners and best friends, Anna Machin found that women expressed greater intimacy than men in respect of their best friends, although the two sexes did not differ in respect of their romantic partners. Women's intimacy towards their best friend was associated with similarity in educational level, humour, dependability and happiness, whereas men's relationships with their best friends were associated with the duration of the friendship, the similarity of their financial potential, gregariousness, dependability and their social connections, suggesting that intimacy in men's relationships is underpinned by very different dynamics than those in women's relationships.

These differences in friendship style have implications for another curious aspect of human behaviour, namely the formation of clubs. Clubs seem to form an especially important feature of human social organisation, in many cases playing an important role in who becomes friends with who. Indeed, they often seem to provide an environment in which close friendships are built up between people who have been arbitrarily thrown together through membership of the club. Kinship (the extended family) is a club in this sense; so are the professions, religions, hobby and sports clubs, dining clubs, debating clubs, and every other interest group you can think of from Rotary and Round Table to the Masons and the secret societies of tribal societies. They are all about fellowship in one form or another. Some of these we choose to join, others, like the extended family or Hindu castes, we are born into and have no choice over whom we share membership of the club with. However, there are striking differences in how the two sexes relate to clubs. Men seem to enjoy, and work more effectively, in clubs. A set of experiments on cooperation in groups by the American evolutionary psychologist Rob Kurzban suggested that men formed a coordinated group much more readily and cooperated more effectively as a group than women did, when success on a task (and hence the money earned) depended on the degree of coordination as a group.

Clubs are often associated with rituals and other paraphernalia (such as forms of dress or special tableware) designed to differentiate social groups within the community by creating a sense of exclusivity. This kind of clubbishness seems to be especially congenial to men, who seem to enjoy the ritual aspects offered by formal speeches, songs, toasts and parades that require a level of self-discipline, attention to a master of ceremonies and willingness to be silent – especially so when these groups are all-male. In such contexts, men are often content to sit in silence even during periods between phases of the event when conversation would in fact be possible. Women do not seem to find these kinds of social environments so congenial, and would rather form small conversational groups. It's a pattern very familiar to late-night taxi drivers: a group of boys being taken home after a night out almost always travel in silence, whereas a group of girls will talk nineteen to the dozen, with several conversations running over the top of each other. If you don't believe me, try asking your driver next time you are in a taxi. This seems to reflect the sex difference in friendship style, where women's friends are focused and intimate (individual relationships are more important than membership of the group), while men's friendships are casual and involve what is almost an anonymous group (membership of the group is more important than the individual members themselves).

A mind of her own

Anne Campbell (the title of whose classic book I have used as my section title in tribute to her) was, until she died just a couple of years ago, one of the leading British evolutionary psychologists. She had a particular interest in women's psychology and behaviour, and made a very strong pitch for the view that, notwithstanding feminism's reluctance to endorse evolutionary psychology, in actual fact the two approaches were in very close agreement, with the one providing the evidence needed to support the other's claims. Most of the work that informed her book, done while she was in the US, had been on girl gangs in New York – a real-life version of *West Side Story*. One of her key observations was that women were often just as aggressive as men, but their aggression was triggered by different circumstances and typically expressed in different ways. Although threats to romantic partners were the ultimate drivers of aggression in both sexes in this particular context, in men it was usually triggered by threats to status, whereas in young women it was more likely to be initiated by threats to their relationships with a boyfriend. Boyfriends provided these girls with access to the resources they wanted (and ultimately needed for their reproductive careers as adults), and they would be fought over just as viciously as boys might fight over territory or reputations. However, when boys fought, they invariably did so physically; in contrast, girls did so psychologically, often by attempting to undermine the sexual reputation and self-confidence of their opponent.

These ethnographic findings have been confirmed in a number of experimental studies. Tania Reynolds and Roy Baumeister (perhaps the leading experimental social psychologist interested in relationships) ran a series of experiments that looked at women's responses to explicit threats to their personal social world. For example, they were shown a photograph of an attractive female labelled with the statement either that 'She has just joined your social group' (a no-threat condition) or 'She has been flirting with your boyfriend' (a threat condition), together with a further set of statements, half of which were positive ('She donates to charity') and half negative ('She cheated on her last boyfriend'). They were then asked to rate how likely they would be to pass on these titbits of gossip to others in their social group. Women were much more likely to gossip about the negative information in the threat condition and the positive information in the no-threat condition, and especially so if they were themselves of a competitive disposition; moreover, they were more likely to do so if the rival was physically attractive or dressed provocatively. In other words, women are more willing to strategically repeat social information about romantic rivals if the rivals are perceived as directly threatening their own romantic relationships.

In a recent, extremely comprehensive review of sex differences in behaviour, John Archer found that while men are more prone to using violence in aggression, are more object-oriented and consistently more sexually oriented than women, women invariably perform better on tests of language competence, are more prosocial and empathic, and are more focused on making careful mate choices. Women are also better at inhibitory and effortful control, especially early in life. One of the studies he cites found large consistent sex differences in risk-taking for potential gain in favour of males in fifty-three countries. Another experimental study of Hadza hunter–gatherers from East Africa found similar sex differences in the male direction for risk-taking in two gambling games.

The relationship between physical violence and males is one of the most consistent universals. This is not to say that women never fight physically and never murder using violent means, but their weaker upper-body strength means that such fights are invariably less damaging than those that involve males. For better or worse, as we saw in chapter 11, physical violence, or even just the threat of violence, is an effective first-pass strategy in any conflict for men, and often works – especially if you have the advantage of physical strength or numbers on your side. Women, however, often play an indirect role in this by inciting their menfolk to violence on their behalf.

This contrast is well illustrated in the family sagas of the medieval Icelandic Vikings. Although all but a tiny handful of the murders were perpetrated by men, women often played a crucial role in the background. In the *Völsungasaga*, for example, Brynhild incites her husband Gunnar to kill her former lover, his blood-brother Sigurd, for deceiving her, while in the *Laxdaellasaga* Thorgerd and Gudrun goad their respective menfolk into avenging them for slights they have each received from the other family, with Gudrun even threatening her husband Bolli with divorce if he doesn't join in against his own foster brother Kjartan whom she wants to have killed. In Norse society, male children were often sent to live in an ally's household so as to grow up with the ally's son; this created a lifelong bond between the boys and greatly enlarged the circle of social support on which they could depend later in life. Because of this, both men were very reluctant to become involved in the dispute, but in the end were pressured into doing so – a triumph of romance over friendship.

The impression we have from the sagas (and they are family histories, not fiction) is of men who can easily be goaded into action even against their better judgment, and women who are much more calculating and vengeful. The philosopher Aristotle came to a similar conclusion in 350 BC. Based on close observation of human behaviour, he suggested that men are inclined to act on impulse, whereas women are often cool and calculating. In the memorable lines of the Restoration poet William Congreve:

> Heav'n has no rage, like love to hatred turn'd,
> Nor Hell a fury, like a woman scorn'd.

The two sexes even differ in what triggers jealousy. Analyses by the evolutionary psychologist David Buss, among others, suggest that men are more likely to be upset by a partner's sexual infidelity, whereas women are more likely to become upset by a partner's emotional infidelity. This difference has been attributed to the fact that men are more concerned about the risk of cuckoldry (investing in offspring sired by other males), whereas women are more concerned about their man's limited resources being shared among offspring that are not theirs. This difference in jealousy may, in fact, have an early onset that reflects the emotional intensity and focus of female relationships: girls are likely to become jealous if a close friend starts to form a friendship with someone else, whereas, for boys, it tends to be more an issue of out-of-sight/out-of-mind and who cares (for more on this, see chapter 15).

In large part, we might attribute these differences in social – even if not sexual – jealousy to the fact that women's social skills are markedly better than men's. Men are often astonished and mystified by women's intuition about someone else's mental state. Women just seem to *know* when something isn't quite right, sometimes even when the person is not actually physically present. They often can't tell you why they know, or what it is that made them think this. But they do know it, and they are usually right. It's as though they have a sixth sense that men don't seem to have.

In fact, there is considerable experimental evidence to suggest that women are much more accurate than men in correctly identifying the emotion being expressed in a face. Some years ago, Judith Hall carried out a review of seventy-five studies of sex differences in the ability to decode nonverbal signals, and found a consistent difference in favour of women. Of particular interest, given the sex difference in brain white-matter volume (see chapter 3), women were considerably better than men when both visual and auditory channels were available together than when just one of these was available. They could mix and match information from different sources in ways that men did not seem to be able to do. More recently, she and David Matsumato tested American students on both Caucasian and Japanese photographs of facial expressions, and found that females were more accurate than males even when the photograph was presented so briefly (for just 0.2 seconds) that it was on the very edge of consciousness. In one of many studies carried out by Lisa Feldman Barrett's lab, over 900 people were asked to report on the emotions they felt in response to twenty different social scenarios, as well as the emotions experienced by the person in the scenario. When scored by independent raters, women's responses were consistently marked higher on emotional awareness and depth than the men's responses, even after controlling for age, socio-economic status and verbal intelligence (on which women generally score higher).

This ability to be able to infer other people's emotions is likely to be related to mentalising abilities, a cognitive capacity that we met in chapter 6 as being one of the key determinants of the size of your social network. We have carried out half a dozen studies in which we have measured people's mentalising skills using our multilevel mentalising vignettes task. In every single case except one, women scored significantly higher on mentalising skills than men, and even in the exceptional case the direction was in favour of the women. As with almost all psychological and physical traits, there is considerable overlap between the two sexes (some men are better than some women), but the overall pattern is very consistent (some women are better than all men).

Tina Strombach and Tobias Kalenscher asked subjects in an experiment to decide whether to split a reward with someone from their social circle or take the whole reward for themselves. They were interested in how people coped when making this decision while being asked to do something else at the same time. This design creates what psychologists refer to as a cognitive load: the brain is having to devote some of its resources to another task – much as happens in real life when we are engaged in multi-tasking. An everyday example would be driving while holding a conversation with someone or while listening to the radio. Paying attention to something else inevitably creates a distraction that makes it harder to concentrate on the task we are supposed to be doing. They found that men's performance on the decision task (whether to share the reward or not) was significantly affected by the distraction task (the cognitive load), whereas the women's performance was not (in fact, they even did slightly better when under cognitive load). In other words, women really can multi-task, whereas men do better if they focus on one thing at a time.

It seems that at least some of these sex differences in sociality appear very early in life, and so cannot be a consequence of enculturation or rearing. Jennifer Connellan and Simon Baron-Cohen tested a hundred newborn babies on the attention they showed to a photo of Jennifer's face compared with a mobile which had all the same key face elements (Jennifer's eyes, mouth, etc.) but in a jumble. They measured how much time the babies spent looking when shown each of the shapes in turn (with half seeing the face first and half seeing the mobile first). Around a third of the babies exhibited no preference, but of those that did, male babies showed a stronger preference for the mobile, whereas the girl babies preferred the human face, in both cases with a 2:1

preference ratio. Other studies have shown that young girls are more likely to maintain eye contact with caregivers than boys are, and to understand social faux pas earlier than boys. Broadly speaking, girls and women are more vocal than boys and men, develop language earlier and more effectively than boys, and typically spend more time in conversation – something exemplified by the familiar teenage boys' grunt responses whenever parents try to engage them in conversation. This is also true of monkeys, as Natalie Greeno and Stuart Semple showed in a neat little study of vocalisation frequencies in rhesus macaques: the females just seemed to be more social than the males, suggesting that this trait long pre-dates the appearance of our species and its peculiar parenting habits.

Sex and social style

Ellie Pearce used the data from our big genetics study to look at the factors that correlated with one key index of romantic relationship quality (the Sociosexual Orientation Index) and one index that reflected engagement with the wider social network (the number of close friends in the 5-layer). She found that these two seemed to be underpinned by two very different psychological systems – the first by the level of impulsivity and the anxiety dimension of the Experience of Close Relationships Scale (an index of how warm or cool your relationship style is), the second by the avoidance dimension of the Attachment Scale (a measure of how immersed you feel in your local community and how empathic you are). This was true for both men and women. However, while these two systems appeared to be completely separate in men, they were interconnected in women. In women, the empathy scale interacted rather strongly with the impulsivity scale, suggesting that women considered the implications of their romantic relationships for their wider social networks, allowing them to integrate their love lives with the interests of family and friends in a more effective way than men did.

In Anna Machin's study of close relationships, homophily was important for both romantic relationships and same-sex best friendships. Although sense of humour was a predictor of intimacy in best friendships for women, it had no effect on the intimacy of romantic relationships for either sex. Nor did physical attractiveness or athleticism. For women, intimacy with their romantic partner (as opposed to their best friend) was best predicted by similarity in financial potential, outgoingness, dependability and kindness. It seems that personality, traits related to status and resources, mutual support, interests and shared activities may be more important than anything else. Yet none of these variables had any effect at all on the intimacy of men's romantic relationships, although cooperativeness on the part of the partner came closest to having a significant effect. The only factor that significantly influenced the perceived intimacy of men's relationships was the frequency of contact. That might have as much to do with the fact that men's friendships are dominated, at the best of times, by an out-of-sight-out-of-mind effect.

Intriguingly, gift-giving and the provision of emotional support had opposite effects on intimacy in women's relationships: the more gifts received, the less intimate the relationship, whereas the reverse was true for emotional support (the more support received, the more intimate the relationship). One can understand the second, but the first seems puzzling. A plausible explanation, however, may simply be that gifts are only ever part of the process of *developing* a relationship, not of *maintaining* the relationship once established. Gifts may also be more directly targeted. When he was one of our graduate students, Mark Dyble looked at how much money people actually spent on presents for different people one Christmas. Men and women did not differ in how much they spent on close relatives and friends, but they did differ significantly on how much they spent on less close relatives and friends; women were much more generous than men. And they put much more effort into thinking about suitable presents for each person, and spent more time choosing, than men.

In Anna Machin's friendship study, we were intrigued to find that the two sexes focused on quite different criteria. For women, best friendships were most strongly predicted by the degree of similarity in education, sense of humour, dependability, a happy disposition, number of shared activities, how much mutual support was exchanged and, specifically for same-sex best friends, the frequency of contact via digital means (phone, Facebook, email, etc.). Interestingly, a shared history had a *negative* effect on intimacy in these relationships. For men, best friendships were best predicted by the duration of the friendship, having a shared history, the amount of mutual support exchanged, the number of shared activities and the degree of similarity in financial status (presumably important for sharing rounds at the pub or other social events), outgoingness, dependability and number of social connections. These results held irrespective of the sex of the best friend.

Notice the differences between men and women in this, though. It suggests that intimacy in men's friendships may be underpinned by very different dynamics than intimacy in women's friendships. The fact that shared history had opposite effects on intimacy in men and women is especially notable. Whereas this relationship was positive in men, in women it was negative (the greater the emphasis on a shared history, the lower the level of intimacy). This might reflect the difference between men's preference for group-based activities (for which shared history is usually a strong basis – the club has a history) and women's preference for more intimate dyadic ones (for which shared history might be less important than, for example, current levels of mutual disclosure).

These differences in the underlying dynamics of relationships in the two sexes are well illustrated by some of Joyce Benenson's studies. She has devoted a career to exploring the nature of friendships, and two of her studies are particularly relevant here. In one, she allowed two same-sex friends to spend a short time relaxing together before competing against each other in a gender-neutral online computer game. She found that males spent more time than women did engaged in close proximity and even in physical contact both before competing and while engaged in a short cooperative task after the game. She argued that by exhibiting friendly behaviours both before and after being forced to compete, male pairs are able to communicate willingness to accept the outcome of a competitive event and still cooperate afterwards, thereby limiting the risk that an opponent will take pre-emptive or retaliatory action. Indeed, the men seemed to anticipate the disruption of the competitive task by deliberately being in contact more before it, as though to establish that whatever happened afterwards was not to be taken amiss. The women, at least in this sample, seemed to be less able to do this. Benenson and her co-authors attributed this to the fact that, in our evolutionary history, men, but not women, have had to be able to form functional alliances in order to protect the social group and their interests in it from outside attack – something that is, without exception in ethnographic societies, an exclusively male task and duty. In an earlier study, she had found that males had higher tolerances for the stresses and strains that occur within relationships. We will see in the next chapter that this may have implications for why and when relationships break down.

In another of her studies, two same-sex adults competed in a computer game against a pair of virtual opponents. They were told that they could pursue their own individual strategies or form an alliance, but that their monetary reward for taking part would be determined by how well they did in the game individually. She found that, when the women were told that the opponents had formed an alliance against them, they were much more likely to form a counter-alliance in an attempt to exclude the opponents than men were. When there was no threatened attempt to exclude them, however, males and females behaved identically. These results were similar to ones she had found previously in four-year-old children, where girls were much more likely to respond to social threats by forming exclusionary alliances.

In her book *Women, Men and Language*, the social linguist Jennifer Coates observes that men and women differ radically in their conversational style. Women's conversations have a distinctively cooperative character, with frequent use of 'back-channel' comments ('Yes!', 'Uh-huh!', 'You're so right!') given over the speaker's statements, combined with frequent use of simultaneous endings where the listener repeats the last phrase as the speaker utters it. In contrast, men's conversations are more competitive, even combative, in tenor: their conversations have a more bantering style, back-channel is almost unknown, and speech overlaps are considered plain rude. With these very different conversational styles, it is perhaps not surprising that the two sexes segregate so readily as soon as the conversation group is large enough to allow it. It does, however, mean that conversations between romantic dyads are in danger of crashing headlong into conflict. How on earth do we manage? Sarah Grainger, once one of my graduate students and now a senior Scottish government statistician, watched couples in cafés to see how mixed-sex couples managed this. Half the population won't be surprised to learn that the women typically adjusted their conversational style to suit the man's.

Risk-taking is another aspect of behaviour where there seems to be a consistent sex difference. As teenagers and young adults, boys are generally more willing to take risks, and to take much greater risks, than girls. A rather innocuous example is provided by a couple of studies that Boguslaw Pawlowski, Rajinder Atwal and I carried out some years ago. One looked at how willing people were to risk missing the morning bus into the city centre, given that both its departure time from a particular stop and the delay to the next bus varied unpredictably – with an added piquancy that the study was done in winter, so that missing a bus and having to wait for the next bus incurred not just a time cost but also the cost of hanging around longer in the cold. The other study looked at the slightly more serious risks that adults were willing to take in crossing a busy city-centre road on a pedestrian crossing. In both cases, males made much riskier decisions. Even though the cost of missing the bus and having to wait around in the cold for the next one was not enormous, the men cut it much finer than the women did, and as a result ended up having to hang around longer in the cold waiting for the next bus. In the second case, males, irrespective of age, were much less willing than females to wait for the crossing sign to change, and when they did cross against the lights did so under much riskier conditions (indexed as the distance to an approaching car) than the women. More importantly, males' willingness to cross when cars were close and approaching fast turned out to be a function of whether there were any women standing waiting to cross: they were *much* more willing to take risks when they had a female audience. It seems that risk-taking is a form of mate advertising: see how good my genes are – I can afford to take real risks and get away with it.

There are similarly robust differences in sensation-seeking. One classic, well regarded test for this is Zuckerman's Sensation Seeking Scale, which consists of four subscales: *Thrill and Adventure Seeking* (TAS, indexing activities such as sky-diving and mountain climbing), *Disinhibition* (DIS, indexing behaviours like drug and alcohol abuse, vandalism or unsafe sex), *Experience Seeking* (ES, indexing travel, psychedelic drugs and music) and *Boredom Susceptibility* (BS, indexing proneness to boredom and the need to be doing things such as going to the cinema). Though many of its questions now seem dated, it has been widely used since it was created in the 1970s. This allowed Catharine Cross and Gillian Brown to ask whether sex differences in these aspects of personality had changed in response to changes in cultural aspects of sociality over the thirty-five-years since it was first used. They found that the sex difference in the overall scores had not changed at all. In particular, the differences in the DIS and BS subscale scores had remained very stable. The sex difference in TAS had consistently declined (though it was still detectable), but mainly due to a decline in males' willingness to take part in high-risk activities. In short, there are some sex differences in risk taking which seem to have an underlying biological basis, and it is not at all clear that these can easily be modified.

One final example is the striking sex difference in the form of speech known as 'motherese'. This is the very characteristic speech style that women use naturally when talking to babies. It has a high-pitched, very sing-song, melodious quality with exaggerated pitch contours, and is very repetitive. Babies find it calming. A study by Marilee Monnot showed that babies whose mothers spent more time speaking in this way gained weight faster and passed key developmental stages earlier. No matter how hard they try, men are very bad at this, not least because their natural voice pitch is too low and they cannot raise it anywhere near high enough. As a result, they tend to frighten rather than calm babies. Which rather undermines recent well-meaning but misguided attempts to rename it 'parentese'. Alas, a change in name doesn't obviate the inconvenient fact that men's voice pitch is an octave lower than women's.

Sex differences in cognition

Here are two anatomical differences between the sexes that might surprise you. You're off to buy shower gel and you look along the shelves for the one you like. You might notice that soaps and shower gels are shelved by sex, and the ones on the women's shelves are completely different (and probably more expensive). Have you ever wondered why there are separate shower gels for men and women? It isn't just so that manufacturers can charge more for women's products. A few years ago they discovered that men are more sensitive to rough textures on the skin, whereas women are more sensitive to smooth textures. So they make men's shower gels coarser and women's smoother. There isn't such thing as a gender-neutral soap that everyone will like.

The second oddity may be even more surprising. You will be aware that colour vision depends on three different kinds of receptor cells (or cones) in the retina at the back of your eye. Each is sensitive to light of a different wavelength – at roughly 430, 545 and 570 nanometres wavelength, which we see as blue, green and red. The green and red receptors are coded on the X chromosome, whereas blue is coded on chromosome 7. This is why red-blindness (the inability to see the colour red) only occurs in males: as males have only one X chromosome, they are in trouble if their red-cone gene is defective, whereas women always have a back-up on their other X chromosome. In addition, the red-cone gene is particularly variable in the precise wavelength of light to which it is most sensitive. As a result, it often happens that women (but never men) can detect two slightly different versions of the colour red – red and near-red – if they have inherited genes for red cones that differ slightly in their peak sensitivity. This condition is known as *tetrachromacy*, or four-colour vision, and is much more common than most people realise: estimates vary, but perhaps as many as a quarter of all women have it. Much rarer is pentachromacy in which women can distinguish five different colours – red, near-red, green, near-green, and blue. This kind of sex difference is not, as it turns out, all that unusual. Although all Old World monkeys and apes have three-colour vision, the females of some New World monkeys have perfectly normal three-colour vision but the males have only two of the three (and not always the same two). So if a man wonders why he sometimes gets into trouble when asked if two items of his partner's clothing go together and he says: 'Yes, of course they do' when it is quite obvious to her that they clash, there may be a very simple explanation. There is an obvious lesson here, guys: be more ambivalent next time.

In fact, the brain is full of sex differences. Here are three for starters: male brains are bigger than female brains (by about 10 per cent, roughly equivalent to the average difference in body size), whereas female brains have much more white matter (the neurons that act as the wiring connecting up different units within the brain) and a larger prefrontal cortex. Female brains also reach adulthood earlier than male brains, paralleling the age difference in social maturity. The white-matter difference has important implications for the ability to integrate processing in different parts of the brain, and so might explain women's better skills at multitasking. It may also mean that they are better at integrating information from different senses, since these are usually processed in different parts of the brain. That may allow women to make more effective discriminations in the social domain between different individuals – and hence to find some kind of balance between competing criteria in mate choice. In addition, there is evidence from neuroimaging studies that women have larger volumes in the right prefrontal cortex, and especially the orbitofrontal cortex – areas that seem to be crucially involved both in managing social emotional responses, mentalising and social network size (as we saw in chapters 3 and 6).

While the two sex chromosomes, X and Y, are clearly responsible for determining our biological sex, these sometimes get duplicated during the production of gametes (or sex cells), leading to unusual combinations. The most common of these are XXY or XXXY (Klinefelter's Syndrome, with frequencies of around one in every 1,000 and one in every 50,000 male births, respectively), XYY (Supermale Syndrome, one in every 1,000 male births), and X0 (Turner Syndrome, one in every 5,000 female births). Many people with these combinations suffer from developmental disabilities of one kind or another, and in some cases may be sterile.

A female body plan and brain is the default in mammals. The switch over to the male phenotype is triggered by the Y chromosome stimulating the production of testosterone part way through foetal development. In fact, this is about the only thing the Y chromosome seems to do. However, it depends on an environmental trigger, known as 'the race to be male'. It will only do this if the foetal body has built up a large enough store of fat cells (one reason why male babies are larger at birth). This can fail to happen, especially if the foetus is starved at some crucial point. When the switch doesn't happen, the gonads fail to produce enough testosterone during foetal development to switch the default female brain over into a male brain, and as a result they fail to develop a male body plan (though they may have a more masculinised body shape after puberty and be unusually good athletes). These women have male XY sex chromosomes but are anatomically and psychologically female, though usually infertile with non-functional gonads – the problem that caused the effect in the first place. This is known as Swyer Syndrome, and has a frequency of around 1 in every 100,000 female births.

Perhaps the most confusing case was that of Foekje Dillema, the Dutch 200m women's world record holder during the 1940s. Although she refused to take a genetic sex test when these were introduced in 1950 (causing much angst among the sports authorities of the day), subsequent tests indicated that, although she was phenotypically female, genetically she was an XX/XY mosaic (some of her cells were XX and some XY). Mosaic genetics of various kinds are by no means rare in animals (and are very common indeed in plants), but a sex mosaic of this kind seems to be extremely unusual, especially in humans. It's a reminder that nothing is ever simple in biology.

These unusual genetic combinations provide us with natural experiments that provide insights into the X and Y chromosomes' respective contributions to cognitive differences between the sexes. Ivanka Savic, at the famous Karolinska Neuroscience Institute in Stockholm, scanned the brains of XY and XXY males (normal and Klinefelter's individuals, respectively) and normal XX females, and measured their circulating sex hormones from blood samples. She found that the more X chromosomes someone had, the smaller were the volumes of the amygdala, caudate, temporal and insular units (many of which are associated with emotional responses) and the larger the volumes of the parietal lobe and parts of the frontal lobe bordering on the orbitofrontal cortex. The Y-chromosome itself seemed to have no detectable effects. There was, in addition, evidence that testosterone levels were associated with some of these differences in a way that suggested a modifying influence. It seems that the cerebellum and parts of the motor cortex are under the control of X chromosome genes which have no equivalents on the Y chromosome, while the limbic structures such as the amygdala and parahippocampus are under the combined influence of testosterone and X chromosome genes that have Y chromosome equivalents. Judy van Hemmen from the Free University, Amsterdam, undertook a similar analysis of Swyer Syndrome (XY) women and found that, essentially, they had brains with a more female-like structure, again suggesting that circulating testosterone normally plays a key role in the switch over to male brains during early development but didn't do so in their case. These results seem to parallel the effects of genomic imprinting, which suggest that our limbic system (our emotional responsiveness) derives from our paternal genes, while those that determine our neocortex (smart-thinking capacity) derive from our maternal genes (see chapter 3).

There is increasing evidence that male and female brains may process tasks in different ways even though they do not differ in performance. Emily Bell and her colleagues at the University of Alberta in central Canada looked at where in the brain men and women processed three different kinds of cognitive task: a word-generation task, a spatial-attention task and a memory task. Even though the cognitive tasks are not, by the remotest stretch of the imagination, social in character and so might not be expected to differ between the sexes, men and women deal with them in different parts of the brain. In the word task, men showed more activity in the prefrontal cortex (suggesting they were having to think harder about it) and in the parietal lobe and cingulate brain areas than women, while in the memory task men exhibited more activity than women in parts of the parietal lobe and the occipital lobe – in both cases without differing in how well they did the task.

The urban myth would have us believe that men do better than women on spatial or mapping tasks. However, this does depend on just what kind of task is involved. In Emily Bell's study, men did better than women on a spatial attention task even though there were no differences in how this task was being processed in the brain. However, when Elizabeth Weiss and her colleagues at Innsbruck University in Austria looked at a spatial rotation task (the ability to imagine how shapes turn in space, a trait important in mapping), they found striking sex differences as to where in the brain the two sexes processed this task: male processing involved much more activation in the parietal cortex whereas female processing involved more in the right frontal cortex (an area especially associated with active thinking). There is some evidence from longitudinal imaging studies that these differences arise quite early in childhood and maintain themselves through adolescence into adulthood.

Alice Proverbio and her colleagues at the University of Milan showed pictures of people and pictures of scenes to men and women and recorded their brains' electrical activity while they looked at them. Women showed a much larger response to the social scenes than men did, especially in parts of the temporal lobe and the cingulate cortex. In other words, women seem to be naturally more responsive to the social world than men are. In his analyses of the UK Biobank (see chapter 3), Danilo Bzdok found that there were striking differences between the two sexes in the way the brain's reward circuit (in particular, the nucleus accumbens) varied with different indices of sociality: men who had few close relationships, had smaller social circles and were of lower socio-economic status had a smaller nucleus accumbens, but there were no such effects in women. The volume of the ventromedial prefrontal cortex was, however, greater in women who expressed greater satisfaction with their family relationships; in men, the volume of this region correlated only with the number of sexual partners. Since the ventromedial cortex is in part associated with the experience of reward, this suggests that men and women may find different parts of the social process rewarding (interacting with others in one case, having sex with them in the other).

These differences in reward-system neuroanatomy are replicated in the physiology of these systems. In a recent study, Tobias Kalenscher found sex differences in how men and women respond to dopamine when engaged in experiments that invited them to share a monetary reward with someone else. When their brains' responsiveness to dopamine was chemically reduced, women became more selfish but men became more prosocial. In a parallel neuroimaging study, they found that women showed an increase in activation in the striatum (a region of the brain associated with dopamine uptake) – but nowhere else – when making prosocial decisions compared with selfish decisions, but men exhibited no changes.

Sometimes the effects of genetics on sociality are mediated by other aspects of personality. In our big genetics study, Ellie Pearce was able to show that the influence of the dopamine receptor genes on the Sociosexual Orientation Index (SOI, measuring the predisposition to promiscuity) in men was mediated by impulsiveness. In contrast, in women, variation in the endorphin receptor and vasopressin genes independently affected Openness to Experience, which in turn influenced SOI score. Similarly, the effect of the endorphin receptor genes on the number of close friends women had was mediated by the extraversion personality dimension – but not in men.

*

It is clear, looking back over this brief summary of some of the evidence for sex differences in sociality and its underpinning neurobiology, that the two sexes effectively live in two very different social worlds. This is not to say that they are incompatible, but simply that they approach relationships in very different ways. That said, it is important to remember that these sex differences are not absolutes: they are simply the means of two distributions that overlap to some extent. The analogy is with stature: men are, on average, taller than women, but not all men are taller than all women. Where stature is the main factor influencing a trait, men and women will differ, but some women will exhibit that trait more than some men. At the same time, we should not over-generalise. The fact that there are deep-rooted sex differences in *social* style does not mean that there are differences in all traits.

Why friendships end

Here's the shortest story ever told, a story in just two sentences:

'I'm leaving you!'
'Who is he/she?'

So attuned are we to the nature of human psychology that we can weave the rest of the story around just these six words with no difficulty at all. We immediately know the back-story, what each of the protagonists is thinking and feeling. We know what will happen next, where it will all end up. Not only is this a tribute to our extraordinary mentalising abilities and the way that these allow us to see into the minds of other people, but it probably also reflects the fact that relationships break down often enough in real life that we are already half-expecting the answer after the first sentence. The UK Office of National Statistics estimated that, in 2012, 42 per cent of all UK marriages ended in divorce.

Relationships die in one of two ways – by gradually fading out or by cataclysmic collapse. We tend to associate the latter with romantic relationships, probably because most of these inevitably do end in very public acrimony. Friendships, on the other hand, typically involve less intimacy, so they have less far to fall. As a result, they more often just fizzle out quietly. I just don't bother seeing you so often, and gradually you fade from my memory as you slide down through the layers of my friendship network to join the passing acquaintances and also-rans in the outermost layers. Close friendships, however, often behave much more like romantic relationships. And so may close family relationships.

That friendship and kinship relationships differ became clear from our study of relationships in young adults moving away to university. Old friendships from school days faded very quickly because they were replaced by new friendships acquired as a result of meeting new people at university. Friendships die when we do not see the people concerned often enough to maintain the relationship at its former level of emotional intimacy – and especially so when neither side can quite muster the energy to do anything about it. So the tendency is for such relationships to fade quietly, almost by accident rather than design. The road to friendship is paved with good intentions to meet up again, and no doubt a good bit of guilt – we *must* get together sometime . . . but somehow sometime never comes because too many other priorities intervene. In contrast, family relationships can weather the social equivalent of being becalmed in mid-Atlantic, in part because of the pull of family (the Kinship Premium) and in part because the closely integrated network of family relationships means that people don't lose track of you completely. The kin-keepers bridge the divide by keeping everyone up to date with everyone else's doings. You can never quite escape – unless you completely cut yourself off.

Family are more forgiving than friends – not just of those repeated failures to contact them, but also of the trickle of small breaches of trust that inevitably occur along the way. We may find our relatives really irritating, but when emergencies occur we will almost always step up and help them out. The downside to this increased tolerance for family, however, seems to be that when we eventually transgress once too often against them, the relationship is likely to fracture with such violence that it is all but irreparable.

The end game

So who does fall out with whom? When we looked into this, we were surprised to find very few studies. There were studies of why relationships end, but these tended to focus on the most intimate relationships – romantic partners and best friends. We could find nothing to tell us whether friendships were more fragile than family relationships, or whether close relationships were more at risk than more distant ones. To try to fill this gap, we set up an online survey asking people to tell us about the relationship breakdowns they had experienced during the past year. Of the 540 people who responded, 413 reported a total of 902 relationship breakdowns in the previous twelve months. That works out at an average of just over one and a half breakdowns per person per year. Though women reported slightly more than men, the difference between the two sexes was small and not statistically significant. Since they were asked to think about their full extended social network of about 150 people, this represents a fairly modest 1 per cent of relationships overall. However, we tend not to have big bust-ups with people we don't see very often, so, not surprisingly, most of the breakdowns were with people in the innermost friendship circles. Since that averages about fifteen people, this probably represents something closer to 10 per cent of that inner core falling by the wayside each year. If you lose 10 per cent of your inner-core relationships each year, that would seem to imply that it will take you about ten years to fall out with all of the members of your inner two layers. However, as with liars, some people are more prone to falling out with people than others are. Of those who declared that they had had at least one relationship breakdown in the last twelve months, 62 per cent had had 1–2 and 30 per cent had had 3–4, with just 8 per cent having between 5 and 10. One person, however, claimed to have had no fewer than twenty-one relationship breakdowns in a year. Twenty in a year means you have pretty much fallen out with everyone important to you – or with one person many times.

Nearly half of all breakdowns occur within the first three years of a relationship, with most of the rest being breakdowns with someone you have known for most of your life – mainly, of course, close family. In other words, breakdowns happen either early or late in a relationship, and are much less likely to occur in between. The data suggest that breakdowns with non-family members are likely to happen earlier than those with kin – typically, after three years with non-kin and after seven years with kin, perhaps reflecting the Kinship Premium and the fact that kin are more willing to put up with your errant ways and have to be pushed right off the edge before they explode.

A surprisingly high proportion of breakdowns (around a quarter) were with close family members. However, since family account for about half our 150 friends and relations, this implies that breakdowns with family are half as likely as breakdowns with friends, again suggesting that family relationships are somewhat buffered against relationship breakdown by the Kinship Premium. Nonetheless, the three closest relationships we can ever have – parents, romantic partner and best friend – accounted for a third of all cases, in roughly equal proportions, with women reporting more cases than men for parents and romantic partners. Since we usually have two parents and only one romantic partner and one best friend, this still suggests that parents are buffered against breakdowns, with each parent experiencing only half the number of breakdowns experienced by a romantic partner or a best friend.

The romantic partners are perhaps understandable, but the extraordinarily high frequency of breakdowns with close family is a little disturbing. Disturbing because these are the only people who will move heaven and earth to help you when the chips are down and all else fails. Relationship breakdowns with siblings or other close relatives like aunts/uncles and nieces/nephews often seem to happen after the death of the last surviving parent. This seems to be such a common occurrence that there are now dozens of websites with names like *When Death Brings Out the Worst: Family Fighting After a Death, How to Handle Siblings After the Death of Your Parents, Till Death (of our parents) Us Do Part* and *How to Avoid Family Conflicts After the Death of a Parent.* It is clearly a much more common problem than one might imagine. A recent large national sample carried out in the USA found that the death of a parent adversely affected the relationship between siblings in almost all cases. Many of these rifts are the result of one of two sources of stress: the fact that one sibling shouldered most of the responsibility for the care of the dying parent and disputes about inheritances – or, occasionally, disputes on exactly what form the funeral should take. It seems as though the parent has been holding the lid down on a festering quarrel, and their death removed the one thing that kept the warring parties on speaking terms. In many cases, these splits seem to be all but permanent.

In some sense, of course, these are a special case. They happen only once in a lifetime, and they are very specific as to whom they involve. Nonetheless, they remind us just how fragile even these most enduring of all relationships can be when put under pressure. The death of a close family member, even when anticipated, is a stressful event and that stress infiltrates into everything we do. Any weaknesses, any fault lines, that would normally be kept below the event horizon are at risk of bursting asunder.

In our survey, there was a striking sex difference in whom people fall out with. We had listed twenty-four different types of relationships from parents and romantic partners to casual acquaintances that subjects could specify in each case. Women reported having fallen out with all twenty-four, but men reported having breakdowns with only fourteen of them. Men reported no cases of falling out with offspring, half-siblings, aunts/uncles, cousins, step-parents or other more distant relatives. Women reported falling out with all these, although the frequency with which they did so with some categories of relatives was very low compared with other types of relationships. Women were more likely than men to have fallen out with an offspring, a romantic partner, a non-best friend and any relative other than a full sibling (brother or sister). In contrast, men were more likely to have fallen out with a full sibling, a colleague or someone they shared a house with. Men were equally likely to have fallen out with males and females, but women were nearly twice as likely to have fallen out with another woman than they were with a man, suggesting that female–female relationships are especially fragile.

Why do friendships fracture?

One of the seminal studies of relationships and relationship breakdown was undertaken by the legendary British social psychologist Michael Argyle (with whom, in the 1960s, I had classes as a student). During the 1980s, he and his collaborator Monika Henderson ran an extended series of experimental studies examining the rules that underpin friendships. They identified six key rules which were essential for maintaining a stable relationship. These were: standing up for the friend in their absence, sharing important news with the friend, providing emotional support when it is needed, trusting and confiding in each other, volunteering help when it is required, and making an effort to make the other person happy. Breaking any of these rules, they suggested, was likely to weaken the relationship, and breaking many was likely to lead to complete relationship breakdown.

They noticed that, when recalling lapsed relationships, people were more likely to attribute negative behaviours to the other person and positive ones to themselves, a classic form of psychological deflection of blame known as the Attribution Error ('It can't be me that is wrong, so it must be you'). They also noticed that younger people (i.e. those under twenty years of age) attached more significance to public criticism than older people did, and that women placed most importance on failure to apportion time equally and give positive regard and emotional support, whereas men placed a greater emphasis on negative events like being the target of jokes or public displays of teasing. Men seem to be less able to cope with this kind of taunting than women, perhaps because reputations mean more to them. This doesn't apply, however, in the context of all-male groups, where banter of just this kind is near-universal and widely enjoyed.

In our relationship breakdown survey, we offered respondents eleven reasons why a relationship might fail. Ranked in order of most to least frequent in their responses, they were: lack of caring, poor communication, drifted apart, jealousy, problems with alcohol or drugs, anxiety about the relationship, competition from rivals, 'stirring' by other people, tiredness, misunderstandings and cultural differences between the couple. The three most frequent causes (i.e. as opposed to just drifting apart) were perceived lack of caring, poor communication and jealousy. Between them, they accounted for over 50 per cent of all cases of relationship breakdown. Some of these clearly identify problems in the dynamics of the relationship, others pinpoint homophily issues related to the Seven Pillars.

One likely reason for this is that we are inclined to take close relationships for granted. Our expectations become too high. One nice illustration of this was inadvertently provided by the linguists Simeon Floyd and Nick Enfield and their colleagues at the Max Planck Institute for Psycholinguistics at Nijmegen in Holland. They had become interested in how often expressions of gratitude are used – do we always thank people for their kindnesses to us? To examine this, they searched databases of conversations from eight different languages drawn from all over the world (South America, Europe, Africa, South Asia and Australia). They located over fifteen hundred conversational exchanges where someone had asked for something, determined whether the request had been acceded to (about a thousand of those) and whether the requestor had responded with some words expressing gratitude (such as 'thank you'). They found that, on average, the requestor had responded with a 'thank you' or the equivalent on only 5.5 per cent of occasions. The English were the most polite (14.5 per cent of requests), and the Cha'palaa Indians of Ecuador the least (0 per cent). They concluded that, despite the urban myth, people don't in fact express gratitude very often, at least for everyday favours. However, almost all of the conversations they examined were between family members or close friends and that is precisely where we don't use these terms. We simply expect family and friends to accede to our requests as a matter of course as part of the friendship 'deal', and so don't need thanking. Indeed, we often don't even preface our requests to these people with a 'please', never mind a 'thank you' afterwards. We simply expect them to do those favours for us out of obligation. Check it out for yourself. Expressions of gratitude are for strangers or less close friends whom we wouldn't normally expect to behave altruistically. But, and here is the rub, *continued* failure to show gratitude in some way (if only with a smile that would never have been recorded in the verbal databases they analysed) can eventually start to rub us up the wrong way. Do it too often, or do it too often without reciprocating the favour, and it becomes a grudge and part of the gradual erosion of trust and obligation.

There was a striking difference in the causes of relationship breakdown identified by the two sexes. Men tended to mention drifting apart, problems with alcohol or drugs, competition from rivals and stirring by others. Women were more likely to mention poor communication, jealousy and tiredness making them less caring. There is a hint here of men tending to blame others and women tending to blame themselves. One of the reasons why close relationships – romantic or otherwise – between the two sexes may be especially vulnerable is that, as Anna Machin's survey suggested, the two sexes come to these relationships with very different expectations: women have higher expectations than men. The social psychologist Jeffrey Hall reviewed thirty-six studies involving nearly 9,000 subjects that explored just this issue. Overall, women had much higher expectations of relationships than men did, especially in respect of reciprocity (of loyalty, trustworthiness, mutual regard and support), genuineness and communion (willingness to engage in self-disclosure and intimacy). The difference in communion reflects a widely recognised quality of women's behaviour that has been referred to as tend-and-befriend.

Men, by contrast, had higher expectations than women in respect of only one category which Jeffrey Hall termed 'agency' (engaging in physical activities and striving for status). The difference was particularly evident in respect of men's greater tendency to seek out friendships with same-sex friends of high status. These differences held up even when controlling for age and ethnicity, though the magnitude of the differences did seem to increase with age. Anna Machin's study of romantic partners and best friends also suggested that differences in the two sexes' expectations about a relationship often became a bone of contention. Even something as simple as differences in social style can give rise to conflict due to mixed messages. Men's friendships, like their conversations, are typically much more confrontational than women's friendships, involving more joking at the other's expense, more attempts to score points over each other, in a way that is perceived by men to be friendly but by women as threatening or even intentionally aggressive. Women will take offence at such behaviour much more quickly than men will.

The divorce statistics tend to reinforce this conclusion. In the UK, nearly two-thirds of divorce petitions for heterosexual couples in 2017 were submitted by women, while three-quarters of all divorce petitions for same-sex couples were for lesbian couples (as opposed to gay men). In both cases, the most common reason for divorce was unreasonable behaviour, with women more likely to use this as the grounds for divorce (52 per cent as against 37 per cent of males). Unreasonable behaviour was also the most common cause of divorce in lesbian marriages (83 per cent of cases, compared with 73 per cent of cases for male gay marriages). This again suggests that women's close relationships may be more fragile, and that men are often more relaxed about, or just take less notice of, destabilising incidents.

One of our early studies of social networks had examined the relationship between personality and close friends and family. The idea for the study had been suggested by Ruth Wilson (then one of our students, who went on to become a school teacher in London). I was quite surprised by one particular finding from this study, but in retrospect it seems to be very germane to the question of why relationships fracture. This was that women who scored high on the neuroticism scale had significantly fewer female relatives than everyone else – yet they had the same number of male kin. (This does not, by the way, mean they were suffering from clinical psychopathologies. The neuroticism dimension simply implies higher-than-average levels of anxiety, moodiness, worry, anger, frustration, loneliness and feeling depressed. Clinically, such people are otherwise perfectly normal.) We were very puzzled by this because it cannot be that everyone who scores high on neuroticism is born into families that have fewer than the average number of girls. That doesn't make any sense biologically. The only plausible explanation is that they had so irritated their female relatives that these wouldn't have any more to do with them.

Anna Heatley's study of loneliness in Mexican and British students suggested a possible reason why this might happen. She found that women reported a greater sense of loneliness than men. Individuals with low attachment security, who commonly felt they received less emotional support and were anxious about their relationships, felt significantly lonelier than those who were more secure. These are exactly the conditions that would lead to an expectation mismatch and an increased risk of relationship breakdown. These are the kind of people who can easily become a nuisance – forever knocking on your door or ringing you up, constantly bemoaning the miseries of their lives. In the end, you crack and go out of your way to avoid them.

If this is the explanation, then it seems like a recipe for a car crash. Your female relatives are the one group of people who will move heaven and earth to help you out when everyone else has abandoned you. So, in effect, these women had alienated their best source of support. This seems like a very counterproductive strategy, but it reminds us how sensitive our relationships can be. Push them too far, and you lose them. Close family will hold out longer than more distant family, but, in the end, everyone has their price. Part of the problem is that we are all busy people, with our own social networks to worry about. If you force me to devote a disproportionate amount of time to you, it means I have less time to devote to my other friends – who may be important to me. As always, everything in life is a trade-off between alternative options. It is also a reminder that simply being a moaning Minnie can be just as damaging for friendships as betrayals of trust.

One important issue that constantly emerges from the literature on marital breakdown is men's susceptibility to depression and suicide in the aftermath of separation and divorce. In part, this may be a consequence of the fact that men's friendships are more casual, and hence do not provide the emotional support that women's friendships with other women provide in these circumstances. However, it is made worse by the fact that women tend, by default as much as anything else, to take over responsibility for creating and managing the couple's combined social network. Because women are socially more proactive than men, men often end up with a social network dominated by their wives' friends simply because the wives arrange the social events and the husbands just go along with it. Wives often try to encourage their husbands to contact old male friends, only to be greeted by a frustrating shrug of the shoulders. Irrespective of the cause, men risk ending up with no social network other than their own family after a divorce or the death of a spouse. Although well-meaning attempts have been made to try and encourage men to be more emotionally expressive – and, indeed, learn how to be so in childhood in anticipation of future problems – the question thrown up here is whether this is simply howling into the wind. It seems to reflect a failure to appreciate that men and women really are very different in this respect.

The pain of rejection

Relationships that end catastrophically are experienced as deeply painful, so painful in fact that it invariably leads to tears. Three-quarters of us would list the loss of a loved one, either through separation or death, as the single most traumatic and emotionally upsetting thing that has ever happened to us. And most of us would describe this experience as a 'broken heart'. This is obviously a psychological phenomenon, yet virtually every culture uses the language of physical pain to describe it. The reason is that the place in the brain where we feel psychological pain is exactly the same place where we feel physical pain.

The person who has, perhaps, been most responsible for appreciating this has been the American neuroscientist Naomi Eisenberger. To explore what was going on in the brain during social rejection, she used a very simple on-screen game called *cyberball* that was developed by Kip Williams at Purdue University in Indiana. The game involves three people – you (usually seen as a pair of hands at the bottom of the screen) and two other 'players' to the right and left at the top of the screen that are actually avatars controlled by the software – and, of course, a virtual ball that gets tossed from one pair of hands to another. You can decide who to throw the ball to when it comes to you by moving a joystick. Usually, the subject is led to believe that they are playing a virtual game of catch with real people mediated via the internet. The three of you toss the ball between you, but at some point the two avatars stop including you and just toss the ball backwards and forwards between themselves. This simple game induces a surprisingly acute sense of negative emotion, a very real sense of rejection.

Eisenberger found that the areas of the brain that were especially active when someone had been socially excluded in the cyberball game were the anterior cingulate cortex (ACC, deep within the fissure formed by the two halves of the brain) and the anterior insular (AI, buried inside the cortex on either side of your head). The more distressed the person said they were, the more active these regions were. These are exactly the same brain regions that respond to physical pain. They are not the same areas where you have the *sensation* of pain (which seems to involve the somatosensory cortex and an area known as the posterior insula); rather they seem to be where you *perceive* pain. When people who suffer chronic pain have the ACC and the AI destroyed, they can still feel pain but it no longer bothers them. Remove the somatosensory cortex and the posterior insula, and they don't feel the pain at all. The ACC and AI are among the areas of the brain with the highest density of endorphin receptors.

Further evidence that one and the same area of the brain is involved in physical and social pain comes from a variety of sources. One study looked at brain activity during both social exclusion and a physical-pain task at the same time, and found that there was considerable overlap in brain activity in both these regions. Other studies have found that social trauma increases sensitivity to physical pain, while physically painful inflammation makes us more sensitive to social pain. In one study, subjects took regular doses of an over-the-counter painkiller (paracetamol) for two weeks: when they were then tested on social exclusion tasks, they were less sensitive to being excluded (they reported fewer hurt feelings) and activity in their ACC and AI was lower. The OPRM1 gene regulates the endorphin receptors, and a few people have an allele for this gene that makes them especially sensitive to physical pain: these people turn out to be unusually sensitive to social rejection and to have greater activity in the ACC and AI during experimental episodes of social exclusion.

Perhaps not too surprisingly, factors that lead to greater sensitivity to social exclusion, including low self-esteem, oversensitivity to other people, a tendency to feel socially disconnected as well as being characterised at the anxious end of the attachment scale are all associated with increased activity in the ACC and AI when faced with social exclusion. Conversely, factors that reduce sensitivity to exclusion, such as being given social support or a more avoidant attachment style (a cool social style), reduce activity in these brain regions. Increased activity in the ACC was also found in subjects who were more sensitive to rejection when they viewed videos of people displaying disapproving facial expressions. In an experiment devised and run by Jennifer Smith (then one of our students) that used the cyberball game, we found that subjects' pain threshold (an indicator of endorphins) increased after rejection, but especially so in people who said they had been bullied in primary (but not secondary) school. Social experiences, it seems, can have a lifelong effect, making us more sensitive to social situations as grown-ups.

The ACC and AI were also found to be especially active in a study that asked people who had recently experienced the break-up of a romantic relationship to think about what had happened while looking at a photograph of the ex-partner. Similarly, viewing pictures of a loved one who has recently died resulted in increased activity in these same two brain regions. Women who had recently had a stillborn baby also showed increased activity in the ACC when asked to look at a photograph of someone else's smiling baby. Even viewing rejection-themed paintings triggered a greater increase in activity in the ACC and AI compared with viewing paintings depicting acceptance scenes.

Interestingly, it seems that the ACC has no equivalent in the reptilian brain, suggesting that it evolved in higher vertebrates (birds and mammals), perhaps at the time that animals first began to engage in parental care and show parental concern for their not-yet-independent offspring. If you surgically remove the ACC in hamsters, maternal behaviour disappears: they show no interest in their pups at all, and won't retrieve them or return them to the nest – even though in all other social respects they behave perfectly normally. Removing the ACC in rodent pups also suppresses the distress calls that pups would normally give when they are away from the mother, while stimulating the ACC electrically suppresses distress calls. So it may well be that the bonding we feel towards others has its origins in a mechanism designed to create and reinforce the mother–offspring bond in mammals: we have simply generalised this mechanism to other adults (including, of course, romantic partners). That the ACC plays a central role in managing our social relationships is indicated by the fact that, in humans, lesions of the ACC reduce our concern for others' opinions. Not a great place to have a stroke: even if it means you have all your other faculties, can speak normally and are physically fighting fit, insulting people because you haven't noticed their response to what you've said, or failing to be solicitous in the right circumstances, is not a recipe for continued friendship.

Have a good cry and feel better

There is one genuinely odd behaviour that we engage in when we are sad or in pain. I mean odd both in the sense that no other species does it and odd in that it doesn't seem to make much biological sense. It's crying, and crying is very relevant to friendships because relationships often end in tears. Most animals' eyes produce tears of some kind to keep the surface moist and to swill out the dust and grime that inevitably accumulate in the eye. But only humans seem to be capable of turning on floods of tears. Crying and tears can be a response to physical pain, but what is genuinely odd is the fact that they are more often a response to psychological pain – the pain of social rejection, the pain associated with the death of a loved one, even just empathy with someone else's plight, are more powerful triggers of tears than a physical wound. Indeed, in these kinds of emotionally charged situations, we are often encouraged to let go and cry. Let it all out is the advice, and you'll feel much better. Even weirder when you think about it is the fact that many of the most successful films are not those that make us laugh, but those that make us cry. Comedies are often viewed as trivial, tragedies as serious art.

Science has never had a very satisfactory explanation for this strange behaviour. One suggestion has been that crying makes someone else sympathise with you and do something about it – or stop doing whatever is causing you to cry. In fact, people don't often cry when being assaulted, so it is unlikely to discourage the person attacking them to lay off. If we cry at all in response to a physical assault, it is likely to be afterwards. Tears certainly arouse a degree of empathy in us, as Robert Provine has shown in one of his many perceptive studies of human emotional behaviour: individuals portrayed with a tearful face are perceived as sadder than when they have the same expression but without tears. A crying toddler soon gets picked up and soothed. The elephant in the room here, however, is why a good cry should make you feel better in situations that aren't life-threatening? Why would you cry just because Romeo and Juliet died in each other's arms?

In fact, currying sympathy may be just an evolutionary by-product of something much more important. The real benefit of crying arises from the fact that we feel psychological pain. It looks suspiciously as though the endorphin system might be involved. And since the endorphin system provides the brain's own built-in aspirin, psychological pain naturally triggers an endorphin response that both dampens the pain and makes us feel better by giving us a slight opioid high. In other words, the origins of crying may lie in what it does for us directly by making us feel better rather than in what it does for us indirectly by rousing sympathy in someone else.

Reconciliation

It seems that close family relationships, as well as romantic relationships, are especially at risk of ending catastrophically. They are also the ones that are most difficult to reconcile, precisely because they end with such an acrimonious rupture. Of the 900 or so break-ups in our online sample, nearly 45 per cent were unreconciled at the time of the survey. Of course, some of these would have been recent and there might not have been sufficient time for reconciliation to occur. Around 40 per cent of break-ups were reconciled within a week, but after that the proportion fell dramatically to only 1 per cent of those that had lasted a year. Our data suggest that, on average, you could expect to have one terminal (i.e. unreconciled) relationship breakdown every 2.3 years. That's roughly equivalent to thirty or so during your adult life. It seems that if a reconciliation is going to happen, it happens within the first few weeks after the break-up, otherwise it becomes semi-permanent with the two sides not even willing to initiate the process of reconciliation.

In our survey of relationship breakdowns, we had asked our respondents to tell us about how reconciliation had been achieved. By far the most common behaviour was a simple apology (almost half of all successful reconciliations). The next most common did not involve any apology or peace-making: typically, these involved a frank discussion of differences, financial reparations for a loss, or simply 'time out' (the two didn't see each other for a while and that allowed things to calm down). These accounted for a fairly substantial 40 per cent of all reconciliations. Surprisingly perhaps, turning up with a bunch of flowers or the equivalent was least common: giving gifts or engaging in some physical or social activity of the kind normally associated with social bonding accounted for less than 15 per cent of reconciliations.

There was a strong tendency for women's break-ups to remain unreconciled longer than men's. For women, 47 per cent of their break-ups with women remained unreconciled, compared to 40 per cent of their break-ups with men, while 37 per cent of men's break-ups with women and 33 per cent of their break-ups with other men remained unreconciled. In either case, break-ups with spouses were much more likely to be reconciled than were those with parents or best friends. Those with best friends, however, were the least likely of these to be reconciled. Not surprisingly, the parties felt most aggrieved where a break-up had not been reconciled, and the difference in the emotional closeness of the relationship since the break-up was inevitably greatest in these cases, and especially so for women compared with men. Women were also more demanding than men in what they were prepared to accept as evidence of reconciliation.

It seems that women are less forgiving than men. It's a theme to which poets and playwrights have repeatedly returned. Writing as long ago as 430 BC, Euripides has his anti-hero Medea so outraged when her unfaithful husband Jason abandons her for a Greek princess despite the fact that she has sacrificed everything for him that she wreaks a terrible vengeance by murdering her own (and Jason's) children as well as his new mistress, simultaneously turning herself into both assassin and victim.

This raises some fundamental questions of causality. Were it true only of romantic relationships, one might view it simply as a consequence of the fact that women are more often the victims of men's careless betrayals and suffer most from their indifference and lack of attention. However, it seems that this is as true of women's relationships with female best friends as it is of romantic partners. This might be because best friendships (the Best Friend Forever) can be as intense and emotionally intimate as a romantic relationship. Or it may be that all women's relationships are more socially intense than the rather casual relationships that men have, and this causes them to take umbrage more readily and deeply than men do.

There has, in fact, been a longstanding consensus among those studying relationships that women's relationships are more fragile than men's, perhaps because they are much more intimate and emotionally charged – a finding that has even been reported cross-culturally. A study of teenagers' same-sex best friends by Joyce Benenson and Athena Christakos, for example, found that girls' friendships were of shorter duration than those of boys, that girls were more distressed than boys when imagining the potential termination of a friendship, that they were more likely to have done something to hurt a friend, and that they had experienced more friendship terminations than boys had.

This may, however, depend on circumstance and the level of conflict that occurs in the relationship. Benenson ran an experimental study with the anthropologist Richard Wrangham in which they made pairs of same-sex friends compete with each other in a word game. After the competitive game, the pair were either allowed to reconcile or not and then tested on a cooperative word-finding game. They found that immediate contact (moving to sit side by side and chatting) after the competitive games preserved, or even enhanced, performance in the following cooperative task in the women's dyads but not in the men's. Conversely, when no physical contact was allowed after the competitive game, cooperation was adversely affected in the women's case, but not in the men's. Men's relationships seemed to be less deeply affected by whether or not there were opportunities to interact amicably – not surprisingly, perhaps, given our evidence that conversation has almost no impact at all on the persistence of males' relationships. Although this was a very different context to the kinds of emotionally laden events that can cause relationships, and especially women's relationships, to be destabilised in the social world, it is significant that even this mild intervention was enough to shift women's cooperativeness as a function of whether or not they were allowed to talk to each other afterwards.

That women's relationships are more fragile is borne out by the national divorce statistics: opposite-sex marriages do seem to last longer than same-sex relationships. According to the UK Office of National Statistics, the median duration of marriage at divorce in 2017 was 12.2 years for opposite-sex marriages, but only 3.5 years for male same-sex couples and 2.8 years for female same-sex couples. In fact, the rate at which female same-sex marriages dissolved is higher than the rate at which male same-sex marriages dissolved in all the countries of western Europe. Together with the fact that women were responsible for nearly two-thirds of opposite-sex divorce petitions, this suggests that women's relationships may generally be more fragile and prone to fracture.

*

Much of this chapter has reinforced the suggestion that men and women live in two rather different social worlds. This raises the deep philosophical question of how on earth they manage to stay together in romantic relationships, and whether, aside from the minor matter of biological reproduction, they might not do better to have same-sex relationships instead. The divorce statistics suggest that this isn't, in fact, so. Something else seems to make heterosexual relationships work better. One possibility may simply be the presence of children. Divorce statistics suggest that childless couples are much more likely to divorce (especially if childlessness is involuntary) than couples which have children (albeit with some evidence for an upturn in divorce rates for couples with large families of more than five children – evidence, perhaps, of the stresses imposed by the demands of parenthood). Shared interest in, and responsibility for, children may reduce the risk of divorce by making the respective parties more willing to put up with a less than satisfactory relationship in the interests of the children's future.

15

Friendship as we age

Nothing can be more poignant than the remarkable ninth-century Irish poem *An Chailleach Bhéara*, variously translated as the 'Veiled Nun* of Beara', the 'Old Woman of Dingle' or, in the late John Montague's wonderful translation, simply as 'The Hag of Beare'. It is a sustained lament on the inevitability of old age and the social isolation it brings, and must rank as one of the most evocative poems ever written in any language. *Is mé Caillech Bérri Buí, no-meilinn léini mbithnuí* ('I am the Old Woman of Beare from [the island of] Buí, I used to wear smocks that were renewed each day') the poem opens. With blunt candour, she goes on to mourn her inexorable decline from one who flaunted beautiful clothes as she wined and dined and danced with royalty, the social centre of the party, into her present condition in old age, starved, bony, grey-haired, with no more than rags to cover her. Where royalty and young gentlemen once queued at her door to court her, now not even a slave† would pause to bat an eyelid at her. God, she laments, is welcome to have his deposit

---

* *Chailleach* means 'the veiled one' in Old Irish, and so was used as a synonym both for a nun and for an old woman.
† Slaves in this context would be Celts from mainland Britain sold by Viking slavers, or Irish from other clans captured in battle. They were common among the wealthy until well into the medieval period.

back for the body she has now. He's already had one of her eyes as a down payment on the next life, so He might just as well claim the rest and be done with it.

It's a tale that has been repeated many times over many millennia: as age and infirmity make it more difficult for the elderly to get out, they are left to brood and fester alone in their rooms. In some traditional societies, even as the twentieth century dawned, the elderly took it upon themselves to end their own lives voluntarily before they reached the point of becoming a burden. Among the Maasai of East Africa, the elderly might walk out into the bush when they felt their time had come and settle themselves at the base of a thorn tree to await the inevitable – peacefully by starvation and dehydration if they were lucky, at the hands of a hyena if not. In the climatically demanding environment of the Arctic, elderly Inuit who could no longer pull their weight rapidly became a burden and might ask to be killed (usually by stabbing or strangulation), or might just be left behind when the camp moved on, allowing hypothermia to take its inevitable toll. In traditional Japan, poor families left their senile elderly on the upper slopes of mountains in a traditional practice known as *ubasute*.

These ancient practices might seem cruel in the context of the contemporary world, but most of us now live in times that are uniquely economically unstressed, and we should not judge the past by the standards of the present. A second reason for a more charitable view of the past is that it does not take much for such behaviour to resurface in the present. When the economic climate deteriorated in the 1990s, some 70,000 elderly Americans were deposited on the doorsteps of hospitals by their relatives. In Japan, there was a sharp rise in the frequencies with which the elderly were abandoned at hospitals and charities after the Japanese economy took a downturn in the new millennium. Granny dumping, as it is usually known, is simply the tip of an iceberg. The villages and cities of the industrial West are full of elderly who cannot get out and see no one from one week to the next, other than the person who delivers their free meals or someone from an agency sent in for a fifteen-minute visit once a day to get them up and dressed. The rest of the time they are alone. Loneliness, as we saw in chapter 1, is the biggest killer in the modern world.

Let us begin, however, at the beginning, with the friendships we develop in childhood.

Learning to navigate the social world

The social world is probably the single most complex thing that we ever have to deal with in everyday life. A surprising number of scientists think that finding food is the most complex thing animals have to face. I am inclined to observe that the problem with most such scientists is that they don't have much of a social life. A more charitable view is that we become so practised at social skills by the time we are adults that they become second nature and we forget how difficult they actually are. Children understand the concept of friendship quite early on (or, at least, they understand how to use the word), but it takes them a long, long time to understand how to *recognise* when someone really is their friend.

The process of acquiring adult-level social skills probably takes two decades or more in humans. This is mainly why primates, and of course we humans, have such long childhoods compared with other animals. Many years ago, while she was a visiting researcher in my group, Tracey Joffe showed that the best predictor of neocortex volume in primates is the length of the period of socialisation – the time between weaning and puberty. It is not enough to have a big computer: you have to fill it with software, and we primates do this by a long process of learning and practice across childhood and adolescence.

In the very first brain-scanning study I was involved with, Quentin Deeley looked to see where in the brain people processed facial expressions of emotions. What he found was that up to about the mid-twenties, this was done mainly in the prefrontal cortex (we have to think hard about it), but after that it gets pushed down below the consciousness horizon because we have become skilled enough to automate it. Rather cheekily, we suggested that this might explain why teenagers have so much trouble with their relationships: they have to crank their way through everything in tedious detail, whereas adults who have mastered the skills do it more or less subconsciously, only pausing to bring it back into conscious focus when faced with an especially tricky case.

As we saw in chapter 6, mentalising or mindreading consists of a series of levels known as the orders or levels of intentionality. Most animals that are in any sense self-conscious live their lives in a stage of first-order intentionality: they know what they are thinking about the world. Toddlers, too, are first-order intentional in just this sense, but at around age five they break through a developmental glass ceiling and acquire second-order intentionality, or theory of mind. At this point, they progress from being good ethologists (they can understand how to predict what you will do from your past behaviour) to being good psychologists (they understand the mind that lies behind that behaviour). As a result, they are able both to predict your behaviour more accurately *and* to use that knowledge to manipulate your behaviour more effectively. They can begin to lie skilfully because they understand how *you* will interpret what they tell you. From here on in, children gradually acquire successive orders of intentionality until they reach full adult functionality at fifth-order intentionality sometime in the mid- to late teens.

When she was a graduate student with us, Dani Hawker-Bond was prompted to wonder what the sequence of development looked like between the age of five and mid-adolescence and whether this influenced the number of children that an individual could play with simultaneously (in effect, their natural group size). Dani first sampled how many other children an individual child was interacting with on average at any given moment during school playtime, and then took the child off to a classroom on its own to test its mentalising abilities on a children's version of our mentalising task. The number of children simultaneously engaged in interacting with each other increased across year groups from an average of about two in five-year-olds to around three and a half in eleven-year-olds. Recall from chapter 9 that four is the upper limit on conversation group size in adults, so by the start of the teens children can just about manage an adult-sized interaction group. This growth in group size mapped well onto the successive levels of intentionality that these children could achieve.

This pattern of increasingly skilled mentalising as children develop has been documented very nicely in a study by Iroise Dumontheil at University College London. She used a task known as the Director's Task that tests people's ability to see the world from someone else's perspective. The subject sits on one side of a set of partially occluded shelves and is instructed by the 'Director' sitting on the other side to move objects from one shelf to another. Since some objects may be duplicated with one on a shelf that is occluded from the Director's view, the crucial point is that only objects that the Director can see should be moved. This is not *quite* the same thing as intentionality – it really tests perspective-taking. However, perspective-taking is a crucial precursor of intentionality, so it does provide an index of intentional capability. Iroise tested children at age eight, eleven, thirteen and sixteen, as well as twenty-five-year-old adults. Accuracy improved steadily with age, with young adults doing best of all, suggesting that these skills do continue to improve right through to the mid-twenties, just as Quentin Deeley's brain-scanning study implied.

These cognitive patterns map neatly onto a number of behavioural aspects of friendship in children. Until they are about five years old and have acquired full theory of mind, for example, children don't appreciate or suffer from a sense of rejection when excluded from a game or other social situation. Nor do they differentiate between their desire to be friends with someone and that person's willingness to reciprocate. For them, friendship is more like a label than a relationship. When they acquire theory of mind at around age five, they seem to shift from an egocentric to a socio-centric perspective that allows them to understand both how others feel and how they themselves fit into the group. Later still, as teenagers, they are still improving.

Two of my former colleagues, Stephanie Burnett-Heyes and Jennifer Lau, compared fourteen- and seventeen-year-olds in how they performed in a classic economics game in which they could either keep the whole of a sum of money they had been given or divide it among their friends. Because they studied whole school classes, they were able to ask each teenager to rate their relationships to all the others, and this allowed them to see how well relationships were reciprocated. The fourteen-year-olds chose to give money to friends with whom they reported stronger social ties (those they liked and trusted more). While the seventeen-year-olds also acted in the same way, they modulated this sense of their own attraction to others by how much these individuals actually reciprocated those feelings. It is only at this point that we begin to understand the fact that relationships are a two-way process, that the other person is a *person*, not some kind of slave (or a parent!) at one's beck and call. The difference is crucial, because social life in the primate sense is only possible once you have achieved this more sophisticated understanding of how the social world works. Yet it seems that most zoological and psychological, not to mention economic, research is based on the assumption that sociality is all and only about me trying to engineer you into doing what is best for me.

In sum, the skills we need to operate successfully in the adult social world are subtle and sophisticated – far more subtle and sophisticated than those we need to survive in the physical world. We are not provided with these skills at birth because they are simply too complex to be routinised. They are context-dependent, and we have to learn the principles that underlie them laboriously by a combination of practice and instruction. It takes an astonishingly long time to become fully competent in them. It is mainly for this reason that we and the other monkeys and apes have such protracted adolescence. Jennifer Lau has pointed out how odd this period of suspended animation between childhood and adulthood actually is. Nothing like it occurs outside the primates, and no species has such a long adolescence as humans do. We don't need adolescence to become competent in anything except the social world.

Growing into friendship

Very young children tend to play in parallel rather than interact with each other, so they rarely show any preferences for particular play partners. However, by the time they acquire theory of mind at the age of four or five, they are beginning to show a distinct preference for their own sex. There are indications that this sex discrimination emerges much earlier: several studies have reported that infants spend longer looking at same-sex babies compared with opposite-sex babies. By age two, toddlers are more likely to respond to a request to play by a child of the same sex than by one of the opposite sex. By the time they start pre-school, this preference for same-sex playmates has become more entrenched, and by the age of eight or nine, single-sex play groups are pretty much the norm. One study found that only 11 per cent of primary-school-age children's self-reported friendship networks contained a child of the opposite sex. By the end of primary school, these preferences even extend to interactions on class projects and whom they prefer to work with, as well as whom they play with.

Inevitably, perhaps, this pattern changes with adolescence, and increasingly the two sexes start to mix as they enter mid- to late teens. This is especially true of girls, who mature earlier, and noticeably less so of boys who continue to prefer the company of their own sex for much longer – leading girls to associate with older boys who show more interest in them. Even so, most adolescents report feeling closer to their same-sex friends than they do to opposite-sex friends. In one study by Clare Mehta and JoNell Strough, 72 per cent of the friends nominated by teenagers were of the same sex. In another study, fourteen- and fifteen-year-olds were asked to list up to ten close friends; on average, they typically listed six of the same sex against just two of the opposite sex. A third study of teenagers found that boys spent two-thirds of their time with boys, and girls spent two-thirds of their time with girls. In late teens, of course, romance trumps everything. Nonetheless, same-sex friendships continue to play an important role in terms of emotional support, especially for girls, and, as we saw in chapter 13, continue to do so into adulthood.

One reason for the early appearance of segregation is that girls tend to withdraw from the increasingly boisterous play of boys. In a study of seven- to ten-year-olds during school playtime, Emma Powell found that boys were much more likely than girls to be playing 'with something' (a football, a piece of playground equipment) and their play was much more likely to involve vigorous activity (running, wrestling). In addition, when boys and girls played with objects, they had a strong tendency to gravitate to different kinds of toys: boys had a clear preference for construction and transportation toys, whereas girls had a strong preference for dolls and toys associated with home activities.

It is frequently claimed that these sex differences in object play and social style are enculturated. This is, however, fanciful. We see exactly the same sex differences in monkeys. Gerianne Alexander and Melissa Hines studied the play activities of juvenile African green monkeys housed in large enclosures at a primate research centre in California. The males spent significantly more time than the females playing with toys predefined as 'male' (balls, a toy car – toys typically preferred by human boys) and the females spent significantly more time playing with toys predefined as 'female' (dolls, a soft toy ape – toys typically preferred by human girls), but there was no difference between them in the time spent playing with 'neutral' toys (books, a soft toy dog). This had nothing to do with the relative dominance of the two sexes and hence differential access, since individual dominance rank did not correlate with the frequency of contact with any of the toys.

The play styles of wild monkeys and apes are very different as well. Elizabeth Lonsdale, working with data from Jane Goodall's famous study site at Gombe on the shores of Lake Tanganyika, found that adolescent male chimpanzees were much more sociable than the females. The females confined their interactions to immediate family and maternal relatives much more than the males, who preferred to interact with a wider variety of juveniles and adults. One reason for this may be that the females tended to steer clear of the often boisterous play groups formed by the males.

We noticed this in gelada baboons. Among infants up to age twelve months, play groups often consisted of both sexes and were very gentle affairs. But as the infants grew older, the males' play became increasingly rough, with vigorous games of chase, 'king of the castle' and wrestling. By the age of three (puberty), juvenile females had pretty much completely withdrawn from play groups, preferring to spend their time interacting with babies, sometimes even carrying sticks or stones clutched to their bellies as though carrying infants. Males never ever did this. Even in the feral goats that I have spent many years studying on the Isle of Rum (off the west coast of Scotland) and the Great Orme (on the northwest corner of Wales), male kids were far more boisterous in their play than female kids.

Sonya Kahlenberg noticed something very similar in another wild chimpanzee population: she collated observations made over a fourteen-year period and found that juvenile females were four times more likely than males to play with and carry sticks. The way they carried and held them suggested that they were treating them as toy infants. Among our gelada, juvenile females (but never males) would frequently cuddle babies and look after them while their mothers fed or socialised. On one occasion, I remember watching a young juvenile female refuse to allow a low-ranking mother to have her baby back, even though the baby was screaming because the juvenile was mishandling it and despite the mother's considerable distress. The mother knew if she tried to take the baby back forcefully and the juvenile protested, its higher-ranking mother would come to her daughter's defence and punish the mother.

In chapter 13, we noted that males tend to form groups whereas females focus on more intense dyadic relationships, and this difference in social style can be observed even in children. One of the most robust findings in the child-development literature is that boys play in larger groups than girls. In her study of seven- to ten-year-olds, Emma Powell found that boys spent significantly more time than girls in larger groups. Although both sexes spent about 13 per cent of their time alone, when girls were in groups they were fourteen times more likely to be in a small group than in a large group, whereas boys were nearly twice as likely to be in a large group as in a small group. Joyce Benenson used attention to puppets to show that four- and five-year-old girls prefer to watch the puppets interacting in pairs, whereas boys prefer to watch them interacting in groups. When she analysed the play networks of these children (based on asking them whom they liked to play with), the average number of play partners was 1.3 for girls compared with 2.0 for the boys (the difference being statistically significant). Boys preferred groups; girls preferred dyads.

In a year-long study of friendships in eleven-year-olds in which the children were asked to nominate their best friends at six-week intervals, Donna Eder and Maureen Hallinan found that the most common pattern for girls' friendships was pairs. Boys were much more likely to be found in triads, even if all the relationships were not necessarily reciprocated. They also found that, when they did occur, girls' triads were much more likely to break up as a result of one member being excluded, whereas boys' dyads were more likely to become a triad as a result of the chance acquisition of a new member. One consequence of this, they suggested, is that girls will find it more difficult to integrate into a new social (or school) environment than boys will. They cite an earlier experimental study of twelve- and thirteen-year-olds that introduced a stranger to an established same-sex pair of friends in a laboratory setting. Boys spoke to the newcomer earlier than girls did, took more notice of the newcomer's views and gave more positive ratings of the newcomer afterwards.

It seems to be the difference in the intensity of male and female friendships that makes girls' friendships more fragile. Joyce Benenson studied this in a sample of young teenagers. The girls' same-sex best friendships were of much shorter duration than those of the boys and they reported having had more broken relationships. Girls reported that they would feel much worse if the relationship broke up than the boys did. And they felt that the break-up would have a much worse impact on their lives. Moreover, the girls were much more likely than the boys to say that their best friend had upset them, even though their relationships had lasted for less long. Boys' and girls' relationships seem to have a very different quality throughout later childhood and early adolescence. Those of girls are much more intense and focused. Boys' friendships have that same more casual 'out of sight, out of mind' quality that we find in adults.

Our childhood experiences set us up for adulthood. Unpopular or badly adjusted children are more likely to appear in psychiatric clinics as adults, to receive bad-conduct discharges from the armed services, or end up before the courts. Around a third of adults with bipolar disorder were social isolates as children (compared to close to zero for normal adults). In one study of eight- to ten-year-olds, popular children had a better understanding of how to make friends and were more skilled at communicating what they wanted to say. They distributed and received more positive reinforcement, and they spent less time daydreaming and more time socially engaged.

We met the husband-and-wife team Terrie Moffitt and Avshalom Caspi and their analyses of the Dunedin longitudinal database in chapter 11. They found that those who were labelled as having conduct disorders as children (by coming to the notice of child agencies or the police) were, by age twenty-one, twice as likely to have had more than one sexual partner as those who had not, and were nearly three times more likely to have become parents. They were also more likely to have resorted to partner violence in their adult relationships, to have engaged in risky sex, and to have contracted sexually transmitted diseases. As many other studies have noted, they found that this condition was often co-morbid with (or expressed as) depression in girls, but more likely to be externalised in boys (e.g. by lashing out at others). Girls were twice as likely as boys to be diagnosed with depression by the time they were twenty-one. Nearly two-thirds of the adults who had been diagnosed as schizophrenic had experienced con-duct disorder problems by the time they were twenty-one.

Of course, not everyone suffers from these problems: only about a quarter of the sample were identified as having engaged in antisocial behaviour at all during childhood or adolescence. Moreover, most of those became good citizens as adults with no further signs of antisocial behaviour. Nonetheless, even though they do not become lifelong delinquents, many of those that do recover later experience difficulties in the transition to adulthood, often because their youthful experiences have left them at an educational disadvantage, because of substance abuse, or because teenage parenthood restricted their future life opportunities.

Sophie Scott has been one of the few neuroscientists to be inter-ested in laughter – and, thanks to our shared interest in laughter, was the person responsible for challenging me to do stand-up comedy (once was enough …). She and her team found that young teenage boys with diagnoses of psychopathic behaviour, or at risk of developing psychopathy, showed a much reduced response when listening to genuine laughter in two key areas of the brain compared with normal boys. These areas were the supplementary motor area and the anterior insula. The latter is particularly interesting because it is a brain region associated with the endorphin system.

Friends across the lifespan

Sociologists have been aware for some considerable time that social networks decline progressively as we enter old age. At the same time, they have been conscious of the fact that each of us has a core of relationships that remain surprisingly stable across much of the lifespan. These are those very close family and friends that provide us with emotional and social support and who, as it were, accompany us through life rather like a group of devoted servants – always at hand when we need them, always anxious to tend to our needs. There have been two rather different theories about this group of key friends: the socio-emotional theory of friendship (which suggests that we become more and more selective as we grow older to focus on those few emotionally valuable friendships) and the convoy theory (that we are accompanied through life by a relatively stable group of supportive friends). These needn't be incompatible, since they might well refer to different parts of our social network, but they do represent contrasting views of the dynamics of these relationships.

Cornelia Wrzus and her colleagues at the Max Planck Institute in Berlin collated 277 different studies of social networks from the literature (including one of my own studies) and used these to see how networks changed across the lifespan. It was a very large sample: over 177,500 individuals, aged between ten and eighty-five. Importantly, their sample included both Western and non-Western populations. Although it is difficult to make exact comparisons because different studies often define relationships and social networks in different ways, average network size was around 125, with a distinct ∩-shape against age: networks initially increase in size as we age, reach a peak between the mid-twenties and early thirties and then decline steadily into old age – just as we had found in our Christmas-card study. They found that while the family component of the network remained stable (as one might expect), it was what they called the personal (that is, the support network) and friendship components that expanded and then declined with age. At least some of the changes could, they thought, be explained by such obvious life events as puberty, marriage and parenthood, most of which occur at around the same age for most people. Other life events, including moving to a new location, divorce and spousal death, which are sporadic and unpredictable, tend to cause a sudden decrease in the size of the friendship network – in the latter two cases mainly because the partner's friends see you less often.

One small-scale study by Helene Fung and others is interesting both because it studied how the different components of the network change and because it also studied two different ethnic groups (European Americans and African Americans) living in the same location (San Francisco). Although they sampled only 185 individuals, they were aged right across the age range from eighteen to ninety-four. They found that the number of close friends (that inner 5-layer) remained remarkably stable at six individuals, but the number of best friends (essentially the sympathy group 15-layer) declined with age, and this was true of both ethnic groups. This again suggests that, as we age, we tend to sacrifice less close friends in order to invest what time and energy we still have in the more important shoulders-to-cry-on friends. Of course, it is always possible that our friends slowly desert us as we become less interesting and less fun to be with, and only those who feel the greatest obligation towards us keep coming round to see us even though we are less interesting to be with.

The analyses of the national mobile-phone database that have come out of my collaboration with Kimmo Kaski and his group at Aalto University have allowed us to look at the changing pattern of social contacts right across the lifespan from the age of eighteen onwards. Although these are necessarily cross-sectional studies, the enormous sample size means that the broad patterns that emerge are likely to be robust and reliable. One study led by Kunal Bhattacharya used the average number of different people phoned during a month (essentially the sympathy group, or 15-layer) to explore changes in network size with age. Kunal found that the average number of contacts was twelve at age eighteen, rose to a peak of eighteen at age twenty-five and then declined steadily to around eight at age eighty. There appeared to be a particularly sharp change at age thirty which we thought might reflect the birth of the first child, because it followed very close on the heels of the average age at marriage (twenty-nine in this southern European country). The evenness with which people called their closest friends decreased dramatically into old age: by age seventy, the great majority of calls were concentrated on just half a dozen people, with other people being called only very, very occasionally, whereas earlier in life calls were distributed more evenly across the individual's social network.

One surprising finding was that males called more different individuals than women did up to the age of thirty-five, after which the ratio reversed. After thirty-five, women contacted around one and a half times the number of people in a month that males did – scaling up to a difference of five extra individuals over the course of a whole year. In part, this seemed to be due to the fact that men called fewer people as they aged, whereas women typically called more people (at least until they reached old age). In other words, there seems to be a divergence in network size with age between the two sexes. Women became more social, men less so.

At age twenty, most calls were to people of similar age (peers), with a small secondary peak to people aged about fifty – clearly the parents. Most of these calls involved males calling other young males, with females calling males (presumably the romantic interest) proving rather less frequent. Surprisingly, females calling other females ranked a distant third in frequency, though still well ahead of calls to females by males. This pattern was maintained consistently until age fifty, at which point there was a dramatic change in calling patterns. There was now a big peak in calls to people in their twenties (presumably the adult children), as well as a secondary peak to fifty-year-olds (spouses and peer friends). In respect of the calls to twenty-year-olds, by far the most frequent were calls by women to younger males, with older-male-to-younger-male calls running a close second. Female-to-female and male-to-female calls lagged far behind. It seems that mothers and, to a lesser extent, fathers were calling their sons and paying much less attention to their daughters at this point. That might be because the sons are living away, whereas the daughters are still nearby (this *is* a Catholic country). Women were calling same-age peers with much lower frequencies, most of their effort being devoted to what we assume were their children. This pattern was maintained almost unchanged into the sixties and seventies, except that the two peaks progressively shifted to the right by a decade at each stage.

Kristine Ajrouch and her colleagues at the University of Michigan examined the close social networks and mental health of 1,700 Americans aged between forty and ninety-three. They found that, as they got older, men's inner-core social networks (essentially their support group) declined from 7.4 to 6.1 while women's declined from 8.1 to 6.4, with the ages of the friends increasing proportionately. While friends surely matter simply as friends, older friends are not a lot better at getting out to shop for you than you are yourself, so cannot be much help in physical terms. Proximity to friends also declined with age, as did the frequency of contact, neither of which is ideal: as you get older, you need your friends to be within shouting distance so they can get to you quickly and easily. Education seemed to have a generally beneficial effect, with people who had had more education having larger networks, especially among men, while, not too surprisingly, women who had largely stayed at home to be homemakers had smaller networks.

Death and divorce

Major life events like divorce and the death of a spouse have a dramatic effect on the survivor's social networks. Both involve forms of grief, and any form of grief causes us to withdraw from social interaction. In both cases, there is a tendency for the partner's half of the network to disappear quite quickly, especially the more casual friendships, thereby exacerbating the effects of loneliness and social isolation.

Research from both Europe and the United States indicates that, not too surprisingly perhaps, divorced individuals are less happy, and report more symptoms of depression, more social isolation and more negative life events, as well as more health problems, compared with married individuals of the same age. It is not clear whether this is due to the trauma of divorce or to the loss of friends who might offer support, since both are likely to damage health and wellbeing. Nor is it clear from these studies whether those who desert their partner suffer less in these respects than those who are deserted, since studies generally do not distinguish between the two. The second might well result in greater psychological shock, trauma and emotional upset. Divorce commonly results in a reduced standard of living and increased stress due to the need to move house, not to mention the costs of single parenthood (or, conversely, loss of contact with one's children), all of which are likely to have negative impacts on psychological and physical health.

In her analysis of the consequences of life events, Cornelia Wrzus found that the reduction in the size of the family network following divorce was mainly due to the in-laws withdrawing contact. Other network layers didn't seem to change that much. Nonetheless, the loss of in-laws must leave a significant hole in the wider network, especially as some of them may have been seen often enough to rank as more than mere casual friends. In our sample of British and Belgian women's networks, about half of the typical network of 150 were family and, of these, 30 per cent (around twenty-three people) were in-laws. So even though you don't include the whole of your spouse's extended family in your network, the ones you do see and try to keep in touch with represent a significant chunk out of your wider 150-layer network. Losing twenty-odd people leaves a significant hole in your social life.

Most people recover from the trauma of divorce with the passage of time, though the speed with which individuals do so seems to depend on the resources available to them. Those who have more supportive friends and family, higher income and higher levels of education tend to experience less trauma and recover more quickly. The divorcee's psychological attitude is also likely to be important: those who view divorce as an opportunity for a new beginning, perhaps even new career opportunities, will fare much better than those who view it as a personal failing. Those who have pre-existing mental-health problems (which may have been the cause of the divorce in the first place) will often have more difficulty adjusting to divorce, even if they initiate it.

Remarriage is likely to play an important role here, since a new romantic partner will inevitably provide emotional and psychological support. The sociological evidence, however, suggests that men are more likely to remarry than women after divorce, and to do so more quickly – and, when they do, to marry women that are typically ten to fifteen years younger than their original partner. In part, this may reflect the fact that women, with their deeper emotional engagement in relationships, are less willing to risk a repeat experience: once bitten, twice shy. However, it may also reflect the fact that mothers more often have custody of the children, and these will inevitably act as a brake on remarriage – given that single men are often reluctant to take on the burden of other men's children.

This is such a strong effect, by the way, that dating agencies used to advise women not to mention their children in their advertisements because they would get no replies at all. I remember one of the agencies telling me that women invariably ignored this advice until they had experienced it at first hand. The historical demographer Eckart Voland, with whom I collaborated on a number of projects, found something very similar in eighteenth- and nineteenth-century data from the Krummhorn region on Germany's Atlantic coast: young widows with one child were significantly more likely to remarry if the child died than if it survived. It seems that the economic benefits of marriage in this rural farming community were so great that it was better to allow the infant to die so as to have a chance of remarriage and more future children than to try and bring the child up alone in poverty. John Lycett and I found a rather similar pattern in respect of the contemporary national UK abortion statistics: the age-specific likelihood of a termination is directly proportional to the statistical chance of a subsequent marriage.

The death of a spouse will usually be just as traumatic as a divorce, and have very similar social and psychological consequences. Cornelia Wrzus found that the death of a spouse resulted in a significant reduction in the size of the wider friendship network, but an increase in the size of the support network, over the following two years. The reduction in the size of the wider network seems to reflect a tendency to reduce the frequency with which casual friends are contacted, probably in part through loss of social motivation and the fact that grief becomes psychologically all-consuming, leaving little room for more casual social interactions. The increase in the size of the support network is what one might expect as friends and family rally round the bereaved.

Much the same advice applies after the death of a spouse as after divorce. Those with more supportive close friends and family, those who are actively religious, and those who have active interests or hobbies that get them out of the house are likely to cope better and emerge from grieving faster. It is an imprecise business, however, since individuals vary in their psychological resilience as well as in the circumstances of the death. Deaths earlier in life will always be more traumatic and harder to get over than a death late in life, when such events are expected. A death at the end of a long illness is easier to come to terms with than one that comes out of the blue. Nonetheless, however it comes, the death of a spouse unavoidably precipitates a period of grieving, sometimes grief that is unexpectedly deep and debilitating.

Friendship in old age

Old age brings its own peculiar terrors. No longer is it possible to believe, as we all did in our younger days, that we are indestructible and will live for ever. We have seen too many friends and family die. We have begun to experience the inevitable frailty of the human body. We lack the energy and the stamina to do what we once did. Being able to dance or drink till dawn has become a faint memory. As the Hag of Beare reminds us, it is a lonely place on a road to nowhere. Increasing social isolation can have serious negative consequences not just for our wellbeing (as we saw in chapter 1), but also for our cognitive abilities, creating a downward spiral that feeds on itself. We see fewer people, so our cognitive functions decline, and as a result we see even fewer people because we have less to offer in terms of interesting conversation.

María-Victoria Zunzunegui and her colleagues interviewed more than 1,500 people aged sixty-five and over living in the municipality of Leganés just outside Madrid, and followed them up over a period of four years. She found that those with few social connections, infrequent participation in social activities, and a lack of social engagement were most at risk of cognitive decline. Such decline was lowest for men and women who had regular face-to-face contact with relatives and a high frequency of social engagement with the wider community. Having regular interaction with friends seemed to be particularly protective of cognitive function in women, although a similar effect was not noted in men.

In 1984, the United States Department of Health and Human Services launched a six-year follow-up study of 7,000 elderly Americans living in residential homes to explore the effect of physical activity and social interaction on physical function. The average age of the interviewees at the start of the project was seventy-seven, so a significant proportion died before the end of the study, allowing them to use whether or not someone died as a blunt but functional measure of their physical health. The level of physical activity and the level of social interaction both independently predicted the future risk of dying. Moreover, these effects were independent of any effects due to gender, age, education, income, ethnicity, and previous history of chronic disease. Both factors also buffered both sexes against the effects of widowhood: people who had recently been widowed had a significantly elevated risk of dying, but this was reduced if they were either physically or socially active. Friendships really do make a difference.

Old age brings on a downward spiral in which all the odds are stacked against you. You find it hard to make new friends as your old ones die or move away because you have less in common with the younger folk who now make up the bulk of the population; your declining energy makes you less willing to get out as often, and less able to take part in physical activities; your failing cognition makes it harder to respond so wittily or so engagingly as you once did in conversation, making you less interesting as a social companion; you are not so familiar with the topics that interest people now because you have not kept up with social and political developments – or the jokes of the latest stand-ups. Having an impoverished social life has adverse consequences for your cognitive wellbeing as well as your physical health, increasing the risk of dementia as well as physical illnesses that require hospitalisation. The prospect is not inviting. These are not conditions that physical medicine can cure, but nor are they psychiatric issues. They fall into an in-between limbo where conventional medicine offers few solutions. It makes the provision of social clubs and activities for the elderly all the more important as a way of maintaining their mental and physical health.

It is physical mobility that, as much as anything, causes our withdrawal from social interaction in older age. We just find it harder to get to places where people gather socially. In the limit, of course, we eventually become housebound. In that respect, the arrival of the internet has offered the possibility of a solution unique to our times. So, in the final chapter of this story of friendship, let's turn to see what opportunities the digital world and social media have to offer, both for the current older generation and for the future prospects of the younger generations that have grown up with the internet.

16

Friends online

S ome years ago, a young American journalist interviewed me about Dunbar's Number for an article she was doing. Her main specialism was the massive online gaming world – games like *Second Life* and *World of Warcraft* that are played by millions of players from all around the world. She was an avid player herself and was anxious to persuade me that the online worlds were a perfect place to study human behaviour. Most of these games involve creating alliances with other players to achieve objectives that allow you to acquire resources, which in turn allow you to take on the next challenge. With the enthusiasm of an aficionado, she told me that the structures of these alliances were all but identical to everyday communities, other than the fact that they formed and broke up much more quickly. Even more important, she said, they evolved their own self-policing mechanisms that allowed them to manage freeloaders and double-dealers.

I was intrigued and made several unsuccessful attempts to get funding to analyse data from these kinds of games. No funder was interested. However, I soon began to realise that the volume of data generated by these gaming worlds was so enormous that it really needed people with the mathematical and computing skills of statistical physicists to do it. It was way out of my league. However, a few years later, several people with just these kinds of skills began knocking on my door expressing an interest in doing exactly these kinds of studies. Some were interested in real friendships in the online world of Facebook, others in the virtual friendships of the gaming world.

Friendship in an online world

I suggested in chapter 2 that most people actually don't have more people signed up as friends on their Facebook page than they have friends in the offline world, and those few who do seem simply to have signed up people whom we would normally consider to be part of our extended face-to-face world as acquaintances rather than friends. In reality, online social networking sites are simply where you interact with your offline friends, not where you meet new friends. Facebook is just the modern equivalent of the telephone to our grandparents – a medium of communication and no more. This is not to suggest that people don't make new friends on the internet. Sometimes they do. But that doesn't happen as often as people like to believe. Rather, by and large, most people prefer to sign up as friends mainly the people they already know.

In reality, the waters have been muddied by the social networking sites because they have pursued a deliberate strategy of trying to persuade you to 'friend' as many people as possible, mainly for the commercial benefit of their advertising business model. Sometime around 2007, people began to question who all these people were that they had befriended on Facebook and other social-networking sites in response to all the system prompts to befriend friends of a friend's friend. Many of them felt uncomfortable that complete strangers could view their postings and what they said in their private 'conversations'. At this point, someone pointed out that there was a theory that we could only manage around 150 relationships at any one time. It seemed to spark a spontaneous realisation that this number had real everyday-life meaning, and a flurry of culling followed as people tried to reduce the number of 'friends' on their pages. It even became a bit of a game, with advertisers challenging us to cull some of our 'friends' in return for a reward. Ever afterwards, the number 150 was known as Dunbar's Number. So at least I have something to thank Facebook for.

In due course, another problem emerged: parents. Parents had begun to be active on Facebook, often as a way of 'keeping up with' (aka monitoring) their children and their children's friends. Younger users began to find that very restricting because it limited their ability to post what they really wanted. Worse still, employers began to check prospective employees out on Facebook. It is said that there was a period when more jobs as teachers were lost than given because District School Boards (the committees that run the local schools in America) were horrified by the photos of summer holidays in Florida or Thailand that people had posted on their Facebook pages. In real life, our contacts partition neatly into small groups that rarely overlap and seldom interact, so it is possible to present very different personas to different constituencies. Facebook allowed many of these people to sign up to the same shared community and this exposed everyone to the different versions of you. It was one of the major causes in the downturn in the popularity of Facebook: younger users, in particular, have switched to more private channels like WhatsApp and Snapchat.

This is certainly the impression given by two very different lines of evidence. One of these is provided by studies that have looked at how and why people use social networking sites. In one such study, Nicole Ellison found that undergraduates overwhelmingly used Facebook to maintain, and even intensify, their relationships with current friends and, importantly, to keep friendships with former dorm mates or classmates ticking over so that they didn't disappear. The other kind of evidence is the growth in networking sites that deliberately restrict you to more intimate circles of friendships. The American social networking site *Path.com* at first limited the number of friends you could have to fifty, though user pressure later persuaded them to increase it to 150. The Dutch site *Camarilla* advertises itself as the smallest social network in the world and limits you to just fifteen friends. The explosive growth in popularity of messaging services like WhatsApp which allow small closed groups to talk to each other and exchange images attests to the desire to have more focused, private conversations. Taken together, the evidence suggests that most users see the open-endedness of large-scale internet environments like Facebook as OK for some kinds of social interactions, but not for many aspects of social life. We still value our privacy.

Still, the question remains: does our online social world actually look anything like our offline, face-to-face world? To what extent do the underlying cognitive dimensions of human psychology underpin and limit both?

Many years after that young American journalist had tried to get me interested in the online gaming world, I met the Austrian physicist Stefan Thurner at a conference organised by a mutual friend, Ralph Kenna, head of the statistical physics group at Coventry University (whose student Padraig MacCarron had become one of my postdocs – science is all social wheels within wheels). It turned out that, as a result of another chance encounter, he had been able to gain access to the data from the Austrian online game *Pardus* – the very kind of project that I had had in mind. *Pardus* is a gaming world set in a futuristic universe, with a player base of some 300,000 people. Players have an individual avatar (so they are personally anonymous, as is usually the case) and compete with each other or form alliances to solve tasks, acquire real estate to mine for wealth, or raid other players' resources. The game is, obviously, played virtually, but it evolves fast and exhibits many of the natural patterns of social behaviour (players keep track of each other's past behaviour, and misbehaviour or failure to fulfil agreements are punished). When Stefan and Didier Sornette (who had been responsible for the original fractal analyses of our social structure datasets) analysed the patterns of alliance formation, they found essentially the same kind of hierarchical circles that we had found in face-to-face and digital world social networks, with very similar circle sizes and essentially the same scaling ratio.

Stefan Thurner and his group looked in much greater detail at the behaviour of the individual players on *Pardus*. They found that women were more positive in their interactions with others and attracted more positive behaviour than men did; conversely, men initiated and received more negative behaviours. They also found that women's trading networks were much more gender-based than men's networks: female–female trades were far more common than expected had players interacted at random with each other. While male trades directed at females were also common, female trades to males and male–male trades were relatively much less common. Women interacted with about 15 per cent more partners than males, and their trading networks were about 25 per cent more clustered than those of males – in other words, they were more likely to trade with other individuals who also traded, suggesting that they had a stronger preference for homophily and stability. However, women were more likely to attack others who were in conflict with their friends than men were. Males preferred people who were themselves well connected more than females did, while females made significantly more effort to reciprocate their relationships than males did. All this chimes remarkably well with the sex differences in social style (as we saw in chapter 13).

What these results tell us is that, even when we play games in a virtual environment with complete strangers who could be anywhere in the world, we impose a set of natural patterns on our interactions that reflect the kinds of social structures we use to manage our real-world face-to-face interactions. This suggests that the structuring arises from something deep inside our brains, and hence that it is probably something that all humans share and cannot easily change.

Channel matters

Mobile phones obviously provide us with all sorts of wonderfully different facilities. You can check your emails, find your way to a pub you have never been to before, locate your phone when you've lost it (without having to ring it!) and of course phone and text your friends, not to mention checking things on Wikipedia. The possibility of phoning someone has been with us for almost a century. Texting, however, is much more recent, and its introduction was quite accidental. The techies who invented it put the capability onto second-generation mobile phones (the rather smaller ones that followed the brick-sized early ones) simply because it could be done and they thought people might find it useful to be sent updates on train times or the weather. Since most programmers in those days were boys, it probably never occurred to any of them that people might actually use the facility for *social* purposes. Yet within a matter of months of its becoming available, people were excitedly texting each other – probably not saying much more than simply 'Hello! I'm here and thinking of you!'

Since then, of course, texting has become a way of life, and so completely embedded in the fabric of everyday social exchange that it would be hard to imagine social life without it. It has become one of the most used channels of communication, perhaps because it can be explicitly directed at particular individuals and so remains very private – though that, of course, has been the downfall of many who assumed it was so private that they sent rather too explicit messages, forgetting that the digital world stores everything for ever. Although texting has a useful element of privacy (after all, you can't be overheard when you text), it doesn't have quite the same sense of intimacy that speech-based communication obviously has. Perhaps as a result, we tend to use texts only for some kinds of communication. We are more likely to use text for good news, but prefer an old-fashioned phone call for bad news – most likely because we want to receive or give some immediate sympathy and comfort. Texting does work as a channel for social communication, but it is slow and clunky. The person you are texting may have switched their phone off while you were composing your elegantly witty reply. You get no response. You are left emotionally high and dry: did you say something that offended them, or were they just not interested in your declaration of eternal love or your diatribe against the world?

There are, of course, many hazards to text-based channels of communication. One is the <SEND> button. It has a lot to answer for. Some years ago, I was asked by the Holocaust Memorial Day Trust (the UK charity dedicated to memorialising the 1940s Holocaust) to help them with their Holocaust Day message for that year. The theme was how digital media could be used for bullying simply because people are too quick to press the <SEND> button without thinking about the consequences – and, with a nod back to the 1930s, why we so often fail to say something about it when we see it. The Trust commissioned a survey of people's use of digital media and asked about their experiences of being bullied or of themselves bullying others, and I was asked to write a report on it. Fully a quarter of the sample admitted that they had said something online that they later regretted – and would never have said in a face-to-face conversation.

Almost half of these respondents regretted what they had sent because it had been inappropriate, and a quarter regretted it because they later realised it could have (or had) upset the other person. Interestingly, there was a striking age effect: 30 per cent of 18- to 25-year-olds had later regretted putting something on a social media site, but only 12 per cent of those aged fifty-five or over did so – more evidence, perhaps, that we have to learn these skills, that they don't come naturally. In part, this was because younger people admitted that they were less likely to reread what they had written before sending it. Men were particularly bad in this respect: 40 per cent of women said they always checked over what they had written, but only 25 per cent of men did so.

This failure to check may be one reason why bullying has become so prevalent on the internet. Over a third of the sample said they had witnessed or been the victim of online bullying. Fewer than half of those had intervened on behalf of the victim, while 13 per cent had admitted encouraging the bullying. In the face-to-face world, there are natural social inhibitions that cause us to hold back before we open our mouths. But alone in our rooms, there are no such inhibitions and we type furiously away in our anger and frustration.

More than half the sample felt that social media had taken over from everyday face-to-face social interaction (and this was 2012!). Half felt that they would much rather see someone face to face when they were in need of support and advice (although a third said they would rather use the phone). Again, there was a strong age effect, with older people preferring face-to-face interactions both with close friends and in times of emotional need.

This raises the interesting question as to whether we use phone calls and texts in the same way when servicing our everyday social networks (as opposed to passing on news or seeking solace). Another of the Aalto PhD students, Sara Heydari, looked at the text traffic in our high-school dataset. It showed exactly the same pattern as the phone calls did. People's texting patterns looked just like their phone-call patterns: each person had an individual fingerprint in the way they distributed their texts among their friends and family, just as they did with their phone calls. Not only did their text fingerprints look identical to their phone-call fingerprints, they had the same persistence over time. However, the list of people called was not completely identical to the list of people texted – or at least the order of preference in the frequencies of contact for calls and texts was not the same. It seems that you call some people (family), and you prefer to text others (friends). A few people, however, were both called and texted with equal frequency, and these tended to be those who were very high in their list of priorities: the people who were contacted most often tended to receive both calls and texts, whereas those who were contacted least often tended to receive only texts.

While she was a graduate student of ours, Tatiana Vlahovic asked a group of people to record all their contacts with their five best friends at the end of each day for a two-week period, noting the media they had used and rating the interaction on a standard social psychology 'happiness' (or satisfaction) scale. Media were identified as face-to-face, phone, Skype, instant messaging, text or email (including in this last category, postings on social-networking sites like Facebook). The results were striking. Interactions that occurred face-to-face or via Skype were rated as much more satisfying and enjoyable than those using any of the other media, with little to choose between these others. Indirect support for this came from Anna Machin's large-scale study of romantic and best-friend relationships: she found that the frequency of telephone and email contacts had no detectable effects on the perceived intimacy of these close relationships. In fact, frequent face-to-face contacts seemed to be what mattered for close friendships, especially for men – you can't play football or drink down the pub virtually.

The fact that Skype did as well as face-to-face suggests two important conclusions about what makes a conversation enjoyable. One is that these two, uniquely, create a sense of what psychologists have called 'co-presence' – you feel as though you are in the same room together. Text-based media, and even the phone, introduce an unavoidable sense of distance. Co-presence creates a sense of intimacy that is inevitably absent at the end of a keyboard. The second point has to do with what is called 'flow'. Flow is a term that derives from music and refers to those occasions when the music just seems to run away with you under its own steam, especially when you are playing music with others. It's that sense where you seem to lose conscious control and the music takes over. People have sometimes referred to conversations having a musical quality in this sense, and this is most obvious when the conversation races along rather than faltering or grinding to a halt in an embarrassed silence while everyone struggles for something to say.

The pacing of conversations, the alternation of speaking turns, depends on very subtle cues, some of which are auditory (for example, the rise in pitch that occurs at the end of a contribution and signals that the speaker is about to stop and cede the floor to someone else), but others are visual (we tend to look away from someone while we are speaking to them, but flash them a glance just before we intend to stop speaking). More than this, however, it is probably the many visual cues we get while we are speaking to someone that matter: we can see the smile breaking on the face before we even finish our joke. Jokes, in particular, don't work anything like as well in print as they do face-to-face: things we would find hilarious in a face-to-face conversation come across as stilted in the cold light of print. And our attempt at a witty reply is even less funny when our text or email is eventually read several days later (and the recipient can no longer remember what it was a reply to).

What seemed to be especially important in this context was laughter. Tatiana had asked everyone to say whether or not laughter had occurred in each of their daily interactions – either real laughter or virtual laughter in the form of smiley emoticons or acronyms like LOL (meaning 'laugh out loud' – although the acronym meant something very different to the baby-boomer generation). It turned out that interactions that involved some form of laughter were all rated as being more enjoyable, more satisfying, than those that did not, irrespective of the medium. In other words, Facebook posts that provoked laughter in response to a comment were appreciated as much as real conversations that provoked laughter. This suggests that it is the way a conversation triggers laughter that is important.

So it seems that there is something especially engaging about face-to-face interactions that rises above the purely verbal content of what you have to say. Indeed, there is something intimate about the simple fact that you are engaging with someone else. What you have to say hardly counts. It's as though there is something important about being able to see the whites of someone's eyes when you converse with them. Hiromi Kobayashi and Shiro Kohshima at the Tokyo Institute of Technology pointed out that human eyes are unique in having a white sclera (the white outer part that surrounds the coloured iris in the centre): all other primates have brown or dark brown ones that are much closer in colour to both the iris and the surrounding fur. Our sclera is also *much* larger, relative to the size of the iris, than in any other species. Our eyes really do stand out in our faces. The white surround with the dark iris means that it is much easier to see whether or not someone is looking directly at you. Indeed, we find conversations with someone who never looks at you, or always looks at the floor, difficult and awkward, just as we find a conversation with someone who has no expression in their voice hard to engage with.

The 'lockdown' associated with COVID-19 has provided us with an unexpected, but very illuminating, natural experiment. Two things have, I think, come out of this – one good, one not so good but nonetheless very informative. The good aspect has been the imaginative way people have used the digital capacity of the internet to keep up their relationships with friends and family while being prevented from meeting up with them – everything from virtual choirs and singalongs to virtual meals. The latter, in particular, has been a classic example of human creativity, just like the social use of texting was. Everyone cooks the same menu, and then they all sit down to have a virtual meal together, course by course. The interesting thing about this is that they seem mostly to have done this with family rather than with friends. Yet again, it seems, family matters. The negative observation has been just how poorly applications like Zoom and Skype actually work for large social groups. It is only really possible for one person to speak at a time, so it tends to default into a bit of a lecture. You can't slip off to the side of the conversation to have a private word with someone the way you can when everyone is sitting round a big table. In other words, the assembled company cannot break up into several different conversations. One consequence of this is a tendency for the more shy and retiring folk to retreat into silence while the extraverts dominate the conversation. It may work fine for work meetings, but it's not obvious that it really functions well as a conversational medium for more than three or four people.

Facebook and other digital media might be very good for keeping a friendship ticking over when you can't meet up so easily, but my feeling is that all it does is slow down the rate at which friendships naturally decay with time when they are not continually reinforced. In the end, unless it is a deeply strong relationship, nothing on the digital earth will prevent that friendship quietly subsiding into an acquaintanceship – someone I once knew. What seems to be essential if you want to keep the friendship going is to meet up from time to time just to renew the 'spark'. It's the emotional quality of face-to-face interactions, those emotional overtones that our voice and facial expression can put into the words, that seems to be so important. Plus that sense of eyeball-to-eyeball engagement that says: 'I've made the effort to spend time with you.'

The ups and downs of social media

Social networking on the internet has obviously been one of the big success stories of the last decade, not just financially for the businesses that own and run these sites, but also for the punters whose lives have been transformed by the capacity to post photographs of their breakfast for their many friends to admire. Yet, bubbling along beneath the glitzy surface has been an element of disquiet at the effect the digital world can have on people's psychological wellbeing or the way in which our moral or political views can be manipulated by both the well-meaning and the unscrupulous. The world, it seems, is divided into digital optimists and digital pessimists. The optimists see the benefits of increased access to knowledge, and the opportunities to meet people from other cultures elsewhere in the world in ways that, up to a point, de-emphasise race, age and socio-economic status as greatly outweighing any disadvantages that there might be. Pessimists point to the fact that much use of the internet isn't social in any meaningful sense. Much of it is just information-seeking or the pursuit of lonely recreations such as pornography, watching films or playing non-social online games. As for the rest, seeing your friends' posts about the exciting time they are having just makes you more depressed.

In one of his seminal studies, Bob Kraut undertook a longitudinal study of adults moving to a new city for work and found that those who made most use of the internet devoted less time to developing new friendships in the face-to-face world, and as a result their levels of depression and loneliness increased. In another study of 169 people in 73 households during the first year or two after becoming regular internet users, he found that the more someone used the internet, the less they communicated with their family members in the household, the smaller the size of their social circle, and the more likely they were to have experienced depression and loneliness.

Most people are aware that there is something not quite satisfactory about interactions via the internet. For one thing, there is something of the Wild West about it: we seem to act before we think. There were two points of particular interest to our present concerns that came out of the Holocaust Memorial Day Trust survey that I mentioned earlier. One was a clear recognition that not all the friends on Facebook were real friends. People typically declared that they had around thirteen 'real' friends no matter how many Facebook friends they had – seemingly identifying the sympathy group (or 15-layer). In fact, the sociologist Cameron

Marlow analysed Facebook's own data and found that most of the directed posting activity is between a core group of around ten (in the case of boys) or sixteen (in the case of girls), irrespective of whether the number of friends listed was 50, 150 or 500. I found the same in the UK survey carried out for Thomas Fudge's: typically, people indicated that only 16–20 per cent of the friends listed on their Facebook page could be considered real friends.

Many people's concerns probably focus on the impact that the digital world has on children. A major element of that is related to the widespread use of the internet for bullying and the posting of extremist propaganda. There is a widespread perception that the seemingly greater mental fragility of the current generation of teenagers and young adults stems from reading endless posts describing the wonderful party time that their friends are having while they are cooped up in the library struggling to write an essay that is already overdue on an incomprehensible topic they don't understand. In reality, everyone else may not actually be having all that much fun, but the internet creates a pressure to *appear* to be doing so. So the whole process gets fuelled by a vortex that quickly drags us down into depression.

However, for the teenage cohort that has been online since birth, things may not always be quite as desperate. Amy Orben (probably my hardest-working PhD student ever, and now a Research Fellow in her own right at the University of Cambridge) analysed several datasets from the UK, Ireland and the USA. These were all very large national surveys (so many tens of thousands of people) with very detailed questions about people's activities and feelings. She was interested in whether the amount of time spent online affected children's sense of wellbeing. The short answer was: yes, there is a negative effect (the more time spent online the lower their wellbeing), but statistically it was quite small. Much bigger negative effects on wellbeing were due to getting into trouble with the police, binge drinking, being bullied online and use of soft drugs. The need to wear glasses had about the same modest negative effect as technology use. In contrast, eating well (especially fruit and vegetables) had a strong positive effect on wellbeing (though I rather suspect that this had as much to do with a home environment that encouraged a more balanced approach to life than simply the effect of diet).

Data from longitudinal studies did, however, suggest some modest but significant long-term effects. Increased satisfaction with life correlated with reduced use of online technology a year later; conversely, increased technology use predicted lower life-satisfaction a year later. Nonetheless, the effect wasn't huge, and led her to conclude that at least some of the media hype over technology use in the younger generation may be just that – hype. Schoolwork and the school environment, and to a lesser extent concerns about friendships, had much stronger negative effects on life satisfaction, and especially so in girls. Boys experienced little or no impact on life satisfaction from the quality of their friend-ships – not too surprisingly.

Much may, however, depend both on *what* adolescents do online and *how* they do it. In an analysis of data for teenagers, Oxford University's Andy Przybylski and Netta Weinstein found a significant decline in mental wellbeing with more time spent online, whether this was time spent watching films, playing video games, using computers more generally or just fiddling with smartphones. Notably, weekday use had a stronger negative effect than weekend use – perhaps because there were knock-on conse-quences with schoolwork not being completed? In each case, they noted a slight downturn in wellbeing when no time at all was spent online. It strikes me that any teenager who spends no time at all online, or even on a smartphone, is rather unlikely to be especially well adjusted as an individual, and hence that the downturn at the low end may be a signal of someone in serious trouble, not some-one who is so excited by their academic work or the church choir that they are giving it their all. In a very recent survey of more than 10,500 adolescents in Iceland, Ingibjorg Thorisdottir and her collaborators found that while active social media use seemed to reduce symptoms of anxiety and depression, *passive* use had the opposite effect and increased the frequency of these symptoms, and this remained so even when controlling for known risk factors like lack of self-esteem, offline peer support and poor body image.

A further consideration is that there may be sex differences in these effects. Cara Booker, Yvonne Kelly and Amanda Sacker analysed data from the UK Millennium Study (a longitudinal study of a sample of infants born into 19,244 British families between September 2000 and January 2002). They found striking sex differences in the relationship between social-media use and wellbeing. In particular, higher social media use at age ten was associated with lower wellbeing at age fourteen for girls, but not for boys. They found both a direct effect of social media use on wellbeing as well as an indirect effect mediated by online harassment. In addition, greater social-media use was associated with poor sleep, low self-esteem and poor body image, all of which also adversely influenced wellbeing.

Lesley Seltzer and her associates at the University of Wisconsin carried out a study that is particularly informative in this context. They measured the levels of cortisol (a stress hormone) and oxytocin (the so-called 'love hormone') in the urine of 8- to 12-year-old girls after they had spoken to their mother either in person or by instant messaging following a stressful task. The task they used is known as the Trier Social Stress Test for Children: it consists of a set of verbal and maths tests with an adult who never shows any emotion, and is known to be experienced as stressful by children. They found that cortisol levels were lower and oxytocin levels higher when the children spoke to the mother than when they could only message them. Using digital media to seek reassurance doesn't calm you down and may, in fact, lead to the steady accumulation of stress rather than its dissipation.

While the jury may still be partially out on this, I do have some concerns about the impact of life on the internet in another respect. We saw in chapter 15 that the social skills we need to navigate the complexities of the adult social world are so complex that, in humans, they take the better part of twenty-five years to master. In effect, we hone these skills in the sandpit of life. And the point about the sandpit is that, when someone kicks sand in your face, you cannot get out of it and walk off in a huff. You simply have to get a grip and learn the skills of diplomacy and compromise that will enable you to work your way through the adult world. Just as important, perhaps, is the fact that the 'sandpit' is a multi-person universe: everything we do in it has repercussions for many others and we have to learn how to balance their various interests and ours against each other.

If children spend a lot of their time online, they may not be gaining the experience they should be having in two important respects. First, most of their interactions online are dyadic rather than involving many individuals in a group. Second, if someone does kick metaphorical sand in their face, they can simply pull the plug; there is no obligation to learn how to compromise. If so, their social skills will be less well developed, and, as a consequence, the size of social network they can handle is likely to be smaller. They may also be less good at dealing with rejection, offence and failure to achieve. The worrying thing is that we won't know for a generation whether this is the case or not. And, by then it will be too late.

*

The rise of social networking sites and the new forms of digital social media has been the single most important social event of the new millennium. It has, quite literally, revolutionised our social lives. Reflecting back on what we have learned in this exploration of friendship, these new ways of interacting socially provide us with two final important insights. One is that these new media provide ways of maintaining friendships under circumstances where, in the past, those friendships would have quietly died because it was no longer possible to meet face to face. This is especially beneficial for our psychological wellbeing when we move as much as we now do, and so inevitably find ourselves in places where we know no one. Being able to contact old friends buffers us against the loneliness that would otherwise engulf us, and helps ease us into the new social environment by buying us time.

The other insight derives from the fact that digital media have provided us with a massive natural experiment that has allowed us to examine how and, more importantly, why our social world is as constrained as it is. The fact that our online social world is virtually identical to our offline social world tells us that the constraints are in our minds and not in the technology of how we communicate: it is the cognitive limits on our capacity to engage socially that limit the size of our social networks and, through the constraints imposed by time, their structure. The inventive technology of the digital world cannot change that. It may allow us to broadcast our opinions to a much wider audience, but, much as the lighthouse merely signals the presence of a hazard and does not engage in talk with passing ships, it cannot allow us to create new relationships or service old ones. That has to be done the old-fashioned way by directed exchanges. Exchanges have meaning only when there is an existing relationship to give them meaning. The processes of creating friendships – and communities – are more complicated than simply posting messages or sending prompted birthday greetings that we would otherwise have forgotten. We have to talk to people and engage in social activities with them, and that often involves a degree of physicality, of touch and casual caresses, that is impossible to do online.

Further reading

Chapter 1. Why friends matter

Arbes, V., Coulton, C. & Boekel, C. (2014). *Men's Social Connectedness*. Hall & Partners: Open Mind.

Burton-Chellew, M. & Dunbar, R.I.M. (2015). Hamilton's Rule predicts anticipated social support in humans. *Behavioral Ecology* 26: 130-137.

Cacioppo, J.T., Fowler, J.H. & Christakis, N.A. (2009). Alone in the crowd: the structure and spread of loneliness in a large social network. *Journal of Personality and Social Psychology* 97: 977.

Cacioppo, J.T. & Patrick, W. (2008). *Loneliness: Human Nature and the Need for Social Connection*. WW Norton & Company.

Christakis, N.A. & Fowler, J.H. (2007). The spread of obesity in a large social network over 32 years. *New England Journal of Medicine* 357: 370-379.

Christakis, N.A. & Fowler, J.H. (2008). The collective dynamics of smoking in a large social network. *New England Journal of Medicine* 358: 2249-2258.

Christakis, N.A. & Fowler, J.H. (2009). *Connected: The Surprising Power of Our Social Networks and How They Shape Our Lives*. Little, Brown Spark.

Cruwys, T., Dingle, G.A., Haslam, C., Haslam, S.A., Jetten, J. & Morton, T.A. (2013). Social group memberships protect against future depression, alleviate depression symptoms and prevent depression relapse. *Social Science & Medicine* 98: 179-186.

Cundiff, J.M. & Matthews, K.A. (2018). Friends with health benefits: the long-term benefits of early peer social integration for blood pressure and obesity in midlife. *Psychological Science* 29: 814-823.

Curry, O. & Dunbar, R.I.M. (2011). Altruism in networks: the effect of connections. *Biology Letters* 7: 651-653.

Curry, O. & Dunbar, R.I.M. (2013). Do birds of a feather flock together? The relationship between similarity and altruism in social networks. *Human Nature* 24: 336-347.

Dunbar, R.I.M. (2019). From there to now, and the origins of some ideas. In: D. Shankland (ed) *Dunbar's Number*, pp. 5-20. London: Royal Anthropological Institute, Occasional Papers No. 45 (Sean Kingston Publishing).

Dunbar, R.I.M. (2020). *Evolution: What Everyone Needs to Know.* New York: Oxford University Press.

Elwert, F. & Christakis, N.A. (2008). The effect of widowhood on mortality by the causes of death of both spouses. *American Journal of Public Health* 98: 2092-2098.

Fowler, J.H. & Christakis, N.A. (2008). Dynamic spread of happiness in a large social network: longitudinal analysis over 20 years in the Framingham Heart Study. *British Medical Journal* 337: a2338.

Granovetter, M. (1973). The strength of weak ties. *American Journal of Sociology* 78: 1360-1380.

Grayson, D.K. (1993). Differential mortality and the Donner Party disaster. *Evolutionary Anthropology* 2: 151-159.

van Harmelen, A.L., Gibson, J.L., St Clair, M.C., Owens, M., Brodbeck, J., Dunn, V., ... & Goodyer, I.M. (2016). Friendships and family support reduce subsequent depressive symptoms in at-risk adolescents. *PloS One* 11: e0153715.

Heatley Tejada, A., Montero, M. & Dunbar, R.I.M. (2017). Being unempathic will make your loved ones feel lonelier: loneliness in an evolutionary perspective. *Personality and Individual Differences* 116: 223-232.

Holt-Lunstad, J., Smith, T. & Bradley Layton, J. (2010). Social relationships and mortality risk: a metaanalytic review. *PLoS Medicine* 7: e1000316.

Holt-Lunstad, J., Smith, T.B., Baker, M., Harris, T. & Stephenson, D. (2015). Loneliness and social isolation as risk factors for mortality: a meta-analytic review. *Perspectives on Psychological Science* 10: 227-237.

Kim, D.A., Benjamin, E.J., Fowler, J.H. & Christakis, N.A. (2016). Social connectedness is associated with fibrinogen level in a human social network. *Proceedings of the Royal Society, London,* 283B: 20160958.

Lally, Maria: https://www.telegraph.co.uk/women/womens-life/11886089/Lonely-Why-are-we-all-feeling-so-lonesome-even-when-surrounded.html

McCullogh, J.M. & York Barton, E. (1991). Relatedness and mortality risk during a crisis year: Plymouth colony, 1620-1621. *Ethology and Sociobiology* 12: 195-209.

Madsen, E., Tunney, R., Fieldman, G., Plotkin, H., Dunbar, R.I.M., Richardson, J. & McFarland, D. (2007). Kinship and altruism: a cross-cultural experimental study. *British Journal of Psychology* 98: 339-359.

Pressman, S.D., Cohen, S., Miller, G.E., Barkin, A., Rabin, B.S. & Treanor, J.J. (2005). Loneliness, social network size, and immune response to influenza vaccination in college freshmen. *Health Psychology* 24: 297.

Rosenfeld, M.J., Thomas, R.J. & Hausen, S. (2019). Disintermediating your friends: How online dating in the United States displaces other ways of meeting. *Proceedings of the National Academy of Sciences* 116: 17753-17758.

Rosenquist, J.N., Murabito, J., Fowler, J.H. & Christakis, N.A.

(2010). The spread of alcohol consumption behavior in a large social network. *Annals of Internal Medicine* 152: 426.

Rosenquist, J.N., Fowler, J.H. & Christakis, N.A. (2011). Social network determinants of depression. *Molecular Psychiatry* 16: 273.

Santini, Z., Jose, P., Koyanagi, A., Meilstrup, C., Nielsen, L., Madsen, K., Hinrichsen, C., Dunbar, R.I.M. & Koushede, V. (2020). The moderating role of social network size in the temporal association between formal social participation and mental health: a longitudinal analysis using two consecutive waves of the Survey of Health, Ageing and Retirement in Europe (SHARE). *Social Psychiatry and Psychiatric Epidemiology* (in press).

Spence, J. (1954). *One Thousand Families in Newcastle.* Oxford: Oxford University Press.

Smith, K.P. & Christakis, N.A. (2008). Social networks and health. *American Journal of Sociology* 34: 405-429.

Steptoe, A., Shankar, A., Demakakos, P. & Wardle, J. (2013). Social isolation, loneliness, and all-cause mortality in older men and women. *Proceedings of the National Academy of Sciences* 110: 5797-5801.

Yang, Y.C., Boen, C., Gerken, K., Li, T., Schorpp, K., & Harris, K.M. (2016). Social relationships and physiological determinants of longevity across the human life span. *Proceedings of the National Academy of Sciences, USA,* 113: 578-583.

Chapter 2. Dunbar's number

Burton-Chellew, M. & Dunbar, R.I.M. (2011). Are affines treated as biological kin? A test of Hughes' hypothesis. *Current Anthropology* 52: 741-746.

Casari, M. & Tagliapietra, C. (2018). Group size in social-ecological systems. *Proceedings of the National Academy of Sciences, USA,* 115: 2728-2733.

Dàvid-Barrett, T. & Dunbar, R.I.M. (2017). Fertility, kinship and the evolution of mass ideologies. *Journal of Theoretical Biology* 417: 20-27.

Dunbar, R.I.M. (1995). On the evolution of language and kinship. In: J. Steele & S. Shennan (eds.) *The Archaeology of Human Ancestry: Power, Sex and Tradition*, pp. 380-396. London: Routledge.

Dunbar, R.I.M. (2016). Do online social media cut through the constraints that limit the size of offline social networks? *Royal Society Open Science* 3: 150292.

Dunbar, R.I.M. & Dunbar, P. (1988). Maternal time budgets of gelada baboons. *Animal Behaviour* 36: 970-980.

Dunbar, R.I.M. & Sosis, R. (2017). Optimising human community sizes. *Evolution and Human Behavior* 39: 106-111.

Dunbar, R.I.M. & Spoors, M. (1995). Social networks, support cliques and kinship. *Human Nature* 6: 273-290.

Dunbar, R.I.M., Arnaboldi, V., Conti, M. & Passarella, A. (2015). The structure of online social networks mirrors those in the offline world. *Social Networks* 43: 39-47.

Gonçalves, B., Perra, N., Vespignani, A. (2011). Modeling users' activity on Twitter networks: validation of Dunbar's Number. *PloS One* 6: e22656.

Haerter, J.O., Jamtveit, B., & Mathiesen, J. (2012). Communication dynamics in finite capacity social networks. *Physics Review Letters* 109: 168701.

Hill, R.A. (2019). From 150 to 3: Dunbar's numbers. In: D. Shankland (ed) *Dunbar's Number*, pp. 21-37. London: Royal Anthropological Institute Occasional Papers No. 45.

Hill, R.A. & Dunbar, R.I.M. (2003). Social network size in humans. *Human Nature* 14: 53-72.

Hughes, A.L. (1988). *Evolution and Human Kinship*. Oxford: Oxford University Press.

Killworth, P.D., Bernard, H.R., McCarty, C., Doreian, P., Goldenberg, S., Underwood, C., et al. (1984). Measuring patterns of acquaintanceship. *Current Anthropology* 25: 381-397.

MacCarron, P., Kaski, K. & Dunbar, R.I.M. (2016). Calling Dunbar's numbers. *Social Networks* 47:151-155.

O'Gorman, R. & Roberts, R. (2017). Distinguishing family from friends. *Human Nature* 28: 323-343.

Pollet, T., Roberts, S.B.G. & Dunbar, R.I.M. (2011). Use of social network sites and instant messaging does not lead to increased offline social network size, or to emotionally closer relationships with offline network members. *Cyberpsychology, Behavior and Social Networking* 14: 253-258.

Pollet, T., Roberts, S.B.G. & Dunbar, R.I.M. (2013). Going that extra mile: individuals travel further to maintain face-to-face contact with highly related kin than with less related kin. *PLoS One* 8: e53929.

Pollet, T.V., Roberts, S.B.G. & Dunbar, RI.M. (2011). Extraverts have larger social network layers but do not feel emotionally closer to individuals at any layer. *Journal of Individual Differences* 32: 161-169.

Rennard, B.O., Ertl, R.F., Gossman, G.L., Robbins, R.A., & Rennard, S.I. (2000). Chicken soup inhibits neutrophil chemotaxis in vitro. *Chest* 118: 1150-1157.

Rhoades, G.K. & Stanley, S.M. (2014). *Before "I Do": What Do Premarital Experiences Have to Do with Marital Quality Among Today's Young Adults?* The National Marriage Project, University of Virginia.

Roberts, S.B.G. & Dunbar, R.I.M. (2015). Managing relationship decay: network, gender, and contextual effects. *Human Nature* 26:426-450.

Roberts, S.B.G., Dunbar, R., Pollet, T.V. & Kuppens, T. (2009). Exploring variations in active network size: constraints and ego characteristics. *Social Networks* 31: 138-146.

Sutcliffe, A.J., Binder, J. & Dunbar, R.I.M. (2018). Activity in social media and intimacy in social relationships. *Computers in Human Behavior* 85: 227-235.

Sutcliffe, A., Dunbar, R.I.M., Binder, J. & Arrow, H. (2012). Relationships and the social brain: integrating psychological and evolutionary perspectives. *British Journal of Psychology* 103: 149-168.

Wolfram, S.: http://blog.stephenwolfram.com/2013/04/data-science-of-the-facebook-world/

Chapter 3. Making friends with your brain

Bickart, K.C., Hollenbeck, M.C., Barrett, L.F., & Dickerson, B.C. (2012). Intrinsic amygdala–cortical functional connectivity predicts social network size in humans. *Journal of Neuroscience* 32: 14729-14741.

Dunbar, R.I.M. (1991). Functional significance of social grooming in primates. *Folia Primatologica* 57: 121-131.

Dunbar, R.I.M. (1992). Neocortex size as a constraint on group size in primates. *Journal of Human Evolution* 22: 469-493.

Dunbar, R.I.M. (1993). Coevolution of neocortex size, group size and language in humans. *Behavioral and Brain Sciences* 16: 681-735.

Dunbar, R.I.M. & MacCarron, P. (2019). Group size as a trade-off between fertility and predation risk: implications for social evolution. *Journal of Zoology* 308: 9-15.

Dunbar, R.I.M. & Shultz, S. (2010). Bondedness and sociality. *Behaviour* 147: 775-803.

Dunbar, R.I.M. & Shultz, S. (2017). Why are there so many explanations for primate brain evolution? *Philosophical Transactions of the Royal Society, London,* 244B: 201602244.

Fox, K.C., Muthukrishna, M. & Shultz, S. (2017). The social and cultural roots of whale and dolphin brains. *Nature Ecology & Evolution* 1: 1699.

Hampton, W.H., Unger, A., Von Der Heide, R.J. & Olson, I.R. (2016). Neural connections foster social connections: a diffusion-weighted imaging study of social networks. *Social Cognitive and Affective Neuroscience* 11: 721-727.

Kanai, R., Bahrami, B., Roylance, R. & Rees, G. (2012). Online social network size is reflected in human brain structure. *Proceedings of the Royal Society, London,* 279B:1327-1334.

Keverne, E.B., Martel, F.L. & Nevison, C.M. (1996). Primate brain evolution: genetic and functional considerations. *Proceedings of the Royal Society, London,* 263B: 689-696.

Kiesow, H., Dunbar, R.I.M., Kable, J.W., Kalenscher, T., Vogeley, K., Schilbach, L., Wiecki., T. & Bzdok, D. (2020). 10,000 social brains: sex differentiation in human brain anatomy. *Science Advances* 6: eeaz1170.

Kwak, S., Joo, W.T., Youm, Y. & Chey, J. (2018). Social brain volume is associated with in-degree social network size among older adults. *Proceedings of the Royal Society, London,* 285B: 20172708.

Lewis, P.A., Rezaie, R., Browne, R., Roberts, N. & Dunbar, R.I.M. (2011). Ventromedial prefrontal volume predicts understanding of others and social network size. *NeuroImage* 57: 1624-1629.

Meguerditchian, A., Marie, D., Margiotoudi, K., Roth, M., Nazarian, B., Anton, J.-L. & Claidière, N. (in press). Baboons (*Papio anubis*) living in larger social groups have bigger brains. *Evolution and Human Behavior.*

Morelli, S.A., Leong, Y.C., Carlson, R.W., Kullar, M. & Zaki, J. (2018). Neural detection of socially valued community members. *Proceedings of the National Academy of Sciences, USA,*115: 8149-8154.

Noonan, M., Mars, R., Sallet, J., Dunbar, R.I.M. & Fellows, L. (2018). The structural and functional brain networks that support human social networks. *Behavioural Brain Research* 355: 12-23.

Parkinson, C., Kleinbaum, A.M. & Wheatley, T. (2017). Spontaneous neural encoding of social network position. *Nature Human Behaviour* 1: 0072.

Pérez-Barbería, J., Shultz, S. & Dunbar, R.I.M. (2007). Evidence for intense coevolution of sociality and brain size in three orders of mammals. *Evolution* 61: 2811-2821.

Powell, J., Lewis, P.A., Roberts, N., García-Fiñana, M. & Dunbar, R.I.M. (2012) Orbital prefrontal cortex volume predicts social network size: an imaging study of individual differences in humans. *Proceedings of the Royal Society, London,* 279B: 2157-2162.

Powell, J., Kemp, G., Dunbar, R.I.M., Roberts, N., Sluming, V. & García-Fiñana, M. (2014). Different association between intentionality competence and prefrontal volume in left- and right-handers. *Cortex* 54: 63-76.

Sallet, J., Mars, R.B., Noonan, M.A., Neubert, F.X., Jbabdi, S., O'Reilly, J.X., Filippini, N., Thomas, A.G. & Rushworth, M.F.S. (2013). The organization of dorsal prefrontal cortex in humans and macaques. *Journal of Neuroscience* 33:12255-12274.

Shultz, S. & Dunbar, R.I.M. (2007). The evolution of the social brain: Anthropoid primates contrast with other vertebrates. *Proceedings of the Royal Society, London,* 274B: 2429-2436.

Shultz, S. & Dunbar, R.I.M. (2010). Social bonds in birds are associated with brain size and contingent on the correlated evolution of life-history and increased parental investment. *Biological Journal of the Linnean Society* 100: 111-123.

Shultz, S. & Dunbar, R.I.M. (2010). Encephalisation is not a universal macroevolutionary phenomenon in mammals but is associated with sociality. *Proceedings of the National Academy of Sciences, USA,* 107: 21582-21586.

Zerubavel, N., Bearman, P.S., Weber, J. & Ochsner, K. N. (2015). Neural mechanisms tracking popularity in real-world social networks. *Proceedings of the National Academy of Sciences, USA,*112: 15072-15077.

Chapter 4. Friendship in circles

Arnaboldi, V., Passarella, A., Conti, M. & Dunbar, R.I.M.

(2015). *Online Social Networks: Human Cognitive Constraints in Facebook and Twitter Personal Graphs*. Amsterdam: Elsevier.

Binder, J.F., Roberts, S.B.G. & Sutcliffe, A.G. (2012). Closeness, loneliness, support: Core ties and significant ties in personal communities. *Social Networks* 34: 206-214.

Buys, C.J. & Larson, K.L. (1979). Human sympathy groups. *Psychological Reports* 45: 547-553.

Cartright, D. & Harary, F. (1956). Structural balance: a generalization of Heider's theory. *Psychological Review* 63: 277-292.

Curry, O., Roberts, S.B.G. & Dunbar, R.I.M. (2013). Altruism in social networks: evidence for a "kinship premium". *British Journal of Psychology* 104: 283-295.

Dunbar, R.I.M., MacCarron, P. & Shultz, S. (2018). Primate social group sizes exhibit a regular scaling pattern with natural attractors. *Biology Letters* 14: 20170490.

Dunbar, R.I.M., Arnaboldi, V., Conti, M. & Passarella, A. (2015). The structure of online social networks mirrors those in the offline world. *Social Networks* 43: 39-47.

Grove, M. (2010). Stone circles and the structure of Bronze Age society. *Journal of Archaeological Science* 37: 2612-2621.

Hamilton, M.J., Milne, B.T., Walker, R.S., Burger, O. & Brown, J.H. (2007). The complex structure of hunter-gatherer social networks. *Proceedings of the Royal Society, London*, 274B: 2195-2202.

Hill, R., Bentley, A. & Dunbar, R.I.M. (2008). Network scaling reveals consistent fractal pattern in hierarchical mammalian societies. *Biology Letters* 4: 748-751.

Jenkins, R., Dowsett, A.J. & Burton, A.M. (2018). How many faces do people know? *Proceedings of the Royal Society*, London, 285B: 20181319.

Klimek, P. & Thurner, S. (2013). Triadic closure dynamics drives scaling laws in social multiplex networks. *New Journal of Physics* 15: 063008.

Kordsmeyer, T., MacCarron, P. & Dunbar, R.I.M. (2017). Sizes of permanent campsites reflect constraints on natural human communities. *Current Anthropology* 58: 289-294.

MacCarron, P., Kaski, K. & Dunbar, R.I.M. (2016). Calling Dunbar's numbers. *Social Networks* 47:151-155.

Miritello, G., Moro, E., Lara, R., Martínez-López, R., Belchamber, J., Roberts, S.B.G. & Dunbar, R.I.M. (2013). Time as a limited resource: communication strategy in mobile phone networks. *Social Networks* 35: 89-95.

Molho, C., Roberts, S.G., de Vries, R.E. & Pollet, T.V. (2016). The six dimensions of personality (HEXACO) and their associations with network layer size and emotional closeness to network members. *Personality and Individual Differences* 99: 144-148.

Pollet, T.V., Roberts, S.B.G. & Dunbar, RI.M. (2011). Extraverts have larger social network layers but do not feel emotionally closer to individuals at any layer. *Journal of Individual Differences* 32: 161-169.

Sutcliffe, A., Bender, J. & Dunbar, R.I.M. (2018). Activity in social media and intimacy in social relationships. *Computers in Human Behavior* 85: 227-235.

Sutcliffe, A., Dunbar, R.I.M. & Wang, D. (2016). Modelling the evolution of social structure. *PLoS One* 11: e0158605.

Sutcliffe, A., Dunbar, R.I.M., Binder, J. & Arrow, H. (2012). Relationships and the social brain: integrating psychological and evolutionary perspectives. *British Journal of Psychology* 103: 149-168.

Takano, M. & Fukuda, I. (2017). Limitations of time resources in human relationships determine social structures. *Palgrave Communications* 3: 17014.

Tamarit, I., Cuesta, J., Dunbar, R.I.M. & Sánchez, A. (2018). Cognitive resource allocation determines the organisation of personal networks. *Proceedings of the National Academy of Sciences, USA,* 115: 1719233115.

Wellman, B. & Wortley, S. (1990). Different strokes from different folks: Community ties and social support. *American Journal of Sociology* 96: 558-588.

Whitmeyer, J.M. (2002). A deductive approach to friendship networks. *Journal of Mathematical Sociology* 26: 147-165.

Zhou, W-X., Sornette, D., Hill, R.A. & Dunbar, R.I.M. (2005). Discrete hierarchical organization of social group sizes. *Proceedings of the Royal Society, London,* 272B: 439-444.

Chapter 5. Your social fingerprint

Aledavood, T., López, E., Roberts, S.B.G., Reed-Tsochas, F., Moro, E., Dunbar, R.I.M. & Saramäki, J. (2015). Daily rhythms in mobile telephone communication. *PLoS One* 10: e0138098.

Aledavood, T., López, E., Roberts, S.B.G., Reed-Tsochas, F., Moro, E., Dunbar, R.I.M. & Saramäki, J. (2016). Channel-specific daily patterns in mobile phone communication. In: S. Battiston, F. De Pellegrini, G. Caldarelli & E. Merelli (Eds.) *Proceedings of ECCS 2014,* pp. 209-218. Berlin: Springer.

Barrett, L., Dunbar, R.I.M. & Lycett, J. (2000). *Human Evolutionary Psychology.* Macmillan/Palgrave and Princeton University Press.

Bhattacharya, K., Ghosh, A., Monsivais, D., Dunbar, R.I.M. & Kaski, K. (2017). Absence makes the heart grow fonder: social compensation when failure to interact risks weakening a relationship. *EPJ Data Science* 6: 1-10.

Dàvid-Barrett, T. & Dunbar, R.I.M. (2014). Social elites emerge naturally in an agent-based framework when interaction patterns are constrained. *Behavioral Ecology* 25: 58-68.

Devaine, M., San-Galli, A., Trapanese, C., Bardino, G., Hano, C., Saint Jalme, M., ... & Daunizeau, J. (2017). Reading wild minds: A computational assay of Theory of Mind sophistication across seven primate species. *PLoS Computational Biology* 13: e1005833.

Dunbar, R.I.M. (1998). Theory of mind and the evolution of language. In: J. Hurford, M. Studdart-Kennedy & C. Knight (eds) *Approaches to the Evolution of Language*, pp. 92-110. Cambridge: Cambridge University Press.

Ghosh, A., Monsivais, D., Bhattacharya, K., Dunbar, R.I.M. & Kaski, K. (2019). Quantifying gender preferences in human social interactions using a large cellphone dataset. *EPJ Data Science* 8: 9.

Jo, H.-H., Saramäki, J., Dunbar, R.I.M. & Kaski, K. (2014). Spatial patterns of close relationships across the lifespan. *Scientific Reports* 4: 6988.

Kraut, R., Patterson, M., Lundmark, V., Kiesler, S., Mukophadhyay, T. & Scherlis, W. (1998). Internet paradox: A social technology that reduces social involvement and psychological well-being? *American Psychologist* 53: 1017.

Lu, Y-E., Roberts, S., Lió, P., Dunbar, R.I.M. & Crowcroft, J. (2009). Size matters: variation in personal network size, personality and effect on information transmission. In: *Proceedings of IEEE International Conference on Social Computing, Vancouver, Canada, 2009*. IEEE Publications.

Martin, J.L. & Yeung, K.T. (2006). Persistence of close personal ties over a 12-year period. *Social Networks* 28: 331-362.

Mok, D. & Wellman, B. (2007). Did distance matter before the Internet?: Interpersonal contact and support in the 1970s. *Social Networks* 29: 430-461.

Monsivais, M., Bhattacharya, K., Ghosh, A., Dunbar, R.I.M. & Kaski, K. (2017). Seasonal and geographical impact on human resting periods. *Scientific Reports* 7: 10717.

Monsivais, D., Ghosh, A., Bhattacharya, K., Dunbar, R.I.M. & Kaski, K. (2017). Tracking urban human activity from mobile phone calling patterns. *PLoS Computational Biology* 13: e1005824.

Roberts, S.B.G. & Dunbar, R.I.M. (2015). Managing relationship decay: network, gender, and contextual effects. *Human Nature* 26: 426-450.

Saramäki, J., Leicht, E., López, E., Roberts, S.B.G., Reed-Tsochas, F. & Dunbar, R.I.M. (2014). The persistence of social signatures in human communication. *Proceedings of the National Academy of Sciences, USA* 111: 942-947.

DeScioli, P. & Kurzban, R. (2009). The alliance hypothesis for human friendship. *PloS One* 4: e5802.

Smoreda, Z. & Licoppe, C. (2000). Gender-specific use of the domestic telephone. *Social Psychology Quarterly* 63: 238-252.

Sutcliffe, A., Dunbar, R.I.M. & Wang, D. (2014). Modelling the evolution of social structure. *PLoS One* 11: e0158605.

Chapter 6. Friends in mind

Amiez, C., Sallet, J., Hopkins, W.D., Meguerditchian, A., Hadj-Bouziane, F., Hamed, S.B., et al. (2019). Sulcal organization in the medial frontal cortex provides insights into primate brain evolution. *Nature Communications* 10: 3437.

Astington, J.W. (1993). *The Child's Discovery of the Mind.* Cambridge (MA): Cambridge University Press.

Baron-Cohen, S., Leslie, A.M. & Frith, U. (1985). Does the autistic child have a theory of mind? *Cognition* 21: 37-46.

Carlson, S.M., Moses, L.J. & Breton, C. (2002). How specific is the relation between executive function and theory of mind? Contributions of inhibitory control and working memory. *Infant and Child Development* 11: 73-92.

Casey, B.J., Somerville, L.H., Gotlib, I.H., Ayduk, O., Franklin, N.T., Askren, M.K., Jonides, J., Berman, M.G., Wilson, N.L., et al. (2011). Behavioral and neural correlates of delay of gratification 40 years later. *Proceedings of the National Academy of Sciences, USA*, 10: 14998-15003.

Crockett, M.J., Braams, B.R., Clark, L., Tobler, P.N., Robbins,

T.W. & Kalenscher, T. (2013). Restricting temptations: neural mechanisms of precommitment. *Neuron* 79: 391-401.

Dunbar, R.I.M., & Launay, J. & Curry, O. (2016). The complexity of jokes is limited by cognitive constraints on mentalizing. *Human Nature* 27: 130-140.

Dunbar, R.I.M., McAdam, M. & O'Connell, S. (2005). Mental rehearsal in great apes and humans. *Behavioral Processes* 69: 323-330.

Happé, F. (1994). *Autism: An Introduction to Psychological Theory*. London: University College London Press.

Hardin, G. (1968). The tragedy of the commons. *Science* 162: 1243-1248.

Kinderman, P., Dunbar, R.I.M. & Bentall, R.P. (1998). Theory-of-mind deficits and causal attributions. *British Journal of Psychology* 89: 191-204.

Krupenye, C., Kano, F., Hirata, S., Call, J. & Tomasello, M. (2016). Great apes anticipate that other individuals will act according to false beliefs. *Science* 354: 110-114.

Launay, J., Pearce, E., Wlodarski, R., van Duijn, M., Carney, J. & Dunbar, R.I.M. (2015). Higher-order mentalising and executive functioning. *Personality and Individual Differences* 86: 6-14.

Lewis, P.A., Rezaie, R., Browne, R., Roberts, N. & Dunbar, R.I.M. (2011). Ventromedial prefrontal volume predicts understanding of others and social network size. *NeuroImage* 57: 1624-1629.

Lewis, P., Birch, A., Hall, A. & Dunbar, R.I.M. (2017). Higher order intentionality tasks are cognitively more demanding. *Social, Cognitive and Affective Neuroscience* 12: 1063-1071.

Mars, R.B., Foxley, S., Verhagen, L., Jbabdi, S., Sallet, J., Noonan, M.P., Neubert, F-X., Andersson, J., Croxson, P., Dunbar, R.I.M., et al. (2016). The extreme capsule fiber complex in humans and macaque monkeys: a comparative diffusion MRI tractography study. *Brain Structure and Function* 221: 4059-4071.

Passingham, R.E., & Wise, S.P. (2012). *The Neurobiology of the Prefrontal Cortex: Anatomy, Evolution, and the Origin of Insight*. Oxford: Oxford University Press.

Powell, J., Lewis, P., Dunbar, R.I.M., García-Fiñana, M. & Roberts, N. (2010). Orbital prefrontal cortex volume correlates with social cognitive competence. *Neuropsychologia* 48: 3554-3562.

Powell, J., Kemp, G., Dunbar, R.I.M., Roberts, N., Sluming, V. & García-Fiñana, M. (2014). Different association between intentionality competence and prefrontal volume in left- and right-handers. *Cortex* 54: 63-76.

Santiesteban, I., Banissy, M.J., Catmur, C. & Bird, G. (2012). Enhancing social ability by stimulating right temporoparietal junction. *Current Biology* 22: 2274-2277.

Shultz, S. & Dunbar, R.I.M. (2010). Species differences in executive function correlate with hippocampus volume and neocortex ratio across non-human primates. *Journal of Comparative Psychology* 124: 252-260.

Stiller, J. & Dunbar, R.I.M. (2007). Perspective-taking and memory capacity predict social network size. *Social Networks* 29: 93-104.

Chapter 7. Friendship and the magic of touch

Carter, C.S., Grippo, A.J., Pournajafi-Nazarloo, H., Ruscio, M.G. & Porges, S.W. (2008). Oxytocin, vasopressin and sociality. *Progress in Brain Research* 170: 331-336.

Charles, S., Dunbar, R. & Farias, M. (2020). The aetiology of social deficits within mental health disorders: The role of the immune system and endogenous opioids. *Brain, Behavior and Immunity – Health* 1: 100003.

Donaldson, Z.R. & Young, L.J. (2008). Oxytocin, vasopressin, and the neurogenetics of sociality. *Science* 322: 900-904.

Dunbar, R.I.M. (1991). Functional significance of social grooming in primates. *Folia Primatologica* 57: 121-131.

Dunbar, R.I.M. (2010). The social role of touch in humans and primates: behavioural function and neurobiological mechanisms. *Neuroscience & Biobehavioral Reviews* 34: 260-268.

Dunbar, R.I.M., Korstjens, A. & Lehmann, J. (2009). Time as an ecological constraint. *Biological Reviews* 84: 413-429.

Gursul, D., Goksan, S., Hartley, C., Mellado, G.S., Moultrie, F., Hoskin, A., Adams, E., Hathway, G., Walker, S., McGlone, F. & Slater, R. (2018). Stroking modulates noxious-evoked brain activity in human infants. *Current Biology* 28: R1380-R1381.

Henrich, J., Boyd, R., Bowles, S., Camerer, C., Fehr, E., Gintis, H., et al. (2005). "Economic man" in cross-cultural perspective: Behavioral experiments in 15 small-scale societies. *Behavioral and Brain Sciences* 28: 795-815.

Inagaki, T.K. & Eisenberger, N.I. (2013). Shared neural mechanisms underlying social warmth and physical warmth. *Psychological Science* 24: 2272-2280.

Inagaki, T.K., Ray, L.A., Irwin, M.R., Way, B.M., & Eisenberger, N. I. (2016). Opioids and social bonding: naltrexone reduces feelings of social connection. *Social Cognitive and Affective Neuroscience* 11: 728-735.

Johnson, K. & Dunbar, R.I.M. (2016). Pain tolerance predicts human social network size. *Scientific Reports* 6: 25267.

Keverne, E.B., Martensz, N. & Tuite, B. (1989). Beta-endorphin concentrations in cerebrospinal fluid of monkeys are influenced by grooming relationships. *Psychoneuroendocrinology* 14: 155-161.

Lehmann, J., Korstjens, A.H. & Dunbar, R.I.M. (2007). Group size, grooming and social cohesion in primates. *Animal Behaviour* 74: 1617-1629.

Loseth, G.E., Ellingsen, D.M. & Leknes, S. (2014). State-dependent μ-opioid Modulation of Social Motivation—a model. *Frontiers in Behavioral Neuroscience* 8: 430.

Machin, A. & Dunbar, R.I.M. (2011). The brain opioid theory

of social attachment: a review of the evidence. *Behaviour* 148: 985-1025.

Nave, G., Camerer, C. & McCullough, M. (2015). Does oxytocin increase trust in humans? A critical review of research. *Perspectives on Psychological Science* 10: 772-789.

Nummenmaa, L., Manninen, S., Tuominen, L., Hirvonen, J., Kalliokoski, K.K., Nuutila, P., Jääskeläinen, I.P., Hari, R., Dunbar, R.I.M. & Sams, M. (2015) Adult attachment style is associated with cerebral μ-opioid receptor availability in humans. *Human Brain Mapping* 36: 3621-3628.

Nummenmaa, L., Tuominen, L., Dunbar, R.I.M., Hirvonen, J., Manninen, S., Arponen, E., Machin, A., Hari, R., Jääskeläinen, I.P. & Sams, M. (2016). Reinforcing social bonds by touching modulates endogenous μ-opioid system activity in humans. *NeuroImage* 138: 242-247.

Olausson, H., Wessberg, J., Morrison, I., McGlone, F. & Vallbo, A. (2010). The neurophysiology of unmyelinated tactile afferents. *Neuroscience and Biobehavioral Reviews* 34: 185-191.

van Overwalle, F. (2009). Social cognition and the brain: a metaanalysis. *Human Brain Mapping* 30: 829-858.

Pearce, E., Wlodarski, R., Machin, A. & Dunbar, R.I.M. (2017). Variation in the β-endorphin, oxytocin, and dopamine receptor genes is associated with different dimensions of human sociality. *Proceedings of the National Academy of Sciences, USA,* 112 114: 5300-5305.

Pearce, E., Wlodarski, R., Machin, A. & Dunbar, R.I.M. (2018). The influence of genetic variation on social disposition, romantic relationships and social networks: a replication study. *Adaptive Human Behavior and Physiology* 4: 400-422.

Pellissier, L.P., Gandía, J., Laboute, T., Becker, J.A. & Le Merrer, J. (2018). μ opioid receptor, social behaviour and autism spectrum disorder: reward matters. *British Journal of Pharmacology* 175: 2750-2769.

Resendez, S.L. & Aragona, B.J. (2013). Aversive motivation and the maintenance of monogamous pair bonding. *Reviews in the Neurosciences* 24: 51-60.

Resendez, S.L., Dome, M., Gormley, G., Franco, D., Nevárez, N., Hamid, A.A. & Aragona, B.J. (2013). μ-opioid receptors within subregions of the striatum mediate pair bond formation through parallel yet distinct reward mechanisms. *Journal of Neuroscience* 33: 9140-9149.

Seyfarth, R.M. & Cheney, D.L. (1984). Grooming, alliances and reciprocal altruism in vervet monkeys. *Nature* 308: 541.

Sutcliffe, A., Dunbar, R.I.M., Binder, J. & Arrow, H. (2012). Relationships and the social brain: integrating psychological and evolutionary perspectives. *British Journal of Psychology* 103: 149-168.

Suvilehto, J., Glerean, E., Dunbar, R.I.M., Hari, R. & Nummenmaaa, L. (2015). Topography of social touching depends on emotional bonds between humans. *Proceedings of the National Academy of Sciences, USA,* 112: 13811-16.

Suvilehto, J., Nummenmaa, L., Harada, T., Dunbar, R.I.M., Hari, R., Turner, R., Sadato, N. & Kitada, R. (2019). Cross-cultural similarity in relationship-specific social touching. *Proceedings of the Royal Society, London,* 286B: 20190467

Chapter 8. Binding the bonds of friendship

Bandy, M.S. (2004). Fissioning, scalar stress, and social evolution in early village societies. *American Anthropologist* 106: 322-333.

Brown, S., Savage, P.E., Ko, A.M.S., Stoneking, M., Ko, Y.C., Loo, J.H. & Trejaut, J.A. (2014). Correlations in the population structure of music, genes and language. *Proceedings of the Royal Society, London,* 281B: 20132072.

Cohen, E., Ejsmond-Frey, R., Knight, N. & Dunbar, R.I.M. (2010). Rowers' high: behavioural synchrony is correlated with elevated pain thresholds. *Biology Letters* 6: 106-108.

Davila Ross, M., Owren, M.J. & Zimmermann, E. (2009). Reconstructing the evolution of laughter in great apes and humans. *Current Biology* 19: 1-6.

Dezecache, G. & Dunbar, R.I.M. (2012). Sharing the joke: the size of natural laughter groups. *Evolution and Human Behaviour* 33: 775-779.

Dunbar, R.I.M. (2012). Bridging the bonding gap: the transition from primates to humans. *Philosophical Transactions of the Royal Society, London,* 367B: 1837-1846

Dunbar, R.I.M. (2014). *Human Evolution.* Harmondsworth: Pelican and New York: Oxford University Press.

Dunbar, R.I.M. (2017). Breaking bread: the functions of social eating. *Adaptive Human Behavior and Physiology* 3: 198-211.

Dunbar, R.I.M., Kaskatis, K., MacDonald, I. & Barra, V. (2012). Performance of music elevates pain threshold and positive affect. *Evolutionary Psychology* 10: 688-702.

Dunbar, R.I.M., Baron, R., Frangou, A., Pearce, E., van Leeuwen, E.J.C., Stow, J., Partridge, P., MacDonald, I., Barra, V., & van Vugt, M. (2012). Social laughter is correlated with an elevated pain threshold. *Proceedings of the Royal Society, London, 279B,* 1161-1167.

Dunbar, R.I.M., Launay, J., Wlodarski, R., Robertson, C., Pearce, E., Carney, J. & MacCarron, P. (2017). Functional benefits of (modest) alcohol consumption. *Adaptive Human Behavior and Physiology* 3: 118-133.

Dunbar, R.I.M., Teasdale, B., Thompson, J., Budelmann, F., Duncan, S., van Emde Boas, E. & Maguire, L. (2016). Emotional arousal when watching drama increases pain threshold and social bonding. *Royal Society Open Science* 3: 160288.

Gray, A., Parkinson, B. & Dunbar, R. (2015). Laughter's influence on the intimacy of self-disclosure. *Human Nature* 26: 28-43.

Hockings, K. & Dunbar, R.I.M. (Eds.) (2019). *Alcohol and Humans: A Long and Social Affair.* Oxford: Oxford University Press.

Keverne, E.B., Martensz, N. & Tuite, B. (1989). Beta-endorphin concentrations in cerebrospinal fluid of monkeys are influenced by grooming relationships. *Psychoneuroendocrinology* 14: 155-161.

Manninen, S., Tuominen, L., Dunbar, R.I.M., Karjalainen, T., Hirvonen, J., Arponen, E., Hari, R., Jääskeläinen, I., Sams, M. & Nummenmaa, L. (2017). Social laughter triggers endogenous opioid release in humans. *Journal of Neuroscience* 37: 6125-6131.

Pearce, E., Launay, J. & Dunbar, R.I.M. (2015). The ice-breaker effect: singing mediates fast social bonding. *Royal Society Open Science* 2: 150221.

Pearce, E., Launay, J., van Duijn, M., Rotkirch, A., Dàvid-Barrett, T. & Dunbar, R.I.M. (2014). Singing together or apart: The effect of competitive and cooperative singing on social bonding within and between sub-groups of a university fraternity. *Psychology of Music* 44: 1255-73.

Provine, R.R. (2001). *Laughter: A Scientific Investigation.* Harmondsworth: Penguin.

Rennung, M. & Göritz, A.S. (2015). Facing sorrow as a group unites. Facing sorrow in a group divides. *PloS One* 10: e0136750.

Robertson, C., Tarr, B., Kempnich, M. & Dunbar, R.I.M. (2017). Rapid partner switching may facilitate increased broadcast group size in dance compared with conversation groups. *Ethology* 123: 736-747.

Sherif, M., Harvey, O.J., White, B.J., Hood, W. & Sherif, C.W. (1961). *Intergroup Conflict and Cooperation: The Robbers Cave Experiment.* Norman OK: The University Book Exchange.

Tarr, B., Launay, J. & Dunbar, R.I.M. (2014). Silent disco: dancing in synchrony leads to elevated pain thresholds and social closeness. *Evolution and Human Behavior* 37: 343-349.

Tarr, B., Launay, J., Cohen, E., & Dunbar, R.I.M. (2015). Synchrony and exertion during dance independently raise pain threshold and encourage social bonding. *Biology Letters* 11: 20150767.

Tarr, B., Launay, J. & Dunbar, R.I.M. (2017). Naltrexone blocks endorphins released when dancing in synchrony. *Adaptive Human Behavior and Physiology* 3: 241-254.

Weinstein, D., Launay, J., Pearce, E., Dunbar, R. & Stewart, L. (2014). Singing and social bonding: changes in connectivity and pain threshold as a function of group size. *Evolution and Human Behavior* 37: 152-158.

Chapter 9. The languages of friendship

Anderson, E., Siegel, E.H., Bliss-Moreau, E. & Barrett, L.F. (2011). The visual impact of gossip. *Science* 332: 1446-1448.

Beersma, B. & Van Kleef, G.A. (2011). How the grapevine keeps you in line: Gossip increases contributions to the group. *Social Psychological and Personality Science* 2: 642-649.

Bryant, G.A. & Aktipis, C.A. (2014). The animal nature of spontaneous human laughter. *Evolution and Human Behavior* 35: 327-335.

Bryant, G.A., Fessler, D.M.T., Fusaroli, R., Clint, E., Aarøe, L., Apicella, C.L.; et al. (2016). Detecting affiliation in colaughter across 24 societies. *Proceedings of the National Academy of Sciences, USA* 113: 1524993113.

Carney, J., Wlodarski, R. & Dunbar, R.I.M. (2014). Inference or enaction? The influence of genre on the narrative processing of other minds. *PLoS One* 9: e114172.

Cowan, M.L., Watkins, C.D., Fraccaro, P.J., Feinberg, D.R. & Little, A.C. (2016). It's the way he tells them (and who is listening): men's dominance is positively correlated with their preference for jokes told by dominant-sounding men. *Evolution and Human Behavior* 37: 97-104.

Curry, O. & Dunbar, R.I.M. (2011). Altruism in networks: the effect of connections. *Biology Letters* 7: 651-653.

Dahmardeh, M. & Dunbar, R.I.M. (2017). What shall we talk about in Farsi? Content of everyday conversations in Iran.

Human Nature 28: 423-433.

Dàvid-Barrett, T. & Dunbar, R.I.M. (2014). Language as a coordination tool evolves slowly. *Royal Society Open Science* 3: 160259.

Dezecache, G. & Dunbar, R.I.M. (2013). Sharing the joke: the size of natural laughter groups. *Evolution and Human Behavior* 33: 775-779.

Dunbar, R.I.M. (2009). Why only humans have language. In: R. Botha & C. Knight (Eds.) *The Prehistory of Language*, pp. 12-35. Oxford: Oxford University Press.

Dunbar, R.I.M. (2014). *Human Evolution.* Harmondsworth: Pelican and New York: Oxford University Press.

Dunbar, R.I.M. (2016). Sexual segregation in human conversations. *Behaviour* 153: 1-14.

Dunbar, R.I.M., Duncan, N. & Nettle, D. (1995). Size and structure of freely forming conversational groups. *Human Nature* 6: 67-78.

Dunbar, R.I.M., Duncan, N. & Marriot, A. (1997). Human conversational behaviour. *Human Nature* 8: 231-246.

Dunbar, R.I.M., Robledo del Canto, J.-P., Tamarit, I., Cross, I. & Smith, E. (in press). Nonverbal auditory cues allow relationship quality to be inferred during conversations.

Dunbar, R.I.M., Baron, R., Frangou, A., Pearce, E., van Leeuwen, E.J.C., Stow, J., Partridge, P., MacDonald, I., Barra, V., & van Vugt, M. (2012). Social laughter is correlated with an elevated pain threshold. *Proceedings of the Royal Society, London,* 279B, 1161-1167.

Freeberg, T.M. (2006). Social complexity can drive vocal complexity: group size influences vocal information in Carolina chickadees. *Psychological Science* 17: 557-561.

Gray, A., Parkinson, B. & Dunbar, R.I.M. (2015). Laughter's influence on the intimacy of self-disclosure. *Human Nature* 26: 28-43.

Kniffin, K.M. & Wilson, D.S. (2005). Utilities of gossip across organizational levels. *Human Nature* 16: 278-292.

Krems, J. & Dunbar, R.I.M. (2013). Clique size and network characteristics in hyperlink cinema: constraints of evolved psychology. *Human Nature* 24: 414-429.

Krems, J., Neuberg, S. & Dunbar, R.I.M. (2016). Something to talk about: are conversation sizes constrained by mental modeling abilities? *Evolution and Human Behavior* 37: 423-428.

Mehl, M.R., Vazire, S., Holleran, S.E. & Clark, C.S. (2010). Eavesdropping on happiness: Well-being is related to having less small talk and more substantive conversations. *Psychological Science* 21: 539-541.

Mehrabian, A. (2017). *Nonverbal Communication*. London: Routledge.

Mehu, M. & Dunbar, R.I.M. (2008). Naturalistic observations of smiling and laughing in human group interactions. *Behaviour* 145: 1747-1780.

Mehu, M., Grammer, K. & Dunbar, R.I.M. (2007). Smiles when sharing. *Evolution and Human Behavior* 6: 415-422.

Mehu, M., Little, A. & Dunbar, R.I.M. (2007). Duchenne smiles and the perception of generosity and sociability in faces. *Journal of Evolutionary Psychology* 7: 183-196.

Mesoudi, A., Whiten, A. & Dunbar, R.I.M. (2006). A bias for social information in human cultural transmission. *British Journal of Psychology* 97: 405-423.

Oesch, N. & Dunbar, R.I.M. (2017). The emergence of recursion in human language: mentalising predicts recursive syntax task performance. *Journal of Neurolinguistics* 43: 95-106.

O'Nions, E., Lima, C.F., Scott, S.K., Roberts, R., McCrory, E.J. & Viding, E. (2017). Reduced laughter contagion in boys at risk for psychopathy. *Current Biology* 27: 3049-3055.

Provine, R.R. (2001). *Laughter: A Scientific Investigation*. Harmondsworth: Penguin.

Redhead, G. & Dunbar, R.I.M. (2013). The functions of language: an experimental study. *Evolutionary Psychology* 11: 845-854.

Reed, L.I., Deutchman, P. & Schmidt, K.L. (2015). Effects of tearing on the perception of facial expressions of emotion. *Evolutionary Psychology* 13: 1474704915613915.

Scott, S.K., Lavan, N., Chen, S. & McGettigan, C. (2014). The social life of laughter. *Trends in Cognitive Sciences* 18: 618-620.

Stiller, J., Nettle, D., & Dunbar, R.I.M. (2004). The small world of Shakespeare's plays. *Human Nature* 14: 397-408.

Waller, B.M., Hope, L., Burrowes, N. & Morrison, E.R. (2011). Twelve (not so) angry men: managing conversational group size increases perceived contribution by decision makers. *Group Processes & Intergroup Relations* 14: 835-843.

Wiessner, P.W. (2014). Embers of society: firelight talk among the Ju/'hoansi Bushmen. *Proceedings of the National Academy of Sciences, USA,* 111: 14027-14035.

Chapter 10. Homophily and the seven pillars of friendship

Argyle, M. & Henderson, M. (1984). The rules of friendship. *Journal of Social and Personal Relationships* 1: 211-237.

Backstrom, L., Bakshy, E., Kleinberg, J.M., Lento, T.M. & Rosenn, I. (2011). Center of attention: How facebook users allocate attention across friends. In *Fifth International AAAI Conference on Weblogs and Social Media.*

Burton-Chellew, M. & Dunbar, R.I.M. (2015). Hamilton's Rule predicts anticipated social support in humans. *Behavioral Ecology* 26: 130-137.

Cosmides, L., Tooby, J. & Kurzban, R. (2003). Perceptions of race. *Trends in Cognitive Sciences* 7: 173-179.

Curry, O. & Dunbar, R.I.M. (2013). Sharing a joke: the effects of a similar sense of humor on affiliation and altruism. *Evolution and Human Behavior* 34: 125-129.

Curry, O. & Dunbar, R.I.M. (2013). Do birds of a feather flock together? The relationship between similarity and altruism in social networks. *Human Nature* 24: 336-347.

Devine, T.M. (2012). *Scotland's Empire*. Harmondsworth: Penguin.

Domingue, B.W., Belsky, D.W., Fletcher, J.M., Conley, D., Boardman, J.D. & Harris, K.M. (2018). The social genome of friends and schoolmates in the National Longitudinal Study of Adolescent to Adult Health. *Proceedings of the National Academy of Sciences, USA*, 115: 702-707.

Dunbar, R.I.M. (2016). Sexual segregation in human conversations. *Behaviour* 153: 1-14.

Dunbar, R.I.M. (2018). The anatomy of friendship. *Trends in Cognitive Sciences* 22: 32-51.

Dunbar, R.I.M. (2019). From there to now, and the origins of some ideas. In: D. Shankland (ed.) *Dunbar's Number*, pp. 5-20. Royal Anthropological Institute Occasional Papers No. 45. Canon Pyon: Sean Kingston Publishing.

Floccia, C., Butler, J., Girard, F. & Goslin, J. (2009). Categorization of regional and foreign accent in 5- to 7-year-old British children. *International Journal of Behavioral Development* 33: 366-375.

Fowler, J.H., Settle, J.E. & Christakis, N.A. (2011). Correlated genotypes in friendship networks. *Proceedings of the National Academy of Sciences, USA*, 108: 1993-1997.

Hall, J.A. (2012). Friendship standards: The dimensions of ideal expectations. *Journal of Social and Personal Relationships* 29: 884-907.

Kinzler, K.D., Dupoux, E., & Spelke, E.S. (2007). The native language of social cognition. *Proceedings of the National Academy of Sciences, USA*, 104: 12577-12580.

Kinzler, K.D., Shutts, K., DeJesus, J. & Spelke, E.S. (2009). Accent trumps race in guiding children's social preferences. *Social Cognition* 27: 623-634.

Laakasuo, M., Rotkirch, A., van Duijn, M., Berg, V., Jokela, M., Dàvid-Barrett, T., Miettinen, A., Pearce, E. & Dunbar, R. (2020). Homophily in personality enhances group success among real-life friends. *Frontiers in Psychology* 11: 710.

Laniado, D., Volkovich, Y., Kappler, K. & Kaltenbrunner, A. (2016). Gender homophily in online dyadic and triadic relationships. *EPJ Data Science* 5: 19.

Launay, J. & Dunbar, R.I.M. (2016). Playing with strangers: which shared traits attract us most to new people? *PLoS One* 10: e0129688.

Machin, A. & Dunbar, R.I.M. (2013). Sex and gender in romantic partnerships and best friendships. *Journal of Relationship Research* 4: e8.

McPherson, M., Smith-Lovin, L. & Cook, J.M. (2001). Birds of a feather: homophily in social networks. *Annual Review of Sociology* 27: 415-444.

Nettle, D. & Dunbar, R.I.M. (1997). Social markers and the evolution of reciprocal exchange. *Current Anthropology* 38: 93-99.

Oates, K. & Wilson, M. (2002). Nominal kinship cues facilitate altruism. *Proceedings of the Royal Society, London,* 269B: 105-109.

Parkinson, C., Kleinbaum, A.M. & Wheatley, T. (2018). Similar neural responses predict friendship. *Nature Communications* 9: 332.

Pearce, E., Machin, A. & Dunbar, R.I.M. (2020). Sex differences in intimacy levels in best friendships and romantic partnerships. *Adaptive Human Behavior and Physiology* (in press).

Tamarit, I., Cuesta, J., Dunbar, R.I.M. & Sánchez, A. (2018). Cognitive resource allocation determines the organisation of personal networks. *Proceedings of the National Academy of Sciences, USA*, 115: 1719233115.

Thomas, M.G., Stumpf, M.P., & Härke, H. (2006). Evidence for an apartheid-like social structure in early Anglo-Saxon England. *Proceedings of the Royal Society, London,* 273B: 2651-2657.

Trudgill, P. (2000). *The Dialects of England.* New York: Wiley.

Chapter 11. Trust in friendship

Bacha-Trams, M., Glerean, E., Dunbar, R.I.M., Lahnakoski, J., Ryyppö, E., Sams, M. & Jääskeläinen, I. (2017). Differential inter-subject correlation of brain activity when kinship is a variable in moral dilemma. *Scientific Reports* 7: 14244.

Barrio, R., Govezensky, T., Dunbar, R.I.M., Iñiguez, G. & Kaski, K. (2015). Dynamics of deceptive interactions in social networks. *Journal of the Royal Society Interface* 12: 20150798.

Carlisi, C.O., Moffitt, T.E., Knodt, A.R., Harrington, H., Ireland, D., Melzer, T.R., Poulton, R., Ramrakha, S., Caspi, A., Hariri, A.R. & Viding, E. (2020). Associations between life-course-persistent antisocial behaviour and brain structure in a population-representative longitudinal birth cohort. *Lancet Psychiatry* 7: 245-253.

Cikara, M. & Fiske, S.T. (2012). Stereotypes and schadenfreude: Affective and physiological markers of pleasure at outgroup misfortunes. *Social Psychological and Personality Science* 3: 63-71.

Combs, D.J., Powell, C.A., Schurtz, D.R. & Smith, R.H. (2009). Politics, schadenfreude, and ingroup identification: The sometimes happy thing about a poor economy and death. *Journal of Experimental Social Psychology* 45: 635-646.

Devine, T.M. (2012). *Scotland's Empire.* Harmondsworth: Penguin.

Dunbar, R.I.M. (2020). *Evolution: What Everyone Needs to Know.* New York: Oxford University Press.

Dunbar, R.I.M., Clark, A. & Hurst, N.L. (1995). Conflict and cooperation among the Vikings: contingent behavioural decisions. *Ethology and Sociobiology* 16: 233-246.

Farrington, D.P. (2019). The development of violence from age 8 to 61. *Aggressive Behavior* 45: 365-376.

Iñiguez, G., Govezensky, T., Dunbar, R.I.M., Kaski, K. & Barrio, R. (2014). Effects of deception in social networks. *Proceedings of the Royal Society, London,* 281B: 20141195

Jensen, L.A., Arnett, J.J., Feldman, S.S. & Cauffman, E. (2004). The right to do wrong: lying to parents among adolescents and emerging adults. *Journal of Youth and Adolescence* 33: 101-112.

Knox, D., Schacht, C., Holt, J. & Turner, J. (1993). Sexual lies among university students. *College Studies Journal* 27: 269-272.

Little, A., Jones, B., DeBruine, L. & Dunbar, R.I.M. (2013). Accuracy in discrimination of self-reported cooperators using static facial information. *Personality and Individual Differences* 54: 507-512.

Machin, A. & Dunbar, R.I.M. (2016). Is kinship a schema? Moral decisions and the function of the human kin naming system. *Adaptive Human Behavior and Physiology* 2: 195-219.

Madsen, E., Tunney, R., Fieldman, G., Plotkin, H., Dunbar, R.I.M., Richardson, J. & McFarland, D. (2007). Kinship and altruism: a cross-cultural experimental study. *British Journal of Psychology* 98: 339-359.

Mealey, L., Daood, C. & Krage, M. (1996). Enhanced memory for faces of cheaters. *Ethology and Sociobiology* 17: 119-128.

Moffitt, T., Caspi, A., Rutter, M. & Silva, P. (2001). *Sex Differences in Antisocial Behaviour: Conduct Disorder, Delinquency, and Violence in the Dunedin Longitudinal Study.* Cambridge: Cambridge University Press.

Ostrom, E., Gardner, R. & Walker, J. (1994). *Rules, Games and Common-Pool Resources.* Ann Arbor: University of Michigan Press.

Palmstierna, M., Frangou, A., Wallette, A. & Dunbar, R.I.M. (2017). Family counts: deciding when to murder among the Icelandic Vikings. *Evolution and Human Behavior* 38: 175-180.

Reynolds, T., Baumeister, R.F., & Maner, J.K. (2018). Competitive reputation manipulation: Women strategically transmit social information about romantic rivals. *Journal of Experimental Social Psychology* 78: 195-209.

Serota, K.B., Levine, T.R., & Boster, F.J. (2010). The prevalence of lying in America: three studies of selfreported lies. *Human Communication Research* 36: 2-25.

Singer, T., Seymour, B., O'Doherty, J.P., Stephan, K.E., Dolan, R.J., & Frith, C.D. (2006). Empathic neural responses are modulated by the perceived fairness of others. *Nature* 439: 466.

Sofer, C., Dotsch, R., Wigboldus, D.H., & Todorov, A. (2015). What is typical is good: The influence of face typicality on perceived trustworthiness. *Psychological Science* 26: 39-47.

Sutcliffe, A., Wang, D. & Dunbar, R.I.M. (2015). Modelling the role of trust in social relationships. *Transactions in Internet Technology* 15: 2.

Wiessner, P. (2005). Norm enforcement among the Ju/'hoansi Bushmen. *Human Nature* 16: 115-145.

Wlodarski, R. & Dunbar, R.I.M. (2016). When BOLD is thicker than water: processing social information about kin and friends at different levels in the social network. *Social, Cognitive and Affective Neuroscience* 11: 1952-1960.

Chapter 12. The romance of friendship

Acevedo, B.P., Aron, A., Fisher, H.E. & Brown, L.L. (2012). Neural correlates of long-term intense romantic love. *Social, Cognitive and Affective Neuroscience* 7: 145-159.

Bartels, A. & Zeki, S. (2000). The neural basis of romantic love. *NeuroReport* 11: 3829-3834.

Bartels, A. & Zeki, S. (2004). The neural correlates of maternal and romantic love. *NeuroImage* 24: 1155-1166.

Burton-Chellew, M. & Dunbar, R.I.M. (2015). Romance and reproduction are socially costly. *Evolutionary Behavioral Science* 9: 229-241.

Del Giudice, M. (2011). Sex differences in romantic attachment: A meta-analysis. *Personality and Social Psychology Bulletin* 37: 193-214.

Dunbar, R.I.M. (2012). *The Science of Love and Betrayal*. London: Faber & Faber.

Dunbar, R.I.M. & Dunbar, P. (1980). The pairbond in klipspringer. *Animal Behaviour* 28: 251-263.

Goel, V. & Dolan, R. J. (2003). Explaining modulation of reasoning by belief. *Cognition* 87: B11-B22.

Grammer, K. (1989). Human courtship behaviour: Biological basis and cognitive processing. In: A. Rasa, C. Vogel & E. Voland (Eds.) *The Sociobiology of Sexual and Reproductive Strategies*, pp. 147-169. New York: Chapman & Hall.

Harcourt, A.H., Harvey, P.H., Larson, S.G. & Short, R.V. (1981). Testis weight, body weight and breeding system in primates. *Nature* 293: 55-57.

Helle, S. & Laaksonen, T. (2009). Latitudinal gradient in 2D:4D. *Archives of Sexual Behavior* 38: 1-3.

Judge, T.A. & Cable, D.M. (2004). The effect of physical height on workplace success and income: preliminary test of a theoretical model. *Journal of Applied Psychology* 89: 428-441.

Kelly, S. & Dunbar, R.I.M. (2001). Who dares wins: heroism versus altruism in female mate choice. *Human Nature* 12: 89-105.

Machin, A. & Dunbar, R.I.M. (2013). Sex and gender in romantic partnerships and best friendships. *Journal of Relationship Research* 4: e8.

Manning, J.T., Barley, L., Walton, J., Lewis-Jones, D.I., Trivers, R.L., Singh, D., Thornhill, R., Rohde, P., Bereczkei, T., Henzi, P., Soler, M. & Szwed, A. (2000). The 2nd:4th digit ratio, sexual dimorphism, population differences, and reproductive success: evidence for sexually antagonistic genes? *Evolution and Human Behavior* 21: 163-183.

Markey, P.M. & Markey, C.N. (2007). Romantic ideals, romantic obtainment, and relationship experiences: The complementarity of interpersonal traits among romantic partners. *Journal of Social and Personal Relationships* 24: 517-533.

Murray, S.L. & Holmes, J.G. (1997). A leap of faith? Positive illusions in romantic relationships. *Personality and Social Psychology Bulletin* 23: 586-604.

Murray, S.L., Griffin, D.W., Derrick, J.L., Harris, B., Aloni, M. & Leder, S. (2011). Tempting fate or inviting happiness? Unrealistic idealization prevents the decline of marital satisfaction. *Psychological Science* 22: 619-626.

Nelson, E., Rolian, C., Cashmore, L. & Shultz, S. (2011). Digit ratios predict polygyny in early apes, *Ardipithecus,* Neanderthals and early modern humans but not in *Australopithecus. Proceedings of the Royal Society, London,* 278B: 1556-1563.

Palchykov, V., Kaski, K., Kertész, J., Barabási, A.-L. & Dunbar, R.I.M. (2012). Sex differences in intimate relationships. *Scientific Reports* 2: 320.

Park, Y. & MacDonald, G. (2019). Consistency between individuals' past and current romantic partners' own reports of their personalities. *Proceedings of the National Academy of Sciences* 116: 12793-12797.

Pawlowski, B. & Dunbar, R.I.M. (1999). Withholding age as putative deception in mate search tactics. *Evolution and Human Behavior* 20: 53-69.

Pawlowski, B. & Dunbar, R.I.M. (1999). Impact of market value on human mate choice decisions. *Proceedings of the Royal Society, London,* 266B: 281-285.

Pawlowski, B. & Dunbar, R.I.M. (2001). Human mate choice strategies. In: J. van Hooff, R. Noë & P. Hammerstein (Ed.) *Economic Models of Animal and Human Behaviour,* pp. 187-202. Cambridge: Cambridge University Press.

Pawlowski, B., Dunbar, R.I.M. & Lipowicz, A. (2000). Tall men have more reproductive success. *Nature* 403: 156.

Pearce, E., Machin, A. & Dunbar, R.I.M. (2020). Sex differences in intimacy levels in best friendships and romantic partnerships. *Adaptive Human Behavior and Physiology* (in press).

Pearce, E., Wlodarski, R., Machin, A. & Dunbar, R.I.M. (2017).

Variation in the β-endorphin, oxytocin, and dopamine receptor genes is associated with different dimensions of human sociality. *Proceedings of the National Academy of Sciences, USA*, 114: 5300-5305.

Pearce, E., Wlodarski, R., Machin, A. & Dunbar, R.I.M. (2018). Associations between neurochemical receptor genes, 2D:4D, impulsivity and relationship quality. *Biology Letters* 14: 20180642.

Pew Research Center: https://www.pewresearch.org/fact-tank/2019/02/13/8-facts-about-love-and-marriage/

Smith, A. & Duggan, M. (2013). *Online Dating and Relationships*. Report of Pew Research Center.

Stone, E.A., Shackleford, T.K. & Buss, D.M. (2007). Sex ratio and mate preferences: A cross-cultural investigation. *European Journal of Social Psychology* 37: 288-296.

Versluys, T.M., Foley, R.A. & Skylark, W.J. (2018). The influence of leg-to-body ratio, arm-to-body ratio and intra-limb ratio on male human attractiveness. *Royal Society Open Science* 5: 171790.

Vohs, K.D., Finkenauer, C. & Baumeister, R.F. (2011). The sum of friends' and lovers' self-control scores predicts relationship quality. *Social Psychological and Personality Science* 2 138-145.

Waynforth, D. & Dunbar, R.I.M. (1995). Conditional mate choice strategies in humans: evidence from 'Lonely Hearts' advertisements. *Behaviour* 132: 755-779.

Whitty, M.T. (2015). Anatomy of the online dating romance scam. *Security Journal* 28: 443-455.

Whitty, M.T. (2018). Do you love me? Psychological characteristics of romance scam victims. *Cyberpsychology, Behavior, and Social Networking* 21: 105-109.

Whitty, M.T. & Buchanan, T. (2012). The online romance scam: a serious cybercrime. *CyberPsychology, Behavior, and Social Networking* 15: 181-183.

Wlodarski, R. & Dunbar, R.I.M. (2015). Within-sex mating strategy phenotypes: evolutionary stable strategies? *Human Ethology Bulletin* 30: 99-108.

Wlodarski, R., Manning, J. & Dunbar, R.I.M. (2015). Stay or stray? Evidence for alternative mating strategy phenotypes in both men and women. *Biology Letters* 11: 20140977.

Zahavi, A. & Zahavi, A. (1997). *The Handicap Principle: A Missing Part of Darwin's Puzzle*. Oxford: Oxford University Press.

Chapter 13. The gendering of friendship

Archer, J. (2004). Sex differences in aggression in real-world settings: A meta-analytic review. *Review of General Psychology* 8: 291-322.

Archer, J. (2019). The reality and evolutionary significance of human psychological sex differences. *Biological Reviews* 94: 1381-1415.

Bell, E.C., Willson, M.C., Wilman, A.H., Dave, S., & Silverstone, P.H. (2006). Males and females differ in brain activation during cognitive tasks. *Neuroimage* 30: 529-538.

Benenson, J.F. & Wrangham, R.W. (2016). Cross-cultural sex differences in post-conflict affiliation following sports matches. *Current Biology* 26: 2208-2212.

Benenson, J.F., Markovits, H., Thompson, M.E. & Wrangham, R.W. (2011). Under threat of social exclusion, females exclude more than males. *Psychological Science* 22: 538-544.

Benenson, J.F., Markovits, H., Fitzgerald, C., Geoffroy, D., Flemming, J., Kahlenberg, S.M., & Wrangham, R.W. (2009). Males' greater tolerance of same-sex peers. *Psychological Science* 20: 184-190.

Buss, D.M., Larsen, R.J., Westen, D., & Semmelroth, J. (1992). Sex differences in jealousy: evolution, physiology, and psychology. *Psychological Science* 3: 251-256.

Buss, D.M. (1989). Sex differences in human mate preferences: Evolutionary hypotheses tested in 37 cultures. *Behavioral and Brain Sciences* 12: 1-14.

Byock, J.L. (Ed.) (2004). *The Saga of the Volsungs*. Harmondsworth: Penguin.

Campbell, A. (2013). *A Mind of Her Own: The Evolutionary Psychology of Women*. Oxford: Oxford University Press.

Coates, J. (2015). *Women, Men and Language: A Sociolinguistic Account of Gender Differences in Language*. London: Routledge.

Connellan, J., Baron-Cohen, S., Wheelwright, S., Batki, A. & Ahluwalia, J. (2000). Sex differences in human neonatal social perception. *Infant Behavior and Development* 23: 113-118.

Cross, C.P., Cyrenne, D.L.M. & Brown, G.R. (2013). Sex differences in sensation-seeking: a meta-analysis. *Scientific Reports* 3: 2486.

Dàvid-Barrett, T., Rotkirch, A., Carney, J., Behncke Izquierdo, I., Krems, J., Townley, D., McDaniell, E., Byrne-Smith, A. & Dunbar, R.I.M. (2015). Women favour dyadic relationships, but men prefer clubs. *PLoS-One* 10: e0118329.

Del Giudice, M. (2011). Sex differences in romantic attachment: a meta-analysis. *Personality and Social Psychology Bulletin* 37: 193-214.

Dunbar, R.I.M. (2016). Sexual segregation in human conversations. *Behaviour* 153: 1-14.

Dunbar, R.I.M. & Machin, A. (2014). Sex differences in relationship conflict and reconciliation. *Journal of Evolutionary Psychology* 12: 109-133.

Dyble, M., van Leeuwen, A. & Dunbar, R.I.M. (2015). Gender differences in Christmas gift-giving. *Evolutionary Behavioral Science* 9: 140-144.

Barrett, L.F., Lane, R.D., Sechrest, L. & Schwartz, G.E. (2000). Sex differences in emotional awareness. *Personality and Social Psychology Bulletin* 26: 1027-1035.

Gardner, W.L. & Gabriel, S. (2004). Gender differences in relational and collective interdependence: implications for self-views, social behavior, and subjective well-being. In: A.H. Eagly, A.E. Beall, & R.J. Sternberg (Eds.) *The Psychology of Gender*, pp. 169-191. New York: Guilford Press.

Ghosh, A., Monsivais, D., Bhattacharya, K., Dunbar, R.I.M. &

Kaski, K. (2019). Quantifying gender preferences in human social interactions using a large cellphone dataset. *EPJ Data Science* 8: 9.

Grainger, S. & Dunbar, R.I.M. (2009). The structure of dyadic conversations and sex differences in social style. *Journal of Evolutionary Psychology* 7: 83-93.

Greeno, N.C. & Semple, S. (2009). Sex differences in vocal communication among adult rhesus macaques. *Evolution and Human Behavior* 30: 141-145.

Hall, J.A. (1978). Gender effects in decoding nonverbal cues. *Psychological Bulletin* 85: 845-857.

Hall, J. A. & Matsumoto, D. (2004). Gender differences in judgments of multiple emotions from facial expressions. *Emotion* 4: 201-206.

van Hemmen, J., Saris, I.M., Cohen-Kettenis, P.T., Veltman, D.J., Pouwels, P.J.W. & Bakker, J. (2016). Sex differences in white matter microstructure in the human brain predominantly reflect differences in sex hormone exposure. *Cerebral Cortex* 27: 2994-3001.

Kiesow, H., Dunbar, R.I.M., Kable, J.W., Kalenscher, T., Vogeley, K., Schilbach, L., Wiecki., T. & Bzdok, D. (2020). 10,000 social brains: sex differentiation in human brain anatomy. *Science Advances* 6: eeaz1170.

Lycett, J. & Dunbar, R.I.M. (2000). Mobile phones as lekking devices among human males. *Human Nature* 11: 93-104.

Machin, A. & Dunbar, R.I.M. (2013). Sex and gender in romantic partnerships and best friendships. *Journal of Relationship Research* 4: e8.

McClure, E.B., Monk, C.S., Nelson, E.E., Zarahn, E., Leibenluft, E., Bilder, R.M., et al. (2004). A developmental examination of gender differences in brain engagement during evaluation of threat. *Biological Psychiatry* 55: 1047-1055.

McGauran, A. M. (2000). Vive la différence: the gendering of occupational structures in a case study of Irish and French retailing. *Women's Studies International Forum* 23: 613-627.

Madsen, E., Tunney, R., Fieldman, G., Plotkin, H., Dunbar, R.I.M., Richardson, J. & McFarland, D. (2007). Kinship and altruism: a cross-cultural experimental study. *British Journal of Psychology* 98: 339-359.

Mehta, C.M. & Strough, J. (2009). Sex segregation in friendships and normative contexts across the life span. *Developmental Review* 29: 201-220.

Monnot, M. (1999). Function of infant-directed speech. *Human Nature* 10: 415-443.

Pálsson, H. & Magnusson, M. (trans.) (1969) *Laxdaela Saga*. Harmondsworth: Penguin.

Pawlowski, B., Atwal, R. & Dunbar, R.I.M. (2007). Gender differences in everyday risk-taking. *Evolutionary Psychology* 6: 29-42.

Pearce, E., Wlodarski, R., Machin, A & Dunbar, R.I.M. (2019). Exploring the links between dispositions, romantic relationships, support networks and community inclusion in men and women. *PLoS One* 14: e0216210.

Proverbio, A.M., Zani, A. & Adorni, R. (2008). Neural markers of a greater female responsiveness to social stimuli. *BMC Neuroscience* 9: 56.

Reynolds, T., Baumeister, R. F. & Maner, J.K. (2018). Competitive reputation manipulation: Women strategically transmit social information about romantic rivals. *Journal of Experimental Social Psychology* 78: 195-209.

Rose, S. M. (1985). Same- and cross-sex friendships and the psychology of homosociality. *Sex Roles* 12: 63-74.

Savic, I., Garcia-Falgueras, A. & Swaab, D.F. (2010). Sexual differentiation of the human brain in relation to gender identity and sexual orientation. *Progress in Brain Research* 186: 41-62.

Schmitt, D.P., and 118 others. (2003). Universal sex differences in the desire for sexual variety: tests from 52 nations, 6 continents, and 13 islands. *Journal of Personality and Social Psychology* 85: 85-104.

Strombach, T., Weber, B., Hangebrauk, Z., Kenning, P., Karipidis,

I. I., Tobler, P. N. & Kalenscher, T. (2015). Social discounting involves modulation of neural value signals by temporoparietal junction. *Proceedings of the National Academy of Sciences, USA*, 112: 1619-1624.

Vigil, J.M. (2007). Asymmetries in the friendship preferences and social styles of men and women. *Human Nature* 18: 143-161.

Weiss, E., Siedentopf, C.M., Hofer, A., Deisenhammer, E.A., Hoptman, M.J., Kremser, C., ... & Delazer, M. (2003). Sex differences in brain activation pattern during a visuospatial cognitive task: a functional magnetic resonance imaging study in healthy volunteers. *Neuroscience Letters* 344: 169-172.

Chapter 14. Why friendships end

Argyle, M. & Henderson, M. (1984). The rules of friendship. *Journal of Social and Personal Relationships* 1: 211-237.

Benenson, J.F. & Wrangham, R.W. (2016). Cross-cultural sex differences in post-conflict affiliation following sports matches. *Current Biology* 26: 2208-2212.

Dunbar, R.I.M. & Machin, A. (2014). Sex differences in relationship conflict and reconciliation. *Journal of Evolutionary Psychology* 12: 109-133.

Eisenberger, N.I. (2012). The pain of social disconnection: examining the shared neural underpinnings of physical and social pain. *Nature Reviews Neuroscience* 13: 421.

Eisenberger, N.I. (2015). Social pain and the brain: controversies, questions, and where to go from here. *Annual Review of Psychology* 66: 601-629.

Eisenberger, N.I., Lieberman, M.D. & Williams, K.D. (2003). Does rejection hurt? An fMRI study of social exclusion. *Science* 302: 290-292.

Floyd, S., Rossi, G., Baranova, J., Blythe, J., Dingemanse, M., Kendrick, K.H., ... & Enfield, N.J. (2018). Universals and cultural diversity in the expression of gratitude. *Royal Society*

Open Science 5: 180391.

Hall, J.A. (2011). Sex differences in friendship expectations: A meta-analysis. *Journal of Social and Personal Relationships* 28: 723-747.

Heatley Tejada, A., Montero, M. & Dunbar, R.I.M. (2017). Being unempathic will make your loved ones feel lonelier: loneliness in an evolutionary perspective. *Personality and Individual Differences* 116: 223-232.

Master, S.L., Eisenberger, N.I., Taylor, S.E., Naliboff, B.D., Shirinyan, D. & Lieberman, M.D. (2009). A picture's worth: Partner photographs reduce experimentally induced pain. *Psychological Science* 20: 1316-1318.

Provine, R.R., Krosnowski, K.A. & Brocato, N.W. (2009). Tearing: Breakthrough in human emotional signaling. *Evolutionary Psychology* 7: 147470490900700107.

Rasmussen, D.R. (1981). Pair-bond strength and stability and reproductive success. *Psychological Review* 88: 274.

Roberts, S.B.G., Wilson, R., Fedurek, P. & Dunbar, R.I.M. (2008). Individual differences and personal social network size and structure. *Personality and Individual Differences* 44: 954-964.

Rotge, J.Y., Lemogne, C., Hinfray, S., Huguet, P., Grynszpan, O., Tartour, E., ... & Fossati, P. (2014). A meta-analysis of the anterior cingulate contribution to social pain. *Social Cognitive and Affective Neuroscience* 10: 19-27.

UK Government Office of National Statistics: https://www.ons.gov.uk/peoplepopulationandcommunity/birthsdeathsandmarriages/divorce

Chapter 15. Friendship as we age

Alexander, G.M. & Hines, M. (2002). Sex differences in response to children's toys in nonhuman primates (*Cercopithecus aethiops sabaeus*). *Evolution and Human Behavior* 23: 467-479.

Ajrouch, K.J., Blandon, A.Y. & Antonucci, T.C. (2005). Social networks among men and women: The effects of age and socioeconomic status. *Journal of Gerontology: Psychological Sciences and Social Sciences* 60: S311-S317.

Astington, J.W. (1993). *The Child's Discovery of the Mind.* Cambridge MA: Harvard University Press.

Bhattacharya, K., Gosh, A., Monsivais, D., Dunbar, R.I.M. & Kaski, K. (2016). Sex differences in social focus across the life cycle in humans. *Royal Society Open Science* 3: 160097.

Benenson, J.F. (1993). Greater preference among females than males for dyadic interaction in early childhood. *Child Development* 64: 544-555.

Benenson, J.F. & Christakos, A. (2003). The greater fragility of females' versus males' closest same-sex friendships. *Child Development* 74: 1123-1129.

Burnett-Heyes, S., Jih, Y.R., Block, P., Hiu, C.F., Holmes, E.A. & Lau, J.Y. (2015). Relationship reciprocation modulates resource allocation in adolescent social networks: developmental effects. *Child Development* 86: 1489-1506.

Buz, J., Sanchez, M., Levenson, M.R. & Aldwin, C.M. (2014). Aging and social networks in Spain: The importance of pubs and churches. *International Journal of Aging and Human Development* 78: 23-46.

Deeley, Q., Daly, E.M., Azuma, R., Surguladze, S., Giampietro, V., Brammer, M.J., Hallahan, B., Dunbar, R.I.M., Phillips, M., & Murphy, D. (2008). Changes in male brain responses to emotional faces from adolescence to middle age. *NeuroImage* 40: 389-397.

Dumontheil, I., Apperly, I.A., & Blakemore, S.J. (2010). Online usage of theory of mind continues to develop in late adolescence. *Developmental Science* 13: 331-338.

Eder, D. & Hallinan, M.T. (1978). Sex differences in children's friendships. *American Sociological Review* 43: 237-250.

Fung, H.H., Carstensen, L.L. & Lang, F.R. (2001). Age-related patterns in social networks among European Americans and African Americans: Implications for socioemotional selectivity across the life span. *International Journal of Aging and Human Development* 52: 185-206.

Joffe, T.H. (1997). Social pressures have selected for an extended juvenile period in primates. *Journal of Human Evolution* 32: 593-605.

Kahlenberg, S.M. & Wrangham, R.W. (2010). Sex differences in chimpanzees' use of sticks as play objects resemble those of children. *Current Biology* 20: R1067-R1068.

Lonsdorf, E.V., Anderson, K.E., Stanton, M.A., Shender, M., Heintz, M.R., Goodall, J., & Murray, C.M. (2014). Boys will be boys: sex differences in wild infant chimpanzee social interactions. *Animal Behaviour* 88: 79-83.

Lycett, J. & Dunbar, R.I.M. (2000). Abortion rates reflect the optimization of parental investment strategies. *Proceedings of the Royal Society, London,* 266B: 2355-2358.

Mehta, C.M. & Strough, J. (2009). Sex segregation in friendships and normative contexts across the life span. *Developmental Review* 29: 201-220.

Moffitt, T., Caspi, A., Rutter, M. & Silva, P. (2001). *Sex Differences in Antisocial Behaviour.* Cambridge: Cambridge University Press.

Palchykov, V., Kaski, K., Kertész, J., Barabási, A.-L. & Dunbar, R.I.M. (2012). Sex differences in intimate relationships. *Scientific Reports* 2: 320.

Powell, E., Woodfield, L.A. & Nevill, A.A. (2016). Children's physical activity levels during primary school break times: A quantitative and qualitative research design. *European Physical Education Review* 22: 82-98.

Unger, J.B., Johnson, C.A. & Marks, G. (1997). Functional decline in the elderly: evidence for direct and stress-buffering protective effects of social interactions and physical activity. *Annals of Behavioral Medicine* 19: 152-160.

Voland, E. (1988). Differential infant and child mortality in evolutionary perspective: data from 17th to 19th century Ostfriesland (Germany). In: L. Betzig, M. Borgerhoff-Mulder & P.W. Turke (eds) *Human Reproductive Behaviour: A Darwinian Perspective,* pp. 253-262. Cambridge: Cambridge University Press.

Wrzus, C., Hänel, M., Wagner, J. & Neyer, F.J. (2013). Social network changes and life events across the life span: a meta-analysis. *Psychological Bulletin* 139: 53.

Zunzunegui, M.V., Alvarado, B.E., Del Ser, T. & Otero, A. (2003). Social networks, social integration, and social engagement determine cognitive decline in community-dwelling Spanish older adults. *Journal of Gerontology: Psychological Sciences and Social Sciences* 58: S93-S100.

Chapter 16. Friends online

Arnaboldi, V., Passarella, A., Conti, M. & Dunbar, R.I.M. (2015). *Online Social Networks: Human Cognitive Constraints in Facebook and Twitter Personal Graphs.* Amsterdam: Elsevier.

Blease, C.R. (2015). Too many 'Friends,' too few 'Likes'? Evolutionary psychology and 'Facebook Depression'. *Review of General Psychology* 19: 1-13.

Booker, C.L., Kelly, Y.J. & Sacker, A. (2018). Gender differences in the associations between age trends of social media interaction and well-being among 10-15 year olds in the UK. *BMC Public Health* 18: 321.

Camarilla: https://download.cnet.com/Camarilla-the-worlds-smallest-social-network/3000-12941_4-77274898.html

Dunbar, R.I.M. (2012). *Speak Up, Speak Out.* London: Holocaust Memorial Day Trust.

Dunbar, R.I.M. (2012). Social cognition on the internet: testing constraints on social network size. *Philosophical Transactions of the Royal Society, London,* 367B: 2192-2201.

Dunbar, R.I.M. (2016). Do online social media cut through the constraints that limit the size of offline social networks? *Royal Society Open Science* 3: 150292.

Dunbar, R., Arnaboldi, V., Conti, M. & Passarella, A. (2015). The structure of online social networks mirrors those in the offline world. *Social Networks* 43: 39-47.

Ellison, N. B., Steinfield, C. & Lampe, C. (2007). Social capital and college students' use of online social network sites. *Journal of Computer-Mediated Communications* 12: 1143-1168.

Fuchs, B., Sornette, D. & Thurner, S. (2014). Fractal multi-level organisation of human groups in a virtual world. *Scientific Reports* 4: 6526.

Heydari, S., Roberts, S.B.G., Dunbar, R.I.M. & Saramäki, J. (2018). Multichannel social signatures and persistent features of ego networks. *Applied Network Science* 3: 8.

Kobayashi, H. & Kohshima, S. (1997). Unique morphology of the human eye. *Nature* 387: 767.

Kelly, Y., Zilanawala, A., Booker, C. & Sacker, A. (2018). Social media use and adolescent mental health: Findings from the UK Millennium Cohort Study. *EClinicalMedicine* 6: 59-68.

Kraut, R., Patterson, M., Lundmark, V., Kiesler, S., Mukophadhyay, T. & Scherlis, W. (1998). Internet paradox: A social technology that reduces social involvement and psychological well-being? *American Psychologist* 53: 1017.

Marlow, C. (2011). Maintained relationships on Facebook. http://overstated.net/

Orben, A. & Przybylski, A.K. (2019). The association between adolescent well-being and digital technology use. *Nature Human Behaviour* 3: 173.

Orben, A., Dienlin, T. & Przybylski, A.K. (2019). Social media's enduring effect on adolescent life satisfaction. *Proceedings of the National Academy of Sciences, USA,* 116: 10226-10228.

Przybylski, A.K. & Weinstein, N. (2017). A large-scale test of the Goldilocks Hypothesis: Quantifying the relations between digital-screen use and the mental well-being of adolescents.

Psychological Science 28: 204-215.

Seltzer, L.J., Prososki, A.R., Ziegler, T.E. & Pollak, S.D. (2012). Instant messages vs. speech: hormones and why we still need to hear each other. *Evolution and Human Behavior* 33: 42-45.

Szell, M. & Thurner, S. (2013). How women organize social networks different from men. *Scientific Reports* 3: 1214.

Thorisdottir, I.E., Sigurvinsdottir, R., Asgeirsdottir, B.B., Allegrante, J.P. & Sigfusdottir, I. D. (2019). Active and passive social media use and symptoms of anxiety and depressed mood among Icelandic adolescents. *Cyberpsychology, Behavior, and Social Networking* 22: 535-542.

Vlahovic, T., Roberts, S.B.G. & Dunbar, R.I.M. (2012). Effects of duration and laughter on subjective happiness within different modes of communication. *Journal of Computer-Mediated Commununication* 17: 436-450.

Index

9/11 terror attacks, 228–9

Aachen, University of, 66–7
Aalto University (Finland), 30, 97, 143,
   245, 349; mobile-phone dataset,
   30–1, 100–1, 104, 106, 108–10,
   261–2, 334–5
abortion statistics, UK, 338
academics, 125–6; academic job market,
   86; co-authorship networks, 74–5;
   network size of, 36, 73; peer-review
   system, 126
afferent c-tactile (CT) neurons, 139,
   141
Afghans, 215
Africa: agro-pastoralists in, 99, 255;
   Bantu tribes, 213, 215, 239; Robin
   Dunbar's background in East Africa,
   21, 209; evolution of modern
   humans in, 214–15; Hadza hunter–
   gatherers in East Africa, 282; !Kung
   San hunter–gatherers in south, 99,
   183, 238–9; Maasai of East Africa,
   99, 321; pygmies of the Central
   African forests, 52; South Africa,
   157, 217, 246; sub-Saharan Africans,
   99, 214; Swahili and Indian cultures
   in East Africa, 209; wild animals in,
   21, 22–3, 38–9, 84, 104, 116, 135,
   136–7, 161, 173, 179, 328–9
African green monkeys, 327–8
Ajrouch, Kristine, 335
alcohol: addiction treatment, 169–70;
   addiction/abuse, 138, 291, 306, 307;
   African great apes' tolerance of, 173;

and endorphin system, 138, 169–70,
   172–3
*Alcohol and Humans: A Long and Social
   Affair* (eds. Robin Dunbar and Kim
   Hockings), 173
Aledavood, Talayeh, 107, 198
Alfred the Great, 217
altruistic behaviour, 12–13, 43–4, 93–4,
   135, 203, 246
Angles (Germanic tribe), 212–13
Anglo-Saxons, 216–17, 220–1; Anglo-
   Saxon language, 210, 217–18
animal behaviour: bonded social
   relationships, 22–3, 48–50,
   53–6, 79, 84, 87–8, 114, 135–7,
   139–40, 147–8, 153, 158, 159,
   170; brain size and group size, 23,
   48, 49–50, 53, 54, 64; carnivores,
   52, 53, 54; and circles/layers of
   friendship concept, 79–80; computer
   modelling of layer structuring,
   86–9; creation of friendships, 114;
   diurnal species, 107; and Robin
   Dunbar's background, 21–3; greater
   sociality of females, 286; grooming
   in primates, 22, 48–50, 79, 84, 104,
   135–7, 139–41, 147, 153, 155–6,
   158, 170; and language, 175, 179;
   length of socialisation period, 322,
   325–6; pairing and mating patterns,
   53, 54, 55; promiscuous species, 53,
   145, 146, 265–6; sex differences in
   juvenile play activities, 327–9; small
   harem-like arrangements, 53, 79, 88;
   and theory of mind, 113, 114, 116,

animal behaviour – *continued*
117, 118, 125–6, 129; unstructured
herds, 53, 56, 88, 136–7; Zahavi's
Handicap Principle, 258 *see also*
apes; monkeys
anthropoid primates *see* apes; monkeys
antisocial behaviour: and childhood
experiences, 330, 331; and gender,
248; and Norse berserkers, 249–51;
research into origins of, 247–9; risk
factors for, 247–9
anxiety and stress: and autism, 111*,
117, 152, 153; and endorphin
system, 138–9, 147, 152, 315; and
Experience of Close Relationships
Scale, 286; and Five Factor
(OCEAN) Model, 224, 309; gender
differences in responses to, 278,
289; of living in close proximity
with others, 55, 56; and loneliness,
4, 20, 60; and oxytocin, 146–7;
and polyamory/polygamy, 268; and
relationship breakdown, 289, 304,
306, 309–13, 336–7; and social
fingerprint concept, 110; and use of
social media, 357
apes: African great apes, 116, 161, 173;
bonded social relationships, 54–6,
79, 84, 87–8, 114, 136, 158, 159;
brain size of, 48, 49, 50, *51*, 53,
54–6; circles/layers of friendship, 79,
83, 84, 87–8; creation of friendships,
114; as diurnal species, 107; frontal
pole in, 129; and language, 175; play
styles of, 328; protracted adolescence
of, 326; purpose of grooming for,
136, 158; and ROM face, 161, 186;
and Social Brain Hypothesis, *51*, 53,
54–6; and theory of mind, 113, 116,
125–6, 129; three-colour vision of,
293; tolerance of alcohol, 173
archaic humans: controlling of fire by,
199; displaced by migrants from
Africa, 214; Heidelberg folk, 168;
Neanderthals, 168, 177, 214; and
theory of mind, 168, 177
Archer, John, 274–5, 281–2
Argyle, Michael, 305
Aristotle, 242–3, 283
Arnabaldi, Valerio, 73–5
Asperger syndrome, 111*, 112, 113

Atkinson, Quentin, 235
Attachment Scale, 152, 286–7
attachment styles, 20, 150, 286–9,
309–10, 313
Attribution Error, 305
Atwal, Rajinder, 290–1
Australia, 4, 213, 214–15
Australian Aboriginals, 52, 214
Australian Rules football, 69*
autism, 111, 112, 113, 114, 117, 120,
138, 152–3

baboons, 22–3, 38–9, 64, 79, 84, 104,
135, 136–7, 328–9
Bacha-Trams, Mareike, 245
Backstrom, Lars, 102, 205
Balance Theory, 81–3
Bannan, Nick, 157
Bantu tribes, 213, 215, 239
Barnard, Russell, 28, 29
Baron, Rebecca, 162
Baron-Cohen, Simon, 285–6
Barrett, Lisa Feldman, 182, 284
Barrio, Rafael, 231–3
Bartels, Andreas, 263–4
Basques, 215, 216
bats, 53, 54, 79
Baumeister, Roy, 242, 260, 281
the Beatles, 208
Beersma, Bianca, 182
behavioural science, 48; stranglehold of
microeconomics, 148–9
Bell, Emily, 296–7
Benenson, Joyce, 288–9, 318, 329, 330
Bentall, Rich, 120
Bentley, Alex, 79
Berntson, Gary, 15
best friends, 13, 70, 92, 137, 166,
246, 308, 333; in animal kingdom,
104; 'Best Friend Forever,' 76,
104, 277, 317; breakdowns of
relationship, 302, 303, 317–18, 330;
in childhood/adolescence, 329–30;
homophily as important, 278, 287,
288; methods of contact with, 350;
relationship breakdowns among
women, 317–18, 330; sex of, 76,
261–2, 276–7, 288; time invested in,
154, 204–5, 278
Bhattacharya, Kunal, 104, 334
Big Lunch Project, 170–2, 173, 197

Binder, Jens, 29, 73, 92–3
Biobank database, UK, 66–7, 297–8
bipolar disorder, 330
Birch, Amy, 123
Bird, Geoff, 124–5
bird populations, 53, 54, 55, 114, 178–9
Black Urban Vernacular (BUV), 211
bonded social relationships: in the animal kingdom, 22–3, 48–50, 53–6, 79, 84, 87–8, 114, 135–7, 139–40, 147–8, 153, 158, 159, 170; Argyle's six key rules on friendship, 305; as based on trust and obligation, 136, 139, 149–50, 171–3, 202, 206–11, 222, 227, 228–42, 244–7, 251, 307–8; causes of relationship breakdown, 301, 303–4, 305–11; community as extended family, 207; convoy theory of friendship, 332; dealing with antisocial behaviour, 247–51; diplomatic and social skills needed for, 55–6; ending of friendships, 301, 302–3, 304–11, 313–14, 316–19; and endorphin system, 11, 114, 115, 137–8, 237, 263; and expressions of gratitude, 306–7; and feasting, 169–72, 173, 227; Inclusion-of-Other-in-Self (IOS) Index, 163–4; in the military, 16–17, 192; monogamous reproductive relationships, 21, 46, 53, 54, 55, 79, 114, 136–7, 145, 146, 147, 265–8; mother–infant bond, 140–1, 144–5, 263–4, 313–14; and oxytocin, 144–7, 150, 151, 263, 272, 357; primate-like grooming in humans, 140–1; reconciliations, 316–17; role of laughter, 159–63, 195; role of music in evolution of, 157–8; role of singing and dancing, 159, 163–4, 165–9, 224–5, 227; shared emotional experiences, 191–2; significance of night-time, 197–9; social grooming in primates, 22–3, 48–50, 79, 84, 104, 135–7, 139–41, 147, 153, 155–6, 158, 170; socio-emotional theory of friendship, 332; sophisticated cognition underpinning, 55–6, 112, 174;

terminal (unreconciled) breakdowns, 316
Booker, Cara, 357
brain, human: brain-imaging technology, 57–8, 59, 60, 61–3, 130; functional imaging (fMRI) studies, 130; gender differences in, 65–7, 284–91, 292–9; genomic imprinting, 65; left-handed people, 62; male brains as bigger, 65, 66, 294; memory storage, 60; myelinisation, 17–18, 61; Positron Emission Tomography (PET), 142–4, 162, 170; processing and controlling emotions, 60–1, 62; processing of facial expressions of emotions, 313, 315, 322–3, 352; processing of fear/flight response, 60–1; processing of physical and psychological pain, 189, 311, 312–14; processing of social and emotional cues, 60–1, 62–3, 67; processing of social information, 58, 62–3; reward-system neuroanatomy, 297–8; right-handers and left-handers, 61–2; and social rejection, 311, 312–14; 'theory of mind network,' 59, 122–3, 124, 131
brain, human (parts/regions/structure), 58; amygdala, 59, 60, 63, 64, 66–7, 123, 153, 201, 263, 296; anterior cingulate cortex (ACC), 245, 312–14; anterior insular (AI) region, 312–14, 332; caudate nucleus, 201, 296; cerebellum, 296; cingulate cortex, 263, 297; default mode neural network, 59; frontal pole (Brodmann Area 10), 129–31, 249; grey matter, 61, 65; the insula, 140, 153, 263, 296, 312–14, 332; limbic system (emotional machinery), 59, 60–1, 65, 66–7, 123, 153, 201, 296; lingual gyrus, 60; motor cortex, 296; myelin (fatty sheath), 17–18, 61; neocortex, 50, 61, 296; nucleus accumbens, 153, 201, 297–8; occipital lobe, 297; parahippocampus, 296; parietal cortex, 245, 296, 297; posterior insula area, 312; precuneus, 62–3; prefrontal cortex, 17–18, 58–9, 64, 65–6, 124, 125, 152, 236–7,

brain, human (parts/regions/structure) –
    continued
    245, 249, 263–4, 294, 296–7, 323;
    prefrontal cortex (dorsal region
    of), 59–60, 62, 123, 130–1, 153;
    prefrontal cortex (medial region),
    62–3; prefrontal cortex (orbitofrontal
    region of), 59–61, 62, 63, 67,
    122–3, 153, 294, 296; prefrontal
    cortex (ventromedial region of),
    153, 298; processing of social
    information, 59–63; right frontal
    lobe, 129, 297; somatosenory cortex,
    312; striatum, 62–3, 140, 263, 298;
    superior temporal sulcus (STS), 60;
    supplementary motor area, 332;
    temporal lobe, 58, 59, 60, 249,
    263, 296, 297; temporo-parietal
    junction (TPJ), 58, 125, 249; ventral
    striatum, 62–3, 140; white matter,
    61, 284, 294; μ-receptors, 139
Brigham Young University (Utah), 4–6
British Columbia, University of, 53–4
Bronze Age stone circles, 77–8
Brown, Gillian, 291–2
Brown, Steven, 168–9
Bryant, Gregory, 184–5
Buddelman, Felix, 189
burkas, 275
Burnett-Heyes, Stephanie, 325
Burton, Max, 13, 45, 84, 135, 268
business and commerce, 33
Buss, David, 283
Buys, Christian, 68
Byrne, Dick, 49
Bzdok, Danilo, 66–7, 297–8

Cable, Daniel, 257
Cacioppo, John, 15–16, 19
Camarilla (Dutch site), 345
Cambridge University, 164, 225, 355
camel family, 53
Campbell, Anne, 242, 280–1
CAMRA (Campaign for Real Ale), 170,
    171, 172–3
Canada, 32–3, 90–1, 101, 244
Cardiff University, 57
Caribbean patois, 210–11
Carlson, Stephanie, 128–9
Carnegie Mellon University
    (Pittsburgh), 16

Carney, James, 129, 178
Carter, Sue, 145
Cartright, Dorwin, 81
Casari, Marco, 32
Casey, B.J., 129
Caspi, Avshalom, 248–9, 331
cats, 53, 141
Celtic Britain, 216–17
    An Chailleach Bhéara (Irish poem),
        320–1, 339
Cheney, Dorothy, 135
Chicago, University of, 15
chickadees, 178–9
chicken broth, 11
childhood/adolescence: ability to
    delay gratification, 127, 129; child
    mortality rates, 255; and concept
    of friendship, 322, 324–5, 326–7;
    and divorce of parents, 337–8; and
    group formation, 226–7, 329–30;
    group size for play activities, 323–4,
    329–30; impact of digital world,
    355–8; inhibition of prepotent
    responses in, 127, 129; length of
    socialisation period, 322, 325–6;
    'motherese' speech, 292; mother–
    infant bond, 140–1, 144–5, 263–4,
    313–14; negative experiences in, 19,
    330, 331; primate-like grooming
    in humans, 140–1; risk factors for
    antisocial behaviour, 247–8, 249;
    Sally and Ann Test, 113–14, 116;
    sex differences in play activities,
    326, 327–9; and sex differences
    in sociality, 285–6, 327–30; social
    isolation in, 18–19; Trier Social
    Stress Test for Children, 357; US
    National Longitudinal Study of
    Adolescent Health, 200
chimpanzees, 79, 116, 175, 266, 328
Christakis, Nick, 7–8, 9, 12, 17, 200;
    Connected (with James Fowler), 14
Christakos, Athena, 318
Christmas-card lists, 27–8, 70, 153, 333
Church of England, 31–2
circadian rhythm, 107–8
circles/layers of friendship, 69–80,
    71; 1500-layer, 71, 72; 150-layer,
    70, 73, 79, 82, 85, 88, 91–2, 93,
    100, 204, 229; 1.5-layer, 70, 75–7,
    79; 5000-layer, *71*, 72; 500-layer,

71, 72; 50-layer, 70, 73, 91, 100; across primates as a whole, 79–80; age factors in, 80; and altruistic behaviour, 93–4; breakdowns with family members, 301; computer modelling of, 86–9, 90; data from online gaming worlds, 344–5; different benefits offered by layers, 90–4; and distance apart, 100–1; ending of friendships, 301, 302–3, 304–6; and friends on Facebook, 354–5; *Heider's Structural Balance Theory*, 81–3; and length of time apart, 101–3, 104–5, 301; and level of trust, 229, 230, 237; and *moral partiality* problem, 234–7; personality factors in, 80; pure mathematical theory, 88–9, 90; reverse structure in small populations, 89–90, 221; 'scaling ratio,' 72–3, 75, 76–7, 78, 79, 82, 83–4, 346; and Seven Pillars of Friendship, 204–6; and socially complex animal populations, 79–80; 'Thirty-Minute Rule,' 100–1; time factors, 84–90, 154–5, 158–9, 247 *see also* support cliques (the 5-layer); sympathy groups (the 15-layer)

clubs and organisations, 6, 18, 279–80

Coates, Jennifer, 290

cognitive abilities: of anthropoid primates, 50, 116, 125; and antisocial behaviour, 247, 248–9; and autism, 111*, 152; causal reasoning, 129; cognitive load, 285, 294; comparing multiple outcomes, 130; and conversation, 176–8, 180–1, 182–3, 194–7, 290; decline in old age, 339–41; and deep love, 263–4; executive functions, 129–31; gender differences in, 284–91, 292–9; one-trial learning, 129; pre-commitment strategy, 130–1; and Social Brain Hypothesis, 50, 55–6, 114–15, 124; and social isolation, 20; sophisticated underpinning of social world, 55–6, 112; spatial or mapping tasks, 297 *see also* mind, theory of (mentalising or mindreading)

colour-blindness, 293

comedy, 121, 160–1, 162, 163, 189

communication: complexity of and group size, 178–9; conversation, 175–8, 180–1, 182–3, 206, 276, 290, 306–7, 318, 350–1; critical comments (negative gossip), 182, 183, 238–9, 240–1, 281, 305–6; experiments on language and conversation, 178–9, 180–2; experiments on nonverbal cues, 184–6, 284; experiments on smiling, 187, 243–4; expressions of gratitude, 306–7; and human eyes, 352; limitations of applications like Skype/Zoom, 352–3; natural size of conversation groups, 192–7, 290; nonverbal cues, 176, 183–6, 284, 351; origin tales of the tribe, 180; smiling, 186–8, 243–4; storytelling, 159, 178, 179–80, 188–9; women's use of gossip, 242, 281 *see also* language

communities, local: adoption of invaders' names by locals, 220–1; adoption of local names by immigrants, 220; average village size in England, 31–2; balkanisation or ghettoisation of, 89–90, 221; Big Lunch Project, 170–2, 173, 197; dyadic relationships within, 149–50; ethnic origins in ancestral past, 212–18; freeloaders as cause of fragmentation, 209–10; levels of involvement with, 5, 6, 7, 171–3, 286; the local pub, 170, 172–3; natural group size for, 31–4, 42–3, 50–2; neighbours, 8, 171; policing mechanisms within, 150; role of music in evolution of, 157–8; selfish liars as cause of fragmentation, 233; and signals of belonging, 206–11, 212–18, 219–22; village life, 3, 31–2, 33–4, 42, 128, 321–2

competition, 65, 223, 224–5, 226, 256, 289–90, 318; and mating preferences, 261, 266

computer science, 86; agent-based models, 86–9, 90; and facial characteristics/expressions, 243–4; GIGO outcome, 87; modelling of trust, 228, 229–30, 232–4; pervasive-technology problem, 201–2; reverse engineering, 87–8

Congreve, William, 283
Connellan, Jennifer, 285–6
Conti, Marco, 73–5
contraception, 42
Copenhagen, 6, 36
cortisol (stress hormone), 357
COVID-19 lockdown, 352
Cowen, Alan, 185
criticism, social, 182, 183, 238–9, 240–1, 242, 305–6
Crocket, Molly, 130–1
Cross, Catharine, 291–2
Cross, Ian, 185
Cruwys, Tegan, 18
crying, 191, 278, 314–15
cultural and social identity, 201, 206–11, 212–18; adoption of invaders' names by locals, 220–1; adoption of local names by immigrants, 220; group-specific cultural traditions, 224–5, 227, 279; obstacles to multi-ethnic friendship, 221
Cumberbatch, Benedict, 190
Cundiff, Jenny, 19
Curry, Oliver, 12–13, 93, 121, 202–3, 204
cyberball, 311–12, 313

Dahmardeh, Mahdi, 180
dancing, 159, 163–4, 165–7, 169, 174
Darwin, Charles, 23–4
dating sites/agencies, 14, 269–70, 272, 338
Dàvid-Barrett, Tamas, 179, 277
Davies, Alan, 25, 26
Day of the Dead (31 October), 46
Decety, Jean, 15
Deeley, Quentin, 322–3, 324
deer and antelope, 14, 53, 56, 137
deforestation, 128
dementia, 18, 341
democracy, 127
demography, historical, 31–3, 338
Denisovan peoples in Asia, 214
depression, 8, 11, 18, 138, 139, 310; and digital world, 354; after divorce, 336; and gender, 8, 331; and negative childhood experiences, 19, 331
Devaine, Marie, 125–6
Dezecache, Guillaume, 195

Diab, Lutfy, 226
Dillema, Foekje, 295
diplomacy, 127
dog family, 46–7, 53, 141, 254
Dolan, Ray, 264
dolphins, 53, 54, 175
Domesday Book, 31
Domingue, Benjamin, 200
Donner Party in American folklore, 10
dopamine system, 139, 140, 148, 151, 248, 263, 272, 298; receptor genes, 200, 267, 298
Duchenne, Guillaume, 162, 187
Dumontheil, Iroise, 324
Dunbar, James MacDonald, 244
Dunbar surname, 219–20
Dunbar's Number, 23, 25–6, 27–34, 48, 343–4; and the family, 40–6; and online 'friends,' 34–7, 343–4; reasons for variation in number of friends, 37–40
Duncan, Neil, 180
Duncan, Sophie, 189
Dunedin, New Zealand, 248, 248*, 249, 331
dyadic relationships, 50, 83, 118–19, 148, 149–50, 277, 290, 329–30; online, 358

East York (outside Toronto), 90–1, 101
economics, 231, 255, 321; behavioural, 240, 325; classic economic games, 149, 240, 241, 325; discounting the future concept, 128; stranglehold of microeconomics, 148–9
Eden Project, 170–1
Eder, Donna, 329–30
Egilssaga family history, 250
Eisenberger, Naomi, 140, 144, 189, 311–12
Ejsmond-Frey, Robin, 164–5
elephants, 53, 79, 114
Ellison, Nicole, 344
Elwert, Felix, 9
emotional content of relationships: and the amygdala, 59, 60, 63, 64, 66–7, 123, 153, 201, 263, 296; and circles/layers of friendship, 72–3, 80, 91, 92, 93, 101–3, 105; and conversation, 177, 184, 185; emotional capital as finite, 40, 80;

and endorphin system, 11, 114, 115, 137–8, 143–4, 227, 237, 263; face-to-face communication as preferred, 353; and the family, 44–5; gender differences, 65–7, 278–9, 283–91, 294, 306, 310, 311, 317–19, 337–8; gift-giving, 287–8; homophily concept, 200–1, 202–18; intensity of women's relationships, 317–19, 330; and length of time apart, 101–3, 301; limbic system, 59, 60–1, 65, 66–7, 296; negative emotionality, 248–9; and network size, 39–40, 80; and pets, 46–7; and polyamory/polygamy, 268–9; processing and controlling emotions, 60–1, 62, 294; processing of social and emotional cues, 60–1, 62–3, 67, 123; psychological pain of loss/rejection, 311–13, 314–15, 336; right-handed/left-handed people, 61–2; shared emotional experiences, 191–2; significance of night-time, 198; socio-emotional theory of friendship, 332; support from others, 5, 12–13, 40, 59, 91, 92, 287, 305, 306, 309, 327, 332, 337; time as creating closeness, 153–5, 158; and touch, 134, 143–4; and use of social media, 35

empathy, 20, 60, 150, 241, 286–8, 315

endorphin system: abnormal endorphin levels, 138–9; afferent c-tactile (CT) neurons, 139, 141; and alcohol, 138, 169–70, 172–3; and anxiety/stress, 138–9, 147, 152, 315; assaying for endorphins, 141–4; and autism, 152–3; beta-endorphins, 137; and crying, 315; and emotional bonds, 11, 114, 115, 137–8, 143–4, 237, 263; endorphin receptor genes, 150–2, 267, 298, 312–13; and feasting, 159, 169–72, 173; and laughter, 11, 159, 161, 162–3, 189, 332; naloxone (endorphin blocker), 140, 169–70; and natural killer (or NK) cells, 11; nature and purpose of, 11, 114, 115, 137–8; OPRM1 gene, 312–13; and Jaak Panksepp, 147–8, 152, 153; and psychiatric conditions, 138–9; role in context

of pain, 137–8, 140, 151, 162, 163, 164–6, 167, 169, 190, 224, 312–13, 315; and romantic relationships, 263, 267; and rowing crews, 164–5; 'second wind' or the 'runner's high,' 140; and sex, 138, 141, 146, 263, 267, 272; singing and dancing, 11, 159, 163–4, 165–9, 224–5; and social disposition/style, 150–2, 298; and social grooming, 139–40, 147–8, 153, 155–6, 170; and storytelling, 159, 189–90; and touch, 11, 139–40, 141–4, 147, 153, 155–6, 170

Enfield, Nick, 306

Engels, Friedrich, 268

Espi-Sanchis, Pedro, 157–8

Estonians, 215

ethnicity, 205, 211, 212–13, 225; apartheid in South Africa, 217; 'European' subcategory, 215; Hindu caste system in India, 215–16, 279; and historical Mongolian invasions, 215; history of the British Isles, 216–18, 220–2; Indo-Europeans, 215–16; modern sub-Saharan Africans, 214; nineteenth century racial classifications, 213, 214–15; and skin colour, 213–14

Euripides, *Medea*, 317

Evolution: What Everyone Needs to Know (Robin Dunbar), 24, 232

evolutionary science: co-evolutionary relationships, 54; Darwin's natural selection theory, 19, 23–4, 65–6, 232; difference between cues and reality, 212; emergence of *Homo sapiens*, 168; evolution of formal language, 179–80; evolutionary basis of social brain, 64, 65–6, 67, 112, 157–9, 168, 177–80, 199; human mate-choice behaviour, 252–3, 254–62, 265–9, 281–2, 294; loneliness as evolutionary alarm signal, 16, 19–20; loss of most of human fur, 141; and lying/deception, 232; male protection of the social group, 289; question of sex differences, 65–7, 254, 274–5, 280–92; real benefit of crying, 315; risk-taking males, 191–2, 258–9, 282, 290–2; role of music in, 157–8, 168–9; sex differences in

evolutionary science – *continued*
cognition, 292–9; and skin colour,
213–14; theory of kin selection,
43–4, 245, 246–7, 250–1; variation
within species, 56–7; and 'virtual
grooming' techniques, 159

Facebook, 34–6, 40–1, 96, 277, 353,
354–5; datasets, 73–4, 76, 102, 205;
declining popularity among young,
344, 345; and Dunbar's Number,
34–7, 343–4; as modern equivalent
of the telephone, 343; parents as
active on, 344
facial characteristics/expressions: brain's
processing of, 313, 315, 322–3,
352; and computer science, 243–4;
defining of, 243–4; and face-to-face
interactions, 353; folk wisdom on
reading of personality, 242–3; gender
difference in reading of, 284, 285–6;
mechanisms of face recognition,
71–2; ROM face, 161, 186; sclera
in the human eye, 352; smiling,
186–8, 243–4, 351; Taoist art of
face-reading, 242
the family: and altruistic behaviour,
12–13, 43–4; as best cue for
trustworthiness, 244–7; breakdowns
with family members, 301, 303–5;
and churn in network membership,
98, 301; and circles/layers of
friendship concept, 91, 94, 155; and
COVID-19 lockdown, 352; death
of parents, 9, 303–4; and Dunbar's
Number, 40–6; and expressions of
gratitude, 306–7; extended families,
20, 41–2, 91–2, 279; Hamilton's
theory of kin selection, 43–4, 245,
246–7, 277; and health of young
mothers, 9–10; historical cases
of importance of, 10; and infant
health, 9–10; *kinship premium*, 43–4,
245, 301, 303; kinship-naming
systems, 42–3; in-laws (relatives
by marriage), 45, 337; and *moral
partiality* problem, 234–7; negative
family experiences in childhood,
19; nuclear family, 20; parents as
active on Facebook, 344; recently
dead ancestors, 46; and Seven Pillars

of Friendship, 207; in small-scale
societies, 42–3; as special kind of
friend, 9–10, 26; as stable across
time, 44–5, 102, 301, 310, 332, 333
family names, 219–21
Farrington, David, 247–8
feasting, 159, 169–70, 173, 227; Big
Lunch Project, 170–2, 173, 197
feminism, 280
fentanyl, 138
fibrinogen levels, 17
Fieldman, George, 246
film and cinema, 118–19, 189–91, 245,
315; conversation group size in,
195–6
Finland, 134, 143, 215
fishes, 144
Floccia, Caroline, 208
Floyd, Simeon, 306
Fowler, James, 7–8, 12, 17, 200;
Connected (with Nick Christakis),
14
Fox, Kieran, 53–4
Framingham Heart Study, 7–8, 12, 17,
63, 200
Frangou, Anna, 163
Freeberg, Todd, 178–9
Fry, Stephen, 25
Fukuda, Ichiro, 86
Fung, Helene, 333

Gabriel, Shira, 278
Gächter, Simon, 240
Gaelic mouth music, 163
Galton, Sir Francis, 243
Gardner, Wendi, 278
gelada baboons, 22–3, 38–9, 104, 135,
136–7, 328–9
genetics: and 2D4D ratio, 267; and
antisocial behaviour, 248–9, 251;
CYP2A6 gene, 200; dopamine
receptor genes, 200, 267, 298;
endorphin receptor genes, 150–2,
267, 298, 312–13; and ethnicity,
213–17; genomic imprinting, 65–6;
large-scale genetics study (Pearce/
Machin/Wlodarski), 150–1, 263,
267, 286, 298; and loneliness,
19–20; monoamine oxidase A
(MAOA) gene, 248; and music-
making, 168–9; OPRM1 gene,

312–13; oxytocin receptor genes, 20, 145, 146, 147, 150, 263; receptors of six social neurochemicals, 150–1; and risk-prone males, 191–2, 258–9, 282, 290–2; serotonin transporter genes, 20; sex chromosomes, 216–17, 293, 294–6; shared genes and friendship, 200–1; and skin colour, 213–15; and sociality, 298; unusual genetic combinations, 294, 295–6; vasopressin genes, 267, 298

gestation, 145, 254
Ghosh, Asim, 104
gibbons, 266
goats, feral, 21, 56, 136–7, 328
Goel, Vinod, 264
Gombe (Lake Tanganyika), 328
Gonçalves, Bruno, 36
Goodall, Jane, 328
goosebumps, 141
Gore, Willard, 33
Gore-Tex (company), 33
gorillas, 116, 173
Göritz, Anja, 191
gossip theory of language evolution, 23, 179
Grainger, Felix, 163
Grainger, Sarah, 290
Grammer, Karl, 252–3
Granovetter, Mark, 13–15
Gray, Alan, 163
Great Orme (Wales), 21, 328
Greeno, Natalie, 286
Grooming, Gossip and the Evolution of Language (Robin Dunbar, 1996), 179
Grove, Matt, 77–8
guanaco, 53

Haerter, Jan, 36
haka (traditional Maori war dance), 169
Hall, Jeffrey, 154, 308
Hall, Judith, 284
Hallinan, Maureen, 329–30
Hamilton, Bill, 43, 245, 246
Hamilton, Marcus, 31, 77
hamsters, 146
Hang-Hyun Jo, 100–1
Harary, Frank, 81
Hardy, Tom, 190

Harvard University, 7
Hawker-Bond, Dani, 323–4
health and wellbeing: clustering together of unhappy people, 7–8; after divorce, 336–7; importance of friendships, 3–9, 11, 15–20, 172; infant health, 9–10; meaningful conversation, 181; and *quality* of friendships, 4, 6; and size of extended family, 9–10 *see also* psychological wellbeing
Heider, Fritz, *The Psychology of Interpersonal Relations*, 81–3
Henderson, Monika, 305
Hermann, Benedikt, 240
Hewlett Packard, 256
Heydari, Sara, 349
Hill, Russell, 27, 29–30, 79
Hindu caste system, 215–16, 279
hippy communes in 1960s America, 101, 102
Hockings, Kim, 173
Holocaust Memorial Day Trust, 348, 354–5
Holt-Lunstad, Julianne, 4–5, 6–7
Homo sapiens, emergence of, 168
homophily concept, 200–1, 202–18; and family names, 219–21; and gender, 205–6, 224, 225, 275–9, 287, 288; and newly forming communities, 222–7; and online gaming world, 346; and relationship breakdown, 306; and romantic relationships, 260; and sense of humour, 203, 204, 278, 287, 288
honeybees, 175
horse family, 49, 53, 65, 114
howler monkeys, 161
Hudson's Bay Company, 244
Hughes, Austin, *Evolution and Human Kinship*, 45
Huguenots, 221–2
Human Evolution (Robin Dunbar), 141, 168, 199
Hungarians, 215
hunter–gatherer societies: banishment in, 239; characteristic form of settlement, 50–2; community size in, 31, 52, 70, 207; conversation in, 183; and ethnicity, 212; Hadza in East Africa, 282; hierarchically

hunter–gatherer societies – *continued*
nested structures, 77; importance
of kinship, 42–3, 46, 207, 212;
!Kung San in southern Africa, 99,
183, 238–9; 'scaling ratio' in, 76–7;
and siesta tradition, 109; and social
criticism, 238–9; time spent on
social interaction, 99; value of weak
ties in, 14
Hutterites (Anabaptist Christian sect),
32–3, 275
Huxley, Aldous, 268
hydrocodone, 138

Icelandic family sagas, 249–51, 282–3
IJburg College (Amsterdam), 33
immigrant communities, 89, 90, 220–2
immune system, human, 11, 16–17,
55; 'immunophenotypes,' 138;
inflammatory cytokines, 138; natural
killer (or NK) cells, 11
Implicit Association Test (IAT), 44
Inagaki, Tristen, 140, 144
Inclusion-of-Other-in-Self (IOS) Index,
163–4
India, 215–16, 244, 279
Indo-European languages, 215
infant health, 9–10
Iñiguez, Gerardo, 231, 232–3
insectivores, 52
Institut Eurécom (near Nice), 202
internet, 35, 95–6, 311–12, 341;
and COVID-19 lockdown, 352;
extremist propaganda on, 355;
impact on children, 355–8;
limitations of applications like
Skype/Zoom, 352–3; as massive
natural experiment, 359; new friends
made on, 343; online bullying, 348–
9, 355, 357; online dating sites, 14,
269–70, 272; online gaming world,
83, 342–3, 345–6; and psychological
wellbeing, 353–4, 355–8, 359;
romantic scamming on, 269–72
Inuit societies, 52, 321
Iran, 180, 215, 276
Ireland, 77–8, 220, 320†, 320–1
Islam, 275

Jagani, Sheel, 216
Jamestown (in present-day Virginia), 10

Japan, 86, 134, 321
jazz scat singing, 163
Jenkins, Rob, 71–2
Joffe, Tracey, 322
Johnson, Katerina, 151
jokes, 121–2, 160–1, 204, 206, 207,
351
Judge, Timothy, 257

Kahlenberg, Sonya, 328
Kalenscher, Tobias, 130–1, 285, 298
Kanai, Ryota, 60
Karinthy, Frigyes, 'Chains,' 28
Karolinska Neuroscience Institute
(Stockholm), 295–6
Kaski, Kimmo, 30–1, 231, 261, 334
Kelly, Susan, 259
Kelly, Yvonne, 357
Kempnich, Mary, 222–3, 225
Kenna, Ralph, 345
Keverne, Barry, 65, 139–40, 144, 147,
170
Killworth, Peter, 28, 29
Kim, David, 17
Kinderman, Peter, 120
King-To Yeung, 101, 102
Kinzler, Katherine, 208
kith and kin expression, 41*
Klimek, Peter, 83
Klinefelter's Syndrome, 294, 295–6
klipspringer antelope, 21, 136–7, 146
Kniffin, Kevin, 182
Knot's Real Wedding Surveys website,
29–30
Kobayashi, Hiromi, 352
Kohshima, Shiro, 352
Kordsmeyer, Tobias, 78
Kraut, Bob, 101, 354
Krems, Jaimie, 194–6
Krio (Sierra Leone creole), 211
Krummhorn region (Germany), 338
Kudo, Hiroko, 79
!Kung Bushmen of Botswana, 183,
238–9
Kurzban, Rob, 279
Kwak, Seyul, 59–60

lactation, 38–9, 144, 145, 254
Lally, Maria, 3
language: anatomical markers for
speech, 168; and animals, 175,

179; Bantu linguistic group, 213; dialect and local accent, 168–9, 201, 203, 206, 207–10; dialect as fast changing, 210; and emergence of *Homo sapiens*, 168; evolution of in humans, 179–80; evolution of modern English, 210–11, 212–13; gossip theory of evolution of, 23, 179; and history of the British Isles, 217–18; Indo-European languages, 215; kinship-naming systems, 42–3; limits to conversation group size, 192–7, 290, 324; Lowland Scots, 210; and mentalising competences, 176–8, 181–2, 194–7; mimicking of dialect by freeloaders, 209–10; nonverbal cues, 176, 183–6, 284, 351; processes of remembering, 181–2; singing as older than, 163, 168–9; social functions of, 180, 181, 182–3, 188; and theory of mind, 113, 116–17, 121–2; as unique to humans, 175; use of metaphors/allusions, 116, 121–2

Laniado, David, 205
Lapps of northern Scandinavia, 215
Larsen, Kenneth, 68
Lau, Jennifer, 325
laughter, 159–60, 174, 331–2, 351; and conversation group size, 195; Duchenne (involuntary) laughter, 160, 161–3; and endorphin system, 161, 162–3, 189, 332; and gender, 187; non-Duchenne (voluntary) laughter, 162; research on, 160–1, 162–3; round open mouth (ROM) face, 161; and smiling, 186–7
Launay, Jacques, 121, 129, 164, 203, 211
Laxdaellasaga (Icelandic family saga), 282
Lebanon, 226
Lehmann, Sune, 107
Leicht, Elizabeth, 97
Leiden University fraternities, 223–5
Lewis, Penny, 57–8, 124
Licoppe, Christian, 106
life expectancy, 3, 4–8, 17; impact of death of spouse, 9
literature, 117–18, 189–90
Little, Tony, 243

Liverpool, 9–10, 207–8
Liverpool Hope University, 58
Liverpool University, 57
loneliness: and attachment styles, 20, 309–10; and brain size, 60; John Cacioppo's work on, 15–16, 19; and circles/layers of friendship concept, 92–3; and digital world, 354; after divorce, 336–7; effects on immune system, 11, 16; and gender, 4, 74, 309–10; impact on mental health, 4, 16, 17–18, 20; and internet romantic scamming, 269–72; as modern killer disease, 4–9, 322; in modern world, 3–4; neurobiological correlates of, 15–16, 17–18, 19–20, 60–1; processing of social and emotional cues, 60–1
Loneliness: Human Nature and the Need for Social Connection (John Cacioppo and William Patrick), 16
Lonely Hearts advertisements, 253–4, 255, 256–7, 259
Longitudinal Study of Ageing (ELSA), UK, 18
Lonsdale, Elizabeth, 328
Lópes, Eduardo, 97
lumbar punctures, 141–2
Lycett, John, 256, 338
lying/deception, 117, 132, 231–2, 238–42; Barrio-Iñiguez mathematical model, 232–4; and intentionality concept, 323; *moral partiality* problem, 234–7; physical appearance and character, 242–4; selfish lies–'white lies' distinction, 232, 233–4

Maasai of East Africa, 99, 321
macaque monkeys, 64, 125, 286
MacCarron, Padraig, 73, 79, 345
'Machiavellian Intelligence Hypothesis,' 49
Machin, Anna, 76, 150, 235, 276–7, 278, 287, 288, 307–8, 350
Madsen, Elainie, 246, 277
magnetic resonance imaging (MRI), 57–8
Maguire, Laurie, 189
Manchester University, 29, 73, 86
Manninen, Sandra, 162
Manning, John, 266

Māori people, 213
Markey, Patrick and Charlotte, 260
Marlow, Cameron, 354–5
marriage: age at, 333, 334; American wedding data, 29–30; couples meetings online, 272; and cross-sex friendships, 276; divorce, 300, 308–9, 310–11, 318–19, 333, 336–7; endogamy in Hindu caste system, 216; exogamy, 42, 52; impact of death of spouse, 9, 310–11, 333, 336, 338–9, 340; intermarriage in Anglo-Saxon times, 217; in-laws (relatives by marriage), 45, 337; opposite-sex marriages as lasting longer, 318–19; polygamous, 268; remarriage, 337–8; rituals in ethnographic societies, 52; same-sex, 309, 318–19; size of weddings, 30; in small-scale societies, 207, 212; and tall men, 257, 258; and tall women, 258
Marriott, Anna, 180
Martin, John Levi, 101, 102
Masters, Alexander, 190
mathematics: data from online gaming worlds, 83, 342–3, 345–6; of fractals, 70, 78, 79, 345–6; pure mathematical theory, 88–9, 90; and social network theory, 81
Matsumato, David, 284
Matthews, Karen, 19
McGlone, Francis, 139
Mealey, Linda, 238
Medicare database, American, 9
Mehl, Matthias, 180, 181
Mehrabian, Albert, 184, 185–6
Mehta, Clare, 275, 327
Mehu, Marc, 187
menstrual endocrinology system, 55
Mesoudi, Alex, 181
Mexico, 20, 46
Milgram, Stanley, 28–9
military life, 16–17, 192
Millennium Study, UK, 357
mind, theory of (mentalising or mindreading): as all but unique to humans, 112–13; and antisocial behaviour, 248, 249; brain-scan studies of, 60, 62–3, 122–3, 236–7, 245, 322–3, 324; in children, 113–

14, 116, 323–6; and conversation, 176–8, 180–1, 182–3, 194–7, 290; Director's Task, 324; extraordinary human abilities, 300; and 'false belief,' 113–14; inhibition of prepotent responses, 126–31, 248, 282; as key to human sociality, 114, 115–16, 131; and language, 113, 116–17, 121–2; and literature, 117–18; and lying/deception, 117, 132, 231–2; as naturally recursive phenomenon, 119–26, 177; *orders* (or *levels*) *of intentionality*, 119–26, 177, 323–6; perspective-taking, 324; processing of likeability/popularity, 62–3; psychological reflection process, 114–16; *Sally and Ann Test*, 113–14, 116; and smarter monkeys/apes, 113, 114, 116, 125–6, 129; and Social Brain Hypothesis, 124–6; and storytelling, 178, 179–80; 'theory of mind network' in brain, 59, 122–3, 124, 131; women's higher mentalising skills, 242, 281–2, 283–91, 294
Miritello, Giovanna, 85
Mithen, Steven, 157
mobile-phone datasets, 30–1, 73, 95, 104, 106; Aalto University (Finland), 30–1, 100–1, 104, 106, 108–10, 261–2, 334–5; of Danish university students, 107–8; distinct individual patterns (social fingerprint), 97–9, 107–8, 349–50; longitudinal study of high-school students, 44–5, 95, 96–9, 101–2, 105–6, 107, 198, 277, 301
mobile-phone technology, 201–2, 347, 349–50; as status symbol in early 1990s, 256; texting, 347–8, 349–50
Moffitt, Terrie, 248–9, 331
Mogilski, Justin, 259
Mok, Diane, 101
monkeys: bonded social relationships, 22–3, 48–50, 54–6, 79, 84, 87–8, 114, 135–7, 158; circles/layers of friendship, 79, 84, 87–8, 158; creation of friendships, 114; as diurnal species, 107; Robin Dunbar's study of, 21–3, 38–9, 48–50, 135; frontal pole in, 129; protracted

adolescence of, 326; purpose of grooming for, 136–7, 139–40; and ROM face, 161, 186; sex differences in sociality, 286, 327–9; and Social Brain Hypothesis, 48–50, *51*, 53, 54–6, 64; social grooming by, 22, 48–50, 79, 135–7, 139–40, 158; and theory of mind, 113, 114, 125–6, 129; three-colour vision of, 293
Monnot, Marilee, 292
monoamine oxidase A (MAOA) gene, 248
Monsivais, Daniel, 108–10
Montague, John, 320
moral partiality problem, 234–7
Morelli, Sylvia, 62–3
Mormons, 268
Moro, Estaban, 85
Moses, Louis, 128–9
Movember Foundation, 4
Murray, Sandra, 264
music, 157–8; and Seven Pillars of Friendship, 203, 211; singing and dancing, 159, 163–4, 165–9, 174, 224–5; singing as older than language, 163, 168–9
My Sister's Keeper (film, 2009), 245

Nantes, Edict of (1685), 221–2
Nave, Gideon, 145–6
Neanderthals, 168, 177, 214
Nettle, Daniel, 209
neurochemicals, 19–20, 137–48, 200, 248, 263, 267, 298, 357; serotonin, 20, 148, 151, 248; social neurochemicals, 150–1 *see also* dopamine system; endorphin system; oxytocin
neuroendocrines, 248
New Guinea, 46, 211
New Mexico, University of, 31, 77
New York, girl gangs in, 242, 280–1
New Zealand All Blacks, 169
Newcastle upon Tyne, 9
Nietzsche, Friedrich, 268
Njalssaga family history, 250
Noonan, MaryAnne, 61
norepinephrine, 248
Norman Conquest (1066), 217–18, 220–1
Norse (Viking) society of Iceland, 249–51, 282–3
North American Indian tribes, 52
North Carolina, University of, 82
Nummenmaa, Lauri, 143, 151–2, 162, 170

Ochsner, Kevin, 63
Oesch, Nate, 178
O'Gorman, Rick, 44
old age: decline in cognitive abilities, 339–41; and declining social networks, 332, 333, 334, 335–6, 339–41; friendship in, 262, 275, 339–41; granny dumping, 321; sex of best friend in, 262; social isolation in, 19, 39, 320–2, 339
opiates, 138, 139, 140
opioid drugs, 138
orang-utans, 116
Orben, Amy, 355–6
Orkney Isles, 244
Oslo, University of, 36
Ostrom, Elinor, 240
Oxford University, 61, 124, 164–5, 189, 223, 225, 231, 356
oxycodone, 138
oxytocin, 144–8, 150, 151, 263, 272, 357; receptor genes, 20, 145, 146, 147, 150, 263; studies and experiments, 144–7, 148, 150, 151, 263, 357

Palchykov, Vasyl, 261
Panksepp, Jaak, 148, 152, 153
Pardus (Austrian online gaming world), 83, 345–6
parents, 38–9, 91, 274, 286, 313–14, 317, 319, 333, 335, 336; as active on Facebook, 344; custody of children after divorce, 337–8; death of, 9, 303–4; female baboons, 22, 38–9, 104, 328–9; and genomic imprinting, 65; 'motherese,' 292; mother–infant bond, 140–1, 144–5, 263–4, 292, 314; negative experiences for children, 19, 247–8; 'school-gate friends,' 103–4; young mothers, 9–10, 331
Parkinson, Carolyn, 63, 200–1
Passarella, Andrea, 73–5
Path.com, 344–5

Patrick, William, 16
Pawlowski, Boguslaw, 253–4, 256–7, 290
peacocks, 256, 258
Pearce, Ellie, 129, 150, 163, 164, 286, 298
Pellisier, Lucie, 152–3
pentachromacy (five-colour vision), 293
Pérez-Barbería, Javier, 54
personality: addictive, 270; attachment styles, 20, 150, 152, 286–9; and circles/layers of friendship concept, 80; and effects of genetics on sociality, 298; Experience of Close Relationships Scale, 286–7, 298; extraverts and introverts, 39–40, 80, 110, 298; Five Factor Model of (OCEAN), 223–4, 225, 259–60, 309; folk wisdom on facial characteristics, 242–4; and homophily concept, 205, 223–4, 225, 260, 287; and number of friends, 37, 39–40, 60, 80; as psychological construct, 39–40; and relationship breakdown, 309–10, 313; and sensation-seeking, 291–2; social disposition/style, 98–9, 110, 150, 152, 286–9, 298, 313; and social fingerprint, 110
pets, 46–7
philosophy, 118; intentionality concept, 119–26, 177, 323–6; *moral partiality* problem, 234–7
phrenology, 243
'pidgin' English, 211*
Pisa group, 73–5, 76
Plotkin, Henry, 246
the poacher's dilemma, 128
Pocahontas, 10
Poland, 218, 257–8
Pollet, Thomas, 35, 39–40, 43–4, 80
Pomuch community (Mexico), 46
Popchoir, 167–8
Positron Emission Tomography (PET), 142–4, 162, 170
Potter, Beatrix, 188
Powell, Emma, 327, 329
Powell, Joanne, 58, 62, 122–3, 124
Pressman, Sarah, 16
prosimian primates, *51*, 53, 129
Proverbio, Alice, 297

Provine, Robert, 160–1, 187, 315
Przybylski, Andy, 356
psychiatric conditions: and abnormal endorphin levels, 138–9; and childhood experiences, 330, 331–2
psychological wellbeing: as bedrock of success in life, 11–12; clustering together of happy people, 7–8; and digital world, 353–4, 355–8, 359; and divorce, 336–8; and friendships, 4, 6–8, 11, 20–1, 172; involvement in clubs and societies, 18; involvement in local community, 172; and life expectancy, 6–7; loneliness as evolutionary alarm signal, 16, 19–20; and *quality* of relationships, 4, 6; and social isolation, 3, 5, 16, 19–20; underestimation of significance of, 11
psychologists, 23, 39, 113, 114; developmental, 120, 208; evolutionary, 219, 238, 266, 274–5, 279, 280–2, 283; Five Factor Model of personality (OCEAN), 223–4, 225, 259–60, 309; and intentionality concept, 120–2, 323–6; Robbers Cave (*Lord of the Flies*) Experiment, 225–6; social, 44, 68, 81, 153–4, 225–6, 281, 305, 308, 350
Punch magazine, 218
punishment, 238–9, 240–2
pygmies of Central African forests, 52

QI (BBC TV programme), 25
Queensland, University of, 18

racism, 217, 218
reciprocity, 12, 46, 93–4, 114–15, 308, 325
Redhead, Gina, 181
Reed, Lawrence, 187
Reeder, Heidi, 275
religion, 46, 77, 113, 159, 180, 264, 279, 339; Catholic Mexico, 20; Catholicism in southern Europe, 335; Church of England, 31–2; and homophily concept, 203, 206, 211, 212, 255; the Hutterites, 32–3, 275; Protestant French Huguenots, 221–2; sectarian loyalties, 226–7

Rennard, Stephen, 11
Rennung, Miriam, 191
reproduction, human: 269-261,
    269–1; anatomical indices of mating
    systems, 265–7; cues of fertility
    in women, 256, 257, 259; female
    body plan and brain as default in
    mammals, 294–5; fetal testosterone,
    267, 294–5, 296; human mate-
    choice behaviour, 252–3, 254–62,
    265–9, 281–2; male and female
    strategies, 65–6, 261, 262, 266, 268,
    281–2; monogamous relationships,
    21, 46, 53, 54, 55, 79, 114, 136–7,
    145, 146, 147, 265–8; and romantic
    relationships, 272; sex chromosomes
    (X and Y), 216–17, 293, 294–6; and
    wealth/status, 255–6, 261
residential campsites in Germany, 78
Reynolds, Tania, 242, 281
Rheims, 208
rhesus macaques, 286
Rhoades, Galena, 30
rickets, 214
risk-taking, 258–9, 282, 290–2
Robbers Cave State Park (Oklahoma),
    226
Roberts, Anna, 179
Roberts, Ruth, 44
Roberts, Sam, 35, 80, 85, 92–3, 96–7,
    179
Robertson, Cole, 166
Robinson Crusoe Island, 15
Robledo del Canto, Juan-Pablo, 185
Roman Chair position, 151, 224, 246
romantic relationships: and aggressive
    behaviour, 242, 280–3; analysis of
    personal adverts, 253–4, 255, 256–7,
    259; anatomical indices of mating
    systems, 265–7; attractiveness of
    'bad lads,' 259; and best friends, 76,
    276–7, 278, 287, 317, 327; brain
    activity and love, 263–5; courtship,
    253, 269; depression and suicide
    in men after breakdown, 310–11;
    ending of, 300, 303, 308–9, 310,
    313, 316, 318–19; female choice
    as the norm, 261–2; and female
    stature, 258; gay and lesbian, 272–3,
    308–9, 319; gender and wider social
    networks, 76, 276–7, 278, 286–8,

308, 317–18, 327; gender differences
    over choices of partner, 256–9, 294;
    gender-based expectations, 307–9;
    and homophily, 260; human mate-
    choice behaviour, 252–3, 254–62,
    294; importance of commitment,
    255, 259–60; intensity of, 75, 137,
    155, 251, 252, 263, 268–9, 272;
    and IOS index, 164; lying to partner,
    231; and male stature, 257–8; online
    dating sites, 14, 269–70, 272; and
    oxytocin research, 148, 150–1, 263;
    pain and trauma of breakdown,
    311; polyamory/polygamy, 76, 259,
    267–9; presence of children, 319;
    psychological/physiological signs
    of, 252, 263–5, 271–2, 313–14;
    putting reality on hold, 260–1,
    264–5, 271–2; remarriage, 337–8;
    and risk-prone males, 192, 258–9;
    romantic scamming on the internet,
    269–72; and smaller support clique,
    154–5; and social neurochemicals,
    148, 150–1, 263, 267; Sociosexual
    Orientation Index (SOI), 263, 266,
    267, 286, 298; and touch, 134
Rose, Suzanna, 276
Rotkirch, Anna, 167
rowing crews, 164–5, 182
Rum, Isle of, 21, 328
Rutgers University, 11

Sacker, Amanda, 357
Sackville-West, Vita, 268
Safebook security software, 202
Sally and Ann Test, 113–14, 116
San Francisco, 333
Sánchez, Anxo, 88
Santini, Ziggi, 6
Saramäki, Jari, 97
Sarkar, Dipak, 11
Savic, Ivanka, 295–6
schizophrenia, 138, 331
Schrödinger, Erwin, 268
science, 118
The Science of Love and Betrayal (Robin
    Dunbar), 264
Scotland, 210, 219–20; Act of Union
    (1707), 218; kinship in eighteenth/
    nineteenth centuries, 244; Union of
    Crown with England (1603), 218

Scott, Sophie, 331–2
sealions, 79
Second Life (computer game), 342
second-hand car sales, 148–9
Selkirk, Alexander, 15
Seltzer, Lesley, 357
Semple, Stuart, 286
serfdom, 217–18
serotonin, 20, 148, 151, 248
settlements: form of hunter–gatherer societies, 50–2; Framingham, Massachusetts, 7–8; Hutterites in North America, 32–3; Jamestown (in present-day Virginia), 10; medieval English villages, 31–2; natural group size for human communities, 31–4, 42–3, 50–2; size of in small-scale societies, 31, 42–3; urban populations, 50; use of historical records to determine size of, 31–2
Seven Pillars of Friendship, 199, 201–2, 203–6; cultural similarity as more important than ethnicity/race, 218; and ethnicity, 205, 211, 212–18, 225; and family names, 219–21; and human mate-choice behaviour, 255; and judging of strangers, 211, 212–13; and rare traits, 211–12; and relationship breakdown, 306; and signals of belonging, 206–11, 212–18, 219–22
sex/gender: anatomical differences between sexes, 65, 66, 188, 244, 265–7, 274–5, 282, 292–4; and antisocial behaviour, 242, 248; and attitudes to punishment, 241, 242; and childhood friendship, 326–7, 329–30; and circles/layers of friendship concept, 75–6, 80, 286–7; and clubs, 279–80; and cognitive load, 285, 294; and colour vision, 293; and competition, 65, 289–90, 318; and conversation, 180, 194, 206, 276, 290, 318; cues of fertility in women, 256, 257, 259; current fashion to ignore sex differences, 274–5; and death of spouse, 9; and depression, 8, 331; differences in friendship style, 105–6, 224, 275–80, 283, 286–9, 298, 306–11, 317–19, 329–30, 346; and drivers of aggression, 280–1, 282–3; and ending of relationships, 302, 303, 304–5, 306, 307–11, 317–19; and facial expression of emotions, 243–4; female body plan and brain as default in mammals, 294–5; female dress, 275; and Five Factor Model of personality (OCEAN), 224, 309; and forgiveness, 317–18; fragility of female–female relationships, 305, 309–10, 316–19, 330; genomic imprinting, 65; and gift-giving, 287–8; and homophily in social networks, 205–6, 224, 225, 275–9, 287, 288; and jealousy triggers, 283; and laughter, 185, 187; and loneliness, 4, 74, 309–10; and 'motherese' speech, 292; and nonverbal cues, 284; and online gaming world, 346; and oxytocin genes, 263; and promiscuity, 266–9, 298; and reading of facial expressions, 284, 285–6; and reconciliations, 316–17; and remarriage, 337–8; and reproductive strategies, 65–6, 253–9, 261, 262, 266, 268, 281–2; and responses to danger/stress, 278, 289; risk-prone males, 191–2, 258–9, 282, 290–2; and sensation-seeking, 291–2; sex difference in brain white-matter volume, 64–5, 284; sex differences in brains, 64–7, 284–91, 292–9; sex differences in childhood play, 327; sex differences in juvenile animal play, 327–9; sex differences in sociality, 64–7, 80, 285–91, 297–9, 306–11, 317–19, 329–30; sex of best friend, 76, 261–2, 276–7, 288; sexually segregated conversations, 194, 276; significance of night-time, 198; and smiling, 187, 188, 243–4; and social criticism, 238–9, 242; and social media use by young people, 357; and social networks across the lifespan, 334–6; and standards of mate choice, 257–61, 294; and storytelling genres, 190–1; talking and friendship maintenance, 105–6; tall men as more successful, 257, 258; and touch, 134; unusual genetic combinations, 294, 295–6;

and violent behaviour, 282–3; and weighing of romantic cues, 253, 255–9; women's close friendships as more intense than men's, 277, 278, 283, 317–19, 330; women's higher emotional awareness, 281–2, 283–91, 294; women's higher mentalising skills, 242, 281–2, 283–91, 294; women's use of gossip, 242, 281

sexual behaviour: and 2D4D finger-length ratios, 266–7; and brain activity, 263; casual sex, 239, 261; and cross-sex friendships, 118, 276; and endorphin system, 138, 141, 146, 263, 267, 272; fidelity, 259–60; function in romantic relationships, 272; gay and lesbian relationships, 272–3; in hunter–gatherer societies, 238, 239; infidelity, 283; and lying/deception, 231; promiscuity, 53, 76, 145, 146, 150, 239, 263, 265–9, 298; size of canines and testes, 265–6; Sociosexual Orientation Index (SOI), 263, 266, 267, 286, 298; unsafe, 291, 331

Seyfarth, Robert, 135

Shakespeare, William, 195–6

Sherif, Muzafer and Carolyn, 226

Shorter, Stuart, 190

Shultz, Susanne, 52–4, 79

siesta tradition, 108–9

Singer, Tania, 241–2

singing, 159, 163–4, 167–8, 174, 224–5, 227

'six degrees of separation,' 28–9

Skype, 96, 350, 352–3

sleep patterns/habis, 18, 108–10

smiling, 186–8, 243–4, 351

Smith, Emma, 185

Smith, Jennifer, 313

Smith, Joseph, 268

Smoreda, Zbigniew, 106

Snapchat, 344

Social Brain Hypothesis, 23, 33, *51*; alternative hypotheses, 55, 56; as applying *within* species, 56–64; and cognitive abilities, 50, 55–6, 114–15, 124; and different mammalian orders, 52–5; as ecological hypothesis, 55–6; evolutionary basis of, 64, 65–6, 67, 112, 157–9,

168, 177–80, 199; further research confirming, 59–64, 66–7; gender factors, 64–7; and monkeys, 48–50, *51*, 53, 54–6, 64; origins of, 48–50; and psychological reflection process, 114–16; series of four distinct grades in, 50, *51*; Susanne Shultz's work on, 52–4; and theory of mind, 124–6; use of brain-imaging technology, 57–8, 59

social class/status, 207–8, 287, 297–8, 354; and human reproduction, 255–6, 261; and male friendship, 288, 308

social isolation: in childhood/adolescence, 18–19; after divorce, 336–7; nuclear and extended families compared, 20; in old age, 19, 39, 320–2, 339; and psychological wellbeing, 3, 5, 16, 19–20; and risk of death, 7, 17; and the Twitter world, 74

social media/networking sites, 34–7; and advertising business model, 343; age factors in use of, 349; and checking of prospective employees, 344; and circles/layers of friendship concept, 73–4, 76, 86, 354–5; face-to-face communication as preferred, 349, 350, 351–2, 353; and friends in face-to-face world, 34–5, 36–7, 73, 74, 343; limited use of for real relationships, 359; limits on number of friends, 344–5; making friends on, 343; and privacy issues, 343, 344, 345; as slowing down decay of friendships, 353; as way of maintaining friendships, 96, 102, 358–9

social networks: age factors in number of friends, 37–9, 321–2, 332–6, 340–1; and altruistic behaviour, 12–13, 43–4, 93–4; changes across the lifespan, 332–5; Christmas-card lists, 27–8, 70, 153, 333; churn in network membership, 98, 301, 302; common interest friendships, 4; complexity of human world, 112, 114, 118–19, 322–6, 357–8; correlation between sociability and risk of illness, 4, 5–7, 9–10, 11–12,

social networks – *continued*
16–19, 20; as declining in old age,
332, 333, 334, 335–6, 339–41;
determining size of, 27–34; as
dispersed in modern day, 171; dyadic
relationships, 50, 83, 118–19, 148,
149–50, 277, 288, 290; effects on
immune system, 16–17; ending
of friendships, 300–1; face-to-face
communication as preferred, 350,
351–2, 353; hub individuals, 62–3;
of immigrant communities, 89, 90,
221–2; as implicit social contracts,
127–8, 209–10, 240–1; inner-core
networks, 41; *Kaski's Katapult*, 30,
231; 'larks' and 'owls,' 107–8, 110;
in-laws (relatives by marriage), 45,
337; longitudinal study of high-
school students, 44–5, 95, 96–9,
198, 277, 301; maintaining of
friendships, 27, 95–6, 102, 105–6,
110, 111–12, 114, 147, 151, 200,
300–1, 305–6, 358–9; making new
friends, 24, 39, 96, 98–9, 204–5,
211, 301; meaning of word 'friend,'
26–7; and meeting life partner, 14;
in newly forming communities,
222–7; number of guests at
weddings, 29–30; personality factors
in number of friends, 39–40, 60, 80;
pets in, 46–7; reasons for variation
in size, 37–40; recently dead
ancestors, 46; 'school-gate friends,'
103–4; significance of night-time,
197–9; social fingerprint concept,
97–9, 107–8, 110, 349–50; 'Thirty-
Minute Rule,' 100–1; time factors in
interaction with, 44–5, 84–90, 96,
99–100, 153–5, 158–9, 237, 247,
277, 301; triads as basis of, 83–4,
118–19; weak ties, 13–15 *see also*
bonded social relationships; circles/
layers of friendship; communities,
local; the family
social neuroscience, 15–16, 182
social rejection: and the brain, 312–14;
and crying, 314–15; psychological
pain of, 311–13, 314–15, 336;
terminal (unreconciled) breakdowns,
316
social skills: acquiring and maintaining

friendship, 111–12; in childhood,
19, 285–6, 330–1; and complexity
of human world, 55, 56, 64, 112,
114, 118–19, 123, 322–6, 357–8,
359; difficulty in processing social
cues, 60; effects of genetics on
sociality, 298; and evolutionary
selection, 65–6, 112; extraverts and
introverts, 39–40, 80, 110, 298;
grooming in primates, 22–3, 48–50,
79, 84, 104, 135–7, 139–41, 147–8,
153, 155–6, 158, 170; inhibition
of prepotent responses, 126–31,
282; and limbic system (emotional
machinery), 60–1, 65, 66–7; and
prefrontal cortex, 17–18, 58–9,
62–3, 64, 65–6, 125, 152, 153, 245,
249, 296–7; process of acquiring
adult-level, 178, 322–6, 358; and sex
differences, 64–7, 242, 281–2, 283–
91, 294, 297–9, 310, 346; social
disposition/style, 98–9, 110, 150,
152, 286–9, 298, 313; and social
neurochemicals, 150–1, 298; and
stable, permanent groups, 55–6 *see
also* communication; mind, theory of
(mentalising or mindreading)
Sofer, Carmel, 243
Sornette, Didier, 70, 73, 345–6
Sosis, Rich, 33
Spain, 90
Spelke, Elizabeth, 208, 218
Spence, Charles, 9
Spoors, Matt, 41, 69
squirrels, 79
St Andrews University, 49
Stanley, Scott, 30
Steptoe, Andrew, 17
Stewart, Lauren, 167
Stiller, Jamie, 195–6
Stoneking, Mark, 168–9
storytelling, 159, 178, 179–80, 188–9;
dramatic tragedy, 189–90; genre-
specialists, 190–1; at night, 183,
197, 199
Strombach, Tina, 285
Strough, JoNell, 275, 327
Stuart: A Life Backwards (TV film),
189–90
Supermale Syndrome, 294
support cliques (the 5-layer), 70, 88,

91, 92; 1.5-layer within, 70, 75–7, 79; functions of, 92–3; and gender, 75–6, 80, 286–7; impact of death of spouse, 338; and level of trust, 229, 230, 237; and polyamory/polygamy, 76, 268–9; and Seven Pillars of Friendship, 204; size as stable over time, 333; size of, 69, 73, 83–4, 92; and social fingerprint concept, 97; in socially complex animals, 79, 83–4, 88; time spent on social interaction with, 84, 100, 154–5, 158–9

Sutcliffe, Alistair, 29, 73, 86–9, 90, 228, 229

Suvilehto, Juulia, 133–4

Swedish tax-collecting agency, 33

Swyer Syndrome, 295, 296

sympathy groups (the 15-layer), 70, 88, 91, 224; age factors, 80; functions of, 92–3; and level of trust, 229, 237; named by Buys and Larsen, 68; size of, 68, 69, 73, 92, 354–5; size of as declining with age, 333, 334; and social fingerprint concept, 97; in socially complex animals, 79, 88; support cliques within, 69, 73, 91, 92, 100; time spent on social interaction with, 84–5, 100

Tagliapietra, Claudio, 32

Taiwan, 168–9

Takano, Masanori, 86

Tamarit, Ignacio, 88–9, 90, 185

Taoist art of face-reading, 242

Tarr, Bronwyn, 164, 166

team sports, 68–9

Teasdale, Ben, 189–90

Tejada, Ana Heatley, 20

Telefonica, 85–6

testosterone, 148, 151, 267, 294–5, 296

tetrachromacy (four-colour vision), 293

theatre and drama, 162, 189, 197; conversation group size on stage, 195–6

Thomas J. Fudge (boutique Dorset bakers), 35, 37, 355

Thorisdottir, Ingibjorg, 356–7

Thurner, Stefan, 83, 345–6

Tok Pisin (Talk Pidjin), 211

touch: ambivalence of, 133; and autism, 111*, 152; and CT receptors, 139,

141; and endorphin system, 11, 139–40, 141–4, 147, 153, 155–6, 170; intimacy of, 132–3, 134, 158–9, 174; PET experiment on endorphins, 143–4; social grooming in primates, 22, 23, 48–50, 79, 84, 104, 135–7, 139–41, 147, 153, 155–6, 158, 170; universal rules of, 133–4

traditional ethnographic societies: and antisocial behaviour, 249–51; community size in, 31, 52, 77–8, 207; conversation in, 183; friendship in, 12; and gender separation, 275; importance of kinship, 42–3, 46, 207, 212, 244; obligation and trust in, 149; offspring survival rates in, 255; and old age, 321; protection of group as male task, 289; puberty rituals, 191–2; singing and dancing in, 163, 168–9; time spent on social interaction, 99 see also hunter–gatherer societies

tragedy of the commons, 128

Transcranial Magnetic Stimulation (TMS), 124–5, 131

Trentino region of Italian Alps, 32

triads, 80–1, 118–19, 233, 329–30; bridges between, 82, 119; Heider's Structural Balance Theory, 81–3; mathematical theories of social networks, 81; and 'scaling ratio,' 82, 83–4

Trier Social Stress Test for Children, 357

trust, 136, 139, 149–50, 171–3, 202, 227, 228–9, 307–8; behavioural and physical cues of trustworthiness, 206–11, 212, 222, 237, 242–4; and circles/layers of friendship, 229, 230; computer modelling of, 228, 229–30, 232–4; and endorphin system, 140; family as best cue for trustworthiness, 244–7; impact of lying/deception, 230–4, 238–42, 270–2; and moral partiality problem, 234–7; and oxytocin story, 144, 145–6, 147, 263; physical appearance and character, 242–4; as psychological quantity, 229; and punishment, 238–9, 240–2; and social criticism, 238–9, 240–1, 242; and time, 230, 237, 247

Tuenti ('Spanish Facebook'), 205
Tunney, Richard, 246, 277
Turner Syndrome, 294
Tuulari, Jetro, 170
Twitter, 36–7; datasets, 74, 76

ungulates, 53, 54, 136–7
University of Nebraska Medical Center, 11
Untouchables (Dalits) of Northern India, 215–16
Up (cartoon), 190–1

van Duijn, Max, 167, 222, 223
van Emde Boas, Evert, 189
van Harmelen, Anne-Laura, 19
van Hemmen, Judy, 296
van Kleef, Gerban, 182
vasopressin, 148, 151, 267, 298
Vazire, Simine, 180
vervet monkeys, 135
Vespignani, Alessandro, 36
vicuña, 53
Vigil, Jacob, 277–8
violent behaviour, 247–8, 249–51, 282–3
Virginia, University of, 30
vitamin D, 213–14
Vlahovic, Tatiana, 350, 351
Voh, Kathleen, 260
Voland, Eckart, 338
voles, 145, 146, 148
Völsungasaga (Icelandic family saga), 282

Wales, 217
Walker, Rob, 77
Wallace, George, 121
Wallette, Anna, 250
Wang, Diane, 86–9, 230
Wardell, Jane, 17
wedding data, 29–30

Wei- Xing Zhou, 70, 73
Weinstein, Daniel, 167
Weinstein, Netta, 356
Weiss, Elizabeth, 297
Wellman, Barry, 90–1, 101
whales, 54, 79
WhatsApp, 344, 345
When Harry Met Sally (film, 1989), 118–19
Whiten, Andy, 49
Whitmeyer, Joseph, 83
Whitty, Monica, 269, 270, 271–2
Wiessner, Polly, 183, 238, 239
Williams, Kip, 311–12
willpower, 126–31
Wilson, David Sloan, 182
Wilson, Margot, 219
Wilson, Ruth, 309
Wlodarski, Rafael, 129, 150, 236, 266, 267
Wolfram, Stephen, 35–6
Workers' Educational Association (WEA), 167
World of Warcraft (computer game), 342
Wrangham, Richard, 318
Wrzus, Cornelia, 332–3, 336–7, 338

Yang, Claire, 18
Yanomamo people of Venezuela, 52
Young, Larry, 145

Zahavi, Amotz, 258
Zeki, Samir, 263–4
Zerubavel, Noam, 63
zoology, 21–3, 38–9, 48–50; mammalian orders, 52–5
Zoom, 96, 352–3
Zuckerman's Sensation Seeking Scale, 291–2
Zunzunegui, María-Victoria, 339–40